PIRATES, PORTS, AND COASTS IN ASIA

IIAS/ISEAS Series on Maritime Issues and Piracy in Asia

Series Advisory Board

- Professor Alfred Soons
  Institute for the Law of the Sea,
  Utrecht, The Netherlands

- Professor Hasjim Djalal
  Department of Maritime Affairs
  and Fisheries,
  Jakarta, Indonesia

- Professor Dr J.L. Blussé van Oud-Alblas
  Leiden University,
  The Netherlands

- Professor Togo Kazuhiko
  Princeton University/IIAS

- Professor Jean-Luc Domenach
  Sciences-Po, Paris, Italy/
  Tsinghua University, Beijing,
  People's Republic of China

- Dr Mark Valencia
  Maritime Policy Expert,
  Hawaii, United States

- Vice-Admiral Mihir Roy
  Society for Indian Ocean Studies,
  Delhi, India

- Dr Peter Chalk
  Rand Corporation, California,
  United States

- Dr Stein Tönnesson
  International Peace Research Institute,
  Norway

- Dr John Kleinen
  University of Amsterdam,
  The Netherlands

- Professor James Warren
  Murdoch University,
  Australia

- Mr Tanner Campbell
  Maritime Intelligence Group,
  Washington, D.C.,
  United States

The **IIAS/ISEAS Series on Maritime Issues and Piracy in Asia** is an initiative to catalyse research on the topic of piracy and robbery in the Asian seas. Considerable attention in the popular media has been directed to maritime piracy in recent years reflecting the fact/perception that piracy is again a growing concern for coastal nations of the world. The epicentre of global pirate activity is the congested sea-lanes of Southeast Asia but attacks have been registered in wide-scattered regions of the world.

The **International Institute for Asian Studies** (IIAS) is a post-doctoral research centre based in Leiden and Amsterdam, the Netherlands. IIAS' main objective is to encourage Asian studies in the humanities and social sciences — and their interaction with other sciences — by promoting national and international co-operation in these fields. IIAS publications reflect the broad scope of the Institute's interests.

The **Institute of Southeast Asian Studies** (ISEAS) was established in Singapore as an autonomous organization in 1968. It is a regional centre dedicated to the study of socio-political, security and economic trends and developments in Southeast Asia and its wider geostrategic and economic environment. ISEAS Publishing has issued over 2,000 scholarly books and journals since 1972.

IIAS/ISEAS Series on
Maritime Issues and Piracy in Asia

PIRATES, PORTS, AND COASTS IN ASIA

Historical and Contemporary Perspectives

Edited by
John Kleinen and Manon Osseweijer

IIAS | ISEAS

International Institute for Asian Studies | Institute of Southeast Asian Studies
The Netherlands | Singapore

First published in Singapore in 2010 by
ISEAS Publishing
Institute of Southeast Asian Studies
30 Heng Mui Keng Terrace
Pasir Panjang
Singapore 119614

E-mail: publish@iseas.edu.sg
Website: http://bookshop.iseas.edu.sg

First published in Europe in 2010 by
International Institute for Asian Studies
Rapenburg 59
2311 GJ Leiden
P.O. Box 9500
2300 RA Leiden
The Netherlands

E-mail: iias@iias.nl
Website: http://www.iias.nl

All rights reserved. No part of this publication may be reproduced, stored in a retrieval system, or transmitted in any form or by any means, electronic, mechanical, photocopying, recording or otherwise, without the prior permission of the Institute of Southeast Asian Studies.

© 2010 Institute of Southeast Asian Studies, Singapore

The responsibility for facts and opinions in this publication rests exclusively with the authors and their interpretations do not necessarily reflect the views or the policy of the publishers or their supporters.

ISEAS Library Cataloguing-in-Publication Data

Pirates, ports, and coasts in Asia : historical and contemporary perspectives / edited by John Kleinen and Manon Osseweijer.
(IIAS-ISEAS series on maritime piracy).
1. Pirates—Asia.
I. Kleinen, John.
II. Osseweijer, Manon.
III. Title.
IV. Series.
DS526.7 M28   2010

ISBN 978-981-4279-07-9 (soft cover)
ISBN 978-981-4279-11-6 (E-Book PDF)

Photo Credit: Cover photo reproduced courtesy of North Atlantic Treaty Organization (NATO): Marines from the Dutch frigate De Zeven Provinciën freed on 18 April 2009, twenty fishermen from a Yemeni flagged dhow which had been captured by Somali pirates earlier. There was no exchange of fire and Dutch forces seized a number of weapons. Seven pirates were detained, but were eventually released.

Typeset by International Typesetters Pte Ltd
Printed in Singapore by Photoplates Pte Ltd

Contents

Acknowledgements   vii

About the Contributors   ix

Part 1   Introduction

1. Pirates, Ports, and Coasts in Asia   3
   John Kleinen and Manon Osseweijer

2. Piracy in Asian Waters: Problems of Definition   15
   Michael Pearson

Part 2   East Asia

3. Giang Binh: Pirate Haven and Black Market on the Sino-Vietnamese Frontier, 1780–1802   31
   Robert J. Antony

4. Tonkin Rear for China Front: The Dutch East India Company's Strategy for the North-Eastern Vietnamese Ports in the 1660s   51
   Hoang Anh Tuan

5. South Fujian the Disputed Coast, Power and Counter-power   76
   Paola Calanca

6. Maritime Piracy through a Barbarian Lens: Punishment and Representation (the *S.S. Namoa* Hijack Case, [1890–91])   99
   John Kleinen

Part 3   Southeast Asia

7. Violence and Armed Robbery in Indonesian Seas   131
   Adrian B. Lapian

8. Robbers and Traders: Papuan Piracy in the Seventeenth Century 147
    Gerrit Knaap

9. The Port of Jolo: International Trade and Slave Raiding 178
    James Warren

10. Pirates in the Periphery: Eastern Sulawesi 1820–1905 200
    Esther Velthoen

11. Suppressing Piracy in Asia: Decolonization and International 222
    Relations in a Maritime Border Region (the Sulu Sea),
    1959–63
    Stefan Eklöf Amirell

12. Contemporary Maritime Piracy in the Waters off Semporna, 237
    Sabah
    Carolin Liss

13. Piracy in Contemporary Sulu: An Ethnographical Case Study 269
    Ikuya Tokoro

Index 289

Acknowledgements

The chapters in this volume were presented in 2005 at an international conference hosted and organised by the Shanghai Academy of Social Sciences. We are grateful to the staff and Director of SASS, Professor Li Yihai for the hospitality and professional organisation of the conference. We would also like to acknowledge the financial support we have received from the Asia-Europe Workshop Series, a programme run and sponsored by the European Alliance for Asian Studies and the Asia-Europe Foundation (Singapore).

The editors, publisher and the author wish to thank Brill Publishers for permission to use copyright material from Hoang Anh Tuan's book *Silk for Silver: Dutch-Vietnamese Relations, 1637–1700* (2007*b*). Every effort was made to trace the copyright holders of photographs and maps.

Special thanks are due to Wim Stokhof, the Director of the International Institute for Asian Studies at the time of the conference, who was the initiator and motivator of the institute's scientific project on maritime piracy as well as the ISEAS-IIAS Series of which this volume is part.

We would also like to thank Rosemary Robson-McKillop for English language editing of the introduction and two chapters of this volume.

The Editors,
John Kleinen and Manon Osseweijer

About the Contributors

Robert J. Antony is Associate Professor at the University of Macau. He is the author of several books: *Pirates in the Age of Sail* (2007); *Like Froth Floating on the Sea: The World of Pirates and Seafarers in Late Imperial South China* (2003). With Jane Kate Leonard, he co-edited, *Dragons, Tigers, and Dogs: Qing Crisis Management and the Boundaries of State Power in Late Imperial China* (2003).

Paola Calanca is a member of École Française d'Extrême Orient and affiliated to the Institute for the History of Natural Science in Beijing. Her thesis, "Piraterie et contrebande au Fujian: L'administration chinoise face aux problèmes d'illégalité maritime" (17e- début 19e siécle) was published in 2008.

Stefan Eklöf Amirell is Research Fellow at Sweden's Royal Academy of Letters, working at the Swedish Institute of International Affairs in Stockholm. His books include *Pirates in Paradise: A Modern History of Southeast Asia's Maritime Marauders* (2006); *Power and Political Culture in Suharto's Indonesia: The Indonesian Democratic Party (PDI) and the Decline of the New Order (1986–98)* (2003); and *Indonesian Politics in Crisis: The Long Fall of Suharto, 1996–98* (1999).

Hoang Anh Tuan is Researcher and Lecturer at the History Department of Vietnam National University, Hanoi. He obtained his Ph.D. in 2006 at Leiden University (the Netherlands) with his research on the VOC in Tonkin. In 2007, he published *Silk for Silver: Dutch-Vietnamese Relations, 1637–1700*.

John Kleinen is an anthropologist and historian, and serves as an Associate Professor at the Universiteit van Amsterdam. He has published on several aspects of the Vietnamese society and history. His books include *Facing the Future, Reviving the Past: A study of Social Change in a Northern Vietnamese Village*, 1999 (also in Vietnamese); *Lion and Dragon: Four Centuries of Dutch-Vietnamese Relations* (2008). In 2001 he edited *Vietnamese Society in Transition: The Daily Politics of Reform and Change*.

Gerrit Knaap is specialized in Indonesian history and holds a Ph.D. from Utrecht University. At present he is programme director at the Institute for Netherlands History at The Hague, in charge of the Overseas History Programme. His recent publications include *Monsoon Traders: Ships, Skippers and Commodities in Eighteenth-century Makassar* (2004), together with Heather Sutherland; *Grote Atlas van de Verenigde Oost-Indische Compagnie/Comprehensive Atlas of the Dutch United East India Company: Deel/Volume II: Java en Madoera/Java and Madura* (2007), together with colleagues from Asia Maior.

Adrian B. Lapian is Professor of History at Universitas Indonesia in Jakarta, Indonesia. His publications include "Laut Sulawesi: The Celebes Sea, From Center to Peripheries", *Moussons* 7 (2003); "Rechtvaardigheid en de Koloniale Oorlogen: Indonesië", in Madelon de Keizer and Mariska Heijmans-van Bruggen, eds., *Onrecht: Oorlog en Rechtvaardigheid in de Twintigste Eeuw* (2001); and "Research on Bajau Communities: Maritime People in Southeast Asia", *Asian Research Trends: A Humanities and Social Science Review* (1996).

Carolin Liss is a Post-doctoral Research Fellow at the Asia Research Centre, Murdoch University, Australia. For her Ph.D. thesis, *Maritime Piracy in Southeast Asia and Bangladesh, 1992–2006: A Prismatic Interpretation of Security*, Carolin conducted fieldwork in Singapore, Thailand, and Malaysia. Her recent publications include "Privatising the Fight against Somali Pirates", *Working Paper 152*, Asia Research Centre, November 2008; "Abu Sayyaf and US and Australian Military Intervention in the Southern Philippines", *Austral Policy Forum* 07-23A, 29 November 2007; "Southeast Asia's Maritime Security Dilemma: State or Market?", *Japan Focus*, 8 June 2007; and "The Privatization of Maritime Security in Southeast Asia", in Thomas Jäger and Gerhard Kümmel, (eds.), *Private Military and Security Companies* (2007).

Manon Osseweijer who was trained as an anthropologist, is the Deputy Director at the International Institute for Asian Studies and she co-organized the workshop from which the chapters of this book result. She has published on small-scale fisheries and environmental problems in the coastal zones of Indonesia. Her most recent publication is co-edited *The Heart of Borneo* (2009).

Michael Pearson is Professor Emeritus of history at the University of New South Wales and an Adjunct Professor at the University of Technology, Sydney. He is the author of several books on India and the Indian Ocean, including *Merchants and Rulers in Gujarat: The Response to the Portuguese in the Sixteenth Century* (1976); *Port Cities and Intruders: The Swahili Coast, India, and Portugal in the Early Modern Era* (1998); and recently, *The Indian Ocean (Seas in History)* (2003).

Ikuya Tokoro is Associate Professor of Cultural Anthropology at the Research Institute for Languages and Cultures of Asia and Africa (ILCAA), Tokyo University of Foreign Studies (TUFS). His main research field is the maritime world of Southeast Asia. His major research topics are: Islam in Southeast Asia, Moro separatism in Mindanao, and maritime border crossings in Southeast Asia. One of his most recent publications is "Transformation of Shamanic Rituals among the Sama of Tabawan Island, Sulu Archipelago, Southern Philippines,", in S. Yamashita and J.S. Eades (eds.), *Globalization in Southeast Asia: Local, National, and Transnational Perspectives* (2003).

Esther Velthoen is Research Associate of the Wilberforce Institute of Slavery and Emancipation, University of Hull (United Kingdom). Her Ph.D. thesis on which her chapter in this book is based is titled "Contested Coastlines: Diaspora, Trade and Colonial Expansion in Eastern Sulawesi 1680–1905", Murdoch University, 2003. Publications include: "Wanderers, Robbers and Bad Folk: The Politics of Violence, Protection and Trade in Eastern Sulawesi 1750–1850", in Anthony Reid, *The Last Stand of Asian Autonomies, Responses to Modernity in the Diverse States of Southeast Asia and Korea, 1750–1900* (1997), pp. 367–88; "Victims and Veterans in the Nation State; The Print Media in South Sulawesi 1950–1953", in D. Pradidamara and M.A.R. Effendy, (eds.), *Kontinuitas dan Sejarah dalam Sulawesi Selatan* (2003), pp. 41–63. "Hutan and Kota: Contested Visions of the Nation-State in Southern Sulawesi in the 1950s", in Hanneman Samuel and Henk Schulte Nordholt, (eds.), *Indonesia in Transition, Rethinking "Civil Society", "Region" and "Crisis"* (2004), pp. 147–74.

James Warren is Professor in Southeast Asian history at Murdoch University in Perth, Australia. He has held positions at ANU, Yale University, and worked as a professorial research fellow at the Centre for Southeast Asian Studies, Kyoto University, and the Asia Research Institute, National University of Singapore. Professor Warren's major publications include, *The Sulu Zone, 1768–1898* (1981); *Rickshaw Coolie: A People's History of Singapore, 1880–1940* (1986); *At the Edge of Southeast History* (1987); *Ah Ku and Karayuki-San: Prostitution and Singapore Society, 1870–1940* (1993); *The Sulu Zone, the World Capitalist Economy and the Historical Imagination* (1998); *Iranun and Balangingi: Globalization, Maritime Raiding and the Birth of Ethnicity* (2001); and *Pirates, Prostitutes and Pullers: Explorations in the Ethno- and Social History of Southeast Asia* (2008). He teaches units on Southeast Asian social history, on researching and writing history in a trans-disciplinary context, and on colonialism, literature, and social context.

Part 1
Introduction

1

Pirates, Ports, and Coasts in Asia

John Kleinen and Manon Osseweijer

INTRODUCTION

War, trade, and piracy. Three in one, indivisible: Goethe's *Faust's* well known complaint about the English of the seventeenth and eighteenth centuries indicates the contemporaneous, ambiguous use of the term "piracy" which parallels the way the term "terrorist" is employed nowadays.

The limited distance between rulers and pirates is still hailed in the romantic invention of *tradition story*, now eternalized in musicals and Holywood representations, written by William Schwenck Gilbert and Arthur Sullivan's *The Pirates of Penzance* (1879):

> When I sally forth to seek my prey
> I help myself in a royal way.
> I sink a few more ships, it's true,
> Than a well-bred monarch ought to do;
> But many a king on a first-class throne,
> If he wants to call his crown his own,
> Must manage somehow to get through
> More dirty work than ever I do.

The French consequently stigmatized their nationalistically inspired adversaries in colonial Vietnam as "pirates", with not the slightest reference to the sea. Piracy is often used in the same breath as "robbery" and "raiding", but they are not necessarily the same.

The terms "robbery" and "raiding" are not always confined to the high seas, but are also used where human security is threatened in terrestrial areas by the absence of the monopoly of violence in the hands of a single ruler. For a long time, piracy was the extreme instance of marginal coastal and maritime livelihoods and hence assumed a pivotal position in attempts to understand many of the complexities present in coastal and marine settings. Piracy, although it is the most dramatic of marginal(ized) maritime livelihoods available, is just one of the many illegal uses to which the sea can be put, the others being for example, drug smuggling and trafficking in human beings.

Many maritime coastal zones and their hinterlands in Asia started out as frontier societies in which all kinds of illicit and semi-legal activities took place. The political economy of the South China coast, for example, was historically based on an intrinsic cohabitation of rulers, peasants, fisher people, and the "froth of the sea", as pirates were known in those days.

Coastal zones are boundary areas, places of contestation, and cross-fertilization. They are naturally and socially marginal spaces in that they serve to demarcate the limit between sea and land, and the site of contact between cultures. Because of these factors, in contemporary times they have become highly desirable places and consequently areas subject to great social and ecological pressures.

Ports where the loading and unloading of shipments of people and cargo, as well as business transactions, trading, and provisioning, are taking place, are located in these coastal zones. Therefore it is necessary to investigate how port authorities have been operating, combating, condoning, or perhaps even encouraging different forms of piracy and smuggling. Whereas, in certain situations in the past, ports or port towns may have acted as pirate headquarters, in many cases they have also served as places of refuge for the vessels attacked by pirates. The port authorities in East and Southeast Asian ports have been the organizations designated to manage the ports and deal with the suppression of piracy, in cooperation with such (para)-military organizations as the navy and coastguards. Sea ports are also nodes in an emergent world system, and, despite globalization and the liberalization of trade, they are also the markers through which people and goods are controlled. They serve a dual purpose as physical bottlenecks for legitimating a geographical territory, and as identification and interdiction of prohibited commodities and people (see also Heyman 2004).

Social Science Perspective

From a social science point of view, maritime piracy, unlike maritime terrorism, can be regarded as one of many so-called "grey-area" phenomena in Asia. This term borrowed from political scientist Peter Chalk (1997) indicates a "parallel underground economy", comparable with other "grey-area" activities in the socio-economic context of the coastal zone. Like smuggling, trafficking of goods and people, gambling, prostitution, and petty crimes on land, piracy is also pursued in a more or less organized form (Chalk 1997, pp. 15–16). The upshot is that maritime piracy is placed in the context of diminishing human security in the coastal zones of a number of Asian countries. Increasingly, these zones are being distinguished by environmental degradation, high unemployment rates, and livelihoods dependent on government development programmes, which places them under a mounting threat of social problems (crime, prostitution). They are an outgrowth of compensation paid out by (inter)national companies to exploit natural resources (mining, overfishing), or by booming industries (tourism, manufacturing, electronics) which rely on migrant workers. Viewed from this angle, piracy is truly an economic activity whether it be a business concerned with the transportation and distribution or their production. Therefore, in this context, piracy is only one of the many criminal or semi-legal activities in a socio-economic context of a coastal zone, where it is often haphazardly linked to smuggling, trafficking of goods and people, gambling, prostitution, and petty crimes on land. All these activities are carried out in a more or less organized form, but the question remains as to how these activities should be studied and evaluated in the conceptual and material context of a modern nation state.

The recent developments in Somalia showed that the combination of a failed state and the protection of nation-states that serve as local policemen explains the possible motivations of the pirates in the Horn of Africa. The illegal fishing by the West and the dumping of toxic waste in Somali waters are not the only factors at play here. Military bases of the Ethiopian army, a force that is protected by the United States, serve as the recipients of the loot of the Somali pirates. In fact the militant Islamists have repeatedly denounced piracy as an offense to Islam. The question remains who else outside the pirates themselves is interested in the captured spoils of the sea?

Maritime terrorism and maritime piracy may be related phenomena in Asia, but there is no clear proof of a direct link between the two. Maritime piracy turns out to be an element in what was imaginatively called the "tapestry of maritime threats": degradation of coastal inhabitants, pollution of marine environments, illegal fishing, and smuggling. Yet, social scientists still need to understand the knots in this tapestry fully. When undertaking this type of work, researchers should bear in mind that their purposes and priorities fall under the purview of academic research, and not those of Southeast Asian governments or organizations such as the International

Maritime Bureau (IMB). There is an urgent need for research into the human dimension of maritime piracy, the pirates, and their socio-economic context or background in order to understand the situation completely.

So far, where research on contemporary piracy has been concerned, there has been a tendency to overstate the issue on the basis of available evidence (basically the figures the IMB and its U.N. counterpart, the International Maritime Organization [IMO]). In many cases, the absence of thorough research may have led to such a romanticization and a consequent misunderstanding of piracy that "fiction" has overtaken reality. This is not a reason to underestimate the difficulty in undertaking research on pirates. As the American scholar Dian H. Murray (2002, p. 257) has aptly noted, "like other groups for whom written records are anathema, detailed information on pirates and their lives is difficult to come by". And she adds "what pirate would want to keep written accounts of activities which, if the records should fall into government hands, would automatically convict them?"

Conference in Shanghai

This volume is the fourth instalment in the Series on Maritime Issues and Piracy in Asia, a joint collaboration between The International Institute for Asian Studies (IIAS) and the Institute of Southeast Asian Studies (ISEAS) in Singapore. As Graham Gerard Ong-Webb has stated in the second volume, it is hoped the workshops and books will provide "an overview of the current knowledge and key themes in piracy studies vis-à-vis Southeast Asia, in order to provide a reference resource for those working on the topic" (2006, p. xii). The first volume in this series, *Piracy in Southeast Asia: Studies, Issues, and Responses*, edited by Derek Johnson and Mark Valencia (2005), clustered around the characteristics of piracy and the measures to suppress this activity (framed as a security threat) in the region. A second aim was to provide a platform for piracy studies upon which a research agenda could be built and expanded. The authors also presented an elaborate research agenda which was formulated at the first workshop consisting of twenty-five building blocks in piracy research (Ong, ed. 2006, p. xvii). With the publication of the two subsequent books, *Piracy, Maritime Terrorism and Securing the Malacca Straits*, under the editorship of Graham Gerard Ong-Webb, and *Contemporary Maritime Piracy in Southeast Asia: History, Causes and Remedies* by Adam J. Young, we believe that this research agenda has progressed immensely and has fulfilled its ambitions. In conjunction the three books explore the topic of contemporary maritime piracy in Southeast Asia, although the context of historical piracy has been disregarded. With this fourth volume we hope to conclude, at least temporarily, the topic of maritime piracy in Asian waters.

The articles compiled here in the book are based on presentations given at a conference held in Shanghai in November 2005 and organized jointly by the Shanghai Academy of Social Sciences (SASS), IIAS, and the Centre for Maritime Research (MARE) of the University of Amsterdam. The organizers felt that the conference should deal with the broader context of maritime piracy, including the historical and social dimensions.

This volume encompasses a variety of activities ranging from raiding, destroying and pillaging coastal villages and capturing inhabitants to attacking and taking over vessels, robbing, and then trading the cargo. Other activities such as the smuggling of goods and people have also been part of this range of piracy acts. Generally speaking, what connects these activities is the fact that they are carried out at sea, often in the coastal inshore waters (within the twelve-mile zone), by vessels attacking other vessels or raiding coastal settlements. These acts of maritime piracy cannot be regarded as being located outside the relevant framework of the coastal zone. Coastal zones have, therefore, become highly desirable places, a circumstance which has transformed them into places subject to great social and ecological pressures. As piracy is the most dramatic of marginal(ized) maritime livelihood, it is our intention to bring the relationship between pirates, ports, and coastal hinterlands into focus.

Supplementing the former three volumes, this book aims to fill in some of the historical gaps in the coverage of maritime piracy and armed robbery, not only in Southeast Asia, but also in the waters surrounding India and China. The papers presented by Pasoroan Herman, Cees de Bruyne, Hong Nong, Catharina Raymond, Cai Penhang, Zhang Jian, Ota Atsushi, and Thomas Crump were valuable contributions to the Shanghai workshop, but we could not include them here because the number of topics in, and the sheer volume of this book would then make it unreadable. Also, these contributions did not focus specifically on the theme we have chosen for this publication.

Contributions in this Volume

In the opening chapter, Michael Pearson downplays piracy as a threat to world trade when compared with a host of other menaces to maritime trade such as pilfering, and people and drug smuggling, which he claims are more serious than piracy. Broadly speaking, world trade is seriously threatened by the protectionist policies in the United States and the European Union, by climate change, and by military adventurism from the United States. Terrorism and piracy rank far behind these as serious impediments to the ideal of free and unhindered exchange of goods by sea. The author neatly summarizes the various dimensions which contribute to piracy, such as coastal poverty and the complete range of illegal and illicit activities.

This book is divided into two sections which deal respectively with the region of East and Southeast Asia, and they each underline how important it has been to choose this approach. Politically, between 1750 and 1850 Chinese piracy differed from piracy in Southeast Asia because in the latter area, piracy was associated with a multiplicity of small, contending states, whereas piracy in South China was geographically and economically peripheral to a great, but waning empire. (J.L. Anderson 1995). This even led to a surprising development in the transition zone between East and Southeast Asia where Chinese pirates helped the Tay Son rebels (1786–1802) in pre-colonial Vietnam to become state makers and were rewarded for their help. Perhaps it was too early to call them "military entrepreneurs" in the sense Gallant (1999) used in his overview of the historical link between brigandage, piracy, capitalism, and state formation, but in the eyes of the Vietnamese their support helped to unify the country after two centuries of political turmoil (Murray 1987). When the Tay Son rebels were defeated by the Nguyen, the pirates were outlawed once again, but their presence was to leave an indelible imprint on the future of Vietnam. The pirate confederation under the leadership of Zheng Yi Sao and others controlled trade and fishing along the north Vietnamese and southern Chinese coast until the Manchu-Qing government pacified the area and pardoned many of the pirates (Antony 2002, pp. 42–45).

The world in which these pirates lived is vividly described by Robert J. Antony. In his contribution to this volume he deals with the Chinese-Vietnamese port of Giang Binh, twenty-five kilometres north of the modern border town of Mong Cai, which was a frontier in many aspects: From the official Chinese perspective, Giang Binh was beyond the pale of civilization and the pirates were no better than savages. However, Antony has a keen eye for the multicultural, multilinguistic, and multiethnic aspects of a port whose population thrived on illegal activities, especially piracy and smuggling, between 1780 and 1802. It was an international black market. Not only did the economy burgeon on ill-gotten gains, the society and culture in Giang Binh were tied to crime, vice, and violence, and characterized by excessive profanity, intoxication, gambling, brawling, and sexual promiscuity. It was a Far South in every aspect. Giang Binh does not fit very well into our preconceived notions of Southeast Asia or China. It existed uneasily on the outside of any discrete, state-based geographical system. Giang Binh and the pirates and outlaws it supported created a world in itself. As he has done in his other works, Antony puts piracy in the historical context of crime and violence being part of a larger society. For men and women alike, piracy offered a (sub)culture which engendered Southern China's transition to modernity.

In the seventeenth century, the place which Antony describes was part of a larger region and already a rather dangerous place as it was constantly assailed by the raids of the pirate Thun, who persistently attacked vessels sailing between the northern part of Vietnam, called Tonkin or Dang Ngoai at the time, and the southern Chinese ports of Canton and Macau. Vietnamese rulers tried to pacify the waters, but succeeded only partially in their efforts. The Vietnamese author Hoang Anh Tuan reveals an early attempt by Dutch traders to open trade relations with Chinese merchants at a time when the loss of Taiwan, as a result of the activities of corsair Zheng Chong-gong blocking the import of Chinese goods for the United Dutch East India Company (VOC). The VOC had established itself in the capital of Tonkin, Hanoi, and hoped to use this place as a springboard from which to penetrate China from the south. Hoang in this volume argues that piracy and widespread political unrest in southern China had a devastating effect on these attempts.

In a much larger context, Paola Calanca studies the south of Fujian during the eighteenth century in terms of the power and counter-power used to try to gain control of maritime activities. In these fluctuations the local authorities, great lineages, and various coalitions, among them secret societies, struggled for control. Qing/Manchu sovereigns did not show a great interest in seaborne activities at a local level and discouraged many seafarers' activities, including maritime trade in extraterritorial waters. It is obvious that the Manchu emperors failed to take into account the maritime capital which had fallen into their hands following their conquest of China. When they became masters of the land, Fujian was rich in experienced seamen, and above all, a merchant fleet which was fairly active in ocean-going trade. However, it is possible that this "indifference" may also have run parallel to their reticence towards the monopolistic activities of certain lineages or regional groups with respect to the local economy. At the end of the nineteenth century, when the Qing/Manchu Empire had been undermined by foreign Western powers, piracy was still a matter of concern.

The ambiguous concern of Qing magistrates towards maritime piracy is the subject of John Kleinen's detailed account of the case of the hijacking of the *S.S. Namoa*, a vessel which regularly plied between Hong Kong and Amoy at the end of the nineteenth century. The passengers were robbed and some members of the crew killed, crimes which led to a diplomatic exchange between the British and Chinese authorities as to, where, when, and by whom the perpetrators should be punished. Both sets of authorities regarded piracy as a capital offence, but the way the executions were organized forces Kleinen to rethink the Foucaultian discourse on torture and public executions as part of the *Ancien Regime* before they yielded to the development of the (modern) prison system. In China, the transition from a feudal *Ancien Regime* to a revolutionary state has not changed the regulation and punishment of individuals who are accused of criminal activities. The PRC still tops the list of regions where the majority of executions are carried out. At the time it was carried out more than a century ago, the execution of the *S.S. Namoa* pirates followed a pattern which did not deviate from what was being done in the West to punish such crimes. Nor could it be categorized as a pre-modern practice in itself. Where it did differ was in the way Chinese and Westerners viewed the pain of others.

The occurrence of piracy in the waters surrounding Southeast Asia is dealt with historically in a number of contributions which range from the seventeenth and eighteenth to the twentieth century and cover Indonesia, Papua New Guinea, and the remote Sulu Archipelago in the Philippines. Adrian B. Lapian takes the vantage point that the absence of definite boundaries, especially at sea where the margins of territorial waters were still in dispute, produced overlapping claims to jurisdiction. In such circumstances it was inevitable that conflicting claims should emerge about who had the sovereign right to take action against alleged encroachments, and subsequently to resort to the means of violence at their disposal. His message is that "piratical" raids as reported in contemporary colonial records should be scrutinized cautiously, and not taken as fact. The thin line between sea people and sea robbers has caused confusion about the way the monopoly of the means of violence was exercised.

This is illustrated by Gerrit Knaap who deals with Papuan piracy in the seventeenth century as part of complex centre-periphery relations at the eastern end of the expanding sphere of Dutch supremacy in the Indonesian Archipelago. Papuans were deliberately used by local rulers to strengthen the latters' own prestige and authority. They manipulated the pirates — who probably would not have ventured as far west as they did if they had been acting on their own initiative — in their own political games. Since, the Papuan hinterland did not hold great promise compared with the more "developed" parts of Southeast Asia from the economic point of view it is not surprising that its human resources gradually became a prominent export item. Therefore, robbery and barter were two complementary sides of one activity. For a long time, this activity was intrinsic to the political economy of the area. In such circumstances, violence was lingering never far beneath the surface. Those persons acting as pirates, the aggressors as it were, were certainly not part of a marginal criminal group on the fringes of society. On the contrary, the phenomenon was taken for granted and members of the elite were often heavily involved.

James Warren in this volume continues his well known history of the Sulu-Mindanao region by commenting on the consequences of the international trade in slaves around organized markets and ports of which the island of Jolo was the centre. He describes in great detail the pattern of slave imports, the explanation which he adduces as the main reason for the rise in the population of Jolo, which was several times larger than that of the dominant society. The consequence of this demographic development was that captives and their descendants began to dominate the indigenous society. Spanish fears of the encroachment of British and Dutch influence triggered a war on slavery, precipitating not only the demise of Jolo, but also the incorporation of the whole Sulu zone into the Spanish realm of the Philippines.

A survey of the impact of colonial maritime expansion on raiding and raiding networks, and consequently on piracy in general at the end of the nineteenth century around the fringes of the Dutch colonial empire (in Sulawesi), is presented by Esther Velthoen. With a keen eye for detail, she describes the shifting power alliances of the local elites who abandoned mutual raiding to become intermediaries between the colonial power and their local allies or subjects. The subsequent establishment of the *Pax Neerlandica* did not lead to the end of piracy, but relocated it to other parts of the colony until the colonial power also managed to assert its authority in these regions as well.

Three authors deal with contemporary sea piracy. Stefan Eklöf Amirell has studied the development of piracy and its suppression in the Sulu region, still a marginal zone at the time from the perspectives of emergent state powers after World War II. He attributes the failure to achieve efficient naval and police cooperation to curb piracy to a clash between what may be termed the British "trading state" of Malaya on the one side, and the "political states" of Indonesia and the Philippines on the other side. "The former saw free trade as the key to national (or colonial) advancement and the government's role, in that context, was to provide the institutions which allowed free trade to flourish — including to maintain law and order on the sea in order to secure the free passage of traders and goods." Indonesia and the Philippines looked askance at free trade because of its association with predatory capitalism and Western imperialism. His conclusion that the re-emergence of piracy in the Sulu region was the result of this clash is revealing and carries in it a lesson for the future. A recent example of competing state power and unequal development of economic sectors in the region is given by Carolin Liss who deals with maritime piracy in the waters along the coast of Sabah, between Malyasia, Indonesia, and the Philippines. The waters off the district of Semporna have a long history of piracy, ranging from petty smuggling to the violent hijacking of boats and their crews for ransom. The unsolved conflict between Muslim insurgents and the Philippine army hinders efficient cooperation between the two coastal (riparian is more apposite for two states on either side of a river) states, but her conclusion is that the Malaysian government should develop a more comprehensive approach to counter piracy and other illegal activities in Sabah.

The paucity of anthropological material on maritime piracy in spite of the interest in coastal and marine cultures is not a surprise. Like in the study of the Italian mafia, the criminology of piracy is a task which is not without personal danger for the professionals in the field of anthropology. Ikuya Tokoro has studied the activities of robbers and traders in contemporary Sulu to find out how modernity and tradition are combined to secure a paltry livelihood with illegal and illicit trade in copra, and with smuggling. His study shows that anthropological research should create a framework for understanding pirate life on the basis of its own conditions, rules, and body of thought. In his assemblage of the data, Ikuya Tokoro sets the actors — the pirates — in their social, political, economic, and cultural context, and pays attention to the options and motivations of the pirates. It is hoped that others will follow this type of study on those known as small-scale pirates and robbers, who are believed to be disempowered coastal people, most likely, former fishermen and unemployed migrants, who locked out of economic well-being and, excluded, choose piracy for their livelihood.

The purpose of this book is to study maritime piracy from a historical perspective. An important theme is the parallel between state formation processes and the role piracy, or in more general terms, maritime violence, played in these developments. From these historical examples it is possible to learn that the colonial powers made no linguistic distinctions when lumping "piracy" together with generic maritime violence. However, this may not have been the case among the local rulers who tried to defend their realms against intruders, or for whom warfare and indiscriminate maritime violence was a means to establish their power. The well known adage that bandits became state makers and state makers bandits can certainly be aptly applied to some of the historical developments which a number of authors described in this volume and this raises questions about the meaning of piracy as an illegal act. (Also Braudel 1947, De Casparis 1979, and Gallant 1999.) Another theme is the link between piracy and related forms of organized crime (smuggling of goods and people, drug trafficking, and hostage taking, to mention a few), which brings us to the question of what is illegal and illicit in the transnational contexts in which pirates operates.

References

Anderson, J.L. "Piracy and World History: An Economic Perspective on Maritime Predation. *Journal of World History* 6, no. 2 (1995): 175–99.

Anthony, Robert J. and Jane Kate Leonard. *Dragons, Tigers, and Dogs: Qing Crisis Management and the Boundaries of State Power in Late Imperial China*. Ithaca, NY: Cornell East Asia Series, no. 114, 2002.

Braudel, F. "Misère et Banditisme". *Annales* ESC 2 (1947): 129–43.

Casparis, de. *Van avonturier tot vorst: Een belangrijk aspect van de oudere geschiedenis en geschiedschrijving van Zuid- en Zuidoost-Azië [oratie]*. 's-Gravenhage: Universitaire Pers Leiden, 1979.

Chalk, P. *Grey-area Phenomena in Southeast Asia: Piracy, Drug Trafficking and Political Terrorism*. Canberra Papers on Strategy and Defence no. 123. Canberra: ANU Press, 1997.

Gallant, T.W. "Brigandage, Piracy, Capitalism, and State Formation: Transnational Crime from Historical World-Systems Perspective". In *States and Illegal Practices*, edited by J.McC. Heyman, pp. 25–61. Oxford and New York: Berg Publishers, 1999.

Heyman, Joshia McC. *States and Illegal Practices*. Oxford and New York: Berg Publishers, 1999.

———. "Ports of Entry as Nodes in the World System". In *Identities: Global Studies in Culture and Power*, 11 (2004): 303–27.

Johnson, Derek and Mark Valencia. *Piracy in Southeast Asia: Status, Issues, and Responses*, edited by Derek Johnson and Mark Valencia. Singapore: ISEAS and IIAS, 2005.

Kleinen, John, and Manon Osseweijer. Piracy and Robbery in the Asian Seas. Theme introduction. *IIAS Newsletter* 36 (March 2006): 8.

Murray, Dian H. *Pirates of the South China Coast, 1790–1810*. Stanford, CA: Stanford University Press, 1987.

———. "Cheng I Sao in Fact and Fiction". In *Bandits at Sea: A Pirates Reader*, edited by C.R. Pennell, pp. 253–82. New York: New York University Press.

Ong-Webb, Gerard. *Piracy, Maritime Terrorism and Securing the Malacca Straits*, edited by Gerard Ong-Webb. Singapore: ISEAS and IIAS, 2006.

2

Piracy in Asian Waters: Problems of Definition

Michael Pearson

Much contemporary discussion of piracy focuses on the threat today. However, an historical perspective may show that nothing is really new, and that modern concerns can be found far back in history. Perspectives from the past may even illuminate modern problems, dangers, and even solutions.

My first task is to try to define piracy for it is not as simple as it may seem. Consider, for example, the common terms nowadays, "video" or "music piracy", involving what actually seems far from real piracy, for surely piracy must have an aquatic element. This is really copying, which according to some, infringes copyright. So also in our area of concern, where who is a pirate is often very much in the eye of the beholder. The most obvious difficulty is to see if there is a difference between a pirate and a privateer, who, in a Mediterranean context, is called a corsair. A key distinction seems to be that piracy is undertaken for private ends, while a privateer claims sanction from some state. In a European context a privateer would have a letter of marque authorizing action against the seaborne property of an enemy of this state.

But in practice historically it is very blurred and inchoate. As Mitchell points out, "The same person might well be trader, fisherman, pirate and naval employee by turns." Pure pirates, sea-going outlaws playing a lone hand against all comers "without political purpose or official sanction" were very rare.[1] Barendse notes that in an early modern Indian Ocean context the distinction was very ambiguous: "To states privateering was a way of privatizing warfare ..." but many privateers were really pirates. They may have had a letter from some state authority but they gave nothing back to the state and the state had no control over them.[2]

Captain Kidd is a good example of how one person could play various roles at different times. He began as a maritime merchant in the Caribbean. Seeking to get rich, he made an agreement in 1695 with the impoverished Earl of Bellomont, who was soon to be governor of New York. Bellomont gave Kidd a commission as a privateer who could seize any French vessels, and any pirates. King William himself was to get a tenth of any proceeds. Kidd went off to the Indian Ocean, but had little success. Finally he turned pirate and took and plundered the Mughal vessel *Quedah Merchant*, which had an English captain and a local crew. William Kidd had commissions that gave him explicit privateer status, but he chose to exceed this authority. This was his fatal mistake for England was not at war with the Mughals. He later returned to the Caribbean and New York. Imprisoned in New England, he was sent back to England in 1700 and tried. Kidd pointed to his commissions and his original orders from the admiralty as his essential defence to charges of piracy, even though his Indian Ocean targets were not at war with England. His plea was not accepted; he was executed in May 1701.[3]

There were also quite unambiguous acts of piracy, such as that perpetrated by Captain Every and four other ships off the mouth of the Red Sea in 1695. A fabulously wealthy Mughal *hajj* ship, the *Ganj-i Sawai*, was taken, the women on board raped, and a total plunder of £400,000, which included jewels and a saddle and bridle set with rubies meant for the Mughal emperor, was shared out among the crews.[4] On this occasion, and many others, there was no attempt to claim a fig leaf of legality by citing some letter of marque.

The case of the Portuguese in the sixteenth century continues this theme. I will on this occasion avoid the tendentious matter of who introduced violence into the Indian Ocean, and instead simply mention the way in which the Portuguese state paid its men. When a ship was taken there were clear official divisions laid down as to who was to get what. This was then a very cheap way for the crown to pay its sailors; plunder and booty were in effect an informal mechanism for providing pay.[5] It is relevant here to note an account of how a ship trading outside the Portuguese system was caught. The crew offered to surrender if the lives of those on board were spared. The Portuguese captain agreed to this, but the Portuguese sailors then mutinied. They preferred to board a hostile ship and loot it, for in the ensuing confusion there was much more chance of picking up valuable booty. In England the usual division of the spoils was roughly one fifth for the crown, and of the remainder, two thirds for the owners, and the rest for the crew, shared out according to rank. This, however, was mostly theory, for once a ship was taken and the most obvious treasures taken out by the officers, the crews claimed the right to "rummage" it and keep whatever hidden treasures they happened to find.

Sometimes the existence of piracy, however defined, could be beneficial for some agents of the state. In the sixteenth century the Portuguese failed to take Aden and so block access to the Red Sea. Instead they patrolled the entrance each season. However, this worked well for some Portuguese captains; an open Red Sea increased their chances of taking prizes, even if it also undermined the state's ambition to muzzle Muslim trade to this area. So also in the Caribbean in the early eighteenth century. Naval ships quite liked having pirates there for they could be hired to act as very well paid escorts for merchant ships. And this was more or less risk free: pirates never attacked a guarded merchant convoy. Escorting naval ships could also — illegally — carry freight at a hefty premium.

This was clearly unacceptable to the state, but even the relatively less extreme booty and plunder payment method becomes a little dubious when we remember that the ships taken, at least in the sixteenth century, were not those of states with which the Portuguese were at war. Rather they were native ships which had defied, sometimes inadvertently, the Portuguese claim to control and license and tax all trade in the Indian Ocean. It certainly could be argued that this invalidated — except from a very Eurocentric standpoint — the way in which the state allowed and regulated this practice. It then becomes state sponsored piracy rather than privateering. This is not, however, equivalent to Captain Kidd when he took Mughal ships, for he was punished, while neither the Portuguese state nor its sailors were. The key obviously is whether or not a state had given some licence, and then, whether or not the privateer returned something to the licensing authority. The additional requirement presumably is that the licence is given only for attacks on ships belonging to an enemy of the state which issues the licence.

In 1637, after a two-year cruise with a royal licence to plunder "from the Cape to China and Japan, including the Red Sea, the Persian Gulf, and the Coromandel coast", the *Roebuck* and the *Samaritan* returned to England with loot worth £40,000. Unfortunately, I have been unable to find out whether part of the proceeds went to the legitimizing agent, the Crown. However, it would be extraordinary if some "sweetener" was not presented to the Crown, for this was standard practice in Elizabethan and Stuart England. The famous Pirate Round in the late seventeenth century operated under a veneer of legitimacy. The perpetrators had been driven out of North America and the Caribbean to the Indian Ocean. They were meant to be targeting the French enemy, but Muslim ships were much easier to plunder. However, the point is that financiers and, crucially, governors in New England took up to half the profits.[6] At least in European eyes, these men were privateers, but one has to say that when they took French ships they were, but when they took Indian ones they were pirates. In any case, early next century the Dutch and English trading companies combined to stop them, for their operations had led to retaliation from Muslim states, especially in India.

The obligation to have a licence and return part of the proceeds to a state authority is crucial to separate a privateer from a pirate, but then what is a state? Later chapters in this volume touch on this, especially that by Esther Velthoen. Were Islamic states not part of the European state system? If so, could their ships be fair prizes? Could a privateer be summoned to a European court? Or to a Muslim one? South of Calicut were pirates who were ruled by their own rulers and numbered about 1,000 men. They were a people of both land and sea with small boats.[7] If they had their own "rulers", does this make them privateers? Were the Mappila opponents of the Portuguese off the west Indian coast in the sixteenth century acting with the sanction of the ruler of Calicut, and, if so, were they then privateers rather than pirates? And if, say, the English captured an American pirate, where was he to be tried? Were the Qawasim in Ras al-Khaimah in the Gulf a state or, as the British claimed, a confederation of tribes, and if so does this make them less than a state, unable, say, to license privateers? If it was a state then the British were incorrect in calling their naval auxiliaries pirates. To call them pirates was to provide a veneer of legality to what was really a desire to extend British control over the Gulf.[8] Nor was this unusual for the British. Around 1800, Southeast Asia was an ideal location for predation, especially in the Strait of Malacca. For a while the British took no notice, but once Singapore rose, British trade was threatened, so they took action against loosely defined predators, most of whom had some sort of relationship or affinity with local political controllers.

In an earlier work on the Mappilas who defied the Portuguese in the sixteenth century I found that some were privateers, some pirates.[9] Similarly, Risso has written that historians who defend the western Indian "admiral" Kanhoji against all accusations of piracy point to his adjunct position with the Maratha confederation, a position that lent him legitimacy. Kanhoji, however, often functioned in his own best interests and with considerable autonomy.[10] Consider also what Marco Polo found much earlier on the coast near modern Mumbai:

> With the King's connivance many corsairs launch from this port to plunder merchants. These corsairs have a covenant with the King that he shall get all the horses they capture, and all other plunder shall remain with them. The King does this because he has no horses of his own, whilst many are shipped from abroad towards India; for no ship ever goes thither without horses in addition to other cargo. The practice is naughty and unworthy of a king.[11]

The term used, "corsair", is the correct one, for they did return something, that is, horses, to the king who had sanctioned them. Some centuries later, in 1610, there is another example of how "piracy" was sometimes focused and controlled. The sheikh of Qadil on the Makran coast allowed ships from his territory to attack merchant ships, but not those of the Portuguese. The latter called in to Qadil, on the way to Hurmuz, to get refreshments, so the pirates agreed with the sheikh to leave them alone.[12]

Risso has covered in great detail definitions of piracy in a host of languages.[13] As I noted, Europeans had their own notions of legality and legitimacy of states, but Muslim examples seem to point again to ambiguity and fuzziness. According to the *shariah*, Muslim states were obliged to combat pirates, and protect all ships in coastal waters, including ships operated by non-Muslims.[14] To the extent this was achieved, it was only in restricted maritime spaces, such as the Black Sea or the Red Sea. Certainly Muslim powers around the shores of the Indian Ocean had no such obligation. I will return to this matter of coastal waters as compared with deep sea later, but while discussing Muslims we can note the situation described by a Persian envoy near Cochin in the 1680s. He found Muslim "pirates," who followed the *shafi'i madhhab*, and most of whom had learned the *Qur'an* by heart. They had their own eccentric justification for their actions. They attacked any ship they found except, pragmatically, European ones.

> The document which they bring forth to prove the legality of their actions is what the interceding ministers of the Shafi'i sect have published in their Qur'anic commentaries. "It is lawful for man to hunt on land and sea." But according to this group's interpretation, hunting in the sea is taken to mean piracy and thus they have formally decreed that it is permissible to capture foreign ships. They also say that as Muslims it is good to steal unbelievers'

goods. If they find a Muslim's goods, they quote "Indeed all believers of the faith are brothers" and then take their fellow Muslims' goods by right of kinship![15]

So much for the complex matter of separating pirates and privateers. We now need to move on to define piracy *tout court* briefly. There is a certain lack of specificity in the definition provided by the International Maritime Bureau: "an act of boarding any vessel with the intent to commit theft or any crime and with the intent or capability to use force in the furtherance of that act". They usually are despised as scavengers who hinder peaceful trade. Anderson's seminal study claims that piracy is "a subset of violent maritime predation" and he then goes on to find three variants: parasitic, intrinsic, and episodic.[16] As for the first, economic category, they are, as McNeill has it, macroparasites, human groups that draw sustenance from the toil and enterprise of others, offering nothing in return. As parasites they flourish when trade is prospering, and, at least botanically, an efficient parasite at worst debilitates rather than destroys the host that sustains it. Certainly they are predatory, but then fisherfolk are similarly predatory, for unlike peasants they extract but do not cultivate, take, but do not give.

In rather sanguine fashion, Horden and Purcell claim that they are not really separate from others at sea: "Piracy is the continuation of cabotage by other means."[17] Others point out that they are at least a sign of prosperity, for they need something to prey on; similarly, only a rich port is worth plundering. On the other hand, many studies show that piracy is created by coastal poverty, or the denial of access to previously available resources. Indonesian boats fishing in Australian territorial waters are considered to be illegal, and are subject to confiscation, the crews to imprisonment or repatriation. In the deep sea all can fish, for there is no property involved, but presumably once fish enter our territorial zone they become our property, just like anything on land such as a house. Thus those who infringe are indeed pirates, for they steal property found on the sea. Presumably they are considered to be economic pirates, but surely they are a consequence of coastal poverty. Recently, financed by criminal gangs, their boats have got bigger and more sophisticated; how do we categorize them now?

Some have claimed that piracy, and for that matter smuggling also, flourishes when coastal society is under stress. If legitimate trade, or fishing, fails to provide adequate returns, then people will resort to violence. On the other side of the coin, the prevalence of piracy often results from a weak state, one unable to police its waters. A study of recent southeast Asian piracy claims that it is a "grey area" phenomenon. It is like smuggling, gambling, prostitution, trafficking of goods and people, and petty crime on land, in that it exists more or less in organized forms in the context of diminishing human security. Maritime Southeast Asia's coastal zones are increasingly characterized by environmental degradation, illegal fishing, high unemployment, migrant labour, smuggling, crime, and prostitution. Piracy in this context is an economic activity, although it is concerned with the transport and distribution of goods rather than their production.[18]

Today coastal societies may be under stress from essentially economic forces, but in the past as European control spread over the Indian Ocean, stress came not from "impersonal" economic forces, but from the ambitions of the Europeans. The first example of this was the way in which the Portuguese claimed to monopolize the trade in pepper on the west coast of India in the sixteenth century. The pre-existing traders, the local Kerala Muslims called Mappilas, tried to continue their trade. They were called pirates by the Portuguese, and attacked on sight with great savagery. Other Mappilas were naval auxiliaries of the ruler of Calicut, whose trade was forcibly undercut by the Portuguese. Then again, some of the dispossessed traders seem to have turned to indiscriminate attacks on any merchant vessels they came across; maybe they were pirates, even if they took this up as a last resort. Certainly neither the traders nor the guerrilla naval forces can legitimately be called pirates, except from the standpoint of the Portuguese.[19] It is very much in the eye of the beholder, as shown by the way locals thought it was the Portuguese who were pirates. In Bengal a ballad went

> The dreaded Portuguese pirates, the Harmads, were constantly watching the movement of these [grain] boats [in the delta], stealthily following them through the nooks of the coast. They plundered the boats and assassinated their crew, and the boatmen and captains of the seaside trembled in fear of the Harmads.[20]

It could be that the Chinese pirates who were so important between 1520 and 1810 off the South China coast can be equated with the more "official" activities of the Portuguese, though they do seem to have been much more successful. Antony shows how they could be avoided only if they were paid protection money and had issued a passport. Such extortion was a major form of income for them, and was highly institutionalized. This all sounds like the Portuguese *cartaz* system of the sixteenth century.[21]

As European naval power grew in the Indian Ocean in the eighteenth century, "piracy" was more effectively combated, and was sometimes created by arbitrary definition. The Europeans pursued a carefully graduated policy on this matter. Essentially they defined who were their allies or clients, and protected their ships, and, indeed, sometimes turned a blind eye to nefarious activities from such client states. It was the enemies of the clients who were subject to attack. This was well articulated by the leader of a "pirates" stronghold in Kathiawad, western India, in 1807. He lugubriously told the British "In these days, all merchants have taken to the flag and protection of the Honourable Company, and if I abstain from plundering them, where can I procure food, and if I continue I fall under the displeasure of the Company."[22] In the nineteenth century in Southeast Asia, the Dutch first tried to reduce the coastal poverty which bred piracy by resettling people; later, in a way eerily reminiscent of modern discussions on how to combat terrorism, they reversed their focus and tried to use force.[23]

Another example, much studied, is the case of the Qawasim "pirates", based at Ras al Khaima [today Ra's al Khayma]. The Qawasim were a loose confederation of tribes, thus, as we noted, again raising the question of what is a state? Briefly, the British in the early nineteenth century allied themselves with the ruler of Oman, and then dubbed traders from Ras al Khaima, who competed with Oman, as pirates. It is true that some ships from this region raided around the shores of the ocean, which reminds us of the earlier discussion on who is a privateer. In 1816, they had the audacity to attack an English East India Company ship. Retribution followed: In 1820, the "pirate stronghold" was stormed, and British hegemony over the Gulf followed. The British defined one party to a rivalry between two indigenous Gulf states as pirates, and acted accordingly. As Philip Francis said at the time in the House of Commons, "whenever the Governor General and Council (of India) were disposed to make war upon their neighbours they could at all times fabricate a case to suit their purpose". The ruler of Oman also did well, being able to establish a strong maritime state in Zanzibar and East Africa until later in the century when his successors fell out with the British and were brought to heel. Here then overly successful competitors were stigmatized and defeated; again it seems clear they were pirates only in the eyes of the British.[24] Yet we have noted above that sometimes agents of states who were ostensibly combating people they identified as pirates acted contrary to state policy, as in the Caribbean, and earlier, off the mouth of the Red Sea. Indeed, one could legitimately quote St. Augustine to the British in the nineteenth century. It will be remembered that Alexander had captured a pirate chief: "For elegant and excellent was the pirate's answer to the great Macedonian Alexander, who had taken him; the king asking him how he durst molest the seas so, he replied with a free spirit, "How darest thou molest the whole world? But because I do with a little ship only, I am called a thief; thou doing it with a great navy, art called an emperor."

The Europeans were innovative in the Indian Ocean in another way too. Many earlier states had combated piracy in coastal or confined waters. In the seventh century BC, the Assyrian King Sennacherib sent out an expedition against them. Three hundred years later Alexander was harassed by them, and later again the Roman emperor Trajan led a naval expedition in the Gulf. In early modern times the Ottomans and other Muslim states tried to combat piracy in enclosed maritime areas such as the Black Sea, Red Sea, and Gulf, and instituted *mare clausum* policies (closed sea: a navigable body of water under the jurisdiction of a single nation). However, the Europeans, beginning with the Portuguese, expanded this to cover the oceans and the deep sea. Steinberg usefully differentiates between "land-like territorial waters and a non-territorial deep sea …", one territorialized from early on, the other for most of history outside of any state control.[25] This situation continues till today, of course, for the United Nations Convention on Law of the Sea (UNCLOS) gave states a territorial zone of twelve nautical miles (and an Exclusive Economic Zone [EEZ] of 200). In earlier times, Europeans arrogated to themselves the right to combat "piracy", and also people they accused of transporting slaves, wherever found; in effect the whole ocean was territorialized. Today it is more problematic to decide who has the authority to patrol beyond twelve nautical miles.

Yet it seems that today we think we know who is a pirate. There is much less flexibility compared with the many grey areas we have discussed. States have become much stronger, while international agencies have strict definitions of piracy. Now we have only "legitimate", state-sanctioned traders, and pirates, with nothing in between. Even when pirates receive tacit, or corrupt, assistance from governmental authorities,[26] this is still seen as illegal according to internationally accepted norms. Yet past ambiguities may be seen in the putative emerging phenomenon of seafaring terrorism, which some would equate with the corsairs of earlier times.

The much studied attack on the *USS Cole* raises further questions. It was different from what Eklöf calls "political piracy", that is, pirates who have an affiliation with some political group, such as Abu Sayyaf in the Philippines, or GAM. The groups Eklöf mentions are rather different from terrorists, for their objective is usually to commit a crime to raise money for their political cause, not simply to take lives. Note however that the money is not for them, which would be piracy, but for their cause, which makes it political piracy, and in some eyes, a quite legitimate activity. Indeed, Eklöf also claims that the attack on the *USS Cole* was not terrorism anyway, for this was a military target and terrorists by definition attack only civilians.[27] If we accept this, then the current outflow of books and articles warning of the dangers of maritime terrorism may be exaggerating the danger — so far there have been few significant examples of attacks by "terrorists" on civilian maritime targets. Three exceptions are the suicide attack on the French supertanker *MV Limberg* in October 2002, on the Al Basra Oil Terminal in April 2004, and especially Abu Sayyaf's suicide bombing of a Philippines ferry in February 2004, which killed more than 100 people. The last instance is clearly not political piracy, but rather maritime terrorism.

Yet these three examples hardly make up a threat to world trade. They, and piracy itself, are relatively minor problems compared with a host of other detriments to maritime trade. Even within the criminal category one would point to pilfering, and people and drug smuggling as more serious than piracy. More broadly speaking, world trade is seriously threatened by protectionist policies in the United States and the European Union, by climate change, and by military adventurism from the United States. Terrorism and piracy rank far behind these as serious impediments to free and unhindered exchange of goods by sea.

Notes

This article represents a greatly revised version of my Keynote Address to the Shanghai workshop. I am grateful to my colleagues for some factual corrections, and more importantly, for their excellent presentations, which encouraged me to rethink several matters.

1. David Mitchell, *Pirates* (London: Thames and Hudson, 1976), p. 11.
2. R.J. Barendse, *The Arabian Seas: The Indian Ocean World of the Seventeenth Century* (Armonk, NY: M.E. Sharpe, 2002), pp. 471–78.
3. Mitchell, *Pirates*, pp. 110–16 for a readable account, and Patricia Risso's excellent "Cross Cultural Perceptions of Piracy: Maritime Violence in the Western Indian Ocean and Persian Gulf Region during the Long Eighteenth Century", *Journal of World History* 12, no. 2 (2001): 293–319.
4. Mitchell, *Pirates*, pp. 101–08.
5. Luis Filipe F.R. Thomaz, "Portuguese Control over the Arabian Sea and the Bay of Bengal: A Comparative Study", in *Commerce and Culture in the Bay of Bengal, 1500–1800*, edited by Om Prakash and Denys Lombard (New Delhi: Manohar, 1999), pp. 115–62; Sanjay Subrahmanyam, *The Portuguese Empire in Asia 1500–1700: A Political and Economic History* (London: Longman, 1993), p. 61.

6. Mitchell, *Pirates*, pp. 101–03.
7. G.R. Tibbetts, *Arab Navigation in the Indian Ocean before the Coming of the Portuguese* (London: The Royal Asiatic Society of Great Britain and Ireland, 1971), p. 202.
8. See Risso, *passim*, and also Sultan Md. Al-Qasimi, *The Myth of Arab Piracy in the Gulf* (London: Croom Helm, 1986); for the contrary position, see Charles E. Davies, *The Blood-Red Arab Flag: An Investigation into Qasimi Piracy, 1797–1820* (Exeter: Exeter UP, 1997).
9. M.N. Pearson, *Coastal Western India* (Delhi: Concept Publishers, 1981), pp. 30–35.
10. Risso, op. cit.
11. Marco Polo, *The Travels of Marco Polo* (New York: New American Library, 1961), p. 393.
12. R.J. Barendse, "Trade and State in the Arabian Seas: A Survey from the Fifteenth to the Eighteenth Century", *Journal of World History* 11, no. 2 (2000): 191, f.n. 71.
13. Risso, pp. 296–302.
14. Hassan S. Khalilieh, *Islamic Maritime Law* (Leiden: Brill, 1998), pp. 128–48.
15. John O'Kane, trans. and ed., *The Ship of Sulaiman* (London: Persian Heritage Series no. 11, 1972), pp. 223–24.
16. J.L. Anderson, "Piracy and World History: An Economic Perspective on Maritime Predation", *Journal of World History* 6, no. 2 (1995): 175–99; also an interesting analytical and comparative study by Roderich Ptak, "Piracy along the Coasts of Southwest India and Ming China", in *As relações entre a India Portuguesa, a Asia do Sueste e o Extremo Oriente: Actas do VI Seminário Internacional de História Indo-Portuguesa*, edited by Artur Teodoro de Matos and Luís Filipe F. Reis Thomaz (Macau: Instituto de Cultura, 1993), pp. 255–73; and in ibid., Thomaz, "Do Cabo Espichel a Macau: Vicissitudes do corso Português", pp. 537–68.
17. Peregrine Horden and Nicholas Purcell, *The Corrupting Sea: A Study of Mediterranean History*, vol. I (Oxford: Blackwells, 2000), p. 158.
18. John Kleinen and Manon Osseweijer, "Piracy and Robbery in the Asian Seas", *IIAS Newsletter* 36 (March 2005): 6.
19. See work cited in note 9.
20. Lakshmi Subramanian, "Of Pirates and Potentates: Maritime Jurisdiction and the Construction of Piracy in the Indian Ocean", in *The UTS Review: Cultural Studies and New Writing* 6, no. 2 (November 2000): 14–17; and also Devleena Ghosh and Stephen Muecke, "The Indian Ocean", in the same issue of *UTS Review*.
21. Robert Antony, "Piracy in Early Modern China", in *IIAS Newsletter* 36, p. 7.
22. Subramanian, "Of Pirates and Potentates", p. 22
23. Older but still valuable works on Southeast include James Warren, *The Sulu*

Zone, 1768–1898 (Singapore: Singapore UP, 1981), and Nicholas Tarling, *Piracy and Politics in the Malay Work: A Study of British Imperialism in Nineteeneth-century South-East Asia* (Melbourne: Cheshire, 1963). For an excellent recent overview which advances the subject very usefully, see Derek Johnson and Mark Valencia, eds., *Piracy in Southeast Asia: Status, Issues, and Responses* (Singapore: International Institute for Asian Studies (Leiden) and Institute of Southeast Asian Studies, (Singapore) 2005). Stefan Eklöf's stimulating review of this collection in the *IIAS Newsletter* 40 (Spring 2006) raises important general questions and points to possible ways forward.

24. See work cited in f.n. 9, and Frank Broeze, "Trade, Warfare and 'Piracy': The Gulf in the 18th and early 19th Centuries [review article]", *The Great Circle* 9, no. 1 (1987): 61.
25. Philip E. Steinberg, *The Social Construction of the Ocean* (New York: Cambridge University Press, 2001), pp. 15, 138–39.
26. See, for example, Ken Blyth with Peter Corris, *Petro-pirates: The Hijacking of the "Petro Ranger"* (St. Leonards, NSW, Australia: Allen & Unwin, 2000).
27. Stefan Eklöf, "Piracy: A Critical Perspective", *IIAS Newsletter* 36, p. 12. See also a very useful modern analysis by Charles Glass, "The War on Piracy," *London Review of Books* 25 (18 December 2003): 3–7.

References

Anderson, J.L. "Piracy and World History: An Economic Perspective on Maritime Predation". *Journal of World History* 6, no. 2 (1995): 175–99.

Antony, Robert. "Piracy in Early Modern China". *IIAS Newsletter* 36 (March 2005): 7.

Barendse, R.J. "Trade and State in the Arabian Seas: A Survey from the Fifteenth to the Eighteenth Century". *Journal of World History* 11, no. 2 (2000): 471–78.

———. *The Arabian Seas: The Indian Ocean World of the Seventeenth Century*. Armonk, NY: M.E. Sharpe, 2002.

Blyth, Ken and Peter Corris. *Petro-pirates: The hijacking of the "Petro Ranger"*. St. Leonards, NSW: Allen & Unwin, 2000.

Broeze, Frank. "Trade, Warfare and 'Piracy': The Gulf in the 18th and early 19th Centuries [review article]". *The Great Circle* 9, no. 1 (1987): 61.

Davies, Charles E. *The Blood-Red Arab Flag: An Investigation into Qasimi Piracy, 1797–1820*. Exeter: Exeter UP, 1997.

Eklöf, Stefan. "Piracy: A Critical Perspective". *IIAS Newsletter* 36 (March 2005): 12.

———. "Piracy in Southeast Asia". *IIAS Newsletter* 40 (Spring 2006): 29.

Glass, Charles, "The War on Piracy". *London Review of Books* 25 (18 December

2003): 3–7.

——— Muecke. "The Indian Ocean Stories". *UTS Review* 6, no. 2, edited by Develeena Ghosh and Stephen Muecke. (November 2000): 24–43.

Horden, Peregrine and Nicholas Purcell. *The Corrupting Sea: A Study of Mediterranean History*, vol. I (Oxford: Blackwells, 2000).

Johnson, Derek, and Mark Valencia. *Piracy in Southeast Asia: Status, Issues, and Responses*, edited by Derek Johonson and Mark Valencia. Singapore: International Institute for Asian Studies (Leiden) and Institute of Southeast Asian Studies, 2005.

Khalilieh, Hassan S. *Islamic Maritime Law*. Leiden: Brill, 1998.

Kleinen, John and Manon Osseweijer. "Piracy and Robbery in the Asian Seas". *IIAS Newsletter 36* (March 2005): 6.

Mitchell, David. *Pirates*. London: Thames and Hudson, 1976.

O'Kane, John. *The Ship of Sulaiman*, edited and translated by Johon O'Kane. London: Persian Heritage Series no. 11, 1972.

Polo, Marco. *The Travels of Marco Polo*. New York: New American Library, 1961.

Prakash, Om and Denys Lombard. *Commerce and Culture in the Bay of Bengal, 1500–1800*, edited by Om Praskash and Denys Lombard. New Delhi: Manohar, 1999.

Ptak, Roderich. "Piracy along the Coasts of Southwest India and Ming China". *As relações entre a India Portuguesa, a Asia do Sueste e o Extremo Oriente: actas do VI Seminário Internacional de História Indo-Portuguesa*, edited by Artur Teodoro de Matos and Luís Filipe F. Reis Thomaz. Macau: Instituto de Cultura, 1993.

Risso, Patricia. "Cross Cultural Perceptions of Piracy: Maritime Violence in the Western Indian Ocean and Persian Gulf Region during the Long Eighteenth Century". *Journal of World History* 12, no. 2 (2001): 293–319.

Steinberg, Philip E. *The Social Construction of the Ocean*. New York: Cambridge University Press, 2001.

Subrahmanyam, Sanjay. *The Portuguese Empire in Asia 1500–1700: A Political and Economic History*. London: Longman, 1993.

Subramanian, Lakshmi. "Of Pirates and Potentates: Maritime Jurisdiction and the Construction of Piracy in the Indian Ocean". *The UTS Review: Cultural Studies and New Writing* 6, no. 2 (November, 2000): 14–17.

Sultan Md. Al-Qasimi. *The Myth of Arab Piracy in the Gulf*. London: Croom Helm, 1986.

Tarling, Nicholas. *Piracy and Politics in the Malay Work: A Study of British Imperialism in Nineteeneth-Century South-East Asia*. Melboure: Cheshire, 1963.

Thomaz, Luís Filipe F. Reis. "Do Cabo Espichel a Macau: Vicissitudes do corso Português." In *As relações entre a India Portuguesa, a Asia do Sueste e o Extremo Oriente: Actas do VI Seminário Internacional de História Indo-Portuguesa*, edited by Artur Teodoro de Matos and Luís Filipe F. Reis Thomaz. Macau: Instituto de Cultura, 1993.

———. "Portuguese Control over the Arabian Sea and the Bay of Bengal: A Comparative Study". In *Commerce and Culture in the Bay of Bengal, 1500–1800*, edited by Om Prakash and Denys Lombard. New Delhi: Manohar, 1999.

Tibbetts, G.R. *Arab Navigation in the Indian Ocean before the Coming of the Portuguese*. London: The Royal Asiatic Society of Great Britain and Ireland, 1971.

Warren, James. *The Sulu Zone, 1768–1898*. Singapore: Singapore University Press, 1981.

Part 2

East Asia

3

Giang Binh: Pirate Haven and Black Market on the Sino-Vietnamese Frontier, 1780–1802

Robert J. Antony

Depositions

In a routine memorial the governor of Guangdong province, Debao, reported to the Qianlong Emperor a case of piracy along the Sino-Vietnamese border that occurred in 1782. The victim was a merchant named Tong Shengru who had gone to the black market town of Giang Binh to trade, perhaps somewhat clandestinely. He testified that in the summer of that year a gang of pirates had robbed the vessel he had hired from Weng Panda, and on which they were both travelling. The band of pirates was a typical small ad hoc gang composed of impoverished fishermen and sailors who regularly alternated between legitimate work and crime to earn their living. Shortly after the incident, several of the pirates were apprehended and brought to trial. This incident typified the unstable, yet vibrant conditions on the Sino-Vietnamese frontier between 1780 and 1802. What follows are excerpts from the depositions of the victim Tong Shengru and a reluctant pirate named Wang Yade:

> Tong Shengru: I, an unassuming subject, originally came from Jiaying Subprefecture and opened a cosmetics shop in Hengye village in a place called Neighing Horse Hamlet (Masishe). On the ninth day of the sixth lunar month of this year (1782), I hired Weng Panda's boat to transport perfumes and powders to Giang Binh to sell. On the thirteenth day [after completing my business transactions] in Giang Binh I collected my money and goods to return to my shop. That night on the ocean at a place known as Flowing Water (Lizhu) a boatload of pirates robbed us. Their boat suddenly heaved alongside us and then, like a swarm of hornets, they boarded our vessel,

grabbing money and goods and then fleeing. The next morning we repaired to Lizhang where we began searching everywhere for the culprits. On the twentieth day, we spotted the pirate boat in Zhangshan harbour. [After reporting the incident to] the local market head, together we apprehended two culprits, Li Xing and Wang Yade. We also recovered some of our stolen property. The others had already got away. Afterwards, we turned the pirate boat over to the port authorities in Zhangshan.

Wang Yade: I, your humble subject, come from Hepu County. I am 21 years old. I make my living as a sailor. I know Li Xing very well. This year [1782], early in the sixth lunar month, the cost of rice was very high, and so I went to Giang Binh to look for some work. On the tenth day of that month I ran into Li Xing and he took me to see He Xing who was looking to hire sailors on his boat. He agreed to pay me 150 cash (*wen*) each month in wages. Aboard He's boat there were three other sailors and a helmsman, so that the total, including the skipper, Li Xing, and me, was seven men. On the afternoon of the thirteenth, He Xing went to the market to find us a job, but he returned to tell us that there was no work anywhere in that port. What is more we were out of rice to eat. He told us that while at the market he had heard that Weng Panda's boat had on board a passenger named Tong who had money and goods and was about to return to his store in Hengye village. He said why don't we go out to meet them en route at sea and rob them of their money and goods? How's that for a piece of work? Li Xing and the others all agreed, but this humble subject was afraid to join with them. He Xing cursed at me and said he would throw me overboard right then if I didn't agree. I didn't dare refuse and so went along with them. They set off and that evening we awaited our prey at a place offshore near Lizhu harbour. Around midnight Tong arrived and his boat anchored for the night. He Xing, Li Xing, and the others pulled our boat up to his. But when they jumped aboard to rob Tong's boat, I hid myself in the stern, afraid to come out. Afterwards He Xing and the others grabbed money and goods and brought them aboard our boat and we sailed off to a secluded spot in barbarian [that is, Vietnamese] waters to split up the booty. I didn't dare take a share, but He Xing told me that since I went along with them and knew about the heist, if ever a word leaked out to anyone he would kill me. He then gave me 2,000 cash. I was afraid of him so I didn't refuse. On the twentieth we anchored at Zhangshan mart. He Xing and three others went ashore to buy food and provisions. Li Xing, Ge'er, and me remained on board to watch things. We didn't know that the victim had already discovered our whereabouts and was on his way with the market head to arrest us. As soon as Ge'er saw them coming he jumped ashore and ran away. The victim and the others came aboard and nabbed Li Xing and me.[1]

Piracy

Piracy was a violent predatory activity, which in the late eighteenth century seemed to have got out of control in the South China Sea. Beginning in the 1780s, small bands of Chinese and Vietnamese pirates began to coalesce into large, well-organized fleets under the patronage of Tay Son rebels. Lacking a strong navy of their own, rebel leaders commissioned Chinese and other pirates to help them in their war against the reigning Le dynasty. Tay Son rebels, who needed both men and money for their struggle, actively recruited pirates, guaranteed them safe harbours, supplied them with ships, weapons, and provisions, and rewarded them with official ranks and titles so they would engage in piracy as a means of obtaining revenue. In effect, the Tay Son regime created a plunder-based political economy. Following the rhythms of the monsoons, each spring and summer pirate fleets left their bases along the Sino-Vietnamese border for Chinese waters, returning each autumn laden with booty which they shared with their Tay Son patrons. By the time the Tay Son Rebellion was crushed in 1802, there were already more than 50,000 pirates roving around the South China Sea. Nevertheless, throughout those years petty gangs of local pirates, such as He Xing's mentioned above, continued to operate in the shadows of the larger, well-organized fleets of "barbarian pirates" (*yifei*) and "ocean bandits" (*yangdao*).

The intensification of piracy on the Sino-Vietnamese water frontier resulted from several factors.[2] First, there was a combination of changing environmental circumstances, especially China's population explosion and the increased trade with Vietnam and elsewhere in Southeast Asia. Paradoxically, the rise in piracy corresponded to China's "prosperous age", and a time when Vietnam was also benefiting from China's booming economy. Piracy arose not because of a general immiseration of Chinese society, but rather because of the strains that prosperity had placed on the more marginal elements of Chinese (and Vietnamese) society. A second factor important to the growth and development of large-scale piracy was the external patronage of the Tay Son rebels in Vietnam. Third, internally the emergence of talented and charismatic leaders among the pirates assured the cohesion and organization necessary for the expansion of piracy. Contradictions inherent in maritime society created conditions of conflict, violence, and predation. Piracy was an endemic and integral part of maritime society and culture and a logical outcome of early modern China's burgeoning economy.[3]

Inevitably, pirates depended on friendly ports and black markets for survival. Cut off from the land by their life on the seas, pirates not only relied on people on shore to supply them with food, water, weapons, and other necessities, but also to dispose of their booty and provide with them information and recruits. They needed safe harbours where they could careen and repair their vessels, and where they could rest and relax. Wherever there were friendly ports there could be found shops, inns, brothels, and gambling dens that catered to the needs and whims of spendthrift pirates.[4] The worst thing that could happen to outlaws, as Eric Hobsbawm pointed out, was to be cut off from their local sources.[5]

One such pirate haven was Giang Binh (in Chinese, Jiangping), a frontier town that thrived on the piracy and smuggling trade between 1780 and 1802. In this chapter we will examine three important aspects concerning the rise and fall of Giang Binh: one, its connection with the underground economy of the South China Sea; two, its role as a frontier; and three, its transient outlaw population and underworld culture.

Turning to the Sea

Giang Binh was located near the mouth of a small, unnavigable river called the Tielang on the ill-defined Sino-Vietnamese border. The town was a part of Vietnam's An Quang province until it reverted back to China in 1885, as part of the settlement ending the Sino-French War.[6] The illustration in Figure 3.1 depicts Giang Binh in the early nineteenth century. With almost impenetrable mountains at its back and land too poor for agriculture, the people of Giang Binh naturally turned to the sea for their livelihood. Throughout the eighteenth century it was a well known black market town, and at the end of the century it served as a major pirate and smuggling headquarters. By then it was a bustling border town with hundreds of shops and a population of roughly two thousand households, composed of both Chinese and Vietnamese, as well as the occasional aborigine sojourner. There was also a large squatter population of mostly poor Vietnamese, who had settled on the sandy shoals at the entrance to the harbour. Many residents specialized in handling stolen goods and provisioning the pirates who frequented the market and lived on many of the nearby islands. Traders and merchants, such as Tong Shengru mentioned above, travelled from Guangdong, Guangxi, Fujian, and other Chinese provinces specifically to this black market to sell merchandise, and to buy booty, which pirates always sold at bargain prices. So too did Vietnamese traders. Giang Binh was a refuge not only for pirates, criminals, and misfits, but it also attracted

FIGURE 3.1
Qing Representation of Giang Binh

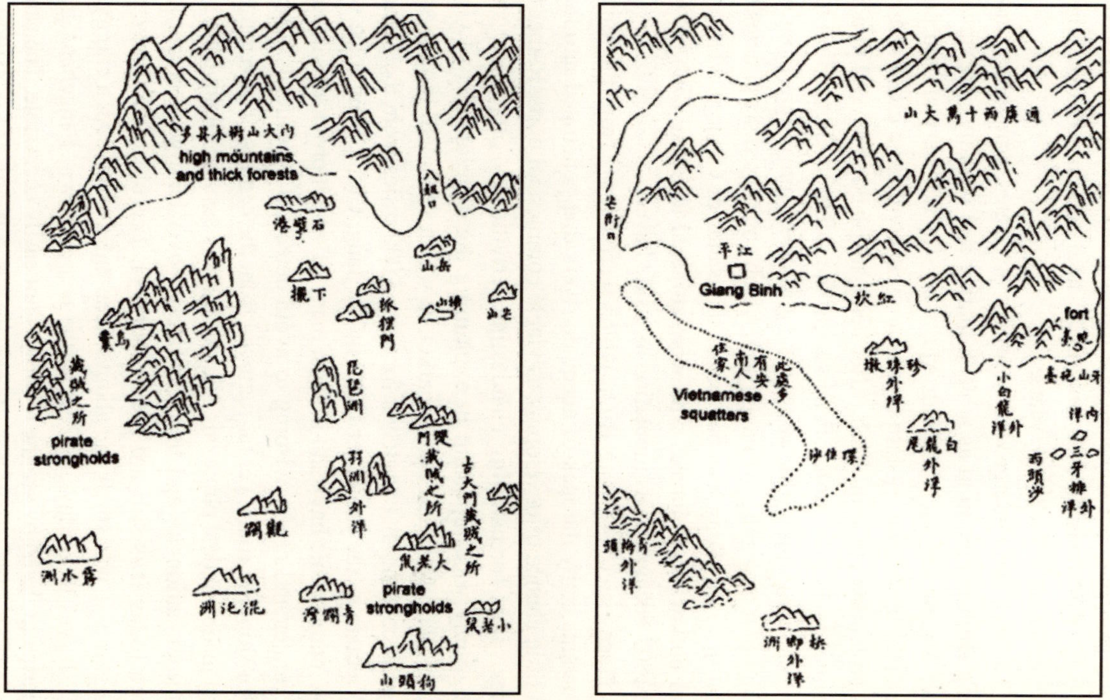

Source: Guangdong tongzhi (Gazetteer of Guangdong province), 1864

large numbers of sailors (such as Wang Yade above), as well as fishermen, labourers, and porters who came in search of work.[7] These were the sorts of men who provided a steady pool of recruits for pirate gangs. In 1802 Giang Binh was razed by royalist troops fighting Tay Son rebels. The destruction of Giang Binh was, in fact, one of the final acts in a devastating rebellion that had lasted over thirty years.

Through the underground networks of pirates, smugglers, and outlaws, Giang Binh's reputation as a black market and friendly port spread far and wide. A gangster such as Peng Aju, who was a fisherman and pirate from Chenghai in faraway eastern Guangdong, knew that he could receive shelter and protection at Giang Binh. After being involved in several piracies on the Guangdong-Fujian border, Peng sought the safety to Giang Binh to hide out from the authorities who were seeking to arrest him. Eight months later, he organized a new gang in Giang Binh, which committed six piracies before his arrest in 1797.[8] Peng was but one of thousands of Chinese, Vietnamese, and other outlaws and outcasts who were attracted to Giang Binh between 1780 and 1802 because of its reputation as a safe haven.

Places such as Giang Binh, which were cut off from the hinterland by mountains or by the lack of adequate rivers that penetrated into the interior, had little chance of developing as viable commercial ports. Rather they were better suited for handling clandestine activities — piracy and smuggling. Geography was important in explaining the development of Giang Binh as a pirate haven and black market. It was a secluded, remote speck on a jagged coastline that stretched for over 3,000 miles from the Mekong Delta in Vietnam to the Ou River Delta in Zhejiang, China. This coast was dotted with innumerable bays and islands, many of which provided safe anchorages for pirates and others wishing to avoid detection by officials. Located on a major shipping route, yet far removed from the centres of government, Giang Binh made an ideal pirate lair. Natural barriers assured Giang Binh's isolation. Communications to and from the interior over land were nearly impossible (even today it is still a difficult journey). The closest military post — at Dongxing — was small and about fifteen miles away over a craggy mountain trail. It was three days by foot to the nearest town, Fangcheng in Qinzhou department. Even by sea the town was not easily accessible. The sandy shoals proved to be dangerous obstacles to shipping.[9] Besides Giang Binh, numerous other clandestine ports and black markets sprung up along the coast of the South China Sea to handle the trade in stolen goods and to service pirate ships and crews. Giang Binh had intimate connections with many of them.

Giang Binh was an integral node in a vibrant underground economy that criss-crossed the South China Sea, linking and forming an extensive network of licit and illicit markets. It was an important part of the larger "water world" of the South China Sea.[10] In its prime (between 1780 and 1802), Giang Binh was the core or hub of a vast water world, a network of black markets, pirate bases, and friendly ports that stretched up the Chinese coast from Hainan Island and Guangdong to Fujian, Taiwan, and Zhejiang, and southward along the Vietnamese coast to Hue, Saigon, and beyond (see the map in Figure 3.2). Some of the well known clandestine ports having connections with Giang Binh included Sanhewo, Baimiao, Haian, Jiazi, Haimen, and Dahao in Guangdong; Meizhou, Baisha, Shage, Shuiao, and Xiahu in Fujian; Jilong, Dagou, Houlong, Suao, and Donggang in Taiwan; and Goutongmen, Shibandian, Dachenshan, and Sanpan in Zhejiang.[11] In Vietnam, Giang Binh's network of friendly ports included Doan Mien, Thi Nai, Hue, and Hoi An.[12]

It is important to point out that in many cases clandestine activities (especially smuggling) were also conducted in some of the larger "legitimate" ports such as Saigon, Macao, Jiangmen, Huangpu, Chenghai, and Amoy. These larger entrepôts that served pirates were cosmopolitan centres and relatively tolerant of outsiders, even criminals, as long as their presence proved to be profitable. In a sense, it would appear, many merchants and even officials made little distinction between legal and illegal enterprises. Piracy and commerce had become indistinguishable. The merchants and traders who travelled to Giang Binh acquired stolen goods, which they then transported and resold in various ports in the same way they sold their other goods.[13] To borrow the words of the Spanish historian Gonçal López Nadal, it would be "difficult to describe these methods of economic activity in terms that are conceptually distinct from commerce in general".[14] Just as Saigon or Amoy functioned as key trans-shipment hubs in the legal trading system, Giang Binh functioned as a key trans-shipment hub in the underground trading system. Although it remained a bustling port during the heyday of piracy in the late eighteenth century, once the pirates had been defeated and their base destroyed, Giang Binh never again recovered its former glory and thereafter devolved into a backwater port and petty black market. Without pirates or smugglers Giang Binh could not survive.

Piracy was important because it allowed marginalized areas, such as Giang Binh, which had otherwise been excluded, to participate in the wider

FIGURE 3.2
Giang Binh's Water World in the Late 18th Century

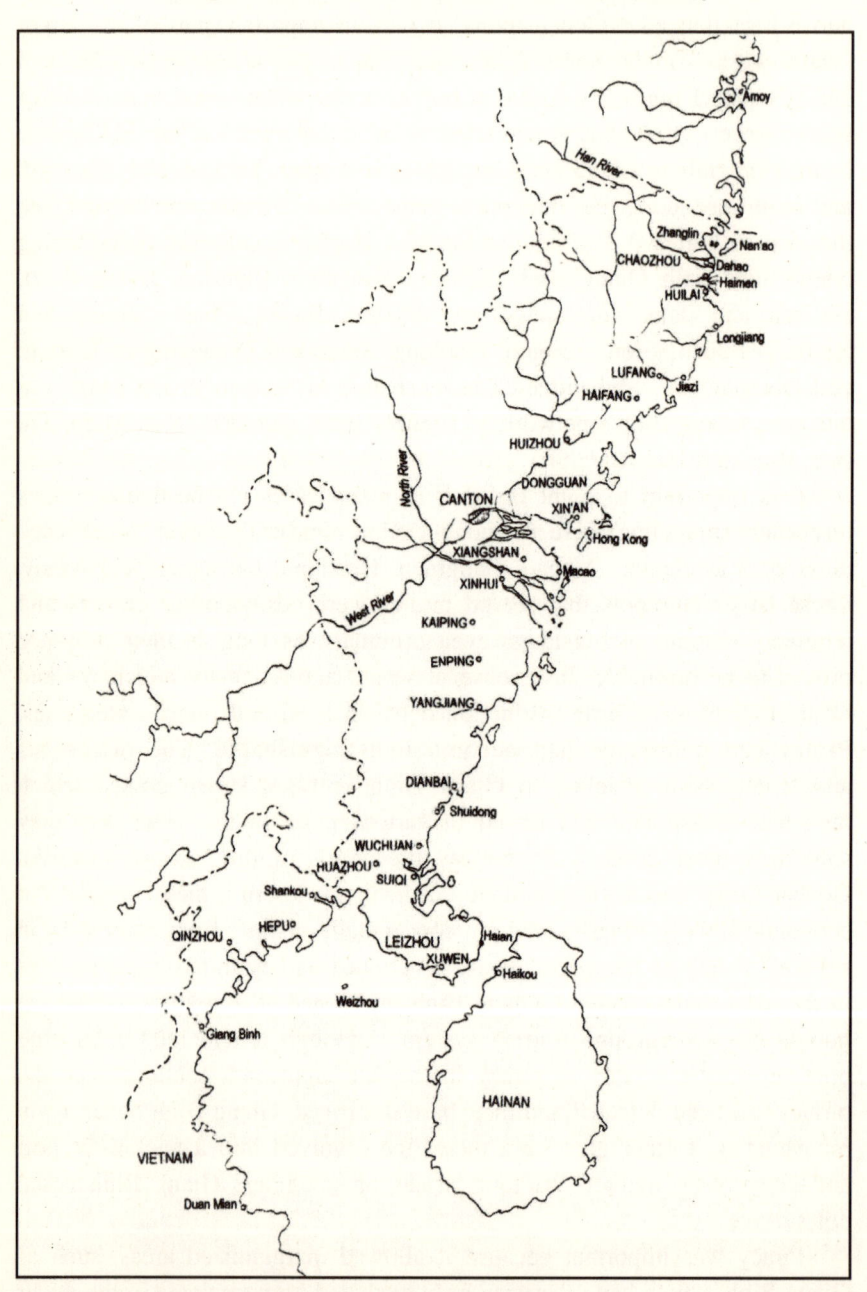

Source: *Guangdong tongzhi* (Gazetteer of Guangdong)

commercial economy. Whenever piracy flourished, so too did the underground economy, providing tens of thousands of jobs to coastal residents. Like the pirates themselves, most of the individuals who traded with them were fishermen and sailors, as well as petty traders, who engaged in both licit and illicit activities as vital for survival. In many instances, extra money gained from clandestine activities provided an important, even major, part of their overall incomes. Because tens of thousands of people on both sea and shore came to depend on piracy for their livelihood, either directly or indirectly, it became a self-sustaining enterprise and a significant feature of life on the South China Sea.

While piracy did detract from legitimate trade and profits, it nonetheless also had important positive economic consequences. Not only did the growth of legitimate commerce promote the development of new ports, but so too did the pirates' illicit trade. Black markets, such as Giang Binh, operated as a shadow economy alongside, and in competition with, legitimate trade centres. Furthermore, this illegal trade also tended to perpetuate piracy. Once pirates generated supplies of goods for sale at discount prices, buyers were attracted to the black markets that arose to handle the trade in stolen goods. Although the scale of illicit trade is impossible to measure, it certainly pumped large amounts of goods and money into many local economies, especially in those areas outside the normal or legitimate marketing system. Large amounts of money and goods flowed in and out of black markets, all of which were outside the control of the state and normal trading networks. The establishment of markets specifically to handle stolen merchandise was a clear indication of weaknesses in the structure of normal, legal markets. Pirates, therefore, made important contributions to the growth of trade and the reallocation of local capital. In a word, piracy had become a normal part of economic life for tens of thousands of people who inhabited the shores of the South China Sea.

Borders and Frontiers

Giang Binh also raises some interesting questions about borders and frontiers, and about cores and peripheries. This place, particularly its location, has long intrigued me because Giang Binh was actually situated just *inside* China's border. Although both Chinese and Vietnamese officials understood that there was a border or boundary separating the two countries, both sides would have been hard pressed to say exactly where that line was at the time. This is not because the notion of borders was an alien concept to Chinese officials, but rather because for them the concept remained imprecise. After all, Chinese rulers were emperors of "all under Heaven" and the Qing imperium viewed Vietnam as a vassal or tributary state. For officials, the question of borders was related more to administrative jurisdictions than to a line of national demarcation, and in the case of Giang Binh, both governments agreed that the town was under Vietnamese jurisdiction.[15] At least that was the theory, and that was how things appeared to officials on both sides of the border in the late eighteenth century.

The rugged terrain also hindered specifying exact boundaries. Both Vietnam and China utilized zones or belts of natural obstacles, such as mountains, deep forests, and rivers, as natural boundaries to separate one from the other. In this area (as in others) the border was simply marked by a series of military posts, which could be moved forward or backward, according to changing circumstances. It was all very imprecise.

Furthermore, it is highly unlikely that the residents of Giang Binh viewed things in the same way officials did. At least, for the fishermen, sailors, pirates, and smugglers, who lived most of their lives on the water, borders and boundaries simply made no sense. The key to their survival, as Dian Murray put it, "lay in the freedom to range back and forth across the border without hindrance".[16] Borders, like laws and regulations, were unnatural to their way of thinking.

Giang Binh can best be understood as a frontier town, in the sense of both place and process. Frontiers were marginal zones of cultural contact where two or more initially distinct peoples coexisted in some sort of developing relationship.[17] In many ways, Giang Binh resembled the pirate stronghold on St. Marie Island off Madagascar during the late seventeenth century.[18] Like St. Marie, Giang Binh had all the earmarks of a typical frontier town. Hemmed in by rugged mountains and thick forests (see Figure 3.1), Giang Binh remained quite remote and isolated from other more settled areas of both China and Vietnam. In the interior there was a buffer zone of "savage" aborigines separating Giang Binh from the "civilized" areas of China. In the eyes of Chinese officials and literati, Giang Binh was on the outskirts of civilization. Many of its Chinese residents had forsaken their queues and had taken Vietnamese or aborigine wives or mistresses.[19] The region, as a whole, was sparsely populated and the population was highly transient. There was little evidence of permanence. Everything seemed makeshift. Most of the people there lacked roots or a place they called home.

Because most of them — the fishermen, sailors, coolies, pirates, smugglers, and itinerant traders who dominated the town — owned no property, they felt little attachment to the land.[20] It was precisely the fluidity and frontier nature of this whole region, Li Tana explained, that "made life uncertain and potentially violent".[21]

Formal government was also weak. Giang Binh fits James Ron's description of a frontier as a "weakly institutionalized and often chaotic setting prone to vigilantism and paramilitary freelancing".[22] Frontiers, after all, were lawless zones. Although the Vietnamese claimed jurisdiction over the area, the government's presence was nearly non-existent. This should not be surprising because it was at the time of the devastating Tay Son Rebellion, and a time of general anarchy throughout much of the region. Because Giang Binh was a backwater on the fringe of the Sino-Vietnamese frontier, neither Vietnamese nor Chinese authorities paid much attention to it. From time to time, the Tay Son rulers, under pressure from the Qing court, sent soldiers to clear Giang Binh of pirates and other outlaws, but this was never done in earnest because the rebels relied on the pirates for money and support.[23] For all practical purposes, it was a town without governance or laws. No wonder the people there were known for their lawlessness, drunkenness, debauchery, and brawling. What Ray Allen Billington said about the "wild" American frontiersmen rings true here as well: "Partly responsible for their antisocial behavior was the inclination of lawless men to concentrate in lawless regions; sparsely peopled frontiers attracted outcasts who rebelled against authority".[24] Under those conditions, Giang Binh was the perfect hideaway for pirates, smugglers, and a host of other malcontents. Outlaws could operate out of there with little fear of detection and arrest.

From the perspective of the heartlands of China and Vietnam, Giang Binh was at the extreme periphery of civilization. From the perspective of Giang Binh's (transient) residents, however, things may have been viewed from a different angle. For them, perhaps Giang Binh was the core, and faraway Canton, Hanoi, and Hue were the peripheries. After all, the terms "core" and "periphery" are relative and mutable. It was truly a no-man's-land, a polyglot community in the process of "creolization", not assimilation.[25] It was neither purely Vietnamese nor purely Chinese in its social, economic, and cultural structures. It was a creation of its own. Though the people of Giang Binh were mostly transients, they (or others) frequently returned to this place for shelter, rest, and play. "Water people" (*shuishang ren*) needed land bases to survive.

Citizens

The "citizens" of Giang Binh, between 1780 and 1802, were a motley bunch of Chinese, Vietnamese, and occasionally even European seafarers, renegades, and misfits. Official documents from both China and Vietnam often used the unflattering term *liumin* to describe these sorts of people. They were homeless wanderers, runaways, displaced persons, vagabonds, fugitives, and refugees. According to Wang Gungwu, the term *liumin* "suggests people whose anti-social behaviour and irresponsible acts had led to their homeless state and to their status as outcasts, vagrants, and even outlaws". The term also referred to people who left China without permission.[26] One such desperado was a monk named Jue Ling, who hailed from Guangdong. In his youth, he was a hoodlum and assassin who first sought the safety of the monastery by becoming a monk and then later fled to Vietnam to avoid arrest. Another Chinese fugitive named He Xiwen was a one-time triad boss who, because of later involvement in the White Lotus Rebellion in Sichuan, fled to Vietnam in 1778, where the Tâysons commissioned him as a commander of a pirate junk.[27]

Pirates were the most important group of transients in Giang Binh in the late eighteenth century. The survival and prosperity of the town depended on them. In one report, dated 1797, Chinese officials estimated that in and around Giang Binh pirates had erected over a hundred shacks where they lived (irregularly) with their families and traded with local and itinerant merchants.[28] Among the 230 individuals arrested for piracy by Guangdong officials whom Dian Murray investigated, 199 had connections in Vietnam, and among those, 127 had direct connections with Giang Binh. Most of those pirates came from south-western Guangdong, particularly from the Leizhou Peninsula, the area in closest proximity to Giang Binh and also one that was notorious for its pirates.[29] Some were from Vietnam, while others came from as far away as Fujian and Zhejiang provinces.

Most of these men were poor fishermen and sailors in their twenties and early thirties; the youngest was fourteen yeas old (*sui*) and the oldest, sixty-eight years old; the average age was 32.8 years. There was also a significant number of peddlers, porters, merchants, and shopkeepers whom the Qing authorities had arrested.[30] Jiang Sheng, a peddler from Zhejiang who sold betel nut in Fujian and engaged occasionally in piracy, returned each year to Giang Binh to sell his booty, rest, and refit his ship.[31] Huang Daxing, who hailed from Xinhui county in the Canton Delta, worked as a porter in Giang Binh before joining the gang of the notorious pirate Zheng

Qi.[32] In general, apart from having a high degree of mobility, most of these men were impoverished; they were individuals who lived on the fringe of society, making barely enough money to survive. Take the case of Wang Yade, mentioned at the start of this chapter. As a hired sailor he earned 150 cash (*wen*) a month, which was about the average wage for hired sailors at that time. Because a male Chinese normally ate one catty (1.3 pounds) of rice each day and a catty of rice cost about five cash, therefore, wages provided a sailor only enough money to buy a day's worth of rice and little else. In short, wages were barely enough for subsistence. Thus, the 2,000 cash Wang received as his share of the booty was an enormous sum of money.

Pirate gangs were seldom fixed or permanent. They were, in this sense, much in tune with the fluid nature of Giang Binh itself. Pirates were not only mobile, but also mostly amateurs. Piracy was typically a part-time job for seafarers who routinely alternated between criminal and legitimate activities (as several of the above mentioned cases have already shown).[33] Wang Ya'er provides a typical case. Originally from Xinhui county in the Canton delta, Wang had gone to Giang Binh with four friends to seek work, but finding none they decided to become pirates. In 1796 they received "certificates" (*zhao*) from Tay Son leaders authorizing them to build ships and recruit gangs ostensibly for piratical activities. They quickly recruited over a hundred men, and in spring, they set sail to plunder the China coast from Guangdong to Zhejiang. After returning to Giang Binh in winter, they disposed of their loot, refitted their ships, and recruited a new gang. Once again they set out early the next year with over a hundred and fifty men, but in June they were apprehended by Chinese naval forces near the coast of Xin'an county.[34]

These Sino-Vietnamese pirates plundered all shipping regardless of nationality, both off the coasts of China and Vietnam. During this period large fleets of pirates from Giang Binh and Vietnam (labelled "barbarian pirates" [*yifei*] by Chinese officials) dominated the Sino-Vietnamese water frontier. Giang Binh pirates routinely cooperated with smaller gangs of "local pirates" (*tufei*) in Guangdong and Fujian provinces who acted as guides and participated in raids in their home areas.[35] So powerful was the Giang Binh network that by 1800, its pirates had nearly shut down the Qing-monopolized salt trade in Guangdong and the Western opium trade in Canton. Through its extensive underground network the pirates also collected annual "tribute" from ports as far away as Zhejiang, between 1796 and 1802.[36]

Other members of Giang Binh's transient community were men such as Luo Yasan, who was a merchant, smuggler, and pirate. Luo, who was thirty-three years old at the time, was a Chinese from Qinzhou, Guangdong, whose family had migrated to Vietnam some three generations earlier. In the summer of 1796, he received a commission from a Tay Son official to transport rice to sell in Giang Binh and then buy medicine, ceramics, and cloth to bring back to the rebel camp. On his way home a month later, however, pirates robbed Luo. Undaunted, he returned to Giang Binh where he was able to procure a boat, weapons, and eighteen men from a friend, a pirate named Liang Er, and so Luo set out once again — this time as a pirate — to recover his losses. Luo and his mixed Sino-Vietnamese gang plundered two junks off the coast of Qinzhou before their ship was wrecked in a storm off Hainan Island.[37] Luo's case shows just how easy it was for someone to move back and forth between criminal and legitimate pursuits in Giang Binh's sociocultural environment.

The people of Giang Binh's water world also shared a common culture. It was a rough and tumble underworld culture of poor, marginalized seafarers, and pirates. They shared a collective culture of their own making, quite different from that of people living in agricultural villages and walled cities on land. Forged out of hardship, prejudice, and poverty, they created a culture of survival based on violence, crime, and vice, and characterized by excessive profanity, intoxication, gambling, brawling, and sexual promiscuity. The culture of seafarers and pirates had its own amusements, sexual mores, and morals. The common language would very likely have been creole, a mixture of southern Chinese and Vietnamese dialects.[38] In defiance of the Qing imperium, and as a political statement perhaps, many Chinese who lived or sojourned in Giang Binh cut off their queues and let their hair hang lose in the fashion of outlaws and rebels.[39] The Qing government was sensitive to the issue of queues because of its policy of using hairstyle as a sign of loyalty. These pirates and sailors were social and cultural transgressors and outcasts, who stood in marked defiance of orthodox values and standards of behaviour.[40]

It was also a male-dominated culture where the place of women was definitely subordinate and submissive, even more so than in the orthodox cultures of China and Vietnam. Pirates acted without restraint. The only sexual conventions they followed were their own. Women and boys were just another type of booty, and could be bought and sold as chattel. Pirate chiefs frequently kept several wives and boys, as many as their fancies dictated. Gang members also took and discarded women and boys like they would empty bottles of wine. Captives were the objects of wanton brutality, being abducted, battered, and raped as their captors saw fit.[41] For many pirates, the acquisition of "wives" was done simply by forceful taking. In the language of official reports pirates, abducted indigenous and occasionally Chinese women whom they "forcefully raped and slept with" (*qiangbi jiansu*). Just as often pirates sodomized young captive boys and forced them to serve them both on and off the ship. In one case, a bankrupted merchant-turned-pirate, Yang Yazhang, kidnapped and raped several Vietnamese women and young boys.[42] In another case, Chen Zhangfa, a fisherman from Xinhui county, Guangdong, had gone to Giang Binh where he joined a gang of pirates in 1795. After plundering a fishing junk off the Dianbai coast, Huang and several cohorts gang raped four captured sailors, while another pirate forced a Dan (Tanka) woman aboard their boat where he raped and kept her against her will.[43] In terms of sexual mores the pirates broke all the rules. Sexual violence against both women and boys was a regular feature of the pirate's trade.

From the official Chinese perspective, Giang Binh was beyond the pale of civilization and the pirates were no better than savages. Like the Christians who joined the Barbary corsairs and "turned Turk" in the seventeenth-century Mediterranean,[44] the Chinese who became pirates were seen as despicable characters for abandoning their own advanced culture in favour of backwardness and depravity among the Vietnamese and non-Sinicized ("raw" [*sheng*]) aborigines. In short, they lacked the redeeming features of Chinese civilization. There was no better "proof" of their debauchery than the extreme cruelty exerted by pirates towards their captives, especially their cannibalistic practices. Take the case of Chen Laosan, a pirate from Suiqi county in south-western Guangdong who operated out of a lair in Vietnam. On more than one occasion Chen brutally murdered his victims by ripping open their chests and extracting their livers, which were then mixed with liquor for the crew to drink. Afterwards he had the corpses thrown overboard. The Qing official who wrote this memorial completely abhorred such outrageous and bloodthirsty acts, and made it clear that Chen had already forsaken China and any semblance of humanity.[45]

Just as seafarers depended on land for their survival, Giang Binh depended on the sea for its survival. It was a multicultural, multilinguistic, and multi-ethnic port whose population thrived on illegal activities, especially piracy and smuggling between 1780 and 1802. It was an international black market. Not only the economy, but also Giang Binh's society and culture were tied to crime, vice, and violence. Giang Binh does not fit in well with our preconceived notions of Southeast Asia or China. It existed uneasily on the outside of any discrete, state-based geographical system. Giang Binh and the pirates and outlaws that it supported created a world unto itself.

Notes

1. Xingke tiben (Routine memorials), QL 11.10.48. First Historical Archives, Beijing. (In the notes, Chinese dates, as above, refer to the eleventh day of the tenth month of the forty-eighth year of the Qianlong Emperor's reign.)
2. The term "water frontier" comes from Nola Cooke and Li Tana, eds., *Water Frontier: Commerce and the Chinese in the Lower Mekong Region, 1750–1880* (Lanham, MD: Rowman and Littlefield, 2004).
3. See the discussions about South China's piracy in the late eighteenth century in Katsuta Hiroko, "Shindai kaiko no kan" (Pirate disturbances in the Qing period), *Shinron* 19 (1967), pp. 27–49; Dian Murray, *Pirates of the South China Coast* (Stanford: Stanford University Press, 1987); and Robert Antony, *Like Froth Floating on the Sea: The World of Pirates and Seafarers in Late Imperial South China* (Berkeley: University of California, Institute of East Asian Studies, China Research Monographs, no. 56, 2003).
4. Ming-Qing shiliao, wubian (Historical materials on the Ming and Qing, *wu* series) (Taibei, undated), pp. 305b, 492–93; *Shichao shengxun* (Imperial edicts of the ten [Qing] reigns [first year of the Jiaqing reign]) (Taibei, undated), 38:1.a-b.
5. Eric Hobsbawm, *Primitive Rebels* (New York: Norton, 1965), p. 17.
6. Suzuki Chusei, "Re Cho koko no sin tono kankei" [Vietnam's relations with the Qing in the late period of the Le dynasty], in *Betonamu Chugoku kankei shi*, edited by Yamamoto Tatsuro (Tokyo, 1975), pp. 480–81.
7. Gongzhongdang (unpublished palace memorials, National Palace Museum, Taiwan) (1074) JQ 1.8.26, (1656) JQ 1.12.11, (2531) JQ 2.6.11 (JQ refers to the Jiaqing Emperor's reign); and *Guangdong haifang huilan* (A conspectus of Guangdong's coastal defence) (Canton, undated), 26:1a-2b.
8. Gongzhongdang (2531) JQ 1.5.29.
9. Suzuki Chusei, op. cit., p. 480.
10. I borrow the term "water world" from Dian Murray, but use it in a slightly different way. I use the term in a broad sense of shared social, economic, and cultural activities and patterns that are not easily defined and delimited by ethnic and linguistic differences or by national boundaries. See Murray, op. cit., pp. 6–17.
11. Thomas C.S. Chang, "Ts'ai Ch'ien, the Pirate King who Dominates the Seas: A Study of Coastal Piracy in China, 1795–1810" (Ph.D. dissertation, University of Arizona, 1983), pp. 218–19; and Antony, op. cit., p. 127.

12. On the friendly ports in Vietnam mentioned in Chinese sources, see Gongzhongdang (137) JQ 1.2.9, (2845) JQ 2.7.6; and (3459) JQ 2.12.1.
13. Gongzhongdang (1047) JQ 1.8.19, (2010) JQ 2.2.14, and (2845) JQ 2.7.6.
14. See Gonçal López Nadal, "Corsairing as a Commercial System: The Edges of Legitimate Trade", in *Bandits at Sea: A Pirates Reader*, edited by C.R. Pennell (New York: New York University Press, 2001), pp. 125–36 (quote on p. 127).
15. Lloyd Eastman, *Throne and Mandarins: China's Search for a Policy during the Sino-French Controversy, 1880–1885* (Cambridge, MA: Harvard University Press, 1967), pp. 43–44.
16. Murray, op. cit., p. 20.
17. For the comparative study of frontiers and the problems they present, see Howard Lamar and Leonard Thompson, *The Frontier in History: North America and Southern Africa Compared* (New Haven: Yale University Press).
18. On the pirates of St. Marie, see Robert Ritchie, *Captain Kidd and the War against Pirates* (Cambridge, MA: Harvard University Press, 1986), pp. 80–111.
19. See examples in *Da Nan shilu Qing-Yue guangxi shiliao hubian* (Material on Sino-Vietnamese relations in the Veritable Records of Vietnam), Xu Wentang and Xie Qiyi, eds. (Nangang, Taiwan: Academia Sinica, 2000), pp. 19–21, 30–31.
20. On Qing frontiers, see James Millward, "New Perspectives on the Qing Frontier", in *Remapping China: Fissures in Historical Terrain*, edited by Gail Hershatter, et al. (Stanford: Stanford University Press, 1996), pp. 113–29.
21. Li Tana, "The Water Frontier: An Introduction", in Nola Cooke and Li Tana, eds., op. cit., p. 8.
22. James Ron, *Frontiers and Ghettos: State Violence in Serbia and Israel* (Berkeley: University of California Press, 2003), p. 16.
23. See, for example, Gongzhongdang (2368) JQ 2.4.24. In another case, Tay Son soldiers cooperated with the Qing navy on a joint expedition to clear the Giang Binh area of pirates. The report mentions the capture sixty-three pirates, but no leaders, and it also claimed that soldiers had killed an unspecified number of pirates besides destroying more than a hundred of their houses in the area. The Tay Son authorities turned over the sixty-three prisoners to the Qing authorities, and as a token gesture, promised to continue to search and arrest pirates in the area. A follow-up memorial details their trial and the sentencing to death of sixty-two of those prisoners; Gongzhongdang (2631) JQ 2.6.16.
24. Ray Allen Billington, *America's Frontier Heritage* (Albuquerque: University of New Mexico Press, 1974), p. 72.
25. See G. William Skinner, "Creolized Chinese Societies in Southeast Asia", in *Sojourners and Settlers: Histories of Southeast Asia and the Chinese*, edited by Anthony Reid (St. Leonards, Australia: Allen and Unwin, 1996), pp. 51–93.

26. Wang Gungwu, "Sojourning: The Chinese Experience in Southeast Asia", in ibid., p. 4.
27. *Da Nan shilu Qing-Yue guangxi shiliao hubian*, pp. 29–31.
28. Gongzhongdang (2368) JQ 2.4.24.
29. *Chiongzhou fuzhi* (Gazetteer of Chiongzhou prefecture, Hainan Island) (1890) 19:28a.
30. Murray, op. cit., pp. 162–65; Murray had 135 cases with information on ages of arrested pirates.
31. Gongzhongdang (2631) JQ 2.6.16.
32. Ibid., (1448) JQ 1.11.10.
33. See the discussion in Antony, op. cit., pp. 82–104.
34. Lufu zouzhe (Copies of palace memorials), First Historical Archives, Beijing, (3854), JQ 2.1.27.
35. For example, see Gongzhongdang (1763) JQ 1.12.29.
36. Antony, op. cit., p. 41.
37. Gongzhongdang (1643 addendum) JQ 1.12.7 (2010) JQ 2.2.14; and Murray, op. cit., p. 187 n. 39.
38. See the discussion on creole languages in Southeast Asia in Skinner, op. cit., pp. 59–61.
39. Gongzhongdang (1047) JQ 1.8.19.
40. For an extensive discussion of the culture of pirates, see Antony, op. cit., pp. 139–63.
41. Although several years later, Chinese pirates under the female chieftain, Zheng Yi Sao, issued a code of conduct that attempted to protect female captives from rape, the evidence is mixed as to just how effective this rule was in actual practice.
42. Gongzhongdang (2845) JQ 2.7.6.
43. Ibid., (1448) JQ 1.11.10.
44. An informative essay about "turning Turk" is Lois Potter, "Pirates and 'Turning Turk' in Renaissance Drama," in *Travel and Drama in Shakespeare's Time*, edited by Jean-Pierre Maquerlot and Michele Willems (Cambridge: Cambridge University Press, 1996), pp. 124–40.
45. Gongzhongdang (2779) JQ 2.6.21. Antony, op. cit., pp. 161–63, discusses the practice of human sacrifice among the pirates of south China.

References

Antony, Robert. *Like Froth Floating on the Sea: The World of Pirates and Seafarers in Late Imperial South China*. Berkeley: University of California, Institute of East Asian Studies, China Research Monographs, no. 56, 2003.

Billington, Ray Allen. *America's Frontier Heritage*. Albuquerque: University of New Mexico Press, 1974.

Chang, Thomas C.S. "Ts'ai Ch'ien, the Pirate King who Dominates the Seas: A Study of Coastal Piracy in China, 1795–1810". Ph.D. dissertation, University of Arizona, 1983.

Chiongzhou fuzhi (Gazetteer of Chiongzhou prefecture, Hainan Island). 1890.

Cooke, Nola, and Tana Li, eds. *Water Frontier: Commerce and the Chinese in the Lower Mekong Region, 1750–1880*. Lanham, MD: Rowman and Littlefield, 2004.

Da Nan shilu Qing-Yue guangxi shiliao hubian (Material on Sino-Vietnamese relations in the Veritable Records of Vietnam), edited by Xu Wentang and Xie Qiyi. Nangang, Taiwan: Academia Sinica, 2000.

Eastman, Lloyd. *Throne and Mandarins: China's Search for a Policy during the Sino-French Controversy, 1880–1885*. Cambridge, MA: Harvard University Press, 1967.

Gongzhongdang (Unpublished palace memorials). National Palace Museum, Taiwan.

Guangdong haifang huilan (A conspectus of Guangdong's coastal defence). Taibei, undated.

Hobsbawm, Eric. *Primitive Rebels*. New York: Norton, 1965.

Katsuta Hiroko. "Shindai kaiko no kan" [Pirate disturbances in the Qing period]. *Shinron*, 19 (1967): 27–49.

Lamar, Howard, and Leonard Thompson. *The Frontier in History: North America and Southern Africa Compared*. New Haven: Yale University Press.

Li, Tana. "The Water Frontier: An Introduction". In *Water Frontier: Commerce and the Chinese in the Lower Mekong Region, 1750–1880*, edited by Nola Cooke and Tana Li. Lanham, MD: Rowman and Littlefield, 2004.

Lufu zouzhe (Copies of palace memorials). First Historical Archives, Beijing.

Millward, James. "New Perspectives on the Qing Frontier". In *Remapping China: Fissures in Historical Terrain*, edited by Gail Hershatter, et al. Stanford: Stanford University Press, 1996.

Ming-Qing shiliao, wubian (Historical materials on the Ming and Qing, *wu* series). Taibei, undated.

Murray, Dian. *Pirates of the South China Coast*. Stanford: Stanford University Press, 1987.

Nadal, Gonçal López. "Corsairing as a Commercial System: The Edges of Legitimate Trade". In *Bandits at Sea: A Pirates Reader*, edited by C.R. Pennell. New York: New York University Press, 2001.

Potter, Lois. "Pirates and 'turning Turk' in Renaissance drama". In *Travel and Drama in Shakespeare's Time*, edited by Jean-Pierre Maquerlot and Michele Willems. Cambridge: Cambridge University Press, 1996.

Ritchie, Robert. *Captain Kidd and the War against Pirates*. Cambridge, MA: Harvard University Press, 1986.

Ron, James. *Frontiers and Ghettos: State Violence in Serbia and Israel*. Berkeley: University of California Press, 2003.
Shichao shengxun (Imperial edicts of the ten [Qing] reigns). Taipei, undated.
Skinner, G. William. "Creolized Chinese Societies in Southeast Asia". In *Sojourners and Settlers: Histories of Southeast Asia and the Chinese*, edited by Anthony Reid. St. Leonards, Australia: Allen and Unwin, 1996.
Suzuki Chusei. "Re Cho koko no sin tono kankei" (Vietnam's relations with the Qing in the late period of the Le dynasty). In *Betonamu Chugoku kankei shi*, edited by Yamamoto Tatsuro. Tokyo, 1975.
Wang Gungwu. "Sojourning: The Chinese Experience in Southeast Asia". In *Sojourners and Settlers: Histories of Southeast Asia and the Chinese*, edited by Anthony Reid. St. Leonards, Australia: Allen and Unwin, 1996.
Xingke tiben (Routine memorials). First Historical Archives, Beijing.

4

Tonkin Rear for China Front: The Dutch East India Company's Strategy for the North-Eastern Vietnamese Ports in the 1660s

Hoang Anh Tuan

>   *In fine*, it is pity so many conveniences and opportunities to make the kingdom [of Tonkin] rich and its trade flourishing should be neglected; for if we consider how this kingdom borders on two of the richest provinces in China, it will appear that, with [final] difficulty, most commodities of that vast Empire might be drawn hither ...; nay, would they permit strangers the freedom of this inland trade, it would be vastly advantageous to the kingdom; but the Chova [*Chúa*] ... has, and will probably in all times to come, impede this important affair.
>
>   — Samuel Baron 1685, p. 664

In the early 1660s, political and military tensions challenged the northern Vietnamese kingdom of Tonkin on both sides.[1] Even as its fifth campaign against Quinam could make no breakthrough on the southern frontier, Tonkin was increasingly being challenged by the Manchu armies on the northern frontier with China. After gradually beating back the restored Ming forces, the Qing armies approached the Tonkin-China border and demanded that the Lê-Trịnh government send tribute to Peking (*DRB 1661*, pp. 49–55). Being exceedingly preoccupied with the conflict with Quinam, Tonkin could not dispatch its first tribute to Peking until 1663 (*Cương mục* II, p. 296). Consequently, the Manchu soldiers attacked Vietnamese merchants trading to southern China and hindered the Chinese in exporting merchandise such as Chinese gold and musk to Tonkin. Bowing to this escalating tension, the Tonkin-China border trade stagnated, which greatly impeded the import and export trade of the factory of the Dutch East India Company (VOC) in Thăng Long (present day Hanoi). Calamity followed calamity and the Company lost Formosa (present day Taiwan) to the Zheng family in 1662. All these negative developments forced the VOC to readjust its strategy towards the Tonkin trade in the first half of the 1660s.

On the basis of the VOC's Tonkin factory records, this chapter aims to draw an insightful picture of the VOC's strategy on the southern China trade. By utilizing its only base in Tonkin as a springboard to penetrate China in the early 1660s. It is done by reconstructing a string of setbacks which the Tonkin factory was facing due to the Chinese civil war and the Company's loss of Formosa in 1662. These impediments forced the Dutch factors in Tonkin to search desperately for Chinese gold and musk and eventually led them to the adventurous expedition to Tinnam (present-day Tiên Yên of Quảng Ninh Province) in 1662. By focusing on these issues, this chapter also seeks to place the VOC's Tonkin trade in the context of regional trade during the eventful 1660s.

THE STAGNATION IN THE TONKIN-CHINA BORDER TRADE AND THE LOSS OF FORMOSA

In the mid-1640s, China became embroiled in a dynastic war between the newly established Qing and the waning Ming, which lasted until the early 1660s. Since the Ming-Qing conflict was largely fought out in the southern provinces of China, it exerted an enormous impact on the politics and economy of Tonkin. At Cao Bằng, the Mạc clan sought the spiritual protection of the Ming Dynasty in their efforts to continue their rivalry with the Lê-Trịnh in Thăng Long. The Ming intervention was the deciding factor which prevented the Lê-Trịnh rulers from toppling their Mạc rivals until the late 1670s (*Lịch triều* IV, pp. 147–50, 204; Wills 1974, pp. 1–28; Struve 2005).

The long-lasting conflict in southern China also affected the commerce of Tonkin, and the border trade between the two countries was the chief victim. Despite the Trịnh's restriction on the border crossing, both Vietnamese and Chinese merchants could still exchange their commodities on a quite large scale. For the most part the goods exported to China from Tonkin included Southeast Asian spices and European textiles which were imported into Tonkin by the Dutch, Chinese, and other foreign merchants. In return, Chinese gold and musk were among the miscellaneous goods which merchants brought to northern Vietnam. From the late 1650s, the Chinese gold exported to Tonkin became one of the most important products on which the VOC set its sights for the Coromandel trade. The reason was that Chinese gold had become scarce in Formosa, reflecting the economic stagnation of the China-Formosa trade. The high government, therefore, ordered the Tonkin factory to purchase as much Chinese gold as possible for the coast factories. Chinese musk was bought for the Netherlands (Hoang 2007*b*, pp. 168–76).

Before long, these two items grew scarce in Tonkin as the border trade declined. In 1655, the Tonkin factory reported to Batavia that although the civil war in China had not caused a complete stagnation in the exportation of Chinese goods over the China-Tonkin border, it had reduced the flow of Chinese gold to northern Vietnam to a remarkable extent (*GM* II, p. 881). The annual volume of the border trade had fallen steadily by the early 1660s. In 1661, Peking reminded the Lê-Trịnh court that should the latter fail to send tribute to Peking within a short time, the border would be violated (*DRB 1661*, pp. 49–55). Because Thăng Long did not dispatch a tribute to Peking in 1662, Chinese soldiers attacked Vietnamese merchants travelling to the border to buy Chinese gold and musk, confiscating all their capital and commodities (*DRB 1663*, p. 71).[2] These merchants were later released and ordered to return to Thăng Long to inform the Lê-Trịnh court that tension on the border would not be resolved until their tribute had arrived at Peking. Consequently, the Tonkin-China border trade was temporarily interrupted. The Tonkin factory, therefore, failed to procure the much wanted Chinese gold and musk (VOC 1240, pp. 1355–74).

During the period of stagnation in the Tonkin-China border trade, the Far Eastern trading network of the VOC was severely affected by the loss of Formosa to the Zheng family in 1662. Indeed, the Dutch Formosa trade had already been in decline from the mid-1640s because of the fall in the annual export volume of Chinese goods to the island (NFJ 57 1 August 1644; NFJ 61 15 September 1648; *GM* II, p. 452; Ts'ao 1997, pp. 94–114). In 1656, in an attempt to control the export of Chinese goods and monopolize the lucrative trade between China and Japan, Zheng Chenggong (alias Coxinga), alleging that the Dutch had molested his junks in Southeast Asian waters, imposed an economic embargo on Dutch Formosa, driving the Company's Formosa trade to a complete standstill. In early 1660 there were rumours that the Zheng armies would invade the island sometime in April of the same year. After gathering enough evidence to convince themselves of this eventuality, Governor Fredrik Coyett and the Council of Formosa prepared for an invasion and requested assistance from Batavia.

The governor general and the Council of the Indies reacted quickly and in late July a fleet of twelve ships arrived in Formosa from Batavia. As the months passed without any invasion from the mainland, the commander and most of the experienced officers in the fleet left Formosa for Batavia in two of the ships despite the vigorous protests of Coyett and the Formosa Council; the rest remained on the island. At the end of April 1661, the Zheng troops invaded the island. After resisting for nine months, the Dutch surrendered. The loss of Formosa was a severe blow to the Company's East Asian trading network (*GM* III, pp. 386–89; Wills 1974, pp. 25–28; Blussé, 1989, pp. 65–72; Andrade 2000, pp. 314–24).

In its efforts to recover from the heavy loss of Formosa to Zheng Chenggong in 1662, the VOC formed a naval alliance with the newly established Qing Dynasty, principally to take revenge on the Zheng clan, but also to obtain trading privileges from the Chinese Court to compensate for the loss of Formosa. Despite sporadic joint naval operations in the years 1662–64, which effectively reduced Zheng's power in Amoy and Quemoy, the final goal of conquering Formosa did not materialize owing to Peking's hesitation. The trading privileges which the Chinese had granted the Company in the early years of the mutual relationship were consequently revoked (Wills 1974, pp. 25–28).

Another way of gaining a niche in the China trade was to attempt to penetrate China from Tonkin. The Company records reveal that besides using the diplomatic channel to Peking, Batavia also instructed its Tonkin factors to cruise along the coastline to explore the seaport system of north-east Tonkin, near the Chinese border, and to look for possibilities to establish a permanent factory there for direct trade with the Chinese. In April 1661, Batavia sent the *Meliskerken* to Tonkin, where she was ordered to obtain a licence from the Trịnh rulers to explore the area called Tinnam in the present north-eastern province of Quảng Ninh.

What was the major aim of this exploration? The answer is directly related to the Company's demand for Chinese gold for its Coromandel trade and, to a lesser extent, Chinese musk for the Netherlands.

CHINESE GOLD AND MUSK AND THE VOC'S STRATEGY TOWARDS THE NORTHERN BORDER TRADE IN THE 1660s

It is important to point out here that from the outset the VOC's utmost aim in trading with Tonkin was to export Vietnamese silk to Japan. Having successfully established its official trading relations with Tonkin in 1637, the VOC regularly exported Tonkinese raw silk and silk piece goods to Japan. From the mid-1640s, the so-called "Tonkinese silk-for-Japanese silver trade" flourished, thanks to China's political crisis which severely hindered the regular influx of Chinese silk from the mainland to Formosa. As a consequence, from 1644 the Company's export volume of Tonkinese silk to Japan increased significantly. This lasted for about one decade, before falling into decline from 1655 because of the marketability of Bengal silk in the Far Eastern market. As the annual export volume of Tonkinese silk declined, the high government in Batavia urged its factors in Thăng Long to import gold for the Coromandel Coast and musk for the Netherlands.[3]

Gold

In the course of the seventeenth and eighteenth centuries, the supply of gold and silver played an indispensable part in the entire commercial activities of the Dutch East India Company in the East. As a fixed rule, right from its foundation in 1602, every chamber of the Company was instructed to send silver pieces of eight (Spanish coins) to Asia as investment capital, and if this specie was not provided in full, then gold was consigned as an alternative (Glamann 1958, pp. 50–72; Gaastra 1983, pp. 447–76). As early as 1602, gold was included in the Company's cargoes dispatched to Asia when 247,500 guilders in rosenobels was exported under the auspices of the Company (Gaastra 1983, p. 453).[4] Silver in the form of both minted coins and bullion was the sort of money which was indispensable to the Company in running its intra-Asian trade throughout the two centuries of its existence. Nevertheless, in some places gold was preferred, especially on the eastern coast of the Indian sub-continent. The Indian trade of the Company required both silver and gold as investment capital: silver was generally in high demand in Bengal and copper was very acceptable in Surat, but gold was desirable in Coromandel. During the seventeenth century, the Coromandel Coast was the most important destination for the gold exported from Europe and by Asian gold exporters. To maximize the profit on the Coromandel trade, or at least to direct this trade into the most profitable channels, the Company was forced to provide its Coast factories with gold. The gold supply from the Netherlands to Asia was not always sufficient to cover demands. During the 1640s, for instance, Batavia's requests for adequate amounts of capital were not always satisfied; its demand for African gold for its Asiatic trade was ignored altogether by the Directors of the VOC, the Gentlemen XVII (Glamann 1958, p. 57).[5]

The Company was not entirely dependent on the Netherlands though, for its supply of precious metals, although during the first thirty years of the Company's existence, its trading capital relied heavily on the money sent from the republic. After this, however, the trend changed significantly. In the case of the gold supply for Coromandel, for instance, a larger proportion of the annual capital by the early 1630s, was being provided by Asian factories which relieved the Coast of its dependence on the Netherlands for the supply of capital (Raychaudhuri 1962, p. 187).

This change can be largely attributed to the developments in the intra-Asian trade, which not only enabled the VOC to make profits on its intra-Asian trading network, but also helped furnish its factories with desirable and marketable commodities (Steengaard 1973, p. 140). One of the key factors which enabled the Company to establish its pre-eminent position in this commerce was the Japan trade. Generally speaking, after this trade had been restructured and strengthened in the early 1630s, the Hirado factory, and, later, the Deshima factory, were able to export a substantial amount of silver every year from Japan. The major part of this silver was shipped to Formosa, where it was exchanged for Chinese commodities which were sought after in both the Asian and European markets. During the 1640–60 period, the Company regularly exported silver valued at about one million guilders per year from Japan. Part of this silver was exchanged for Chinese gold in Formosa, that was then exported mainly to Coromandel, supplementing the gold which was purchased from Java, Malacca, Laos, and Indragiri (Raychaudhuri 1962, p. 189). The gold supply from the island of Formosa to Coromandel proceeded smoothly during the 1630s, before falling into a phase of decline from the early 1640s, induced by the decline in the Formosa trade.

Facing the decline in the gold supply from Formosa, the Company was forced to look for alternative possibilities. In fact, in 1640, the Japan factory, conscious of the importance of providing the Coromandel trade with gold, had already exported some Japanese *koban* (small gold coins) and *oban* (large gold coins), valued at 144,050 taels for the first time. The Dutch export of Japanese gold was short-lived because the Japanese Government issued a ban on the export of gold in the following year, fearing a drain of bullion. Because this ban on the Japanese gold export was strictly enforced until 1665, the Company had to look for a gold supply from other places. When the gold supply from East Asia stagnated, the Company factory in Gamron in Persia started to purchase the gold which arrived there from Europe via the land route. In the 1640s and in the following decade, this Persian factory could provide the Indian factories annually with a substantial sum consisting mainly of silver and gold (Gaastra, 1983, pp. 464–65, 474). In Southeast Asia, the Company itself endeavoured to mine gold on the west coast of Sumatra, and lost no time in procuring this precious metal from various other places such as Manila, Makassar, and Malacca, in its eagerness to supply the Indian Coast with whatever gold it could afford (Gaastra 1983, pp. 464–65, 474; Glamann, 1958, p. 58). In spite of its assiduous efforts, the total amount was inconsiderable.

In the context of this gold shortage, Tonkin emerged as an alternative gold supplier in the late 1650s, born of necessity when the gold supply from the East Asian quarters rapidly declined. In order to comprehend the sudden emergence of Tonkin in this role, some facts should be clarified. In 1651, it was reported to Batavia that the flow of Chinese gold to Formosa had come to a complete standstill. The capital which the headquarters of the VOC at Formosa, Zeelandia Castle could afford to send to the Coromandel Coast struggled to reach around six tons, which was four tons (400,000 guilders) less than had been planned (*GM* II, pp. 451–52). In the middle of the 1650s, the high government was again informed that the VOC servants in Formosa, suffering from the poor trade caused by the civil war in mainland China and Zheng's embargo on Dutch Formosa, were struggling to gather a mere three tons of gold, eight tons less than in 1653. Pertinently, it was noted that the flow of Chinese gold now streamed in the direction of Tonkin instead of Formosa (*GM* II, pp. 451–52).

The Dutch loss of Formosa to Coxinga in 1662 disrupted the regular gold flow from Formosa to eastern India and exacerbated the Company's gold shortage even more severely. In the meantime, the profit margins on gold on the Coromandel Coast revived in the 1660s because the Mughal Emperor demanded his tribute be paid in gold pagodas (Raychaudhuri 1962, pp. 190–91). Batavia, therefore, turned to Tonkin in hopes of solving the gold issue, and urged its factors in Thăng Long to import Chinese gold for Coromandel, where the latest profit was said to be 25.5 per cent (*GM* III, pp. 386–89).

Most of the gold the Company purchased for India in Tonkin was not mined locally. Although in the seventeenth century gold was mined in the present day northern province of Thái Nguyên, the annual gold output was negligible (Van Dam, 1931, pp. 361–65; *Lịch triều*, III, pp. 76–79; Whitmore 1983, pp. 370–73). The major part of the gold available on the Tonkin market was actually imported from China (Baron 1811, p. 663; Dampier, 1931, p. 49). Vietnamese and Chinese merchants trading across the border often travelled to Yunnan and Guizhou to buy Chinese gold. The price of Chinese gold sold in northern Vietnam was said to be reasonable. In 1661, for instance, the purchase price of Chinese gold in Tonkin, according to a Vietnamese merchant trading to Nanking, was lower than that in Guangzhou (*DRB 1661*, pp. 49–55). Ever alert, Batavia, therefore, ordered the Tonkin factors to purchase as much Chinese gold as they could, and, to devise a long-term strategy, penetrating the Chinese gold market from the Tonkin springboard. As the Company's petitions to the Lê-Trịnh rulers for a licence to trade on the border were repeatedly delayed, Batavia repromoted its Tonkin factory to a permanent trading headquarters in the hope that the boost in status would ease the procurement of the Chinese gold pouring to northern Vietnam (VOC 678, 24 April 1663; Hoang 2007*b*, p. 110).

Despite all these strategies, the Tonkin factory often failed to supply the Coast factories with adequate gold cargoes. Rising military tensions in southern China meant Vietnamese and Chinese merchants could not trade across the border. In 1661, under pressure from the increasing demand for gold for the Coast, the high government, while still nurturing the hope of obtaining a licence from the Japanese Government to export Japanese gold to India, urged the Tonkin factors to purchase whatever gold they could find to supply the Coromandel trade (*GM* III, pp. 386, 440). The next year, Batavia again demanded the Tonkin factors spend at least 100,000 guilders on gold. Under such a constraint, the Tonkin factors planned to spend 102,107 guilders on gold, and the idea was to keep another large amount of money ready in stock, awaiting the arrival of another consignment of gold which was expected to come from Yunnan.

Hopes were dashed as the rainy weather impeded the journey of the traders. To make matters worse, Qing soldiers raided the Vietnamese merchants trading on the border in order to punish the Lê-Trịnh court for the delay in sending its tribute to the new dynasty in Peking (VOC 1240, pp. 1355–74; *DRB 1663*, p. 71). As a consequence of these commercial setbacks, the Tonkin factory could purchase only 3,861 taels of gold, valued at approximately 22,716 guilders. Shipped to the Coast factories in 1663, this small sum of gold brought a profit of 23.5 per cent at Paliacatta (*GM* III, pp. 450–51, 457).

Musk

Musk was another highly sought-after item in the Netherlands. Although exported from Tonkin, repeating the story of gold, the major part of musk available on the Tonkin market was not produced locally, but, if we are to believe the Company historian Pieter van Dam, it originated mainly from the Chinese provinces of Yunnan and Sichuan, and to a lesser extent, from the kingdom of Laos (Van Dam, 2-I, pp. 364–65).[6]

When the history of the Company's musk trade is received, it seems that its interest in this product was not awakened until 1652, when the Dutch factors in Tonkin were ordered to purchase some Laotian musk for the Netherlands as an experiment. That same year, Batavia was informed that Bastiaan Brouwer, a Spanish Brabander[7] working the triangular trade between Manila, Tonkin, and Cambodia under the auspices of the governor of Manila, had also bought a large quantity of musk in Tonkin and carried it to Cambodia, where he gained a good price of 80 taels per catty (VOC 1194, pp. 165–239; *GM*, II, pp. 651–52). When it turned out that musk was also a marketable item in Holland, the Tonkin factory was ordered to supply the homeward bound cargoes with whatever musk it could obtain in Tonkin. But after a few halcyon years, in the late 1650s, musk, like gold, became scarce on the Tonkin market. The civil war in southern China severely curtailed the flow of the Chinese musk to Tonkin. Chinese and Vietnamese merchants involved in the cross-border trade were often robbed by the Qing soldiers, acutely exacerbating the scarcity of Chinese musk on the Tonkin market. Laotian musk was, therefore, preferred.

In 1655, the Dutch factors in Thăng Long utilized their good relations with the *capado* (eunuch) Ongiadee to contract with him to buy all the Laotian musk that would be exported to Tonkin through the region governed by him (VOC 1216, pp. 436–42; *GM* III, p. 69). This agreement failed to live up to expectations because the annual quantities of Laotian musk exported to Tonkin were neither regular nor substantial. Consequently, the Dutch factors could purchase for Batavia only twenty-five catties of musk that year (*DRB 1655*, pp. 46–47).

The low export volumes of musk from the Tonkin factory were in part also attributable to a Japanese free merchant, with the name Resimon, who offered stiff competition and speculation. As long as he was still facilitated and protected by local mandarins, the Dutch procurement of musk, not to mention gold and silk piece-goods, would still have to contend with very exacting competition indeed. Between 1650 and 1660, when the Dutch export volume of musk from Tonkin hardly surpassed some thirty catties per year, this entrepreneur experienced no difficulty in sending 112 catties 10 taels of musk to Siam in the year 1659 alone. This portion of musk was then bought by the Dutch factory in Siam at a much higher price.

The next year, the Siam factory again had to buy seventy-two and a half catties of musk which Resimon had sent from Tonkin. To rub salt into the wound, Batavia had to pay interest on its late payment to Resimon (*DRB 1661*, pp. 54–55, 87).

Dissatisfied with the mediocre performance of the Tonkin factors in procuring musk, Batavia in 1661 unrelentingly increased its demands for this product, as well as for Tonkinese silk (*pelings* or *linghs*). Out of the 264,144 guilders Batavia destined for the Tonkin factory during the 1661–62 trading season, 180,000 was earmarked to buy Tonkinese raw silk for Japan, and the rest was to be spent on *pelings* and 1,800 ounces of musk for the Netherlands (*DRB 1661*, pp. 89–90). No matter what Batavia did to encourage some improvement in the purchase of musk in Tonkin, its efforts fell on stony ground. The Tonkin trade was so ailing at the time that the Dutch factors were hard put to buy any musk at all for the domestic market.

In his report to the governor general, Hendrick Baron, the chief factor of the Tonkin factory explained that the current depression in the musk trade in Tonkin was primarily caused by the Manchu military campaigns against the followers of the Nan Ming dynasty who had fled to the South and its staunch supporters, the Zheng clan in south-eastern China. The other fly in the ointment was Resimon and his manipulations. With the full support and connivance of the mandarin Ongiahaen, this merchant did his best to procure all Chinese musk as soon as this product crossed the border (VOC 1240, pp. 1355–74; *DRB 1661*, pp. 89–91; *DRB 1663*, p. 71).

Thus, in order to help the Tonkin factory with its purchase of Chinese gold and musk and, in the long run, to penetrate the southern China market from its Tonkin base, Batavia proposed what was to become the "Tinnam strategy". In 1662, the high government launched an expedition to Tinnam to explore the trading potential of the north-east Tonkin–China border, with the aim of finding an opportunity to establish direct trade with mainland China.

THE UNSUCCESSFUL EXPEDITION AND THE ABORTIVE "TINNAM STRATEGY"

It was, however, neither safe nor easy to make such exploratory voyages in the northern part of the Gulf of Tonkin in the early 1660s. This area had a reputation of being a dangerous place for trading vessels, made unsafe by the daring raids of the pirate Thun. Because of political chaos in southern China, what were known as "Chinese long-hair pirates" gathered around the north-eastern Tonkin-China border to raid trading vessels sailing between Tonkin and such southern Chinese ports as Macau and Guangzhou. In July 1660, the Prince of Tonkin commanded a large fleet of some seventy well armed ships to attack the Thun gang. Although a large number of his men were captured, Thun himself managed to escape (*DRB 1661*, pp. 49–55). The region was, therefore, still not completely safe for ships making passage there.

Despite this risk, the Tonkin factory still managed to explore the area called Nova Macau. After obtaining a licence from the prince to undertake the voyage, Hendrick Baron and his colleagues carried out an exploratory voyage in March 1662. From Doméa, the *Meliskerken* sailed northwards, wove a course among the Archipel Islands, and finally arrived at Tinnam. On 18 April, Baron left Tinnam to travel overland to the province of Loktjouw from where he continued on horseback to travel to Tjoeang, a place in the Province of Ay.[8] At a meeting with the governor of Loktjouw, he was advised to return to the capital because the ambassadorial road was unsafe. Heeding the advice, Baron decided to return to Loktjouw and then to the capital Thăng Long, where he and his men arrived safely on 3 May 1662 (VOC 1236, pp. 829–55; *DRB 1661*, pp. 89–91).

Despite its safe return to Tonkin, the mission was far from successful: no factory was set up mainly because of the chaotic situation on the border and the disapproval of the Tonkin court. Nevertheless, after this voyage of exploration, the Dutch factory continued to observe the area and nourished the hope of making a breakthrough into mainland China from that border market.

On his return, Baron made a meticulous report on the expedition and presented his thoughts on the Tinnam trade. He believed that establishing a permanent factory in that area would in the long run be commercially profitable and strategically important for the Company. He set out a detailed analysis of every place in the area. Ay and Loktjouw were located relatively close to some important provincial cities along the border and would attract local merchants coming to trade with the factory. The drawback was that these places were located relatively far from a waterway, hence, the challenge would be to find ways of reaching them and transporting goods. Tinnam was, therefore, considered to be the most suitable location. Having a permanent factory there would be ideal for the Company for a number of reasons. Principal among them was that Tinnam was close to Thenlongfoe, therefore travelling between the two places would not be inconvenient. This support was bolstered by the fact that local merchants preferred travelling to Tinnam than to other places. Nobody disputed that Tinnam had a good harbour; the Company ships could, therefore anchor conveniently in front of the factory. They would have no difficulty reaching it as the coastal area and its adjacent islands, including the area lying between Vanning and the mouth of the River Tinnam, had been carefully sounded, and was said to be very navigable. Then there was the fact that Tinnam was not so far from Nanning. Those who travelled between these places said that they normally needed twenty-seven days to complete a trip, either on foot or by boat. Finally and also importantly, if a factory were to be founded at Tinnam, not only would goods pour into this place from the south-western provinces and Nanning, but gold would also arrive from Yunnan in a more substantial quantity than ever before. Musk could also be procured without the competition which complicated this trade in the capital Thăng Long. There, Resimon, enjoying the auspices of the local mandarins, often bought up all the musk before the factory could even enter the market. In 1662, for instance, the Tonkin factory failed to procure any musk because the *capado* Ongiahaen had assisted the said speculator to make a clean sweep of all musk that was carried to Thăng Long from Ay and Loktjouw (VOC 1240, pp. 1355–74; *DRB 1663*, p. 71).

The precautions taken by the Trịnh rulers, however, turned the Dutch "Tinnam strategy" into nothing but a distant dream. Highly conscious of the current chaos in southern China, the Trịnh rulers were not happy with the Dutch plan to trade on the north-eastern border, and hence delayed granting them permission to trade at Tinnam. Despite the courtesy shown by Governor General Joan Maetsuycker in sending several letters to him concerning the Company's application for the Tinnam trade, the *chúa*[9] still procrastinated about giving the Company a licence to commence trade on the border. In August 1663, *Chúa* Trịnh summoned several Dutch factors to his palace for a discourse on the Tinnam trade (*DRB 1663*, pp. 689–92).[10] After the dialogue, the *chúa* promised to consider the Dutch petitions, but no official approval was forthcoming. In 1664, the Dutch application to commence trading in Tinnam ended incomplete failure. The Dutch factors lamented to their masters in Batavia that the *capados* in charge of conducting the application for the factory were too timorous to intercede with the *chúa*, and the mandarin Ongdieu had "maliciously" interpreted the Company's "Tinnam strategy" as "very harmful" to Tonkin. Expressing his opinions on this matter during his audience with the *chúa*, the mandarin said that the Dutch presence on the border would undoubtedly entail political disorder, hence, threaten the security of the country. The Trịnh's hesitation to approve

FIGURE 4.1

The Location of Tinnam in North-eastern Vietnam

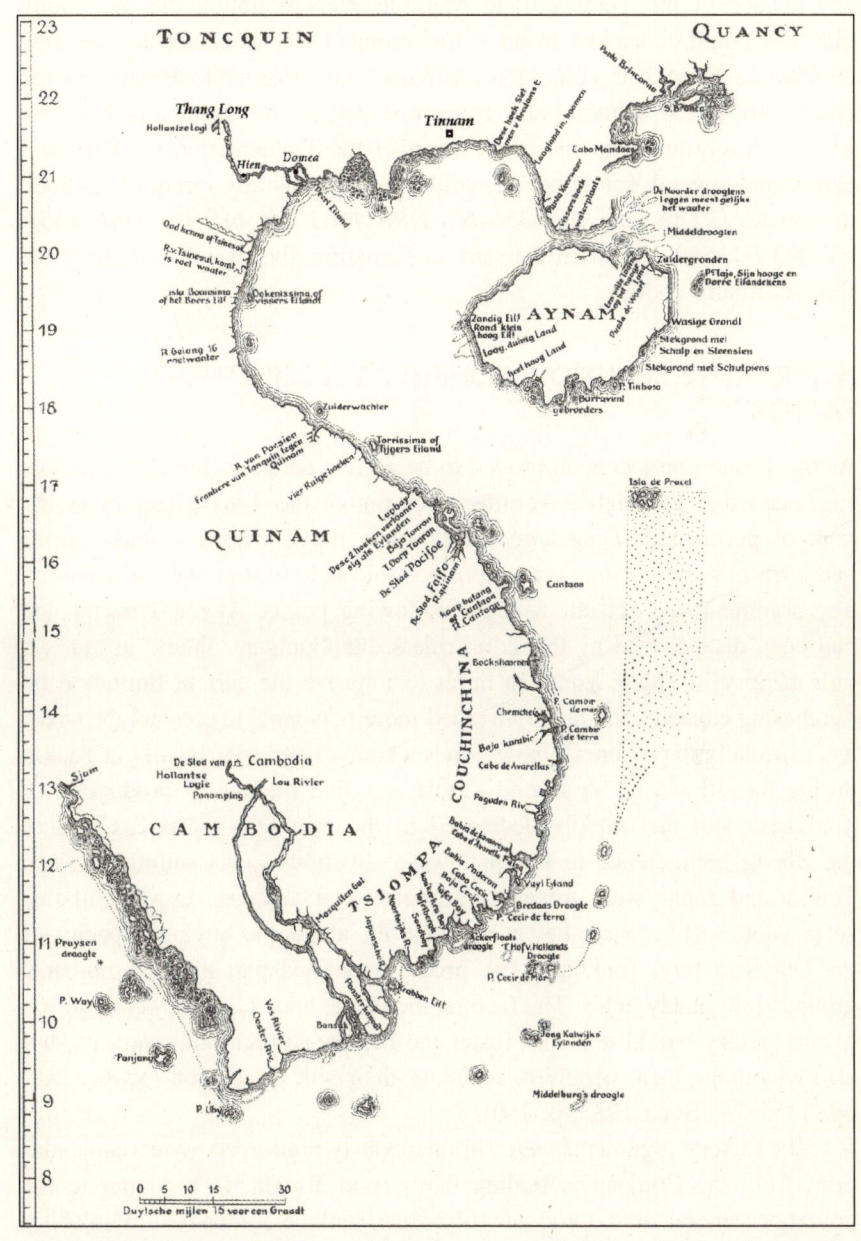

Source: Willem Buch, "De Oost-Indische Compagnie en Quinam: De betrekkingen der Nederlanders met Annam in de 17e eeuw" (dissertation, Amsterdam University, Paris, 1929).

the Dutch petition, therefore, dragged on interminably. Reporting to the high government in early 1664, the Dutch factors in Thăng Long wrote that while any chance of the Tinnam trade was extremely doubtful, the only thing that they could endeavour to do at this moment was to attract the attention of Chinese merchants coming to Tonkin. In their letter to Batavia at the end of 1664, the factors sadly confirmed that it was absolutely hopeless to cherish any hope for the eventuation of the Tinnam strategy. The *chúa* had hinted several times that he would never allow any foreigner to trade in Tinnam (VOC 1241, pp. 356–66; *DRB 1663*, pp. 689–92; *DRB 1664*, pp. 202–04, 548–50). With the said confirmation, the "Tinnam strategy" of Batavia finally ended.

ALTERNATIVE SOLUTION: TONKIN AS A PERMANENT FACTORY

As the Tinnam project soon proved to be a great delusion, the Dutch factors suggested that the high government repromote the Tonkin factory to the rank of permanent. They argued that since the Company's Tonkin trade had been in rapid decline, repromotion would help to improve the situation. The argument was set out with the following points. As the Tinnam plan had been disapproved by the Trịnh rulers, the Company should nurture its only factory in Thăng Long. In order to improve the current limitation on purchasing capacity, the factory needed more personnel to conduct the trade, and especially to procure Chinese goods which arrived sporadically in Tonkin during the off season. A second hurdle was that the annual production of Tonkinese silk had rapidly decreased in the past few years. Because of the Zheng belligerence in regional waters, various junks sailing between Tonkin and Japan were forced to suspend their voyages. In view of this suspension and because they were doubtful about the buying capacity of the Dutch factory, Tonkinese silk producers turned part of their mulberry grounds into paddy fields. The factors, therefore, hoped that the repromotion of the factory would not only foster the factory's purchasing capacity, but also encourage local people to maintain their silk production (VOC 1240, pp. 1355–74; Buch 1937, p. 160).

The factors' arguments were simultaneously reinforced by recommendations from the Company's trading partners in Tonkin. In his letter to the governor general at the end of 1662, the Tonkinese mandarin Plinlochiu informed Batavia that Tonkinese winter silk had been produced abundantly during the past few years, but there had not been enough customers to buy up those great quantities and the purchase price had also been considerably reduced. If the Company ships arrived in Tonkin only in May and left for Japan shortly afterwards as they had been doing hitherto, how could the factors procure enough silk in such a short time? Plinlochiu, therefore, advised the governor general to keep ships, factors, and a substantial capital sum in Tonkin to purchase winter silk to make the silk cargoes for the Japan-bound ships ready before the summer (*DRB 1663*, p. 71). At the same time, Resimon sent a letter to Director General Carel Hartsinck. According to the Japanese middleman, the annual silk production of Tonkin had been quite unstable in recent years because local silk makers for safety's sake only began to work after foreign ships had arrived and the merchants had advanced them money. He, therefore, advised the high government to hold one ship back in Tonkin to encourage local people to produce silk for the Company. Otherwise, Tonkinese farmers would switch over to planting rice and beans which were the staple provisions of the local inhabitants (*DRB 1663*, p. 71).

On the basis of these recommendations it was decided on 24 April 1663 to repromote the Tonkin factory to a permanent station for three cogent reasons: to stimulate the Tonkinese to maintain their annual production of silk for which the Company still had a great demand in both the Netherlands and Japan; to help the factors select raw silk and silk piece goods more carefully; and to attract more Chinese merchants to come to Tonkin with gold and musk in order to increase the export volume of these products from the Tonkin factory. The Tonkin factory would be staffed with fourteen people residing there permanently to conduct trade. Besides the increase in personnel, annual investment capital would also be increased in order to save a certain amount of money for the winter trading season. It was also agreed that half of the annual capital for the Tonkin trade, which consisted mainly of silver and copper coins, would be supplied by the Deshima factory; the rest would be provided by Batavia (VOC 678, 24 April 1663; *DRB 1663*, p. 338; *DRB 1664*, p. 204).

AFTERMATH: CONTINUED DECLINE

As the Tinnam strategy did not work out as expected, the decline in the Company's Tonkin trade which had begun in the latter half of the 1650s continued inexorably. During the first three years of the 1660s, the annual export volume of the Tonkin factory stood relatively low, largely in view of the meagre profit margins the Tonkinese silk cargoes brought on the Japanese market. Because the Tonkinese silk cargo, valued at 185,372 guilders, and sent to Japan in 1659, produced only a 25 per cent profit (*GM* III, pp. 305, 307), Batavia informed the Tonkin factory in 1660 that the investment capital for the Tonkin trade that year would be reduced (*GM* III, pp. 305, 346–47). Because of paucity of the available funding, only 12,038 guilders could be spent on local goods. This depressing export volume was said to be due to the Trịnh's fifth military campaign against Quinam, which had absorbed most of the country's labour forces into the army. Likewise, fearful of sudden conscriptions, a large number of the inhabitants of the capital fled to the countryside (*GM* III, pp. 377–78). The investment capital for the 1662 trading season was sharply increased, totalling 405,686 guilders. Batavia urged its factors in Thăng Long to spend at least 100,000 guilders on gold, which was in high demand for the Coromandel trade. The rest should be invested in raw silk and silk piece goods for both Japan and the Netherlands. The Tonkin factory failed to fulfil these orders. Because the Qing armies had raided merchants trading across the border in retaliation for the Lê-Trịnh's failure to send their first tribute to Peking, there was hardly any Chinese gold or musk on offer on the Tonkin market. The Dutch factors, therefore, had no choice but to spend only 22,761 guilders on gold. The silk cargo for Japan was also much smaller than expected, valued at only 150,000 guilders. The reason for this limited cargo was that a devastating typhoon and subsequent rains had destroyed most of the mulberry groves in the country. The capital Thăng Long was also flooded. The bulk of the silk stored in the Dutch factory was soaked because of the rain. Nor were these natural calamities the only reason. The local silk industry had been heavily eroded in the past few years because of the impoverishment of the people (VOC 1236, pp. 829–55; VOC 1240, pp. 1355–74; *GM* III, pp. 450–51).

All this hit just at a time when the economic depression in Tonkin was worsened by the shortage of copper cash which led to a devaluation of silver (Hoang 2007(a), pp. 149–71). The rapid fall of the silver/cash ratio which began in the early 1650s continued into the first half of the 1660s and caused the Company heavy losses. In 1654, the high government had made an unsuccessful attempt to right the cash equation when it had sent copper *zeni* coins minted in Batavia to Tonkin (VOC 1206, pp. 65–90). Since then, Batavia had found no appropriate solution to cut the loss of silver imported until 1663, when it began to export Japanese copper *zeni* to Tonkin in great quantities (Shimada 2005, p. 95; Hoang 2007*b*, pp. 133–39). In 1660, Resimon blamed the silver devaluation at the time on the VOC, arguing that the great amounts of silver imported into Tonkin by the Company had caused the rapid fall in the silver/cash ratio (*GM* III, pp. 346–47). This accusation was not ungrounded although it was not the main reason for the distortion of the exchange rate. While the shortage of these copper coins was the major factor in the rapid fall of the silver/cash ratio, the large quantities of Japanese silver annually imported into Tonkin by both the Dutch and the Chinese also contributed to the depression of the exchange rate. Batavia was by no means bothered with such a harmless indictment. It was more concerned with how to cut the loss of silver imported into Tonkin and reduce the dependence of the Tonkin factory on the local copper coins. As 400,000 Japanese copper *zeni* sent to Tonkin in 1661 turned out to be profitable, these denomination coins were thereafter regularly imported into Tonkin until the second half of the 1670s (VOC 1236, pp. 829–55; *GM* III, pp. 450–51).

The "discovery" of the efficacy of importing Japanese copper *zeni* into Tonkin did help to relieve the Company's dependence on local coins and reduce the losses on the importation of silver, but it could not revive the Company's steadily declining Tonkin trade. The repromotion of the Tonkin factory in 1663 did not work out as expected either. During the summer of 1663, Tonkin again suffered from heavy rains and high water. Most of the provinces, including the capital Thăng Long, were flooded, which considerably reduced the production of summer silk. Consequently, out of the 373,465 guilders the Company had sent to Tonkin, the factory could spend only 198,974 on silk for the Japan-bound ship. As the Tonkin-China border trade had ground to a complete standstill, the Company's demands for Chinese gold and musk for Coromandel and Europe could not be fulfilled either (*DRB 1663*, pp. 689–92).

The weakness of the Tonkin factory in supplying gold for Coromandel was one of the reasons that prompted Batavia to urge the Gentlemen XVII in the Netherlands to supply gold for the Asian trade of the Company. In 1664, the general missive from Batavia to the directors requested that its demand for minted gold and ducats valued at 500,000 guilders per year be continued (*DRB 1663*, pp. 689–92). As has been demonstrated by Tapan Raychaudhuri, the demand for gold from the Netherlands in the late 1650s and early 1660s by Batavia was temporary because the Deshima factory was officially permitted to export Japanese gold again in 1665 (Raychaudhuri 1962, p. 189).

As mentioned earlier, with the repromotion of the Tonkin factory to the rank of permanent in 1663, Batavia had high hopes its factors in Thăng Long would be able to furnish the returning ships with gold (*DRB 1663*, pp. 158, 209; *DRB 1664*, pp. 2002–04). In December, the *Zeeridder* returned to Batavia with a cargo valued at 148,295 guilders, consisting of approximately 1,900 taels of gold. In the spring, the *Bunschoten* also sailed to Batavia, carrying a small cargo of 31,211 guilders, consisting of 674 taels of gold for Coromandel (VOC 1241, pp. 356–66; *DRB 1664*, pp. 65–67).

Despite these disappointing gold cargoes, in the 1664 trading season Batavia continued to insist that the Tonkin factory endeavour to supply the Coast factories with whatever gold it could procure in Tonkin. In order to fulfil this order, the Dutch factors contracted with the Japanese entrepreneur Resimon to sell all the gold he had at the end of the trading season at the fixed price of 12.5 taels of silver for one tael of 24-carat gold (*DRB 1664*, pp. 548–50). This contract could not be honoured because of the severe shortage of gold on the Tonkin market at the time.

Unable to fulfil the demand, the Dutch factors resolved to use most of their capital to buy silk and piece goods. Consequently, on the departure of the *Zeeridder* for Batavia in November 1664, the Tonkin factors were able to send only 713 taels of gold, while promising their masters to try their best in the coming months to spend around 60,000 to 70,000 guilders on gold (VOC 1252, pp. 209–48). This promise the Tonkin factory also failed to keep: the *Bunschoten*'s cargo for Batavia consisted of only 1,387 taels of gold. In their missive to the governor general in 1665, the Dutch factors confessed that the gold trade in Tonkin had virtually stagnated and, worse, the prospect of improving the procurement of gold in the future seemed hopeless (VOC 1253, pp. 1712–34). In November of the same year, no gold was found in the Tonkin cargo shipped to Batavia. The Tonkin factory lamented that that year's failure had been caused by the complete stagnation of the gold flow from China. Daunted by various difficulties, Chinese gold merchants no longer visited northern Vietnam (*DRB 1665*, pp. 83, 370–72; *GM* III, p. 491).

In order to maintain the gold supply to the Coast after the consecutive failures of the Tonkin factory to procure Chinese gold, the Deshima factory in 1663 ignored the Japanese Government's ban on gold exports and deliberately exported Japanese gold coins (Nachod 1897, p. 357). After the Shogunate authorized their 1664 application for the export of gold, the Dutch began to export Japanese gold in considerable amounts from 1665. From 1668, when the Japanese Government banned the export of silver and lowered the purchase price of Japanese gold, the Dutch export of Japanese gold rose sharply. The problem of the gold supply to Coromandel was now basically solved because the Japanese *koban* could easily be reminted into Indian pagodas as their metallic content was nearly the same (Raychaudhuri 1962, p. 191). Consequently, from the mid-1660s, Tonkin was no longer considered an important gold supplier for the Coast, although Chinese gold was still occasionally procured in Tonkin and exported to Coromandel.

Similarly there was shortage of musk in the Tonkinese market. In 1663, the directors in the Netherlands demanded 3,000 ounces of musk for the next homeward bound voyage. Besides urging its Tonkin factors to supply the bulk of this demand, Batavia also ordered the factory in Agra (India) to provide the Company with supplies of this product. The high government stressed that in order to dispatch musk and Tonkinese piece goods to the Netherlands, the Tonkin factors should send whatever items they could purchase to Batavia before 1 November. To the disappointment of Batavia, Tonkin sent in 1663 and 1664 only 14 taels 2 maas (around 0.9 catty) and 17 17/32 catties of musk respectively. The reasons for these paltry cargoes were a reprise of those of previous years, namely the Manchu violence on and around the border, and Resimon's speculations (VOC 1241, pp. 356–66; *DRB 1663*, pp. 689–92; *DRB 1664*, pp. 65–67).

Despite these meagre supplies, Batavia raised its order for musk at the Tonkin factory in the 1664 trading season, demanding for the Netherlands 50,000 guilders' worth of silk piece goods and 4,000 ounces of musk (*DRB 1664*, p. 298). The Dutch factors in Thăng Long now resolved to contract with Resimon to buy all the gold and musk from him. Despite their efforts, they could procure for Batavia only 8 taels 3 maas of musk in the winter of 1664, and 20 catties more in the summer of 1665, barely fulfilling one sixth of the total demand (*DRB 1664*, pp. 298, 548–50; *DRB 1665*, pp. 83, 193, 222, 370–72).

These tiny cargoes raised the ire of Batavia, especially when it was informed that other foreign merchants trading in Tonkin had been able to purchase more musk than its factors. The Castilian merchant Gonsalvo Discouar, for instance, had percipiently cooperated with Resimon and spent a considerable capital on both Tonkinese silk piece-goods and Chinese musk. Believing that the export volume of musk could be increased if its factors in Tonkin were to do their best, Batavia sternly renewed the order for the previous year and stressed that the Tonkin factory should provide the homeward bound ships with 4,000 ounces of musk. Just as the pressure Batavia exerted on its factors for musk seemed about to hit the ceiling, the Company's Tonkin musk trade started to improve, responding favourably to the revival of the Tonkin-China border trade. A cargo valued at 56,492 guilders that the Tonkin factory sent to Batavia in the winter of 1665 reportedly contained 111 catties 15 taels 1 maas of musk (VOC 1253, pp. 1712–34; *DRB 1665*, p. 370). After this, the annual export volume of musk by the Tonkin factory increased considerably and remained relatively stable until 1700, when the Company finally severed its trading relations with Tonkin.

Concluding Remarks

By the middle of the 1650s, Tonkinese raw silk and piece goods which had been crucial commodities for the VOC's Japan trade throughout the 1640s was no longer a staple merchandize in the Far Eastern market. Therefore, in order to make use of the existence of its only base in Tonkin, the high government urged the Tonkin factors to import Chinese gold for Coromandel and Chinese musk for the Netherlands. All the attempts Batavia made to gear up the import of Chinese gold and musk in Tonkin, however, were not paid off handsomely; the import and export trade of the Tonkin factory stagnated due mainly to the decline of the Tonkin–China border trade caused by political and military turmoil after the dynastic transition in China. Despite inexorable pressure from their masters in Batavia, the Dutch factors in Tonkin constantly failed to fulfil the Company's demands for gold and musk.

The VOC's expedition to the Tonkin–China border and their expectation of the "Tinnam strategy" in the early 1660s not only reveals Batavia's concern for the supply of Chinese gold and musk, but also reflects the Company's long-term desire for a permanent foothold in mainland China. Prior to the early 1660s, the vast market of China still remained a far-flung dream which the Dutch company, just as its English counterpart, had been nourishing for more than half a century (Mantienne 1999, pp. 113–25; Hoang 2005, pp. 73–92). It was mainly this constant longing which encouraged the VOC to maintain its only factory in northern Vietnam until the dawn of the eighteenth century.

Notes

This chapter was originally an article presented at the workshop *Ports, Pirates and Hinterlands in the East and Southeast Asia: Historical and Contemporary Perspectives* in Shanghai, China, in November 2005. In 2007 several parts of this article were incorporated in Chapters 4 and 7 of my book (Hoang 2007*b*). I am grateful to the Academic Brill Publishers for generously allowing me to reprint this article, *Silk for Silver: Dutch-Vietnamese Relations, 1637–1700* (Leiden-Boston: Brill, 2007*b*).

1. From the early seventeenth century, the Vietnamese Kingdom of Đại Việt was split into two kingdoms: Tonkin (present day northern Vietnam) ruled by the Lê-Trịnh and Quinam (today central and southern Vietnam) governed by the Nguyễn family. The Dutch East India Company (VOC) attempted to trade with Quinam between 1601 and 1638, but failed. In 1637, the VOC opened trade relations with Tonkin and maintained a factory in northern Vietnam until 1700.
2. The first Tonkin tribute to Peking was recorded in June 1663: *Cương mục*, II p. 296. *Toàn thư* (III, p. 264) however noted that the 1663 Tonkin tribute was to Ming China. This must have been mistakenly recorded.
3. For a general account of the VOC-Tonkin silk trade in the seventeenth century: See P.W. Klein, "De Tonkinees-Japanse Zijdehandel", pp. 152–77 (Frijhoff and Hiemstra 1986); Hoang Anh Tuan, *Silk for Silver*, pp. 143–64. For the rise of Bengal silk in the Japanese market in the mid- 1650s, see Om Prakas, *The Dutch East India Company*, p. 125.
4. According to Glamann (*Dutch-Asiatic Trade*, p. 51), "not until 1618 gold was sent — intended for the Coromandel Coast — in all 72,000 rials out of the total cargo of the money of 612,000 rials".
5. Gaastra (1983, p. 453), in examining such Company documents as the orders from Batavia, resolutions of the Gentlemen XVII, and receipts in Asia, has stated that 1632 to the end of the 1650s was the "period without gold". The demand for gold from Batavia began once again in 1658, and in 1662 gold was sent from the Netherlands to Asia.
6. For a general account of the musk trade in the early modern period, see Peter Borschberg, "The European Musk Trade with Asia", *The Heritage Journal*, 1 (2004): 1–12.
7. A Dutch living in Antwerp under Spanish rule.
8. Most of the place names found in the Dutch records remain unidentified because of the odd pronunciation and hence orthography.

9. In the 17th and 18th century, Vietnam was ruled by two competing group of rulers, the *Chúa* of the Nguyen in the southern part. Both pretended to rule like kings (for whom the indigenous term *vua* existed).
10. The *Chúa* wanted to know how far Tinnam and Vanning were from the capital Thăng Long, and whether his subjects in those places were vulnerable to the Chinese threat. The Dutch answered the first question, saying that those places did not seem to be terribly far, but did not answer the second.

References

Unpublished Primary Sources

NFJ 57, Dagregister comptoir Nagasaki, 1 August 1644.

NFJ 61, Dagregister comptoir Nagasaki, 15 September 1648.

VOC 1194, Missive [from Tonkin] to Batavia, 8 December 1652, fos. 165–239.

VOC 1206, Missive from Louis Baffart from Tayouan to Batavia, 18 November 1654, fos. 65–90.

VOC 1216, Missive from Gustavus Hanssen to Batavia, 20 February 1656, fos. 436–42.

VOC 1236, Missive from Hendrick Baron to Batavia, 13 November 1661, fos. 829–55.

VOC 1240, Missive from Hendrick Baron to Batavia, 12 November 1662, fos. 1355–74.

VOC 1241, Missive from *Opperhoofd* and Council in Tonkin to Batavia, 6 November 1663, fos. 356–66.

VOC 1252, Missive from Verdonck to Batavia, 23 February 1665, fos. 209–48.

VOC 1253, Missive from Constantijn Ranst to Batavia, 30 October 1665, fos. 1712–34.

VOC 678, Resoluties Gouverneur–Generaal en Raden, 24 April 1663.

Published Primary Sources

[*Cương mục*] *Khâm định Việt sử thông giám cương mục* [Text and Commentary on the Complete Mirror of Vietnamese History as Ordered by the Emperor]. Hanoi: Giáo dục, 1998.

[DRB] *Dagh-register gehouden int Casteel Batavia vant passerende daer ter plaetse als over geheel Nederlandts-India*, 31 vols., edited by Departement van Koloniën. The Hague: Martinus Nijhoff and Batavia: Landsdrukkerij, 1887–1931.

[GM] *Generale Missiven van Gouverneurs-Generaal en Raden aan Heren XVII der Verenigde Oostindische Compagnie*, edited by W. Ph. Coolhaas. The Hague: Martinus Nijhoff, 1960-76.

[*Lịch triều*] Phan, Huy Chú. *Lịch triều hiến chương loại chí* [Annals of the Laws and Institutions of Successive Dynasties]. Hanoi: Sử học, 1961.
[*Toàn thư*] *Đại Việt sử ký toàn thư* [The Complete Book of the Historical Records of Đại Việt]. Hanoi: KHXH, 1998.
Baron, Samuel. "A Description of the Kingdom of Tonqueen". In *A Collection of the Best and Most Interesting Voyages and Travels in All Parts of the World*, edited by John Pinkerton. London, 1811.
Dampier, William. *Voyages and Discoveries*. London: The Argonaut Press, 1931.
Richard, A. "History of Tonquin". In *A Collection of the Best and Most Interesting Voyages and Travels in All Parts of the World*, edited by John Pinkerton. London, 1811.
The Deshima Dagregisters, Vols. XI (1641–50) and XII (1651–60), edited by Cynthia Viallé and Leonard Blussé. Leiden: Intercontinenta, no. 23 & 25, 2001 & 2005.
Van Dam, Pieter. *Beschryvinge van de Oostindische Compagnie*, edited by F.W. Stapel. The Hague: Martinus Nijhoff, 1931.

Secondary Sources

Andrade, Tonio. *Commerce, Culture, and Conflict: Taiwan under European Rule, 1624–1662*. Ph.D. Dissertation, Department of History, Yale University, 2000.
Blussé, Leonard. *Tribuut aan China: Vier eeuwen Nederlands–Chinese betrekkingen*. Amsterdam: Cramwinckel, 1989.
———. "No Boats to China: the Dutch East India Company and the Changing Pattern of the China Sea Trade, 1635–1690". *Modern Asian Studies*, no. 30/1 (1996): 51–70.
Borschberg, Peter. "The European Musk Trade with Asia in the Early Modern Period". *The Heritage Journal*, no. 1 (2004): 1–12.
Buch, W.J.M. "La Compagnie des Indes Néerlandaises et l'Indochine". *Bulletin de l'École Française d'Extrême-Orient* 36 (1936): 97–196 & 37 (1937): 121–237.
Gaastra, Femme. "The Exports of Precious Metal from Europe to Asia by the Dutch East India Company, 1602–1795". In *Precious Metals in the Later Medieval and Early Modern Worlds*, edited by J.F. Richards. California: Carolina Academic Press, 1983.
———. *The Dutch East India Company: Expansion and Decline*. Zutphen: Walburg Pers, 2003.
Glamann, Kristof. *Dutch-Asiatic Trade, 1620–1740*. The Hague: Martinus Nijhoff, 1958.
Hoang, Anh Tuan. "From Japan to Manila and Back to Europe: The Abortive English Trade with Tonkin in the 1670s". *Itinerario: International Journal on*

the History of European Expansion and Global Interaction, no. 29/3 (2005): 73–92.

———. "The VOC Import of Monetary Metals into Tonkin and Its Impact on the Seventeenth-Century Vietnamese Economy". In *Contingent Lives: Social Identity and Material Culture in the VOC World*, edited by Nigel Worden. Cape Town: ABC Press, 2007a.

———. *Silk for Silver: Dutch-Vietnamese Relations, 1637–1700*. Leiden-Boston: Brill, 2007b.

Innes, Robert LeRoy. *The Door Ajar: Japan's Foreign Trade in the Seventeenth Century*. Ph.D. Dissertation, Department of History, The University of Michigan, 1980.

Klein, P.W. "De Tonkinees-Japanse Zijdehandel van de Vereenigde Oostindische Compagnie en het Inter-Asiatische Verkeer in de 17^e eeuw". In *Bewogen en Bewegen*, edited by W. Frijhoff and M. Hiemstra. Tilburg: Gianotten B.V., 1986.

———. "The China Seas and the World Economy between the 16th and 19th Centuries: The Changing Structure of Trade". In *Kapitaal, Ondernemerschap en Beleid: Studie over economie en politiek in Nederland, Europa en Azië van 1500 tot heden*, edited by C.A. Davids, W. Fritschy, and L.A. van der Valk. Amsterdam: NEHA, 1996.

Mantienne, Frédéric. "Indochinese Societies and European Traders: Different World of Trade? (17th–18th Centuries)". In *Commerce et Navigation en Asie du Sud-Est (XIVe-XIXe siècle)*, edited by Nguyễn Thế Anh and Ishizawa Yoshiaki. Tokyo: Sophia University, 1999.

Nachod, Oskar. *Die Beziehungen der niederländischen ostindischen Kompagnie zu Japan im siebzehnten Jahrhundert*. Leipzig: Rob. Friese September, 1897.

Prakas, Om. *The Dutch East India Company and the Economy of Bengal 1630–1720*. Princeton: Princeton University Press, 1985.

Raychaudhuri, Tapan. *Jan Company in Coromandel 1605–1690: A Study in the Interrelations of European Commerce and Traditional Economies*. The Hague: Martinus Nijhoff, 1962.

Shimada, Ryuto. *The Intra-Asian Trade in Japanese Copper by the Dutch East India Company during the Eighteenth Century*. Leiden-Boston: Brill, 2005.

Steengaard, Niels. *The Asian Trade Revolution of the Seventeenth Century: The East India Companies and the Decline of the Caravan Trade*. Chicago: Chicago University Press, 1973.

Struve, Lynn A., ed. *Time, Temporality, and Imperial Transition: East Asia from the Ming to Qing*. Honolulu: Association for Asian Studies and University of Hawaii Press, 2005.

Ts'ao, Yung-ho. "Taiwan as an Entrepôt in East Asia in the Seventeenth Century". *Itinerario: International Journal on the History of European Expansion and Global Interaction*, no. 21/3 (1997): 94–114.

Whitmore, John K. "Vietnam and the Monetary Flow of Eastern Asia, Thirteenth to Eighteenth Centuries". In *Precious Metals in the Later Medieval and Early Modern Worlds*, edited by J.F. Richards. California: Carolina Academic Press, 1983.

Wills, John E. Jr. *Pepper, Guns, and Parleys, The Dutch East India Company and China, 1662–1681*. Cambridge: Harvard University Press, 1974.

5

South Fujian the Disputed Coast, Power and Counter-power

Paola Calanca

The south of Fujian in the eighteenth century provides an interesting field of study to analyse the context in which local authorities operated to ensure coastal security and to study the responsibilities and prerogatives of the various parties involved in the control of maritime activities, that is, local authorities, the great families, and various inhabitants coalitions, among which are secret societies. Our objective is to define the major focal points around which we need to pursue research in order to understand how this sharing of "responsibilities" was articulated and how it functioned. This should enable us to appreciate better who were the real power holders and how they succeeded in assuring a certain social stability. This social stability was probably imposed by the power relations among pressure groups and the local population had to adapt to this, which entailed the loss of a certain amount of its autonomy.

From the time of the Wokou ravages in the mid-sixteenth century, the population was accustomed to rallying around a clan organization, the only means that enabled them to organize a common defence that could stave off pirate attacks.[1] Subsequently, the disastrous (economic and social) effects of the Ming-Qing dynastic transition, the commercial rivalries which intensified with the opening of overseas trade, especially from 1684 onwards, and the exacerbated competition for land and for access to water supplies, etc., crystallized more than ever the adherence of the population to communities and associations that were based on kinship, neighbours, or simple interest groups. These groups, and more exactly those who controlled them, provided the main actors on the coast, the people with whom the government had to deal in order to ensure regional security and prosperity. By the end of the eighteenth century, the clan networks were no longer the only ones managing local communities: various pressure groups, including secret societies, especially the Heaven and Earth Society (*Tiandihui* 天地會), had extended their hold over a part of the economic activities of the coast, and naturally, over the population as well. For its part, the administration found it more and more difficult, except in a few isolated cases, to mobilize the coastal inhabitants and control maritime activities. In order to ensure coastal defence, it is obviously necessary to occupy the field, but who was occupying it in Fujian?

Likewise from the mid-sixteenth century onwards, coastal surveillance took on various forms of organization and progressively developed towards stabilization of naval units and police stations on the continent. The defensive network on the coast was thus indubitably improved, although this was not sufficient to prevent smugglers and pirates from raiding, or the rise of clandestine emigration. In order to ensure an efficient defence system, it was indeed not sufficient to fortify the coastline — it was necessary to occupy the area, including patroling the waters near the coast, and establishing police stations in the appropriate localities along the coast; being able to raise a militia to assist the regular troops, organizing the "quadrillage" of the population (*baojia* 保甲, *aojia* 澳甲), etc. This sort of organization assumes agreement among all the actors in local politics. During the early decades of the eighteenth century, a concrete collaboration, even if it was not always infallible, at least existed as regards the fight against piracy. This situation later gradually deteriorated both in the matter of illegal activities, particularly maritime brigandage, and as regards relations between the local authorities and the population, as well as between the civil and military personnel — the latter often coming from coastal families or were integrated into local society through long presence. What happened? Are these frictions due to the relations between the centre and the periphery or are they more a matter of rivalries — political and economic in nature — that are purely local, or perhaps both at the same time?

THE SOCIAL CONTEXT

From the mid-sixteenth century onward in Fujian (Figure 5.1), both racketeering and violence were nearly omnipresent and they intensified with the development of agreement between the local power holders and secret organizations, along with the multiplication of sworn alliances to settle differences among competing clans and communities, or quite simply, for protection.[2] This was a society in which having the protection of a more

FIGURE 5.1

The Fujian Province

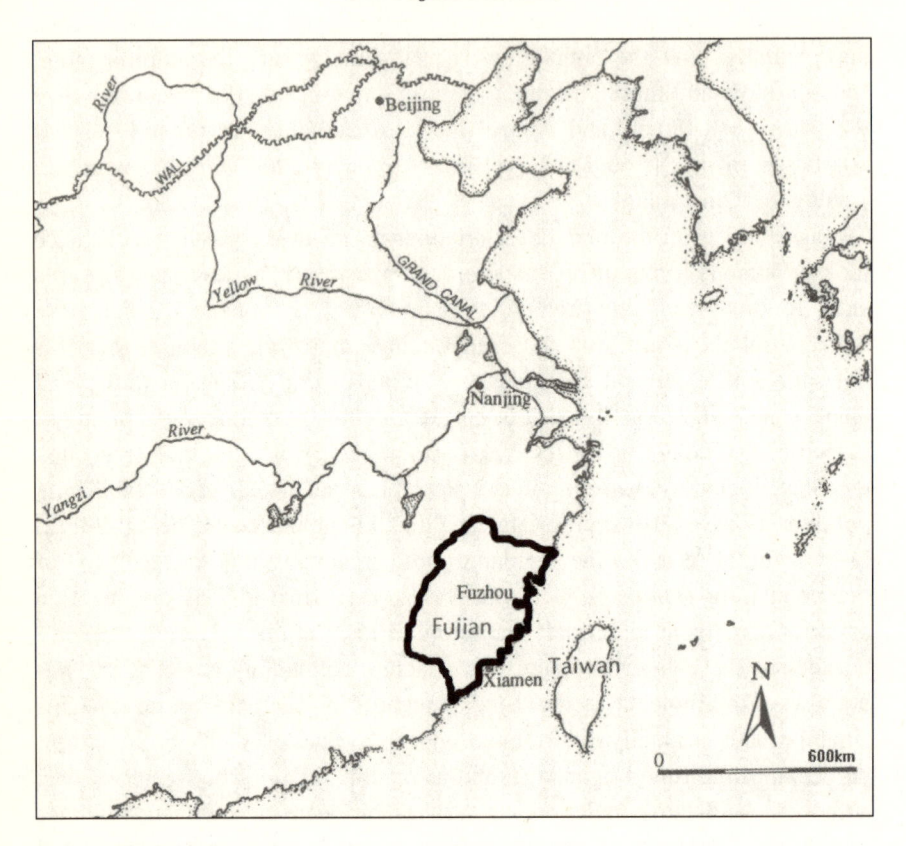

Source: Paola Calanca ©

powerful player was often indispensable, especially in the south of the province, which caused Liu Xingtang to say that although the inhabitants of Quanzhou 泉州 and Zhangzhou 漳州 (Figure 5.2) were bold enough to refuse to pay taxes to the government, they did not have the effrontery to argue about the contributions that certain lineages imposed on them. This was akin to how they feared the persecution of these lineages, but paid no heed to the law.[3] It is quite possible this pressure may have been even more important in maritime activities, since coastal surveillance was carried out by soldiers mainly originating from Quanzhou and Zhangshou. It has indeed been proven that lineages with links to members of the naval forces, the role of which was very important in controlling maritime activities, often acted outside any legal framework and oppressed those who were not so lucky

FIGURE 5.2
The Two Prefectures of Minnan: Quanzhou and Zangzhou

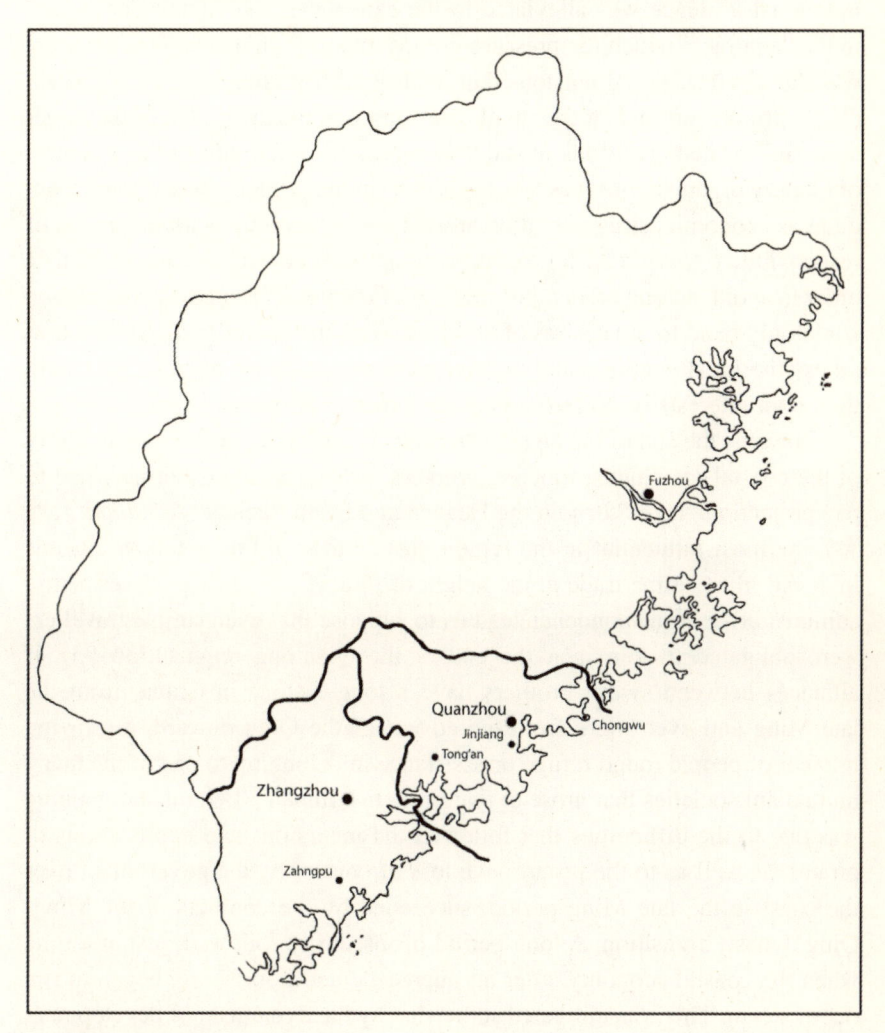

Source: Paola Calanca ©

as to have such links.[4] The same phenomenon can also be observed among local officers as regards the administration of Taiwan. The Min-Zhe general governor Gao Qizhou 高其倬 (1676–1738), when submitting propositions concerning the island in 1727 wondered if it would not be better to enlist men of arms from other regions in order to avoid friction with the population, which was mainly native to these two prefectures.[5]

These interclan or coalition group conflicts (*xiedou* 械鬥) ended up crystallizing the Minnan 閩南 population into subordinate relations in which individual violence was alleviated to the extent that individuals subscribed to the "contract" which the pressure groups imposed on them.[6] This situation was the result of social tensions that intensified from the reign of Yongzhen (1723–36) onward, when the small clans opposed the arrogance of the larger ones and formed coalitions in order to succeed.[7] In the cities where control of tutelary organizations was less territorial (in the property-based sense), but quite as economic, struggles often arose even between the various groups of responsibility (*baojia* 保甲), set up originally to control the population in order to avoid, among others, just this sort of outbreak.[8] Hence, the population could only bend to the desires of those who had the power to dictate the law, unless the local people could arrange alliances enabling them to safeguard their own interests or do business at the expense of others.

Towards the end of the eighteenth century, it is quite likely that a majority of the coastal merchants, itinerant workers, as well as the fishermen, had to pay protection "taxes" or join the Heaven and Earth Society (*Tiandihui* 天地會), the most influential in the region, just as they did their fellow citizens involved in maritime trade at the height of piracy.[9] Some cases described in administrative correspondence lead us to suppose that even simple travellers were obligated to join it at the end of the Qianlong reign (1736–95). If alliances between sworn brothers have a long history in China, from the late Ming and even more from the advent of the Qing onward, a growing number of people found refuge or assistance in belonging to one of the many mutual aid societies that arose at that time. In Minnan 閩南, this burgeoning was due to the difficulties that followed the incursions and depredations of pirates, as well as to the progressive loss of control by the government over the coast in the late Ming period, succeeded by the conflicts of the Ming-Qing dynasty transition. A long period of insecurity followed, just at a time when the coastal economy, after an unprecedented flourishing, began to run out of steam. This was mitigated somewhat by the dynamism of development in Taiwan and the trade between the two sides of the strait. This decline was to be accentuated during the eighteenth century when a shortage of land and the demographic increase were to aggravate a situation that was already precarious for a good part of the population. Population mobility, associated with a large rural exodus, was one of the most significant factors in the period and was to have many social repercussions.

A part of the coastal population — those individuals possessing a specialization — were also concerned with this phenomenon and were on the road seasonally to pursue their activities elsewhere. For example, fishermen who had not succeeded in finding work locally went by road to the ports of Zhejiang, where they were employed on ships working in the Zhoushan 舟山 archipelago.[10] Inter- and intraprovincial emigration, as well as towards countries in Southeast Asia, was in fact the fate of many inhabitants of Fujian, some seeking better working conditions and a livelihood.[11] A large number of peasants streamed into the coastal cities that were unable to integrate all of them. Those who were better off could hope to find employment as travelling peddlers, labourers, workers, craftsmen, and transporters. Those less lucky were to swell the ranks of the population without any definite trade, of whom the local authorities were most especially apprehensive.[12] For this population with or without employment, but most often without any family ties, brotherhood associations represented an answer to their new situation. At least in their initial stages, it was a matter of mutual aid institutions bringing together individuals far from their traditional home who felt the need to create new forms of social belonging.[13]

For that matter, the whole economic life of the province appears to have overlapped completely with the tutelary network. This was probably facilitated by the corporatist or regional organization of a good part of the economic activities, often encouraged and/or desired by the government in order to control them better. Some great families, who opted to play the security card on the side of local authorities, rather benefited from this situation and held a position of privilege.[14] The vast majority of maritime activities as well as legal emigration to Taiwan required a licence that was, in fact, granted to the wealthy or their protégés. Hence, an individual's or even a family's success was intimately linked to their origins (socio-economic situation), but above all to a broader network whose ramifications extended to the holders of key posts controlling economic activities. We are obviously dealing with a politico-economic power here, because mercantile activities alone did not enable people to enjoy such power, as the fortunes thus amassed remained fragile and could collapse as rapidly as they had been built up.[15] The events that marked the Ming-Qing dynastic transition disrupted the socio-economic balance of Fujian, previously dominated mainly by the Zheng 鄭 family in the maritime realm. During the conflict, local alliances underwent numerous turnarounds and some families were "chosen" by the Manchu government to stand on its side at the time of reconstruction. Reinstatement of arable lands, the taking up once again of seaboard activities, and the opening to overseas trade certainly heightened the aspirations of a good part of society and naturally sharpened many rivalries.[16]

In this mixture of social constraints and economic rivalries, it is not always easy to see to what extent the participation of individuals in illegal activities was voluntary or not. As regards the illegal activities on the coast, it is obvious that the coastal inhabitants, like the officials, took advantage of, and were subject to the disadvantages of, the illegal activities associated with the sea; some did not give in to these temptations, others participated only marginally, and still others ran in headlong. On the seacoast, the locals, and even more so, the seamen, had every opportunity to take up illegal activities and become pirates, suppliers, arms dealers, smugglers, etc. At times, these "opportunities" were unavoidable: to counter running the risk of imprisonment or death, it was easier to bend with the wind. It is also likely that the network of personal relations in which the population was bound could have played an important role in the matter.

It is indeed surprising that a good part of the crews in the fleets in the late eighteenth and early nineteenth centuries were made up of victims: kidnapped to satisfy sexual needs or captives taken for ransom, the merchants and sailors captured along with their cargoes, and pressed into service, etc.[17] Some of these groups were even made up of a majority of people who, having been kidnapped, either voluntarily took up banditry or were forced to perpetrate upon others the very acts they had been subjected to themselves. How did it happen that these people, with the greater numbers on their side and being together in a limited space, hence an ideal place to conspire, did not rebel (only cases of individual insubordination are known to us)? The necessary knowledge of navigation could not have represented an obstacle to their rebellion since a good number of these captives were used to the sea. The sources used to investigate this question have not revealed their motivations, so we can only propose some suppositions.

One of the main reasons may have been fear of the law. Although it dealt out punishment in accordance with the acts committed, it indeed foresaw punishment for most of the victims. The lot that justice reserved for them was often humiliating and troublesome and may have motivated them to move on from (active or passive) resistance to illegal acts, bringing them fully into outlaw bands. Why try to escape from the clutches of pirates only to find oneself in a police station where a quite uncertain fate awaited? More materialistic motivations can also be envisioned, as these victims were often of modest means — fishermen, small merchants, etc. Why go on with an activity that could be dangerous in hopes of uncertain profits (considering the climatic and market conditions), subject to both government taxation (official and unofficial) and racketeering by pirates, when it was possible to escape from all that without taking any greater risks than before and perhaps having to work less hard? Some people preferred to acquiesce beforehand to the pirates' demands rather than run the risk of being subjected to their extortion or even to endanger their lives.[18]

Likewise, we must not overlook a social component: in a world where protection from someone more powerful was usually indispensable for economic and, at times, sheer physical survival, people could fear the repercussions of an act of rebellion on both the rebel and his family, if it came to be known among the pirates' accomplices on the mainland. Hence, being unable to count on any protection, the most modest seamen probably accepted their new fate. An important element that may have contributed to the power of Cai Qian 蔡牽 (1761–1809), aside from his unquestionable capacities as a commander, was his alliance with members of the Heaven and Earth Society. More thorough investigation into the way the life of ordinary people was regimented is necessary. If this factor turns out to be as important as many sources suggest it was, it could also explain, through the behaviour of subordination it induces, the importance of the pirate fleets, as well as the docility of many people making up their crews against their will. In such a situation, who provided and how was control over maritime activities maintained?

THE SEA-COASTAL SECURITY

As far as the local authorities were concerned, administrative correspondence reveals that one of the main preoccupations of the bureaucracy was recruiting experienced personnel who knew the south-eastern coast. The central government was aware that in these peripheral areas, it was of primordial import to be able to evaluate the situation in light of local mores. Thus, when a functionary submitted a candidacy, he emphasized both the experience of the applicant in the province or on the coast and his coastal origin, the latter of which was sometimes sufficient to assure his acceptance. This preoccupation is even more evident in regard to the corps of military officers who could request a transfer from civil administration for this reason. The endemic banditry on the south-east coast motivated the choice, even in the civil administration, of men with experience on the ground, who allied good management qualities with considerable talent in conducting repressive expeditions and training troops. At times, high-level functionaries who knew the region, the people, and naval and military techniques well were not subject to the common rule limiting all assignments to a three-year period, and hence remained in the same post for years. For that matter, some military officers spent their entire careers on the seacoast, gradually climbing the rungs of the hierarchical ladder.[19] The considerable number of native-born military officers or of officers well integrated into local society had its consequences on the political developments of the coast. Due to the many tasks they were supposed to carry out — surveillance and defence of strategic sites such as ports, watch fires, control stations on the continent, or on adjacent islands; police operations; escorting official transport vessels; protecting trade and fishing boats, etc. — they were omnipresent and hence played a paramount role in maritime activities.

This situation was directly linked to events that marked the dynastic conflict and to the prudence with which the first Manchu sovereigns approached Fukienese society. There was a need for reconciliation and it was important for the government to ensure the cooperation and submission of a population battered by long years of war, and who had in some districts closely collaborated with the enemy. After the events that had bloodied the coast, the Manchus thus chose to rely on a part of the local elite to reconstruct the region and organize maritime defence. And who, in fact, better to call upon than the Fujian military officers, with their acquaintances among tradesmen, who were sufficiently well regarded by the population, and also had the connections and information indispensable to setting up a coastal defence system oriented towards greater openness to maritime trade? Having the support from both the central government and prominent local families, from which they often came themselves, these officers were invaluable contacts for high-level officials assigned to the south-eastern coast. These functionaries often found the military to be more reliable and well informed about the local situation than their civilian counterparts. Being open to discussion, they also acted as advisors to governors general and governors, in particular in negotiations with Peking on finding a *modus vivendi* that would be acceptable to all involved.

Reading the chronological repertories of the *General history of Fujian* concerning officers, and especially those in the coastal prefectures during the Qing dynasty, reveals that a good many of them served their entire career there, just as many of the commanders of naval forces were active on the coast between Guangdong, Fujian, and Zhejiang.[20] The length of their service, in fact, exceeded that set by the regulations: that of Admiral Huang Shijian 黃仕簡 (1722–89) in Fujian, for example, lasted seventeen years, from January 1770 to April of 1787. Most of the admirals and their direct subordinates were from South Fujian, from the prefectures of Quanzhou 泉州 and Zhangzhou 漳州, and especially the districts of Jinjiang 晉江, Tong'an 同安, and Zhangpu. Others came from the coastal districts of Guangdong and Zhejiang. During the period under study here, only four of these high officers did not have the same background and came from the interior provinces — Wang Jun 王郡, Zhang Wang 張旺 and Li Youyong 李有用, while the last, Hadanga 哈當阿 was a member of the Mongol Plain Yellow Banner.[21] The petty officers of the naval forces were mostly coastal inhabitants and native to the areas they served in. This is due to the necessity of having men used to the sea and familiar with the local area. This latter characteristic was also to be found in the lower-level personnel in the civil hierarchy.

However, the sources reveal a shortage of officials in the ranks of the imperial fleet, probably due to the difficulty of the task, the workload, and the frequency of the risks involved.[22] Even though the Emperors were aware of the dangers these men were subject to in the course of the eighteenth century, the officers knew that unnatural deaths, partial destruction or loss of equipment could lead to sanctions from the imperial government. In order to reduce the risks involved, there was sometimes a propensity to find a *modus vivendi* with partners working on the coast, by limiting the number of expeditions or by tolerating some illegal activities.

This negligence in their work was accompanied by another problem that could perhaps have had more negative consequences: monopolization of the posts by representatives of great families, especially the Shi 施, the Huang, the Lan, etc. The Shi 施 and Huang clans, deeply involved in the struggle against the Zheng 鄭 and the reorganization of maritime defence after the Ming-Qing dynastic transition conflict, were distinguished by their long service. This situation can certainly be explained by the transmission of know-how in a field where competence was rare, but these responsibilities also enabled them to reign as masters over their native prefectures from the conquest of Taiwan onward (1683). This had certain consequences for the hold of the government over the region, considering that Quanzhou for the Shi 施 and Zhangzhou 漳州 for the Huang 黃 and the Lan 藍 were the areas that the vast majority of officers and soldiers in the navy came from. Even though the present state of research does not enable us to determine in detail their influence networks, administrative correspondence reveals the power and arrogance of these lineages. This problem was brought up many times by local authorities, who were obliged both to recruit local men and to enforce respect for the laws.

In 1734, Wang Jun proposed that for the rank above that of colonel (*fujiang* 副將, regional vice commander), naval officers not be native to the region in order to avoid having them act on whim and taking care of their own interests rather than of their mission. He advised the contrary in the case of lieutenant colonels (*canjiang* 參將, assistant regional commander) and other minor command officers, seeing as how it was extremely important to know every nook and cranny of the coast and the tide patterns there.[23] Members of the army native to the coast shared the same interests as their fellow citizens and it is highly probable that they sometimes benefited from their position, to their personal advantage, at the expense of the general interest. The toughness of their lives and their poor pay, often insufficient to say the very least, considering the risks involved, may have encouraged some to infringe the law.[24]

Along with the army, there was another community structure that could assist the authorities, and that was the local mutual responsibility groups. Throughout Chinese history, depending on the period and the region, the government organized local communities into groups of families mutually responsible for one another's actions. These groups had diverse functions ranging from self-defence to self-surveillance. The main object of this system was to isolate wrongdoers in the community and especially to watch the population. At sea, a system equivalent to this *baojia* 保甲 brought together seamen, especially fishermen, to fight against piracy, smuggling, and clandestine emigration: these were the "anchorage groups" (*aojia* 澳甲). The first mention of it that we have found for the Ming dynasty goes back to 1536.[25] This was one of the measures thought up by the censor Bai Ben 白賁 to fight against the Wokou 倭寇. At that time, this form of organization was only meant to apply to the population living on board a ship. In 1616, Xiao Ji 蕭基 suggested utilizing it to assist customs agents and to place maritime activity in a legal framework.[26] In 1628, they were organized in the Tong'an 同安 district according to the instructions of the Supreme Commander Xiong Wencan 熊文燦 and at the instigation of Zheng 鄭 Zhilong 鄭芝龍, doubtless following the campaign he had led with the aid of the Liuwudian 劉五店 (Quanzhou 泉州) fishermen against the pirates.[27]

Under the Qing, the organization of anchorage groups was overseen from 1654 on by the governor of Zhejiang, Qin Shizhen 秦世禎.[28] Adopted generally for defence of the coast and inscribed in the statutes in 1707, the system was experimented with as early as 1703, taking as its model the network of fiscal responsibility (*lijia* 里甲) already organized in the port communities.[29] During the first decades of the eighteenth century, it seems to have been an efficacious means of surveillance and defence. Administrative correspondence indeed reveals close cooperation between the troops in charge of coast guard operations and these units. The rapidity with which the lesser pirates were identified and captured also testifies to good coordination between the government representatives and local society. From the 1780s onward, when piracy again became a major problem along the sea shore, the coastal authorities planned to reinstate this strategy. What then happened during the second third of the eighteenth century, a period of relative peace in the region? The less frequent mention of mutual responsibility groups in documents does not enable us to come to any precise conclusions. The organization was not dissolved, because the innumerable complaints brought against anchor chiefs and the heads of responsibility groups attest to its existence. It is, however, likely that its original objective — surveillance of the population and assisting the army in policing and salvage operations at sea — had been diverted to the benefit of the people in charge of this mission and even to some communities, and that the organization had escaped from the control of the administration and become subject to some misconduct.

We cannot go into all the details here of how the struggle against maritime illegality was organized. We shall limit the discussion to mentioning some practices in order to understand the problems that some of the directives may have raised and the misbehaviour they had also given rise to. In fact, when the Manchu dynasty took its place, the administration became omnipresent and seamen were the victims of innumerable administrative hassles that hindered their activities with a multitude of obstacles and snares. Henceforward, a whole panoply of laws regulated the various types of ships, navigation licences, the time allowed away from port, and so on, and consequently gave rise to an excess of abuses as a corollary. Some of these were perpetrated on seamen by petty administrative personnel responsible for surveillance of ships and licences and ever on the watch for the least opportunity to tap them for money.[30] Other abuses, just as frequent, were due to the unofficial agreements between merchants and officials that permitted and at times even encouraged comings and goings of ships and cargoes that were undeclared in exchange for some gain.

These abuses were the consequence of the ambiguous attitude on the part of the central government when it faced infringements. Indeed, after having recognized the necessity for the coastal regions to develop their potential at sea and the interest of the state in taxing these activities, the court passed laws on how to control the population and showed itself to be tolerant in applying its policies, but still did not lighten up the legislation which enabled the state to take firm command when the situation was getting out of hand or required a call to order. This lack of coherence was accompanied by a naval defence policy that resulted in the deterioration of equipment and the unfitness of troops. Thus, although the authorities managed more or less to control abuses in coastal society until the first decades of the eighteenth century, the economic difficulties that subsequently appeared in the coastal prefectures and the general laxity of the authorities were once again to give rise to behaviour and situations that made real control of the territory difficult. The government's weakness left the population at the mercy of clan hierarchies and the networks of tutelary associations and secret societies that were to take its place.

After the annexation of Taiwan island and the re-establishment of overseas trade, one issue became immediately paramount: controlling exchanges with foreign countries. In the beginning, it was a matter of forbidding clandestine emigration and preventing the Chinese who had gone overseas during the dynastic transition from returning. At that time, a whole series of regulations were adopted, some of which were to become the object of interminable discussions, for instance, the length of absence permitted, how to inspect the crews, or bearing arms on board ships. On the subject of time abroad, once the rules were set out, it was a matter of determining how officers were to judge the delays affecting certain ships. Of course, the authorities were aware of the hazards of navigation and winds, but they also knew that some shipmasters used this as an excuse for delaying their return. At this time, record books were set up for the use of local authorities in which the boat's number, exit date, type of cargo, port visited, etc. were noted. In the control stations and ports, officers were, in fact, supposed to check licences and add the official seal, thus confirming their authenticity and the passage of the boats in question. Quickly, however, it was seen that these measures were only effective for voyages in waters within jurisdiction of the empire, where local authorities could effectively note on the permit that late arrival was involuntary. It was only on this condition that ships would not be investigated by the administration upon their return.[31]

The situation was entirely different for overseas travels: ships' captains could not provide documents verifying the reasons they might be late. In this case, the highest provincial authorities were advised to be particularly vigilant in order to prevent any abuses, such as allowing their subordinates to extort money from captains and passengers of junks or accept bribes. It was also essential to check out the good faith of seafarers. It seems that frauds were, in fact, frequent since ship merchants returning late could arrange matters by paying off civil officials or the former could be the victims of unscrupulous officers who took a percentage of their profits by wielding the threat of denouncing them. The laws and warnings to personnel manning control posts and ports indicate that these practices were not isolated.[32] During the Yongzhen reign (1723–36) and the first decades of the succeeding reign, however, the high civil and military personnel in Fujian proved themselves to be aware of public opinion and especially that of the merchants. They thus frequently took up their defence by explaining to the emperor that late arrival was often inevitable and was a consequence of the normal time necessary for transactions, impossible to shorten unless merchants were to lose money or clients. The reasons given by merchants for delaying their return were indeed often plausible: taking on supplies, poor sales or having to sell at a loss, difficulty being paid for articles, or paying off debts.

It is naturally difficult to determine the extent to which this patronage was devoid of other motivations. Some of the officers in Fujian were able to establish good relations with merchants that enabled the former to pocket so-called "custom surcharges" (*haoxian* 耗羨). These sums usually enhanced the salaries of officials or allowed them to pay some regular expenses not taken into account by the state finances. It would seem that many people participated in, and benefited from, this system and that it was established practice. Most of these surcharges were well known and tolerated by the government as representing a way to counter corruption. It was an established practice and many people benefited from this system, although it was probably a source of disagreement among local authorities. In the 1720s and 1730s, merchants did not seem to have suffered too much from these unofficial taxes or "surplus percentages" (*yingyu* 贏餘 or *xianyu* — a surplus of the customs quota recorded in accounts and paid to the government).[33] Additional taxes were also required from fishermen and seem to have been accepted by the population, doubtless due to a tacit agreement beneficial to all parties involved. It was only when officers went beyond the limits set by the ensemble of the community or when these unofficial profits were not equitably shared out that a scandal would finally break out.

On the other hand, the authorities never really succeeded in cutting off clandestine emigration, even though the subject, especially emigration to Taiwan, was the object of long debate in the central government during the Yongzhen reign (1723–36) and the early years of the following reign.[34] These discussions concerned the selection of official candidates to go to the isle, the conditions of these men's stay, and the methods of checking the crews of ships making the crossing in order to keep crooks from slipping into them. Civilians were not the only ones to be tempted by this illicit transporting of migrants, as is proven by an ordinance of 1717, which permits transport to the isle, but warns the personnel in the coast guard service from taking up this activity themselves.[35] All sorts of infringements were encouraged by the fact that the right to set up household in Taiwan was above all granted to wealthy families, and by the restrictive nature of the measures adopted subsequent to the debates between partisans and adversaries of reinforcing legislation on the matter. Confronted with the deterioration of the social situation on the island and wanting to ensure the protection of the new inhabitants, the authorities alternately proposed to reinforce the rules or make them more flexible.

The extent of the coastline and the complicity of boatmen with the leaders of the responsibility and anchorage groups (*baozhang* 保長 et *aozhang* 澳長) made this a difficult task and prevented an effective and complete surveillance of the coast. The approximate estimation made by the general governor of Guangdong, Hao Yulin 郝玉麟 (1729–40), in 1733 was hardly flattering for the coastal administration: only 10 per cent of the clandestines were captured during the crossing and 20–30 per cent arrived, while 40–50 per cent were abandoned on desert islands or sandbars where they starved to death or were thrown overboard as "fish food" (*yu fu* 魚腹).[36] Beyond these shady local dealings, the mores commissioner of Fujian, Liu Shishu 劉師恕, pointed out an additional reason for this negligence: the judicial impunity of the offenders. The clandestine migrants were, in fact, taken back to the districts they came from, whereas the people who smuggled them across were sentenced to beating and exile, but they could buy their way out by handing over a percentage of their profits to the administration. So, how could these activities be stopped, if the fine was so minimal and the profits so great.[37]

In fact, some of the measures envisioned by the government were diverted or neglected, thanks to these agreements or to the preoccupation with finding a *modus vivendi* acceptable to everyone. The same goes for the directives aiming at reducing infringements at sea and facilitating the work of the coast guards, regulating the size, masting, and crew of ships, as well as the obligation to have distinct signs for their activity and origin. In 1714, all ships were required to have characters on their sails and hulls identifying them as "merchant" (*shang*) or "fisherman" (*yu*), their province, prefecture and district, registration number, and owner's name. Nine years later, these identification elements were completed by the attribution of two colours per province, so that the upper half of the mast had to be painted in blue and the registration number written in white for Jiangnan, in white and green for Zhejiang, in green and red for Fujian, in red and blue for Guangdong.[38] The size of the characters was also regulated so that they would be legible and would enable the authorities to identify offenders.

The governor general of Fujian noted in a memorandum dated 21 July 1771 that responsibility for irregularities was incumbent upon the authorities who did not take inspections seriously and handed over delivery of licences to heads of anchor groups, guarantors, and scribes who indulged in rather obscure practices. No checks were made of masters or crews whose registrations were no longer accurate.[39] A report dated 10 February 1782 indicates that only merchant junks were inspected when they left port and still had their engraved registration, but this was not the case for fishing and transport boats,[40] and even less so in the case of small estuary and river craft which had been subject to the same rules since 1775 because of their role in promoting smuggling.[41] At the end of the eighteenth century and the beginning of the nineteenth, there were increasingly more fishermen supplying pirates at sea. Some of them — according to the confessions they made to the authorities — even did so before being approached to avoid having the pirates rob them of their catch. This voluntary collaboration was as motivated by the lure of profits as by a real fear of reprisals from the outlaws. Fishing and coasting vessels were defenceless against the fleets of pillagers from the 1720s onward, when the government forbade the former to bear arms for their own protection.

***

Management of the coast by the Qing sovereigns, as under their predecessors, was approached in two ways: a military system mainly oriented towards protecting the coastline and a whole series of measures aiming at controlling the coastal population and their activities. Nonetheless, the unquestionable advantages of the system set up from the second half of the sixteenth century onward and reinforced in the early Qing dynasty were severely limited by the weakness of the budget allocated for the upkeep of equipment and troop training on the Fujian coast. Most certainly, the rules about navigation and maritime trade increased in clarity with the Manchu government, but they were overloaded with details that made their implementation even more difficult and resulted in still more negligence on the part of the authorities responsible for applying them. Aside from the pressure from the population subject to these rules, some of them turned out to be inapplicable without the presence of dedicated personnel in sufficient numbers, which was the case in many instances. As the governor of Fujian observed in 1771, management of the coast was being increasingly left to lower-level local personnel who most probably were taking advantage of the situation.[42]

In confiding command of naval forces and control of maritime activities to natives often drawn from the great coastal families, the government gave up a considerable part of its prerogatives in the same stroke. Thus, at the end of the eighteenth century, lacking the personnel necessary for the task, the whole of the coastal economy seems to have been under the control of the inhabitants of Fujian. This situation resulted from decisions taken at the turn of the century and the first consequences only reinforced this state of affairs: during the early decades of the eighteenth century, these measures, in fact, resulted in a genuine cooperation between the various actors in local political life. However, this situation did not continue indefinitely, and even before mid-century, animosity appeared between the civil and military hierarchies, between high-level civil servants and provincial personnel, and there were increasing struggles and conflicts between coalition groups as well. It appears that quite rapidly after the return of peace, local military cadres were no longer participating as previously in the decision making and the judgement of them expressed by their civilian counterparts were rather disdainful.[43] Was the entente that had reigned on the coast at least until the repression of the Zhu Yigui 朱一貴 (d. 1721) insurrection deteriorating due to the return of peace, when all the players were going back to their original occupations without paying enough attention to the overall situation? Is it a matter of friction between the centre and the periphery and, in this case, was the animosity on a political or an economic level or, as is more likely, on both at the same time?

On both sides, the reasons contributing to mutual reticence and distrust were numerous. On the local level, expectations were probably not met. The elite, or at least some of them, who collaborated in the early stages of reconstruction with the government representatives, were soon to realize that the Qing sovereigns, no more than these from the Ming, had no maritime aspirations, and above all, proved to be very distrustful towards seafarers, especially those operating in extraterritorial waters, and perhaps even more so towards the local population. It is obvious that the Manchu emperors did not take into account the maritime capital which they gained following their conquest of China. When they became masters of the land, Fujian had experienced seamen, and above all, a merchant fleet that was quite active in ocean trade. However, it is possible that this "indifference" could also parallel their reticence towards the monopolistic activities of certain lineages or regional groups in respect to the local economy.[44]

It now remains for us to pursue this research by placing it in a context of rivalry where disagreement and dissension are due more to competition than to economic survival, and the real issue seems to be control of the market. Above all, it would be advisable to further the study of the great lineages, for which many aspects remain to be examined more thoroughly. Obviously, evaluation of the real impact of the great clans on society necessitates more extensive quantitative research (the number of their members and evaluation of their holdings and lucrative activities), and qualitative analysis (identification of the families, their development over time, their possible transformation, network of relations, provincial, extraprovincial, and overseas involvements, etc.) It would also be necessary to evaluate the relations that these families maintained with the members of other pressure groups, especially the secret societies, since in the late eighteenth century the latter likewise held considerable power over maritime activities and coastal society. Did these groups share responsibilities or were the masterminds of brotherhood associations none other than representatives of some of the great families of the coast?

Notes

1. The population may have been organized and subjected to such pressures well before this period, if we follow the analysis of economic and political rivalries proposed by Billy So for the tenth to fourteenth centuries (2000).
2. Local life in Minnan 閩南 was widely dominated by personal and clan strategies, not only to the detriment of a large part of the population, but also to that of the power of the state. Many functionaries in Fujian repeatedly described the difficulties of their work, for that matter. Testimony from the period is unanimous in stating that Quanzhou and Zhangzhou were far more disdainful of the laws than the other districts. The manuals written for administrators working in Fujian concentrated mainly on these two prefectures, whose inhabitants were described as intractable, difficult to administer and to subject. A good example of this is provided in *Essay on the Art of Administering the Prefectures of Quanzhou et Zhangzhou* (*Quan Zhang zhifa lun*) written by Xie Jinluan.

    On the subject of secret societies and the renewed interest in research on them, see, among others, Qin Baoqi, 1988; David Ownby and Mary Somers Heidhues, 1993; Dian H. Murray and Qin Baoqi, 1994; and David Ownby, 1996.
3. Ng Chin-keong, 1983, p. 36.

4. Ng Chin-keong, 1983, pp. 34–35. This was the case, for example, of the Huang and Shi 施 clans that became very powerful after the Ming-Qing transition conflicts, due to the actions of two of their representatives, Huang Wu 黃梧 (? –1674) and Shi Lang 施琅 (1621–96), who fought against the Zheng clan. Huang Wu 黃梧 came from the Pinghe 平和 district (Zhangzhou 漳州). He was one of the commanders of Zheng Chenggong 鄭成功 responsible for defending the city of Haicheng 海澄. In 1656, he decided to surrender to the Qing who made him duke of Haicheng 海澄 and he fought with them against his former lord. He is alleged to have been the author of the most extreme propositions which the Manchu government expressed in its policy toward the coast: the execution of Zheng Zhilong 鄭芝龍 and the evacuation of the coast. Shi Lang 施琅, who came from Jinjiang 晉江 (Quanzhou 泉州), was from a great coastal family. He first operated under the orders of Zheng Zhilong 鄭芝龍 and stopped serving the Zheng when Zheng Chenggong 鄭成功 killed part of his family. He then submitted to the Qing and fought at their side in numerous campaigns in Fujian. He was also the prime mover in the conquest of Taiwan.
5. *Gongzhong dang Yongzheng chao zouzhe*, vol. 9, p. 188: 8 December 1727.
6. About *xiedou*, cf.: Harry J. Lamley, 1977, pp. 1–39; 1990, pp. 27–64.
7. *Gongzhong dang Yongzheng chao zouzhe*, vol. 14, p. 717: 6 December 1729.
8. Wang Mingming, 1995, pp. 59–63.
9. Qin Baoqi, 1993, p. 41.
10. Shi Yilong, 2000, p. 26.
11. This migratory movement, in the majority of cases, was towards a few destinations that varied according to the period: in the late Ming and the dynastic transition period, inhabitants of Fujian preferred clearing the mountainous lands of the hinterland and sailing to Southeast Asia, and then in the early eighteenth century, besides the countries of the *Nanyang*, Taiwan became a new land of promise. At the beginning of the Qing dynasty, the government also encouraged emigration to Sichuan in order to resolve the problem of depopulation in the province following the popular rebellions in the late Ming dynasty.
12. Civil officials proposed to enlist them in the army, for that matter: *Neige qian sanchao tiben*, "junwu-fangwu", 0006: 26 March 1737.
13. About this subject, cf. the excellent work of David Ownby (1996).
14. The case of fishermen is quite revealing in this respect, since we can follow the evolution, probably from the early eighteenth century on and perhaps encouraged by the government, from mutual aid associations (*yumin banghui* 漁民幫會) into fishermen guilds (*yumin gongsuo* 漁民公所) that were more restricted and limiting in regards to participation. According to Li Shihao, the latter were presented as being directed by professional fisherman, but in reality, they were under the influence of powerful men who, with the cooperation of local authorities, exploited the workers who were excluded from a share in the

profits, all the while often being oppressed by calamities (Li Shihao et Qu Ruoqian, 1993, p. 96.).
15. *Xiamen zhi*, j. 15, p. 323.
16. For example, the lands suited for "sea farms" were bitterly disputed by the inhabitants and only belonged to the strongest, that is, the powerful clans (Zhang Zhenqian, 1987, pp. 128–43). According to the same author, a good number of the conflicts, lawsuits and feuds that occurred in the seaside villages were principally over the utilization of these sea farms (p. 128).
17. On this subject, see, Robert J. Antony, 1988, ch. 5; Paola Calanca, ch. 3 (2010).
18. This was the case with Chen Shaoyuan 陳紹遠 and Chen Zigong 陳子恭, who made contact with sea pirates and paid them off in rice in order to protect their fishing nets (*Gongzhong zhupi zouzhe*, Nongmin yundong, 1122/11: 21 March 1801).
19. This remark is equally applicable to many officers in the land forces, some of whom operated exclusively in the province from their very first term of office (*Fujian tongzhi*, 1829 edition, j. 120).
20. *Fujian tongzhi*, 1829 edition, j. 120.
21. Wang Jun 王郡, Zhang Wang 張旺, and Li Youyoung 李有用 spent a part of their careers in Fujian and Taiwan, while Hadanga 哈當阿 may have been appointed according to the tendency especially prevalent from the Qianlong reign onward of reserving the best postings in the army to members of the banners, and particularly to the Manchus and Mongols.
22. Private trade employed the best seamen, who, attracted by higher earnings and the opportunity to carry on trade themselves, had no desire to risk their lives in the navy. Furthermore, navigation on the high seas required far more technical personnel: in addition to the captain, his officers and seamen (several dozen), some twenty persons had other precise duties. Cf. Chen Xiyu, 1991, pp. 161–62.
23. *Gongzhong dang Yongzheng chao zouzhe*, vol. 23, pp. 799–801: 16 December 1734. The second-class captain (*shoubei* 守備), lieutenant (*quanzong*), and first lieutenant (*bazong* 把總) were supposed to be on patrol every day, while the colonel (*fujiang* 副將), lieutenant colonel (*canjiang* 參將), and commander (*youji* 遊擊) were supposed to do so only once a month (*Qing shi liezhuan*, vol. 3, j. 11, p. 797).
24. Military personnel and local inhabitants of the coast knew one another so well that dismissal of officers or enlisted men for not respecting the laws could even have a perverse effect, since these men, suddenly idle and unemployed, could be tempted by illegal business. This is why in 1727 the Ministry of War proposed transferring officers, dismissed from their duties for having overlooked illegal trade or taken bribes, to other provinces: officers in Guangdong to Shandong, those in Fujian to Henan, and the officers of the Taizhou and Wenzhou prefectures to Zhili.

25. *Ming shilu leizuan, Fujian-Taiwan juan*, p. 515: 15 August 1536.
26. Zhang Xie, *Dong Xi Yang kao*, j. 7, pp. 135–40; *Ming shilu leizuan, Fujian-Taiwan juan*, p. 549: 5 October 1616. This was one of thirteen measures proposed by Xiao Ji 蕭基 in 1616 in order to place maritime activity in a legal framework. The ensemble of his propositions aimed at "encouraging trade and correcting abuse" (*xu shang li bi* 恤商釐弊).
27. In the same area, the men enrolled on these lists had been divided up into watch squadrons and received three *fen* (1 *fen* = 0,01 *liang*, i.e. tael) daily when they were on duty. This sum was raised to five *fen* when they captured bandits, as well as a reward. They brought part of their own equipment and the rest was provided by the administration. Managing ammunition was the responsibility of their anchorage leader, who handed them out when needed. When they captured enemy ships, the artillery was handed over to the administration, but they were allowed to divide up the edge weapons. If their own ship was damaged during combat with the pirates, the local authorities paid them money for the repairs Ships captured were taken back to port and handed over to the anchorage leader to be used if needed. (Cao Lütai, j. 4, pp. 67–68; pp. 71–76).
28. *Qing shi gao*, vol. 32, j. 240, pp. 9543–44.
29. *Da Qing huidian*, Yongzheng edition, j. 139, p. 6b.
30. On this subject, see for example, *Da Qing huidian*, Yongzheng, ed., j. 139; *Da Qing huidian shili*, Guangxu edition, j. 629 and 630.
31. *Neige qian sanchao tiben*, "junwu-fangwu", 0029: 15 June 1743.
32. Ibid.
33. Ng Chin-keong, 1983, pp. 198–200.
34. In 1770, the authorities again observed considerable emigration from eastern Guangdong (*Qing shi liezhuan*, vol. 6, j. 23, p. 1713).
35. *Da Qing huidian shili*, Guangxu edition, j. 629, p. 1b; *Xiamen zhi*, j. 4, p. 79.
36. *Gongzhong dang Yongzheng chao zouzhe*, vol. 21, pp. 355–56: 18 May 1733; *Ming Qing shiliao*, vol. *wu*, pp. 280–81.
37. *Gongzhong dang Yongzheng chao zouzhe*, vol. 14, p. 716: 6 December 1729.
38. *Da Qing huidian shili*, Guangxu edition, j. 629, p. 2a; *Qingchao wenxian tongkao*, j. 33, p. 5157.
39. *Fujian shengli*, j. 23, pp. 616–18.
40. *Fujian shengli*, j. 23, p. 644. During an inspection the general of division of Fujian, Zhang Tianjun, discovered that many ships had neither the number engraved on their hull, nor the name of their owner on the sails. These were probably ships that were never included in the port registers (*Gongzhong zhupi zouzhe*, "junwu-fangwu", 20: memorandum dated 27 December 1750).
41. *Fujian shengli*, j. 23, p. 618.
42. A similar observation can be seen in Robert Antony's study of Guangdong province (1998, pp. 27–59).
43. *Gongzhong dang Yongzheng chao zouzhe*, vol. IX, pp. 464–65.

44. The authors of the *Yunxiao Monograph* clearly demonstated their preponderance in the regional economy when they declared that fishing and fish farming suffered from the same anomalies as agriculture: wealthy families were increasing their fleets, their fish and shellfish farms and their fortunes, while the lesser-off saw their margin of existence narrow day by day (*Yunxiao xianzhi*, j. 5, p. 4a).

References

Antony, Robert J. "Pirates, Bandits, and Brotherhoods: A Study of Crime and Law in Kwangtung Province, 1790–1830". Ph.D. Dissertation, University of Hawaii, 1988.

———. "Subcounty Officials, the State, and Local Communities in Guangdong Province, 1644–1860". In *Dragons, Tigers, and Dogs. Qing Crisis Management and the Boundaries of State Power in Late Imperial China*, edited by R.J. Antony and J.K. Leonard. Ithaca, New York: Cornell University, East Asia Program, 1998.

Calanca, Paola. *Piraterie et contrebande au Fujian. L'administration chinoise face aux problèmes d'illégalité maritime (17e — début 19e siècle)*. Paris: Editions des Indes Savantes, 2010.

Cao Lütai. *Jinghai jilüe*. Taipei: Taiwan Yinhang, Taiwan Wenxian congkan 33, 1959.

Chen Xiyu. *Zhongguo fanchuan yu haiwai maoyi*. Xiamen: Xiamen daxue chubanshe, 1991.

(*Chongzuan*) *Fujian tongzhi*, rev. Sun Erzhun et al., 1829.

Da Qing huidian, Yongzheng edition, 1733

(*Qinding*) *Da Qing huidian shili* (1899, Guangxu edition), compiled by Li Hongzhang et al. Shanghai: Shangwu yinshuguan, 1908.

Fujian shengli (1873). Taipei: Datong shuju, Taiwan wenxian shiliao congkan (1964): 141–42.

Gongzhong dang Yongzheng chao zouzhe, Taipei, Gugong bowuyuan, 1977–80.

Gongzhong zhupi,"Nongmin yundong" (Peking), n.d.

Lamley Harry J. "Hsieh-tou: the Pathology of Violence in Southeastern China". *Ch'ing-shih wen-t'I* 3–7 (1977): 1–39.

———. "Lineage Feuding in Southern Fujian and Eastern Guangdong under Qing Rule". In *Violence in China. Essays in Culture and Counter culture*, edited by J.N. Lipman and S. Harrel. Albany: State University of New York, 1990.

Li Shihao and Qu Ruoqian. *Zhongguo yuye shi*. Taipei: Taiwan shangwu yinshuguan, 3rd edition, 1993.

Ming Qing shiliao. Peking: Zhonghua shuju, vol. *wu*, 1987.

Ming shilu leizuan, Fujian-Taiwan juan, compiled by Xue Guozhong, Wei Hong, Li Guoxiang, and Yang Chang. Wuhan: Wuhan chubanshe, 1993.

Murray Dian and Qin Baoqi. *The Origins of the Tiandihui. The Chinese Triads in Legend and History*. Stanford: Stanford University Press, 1994.

Ng Chin-keong. *Trade and Society: the Amoy Network on the China Coast, 1683–1735*. Singapore: Singapore University Press, 1983.

Neige qian sanchao tiben, "Junwu-fangwu" (Peking).

Ownby, David and Mary Somers Heidhues, eds., *"Secret Societies" Reconsidered. Perspectives on the Social History of Modern South China and Southeast Asia*. Armonk, New York: An East Gate Book, 1993.

Ownby, David. *Brotherhoods and Secret Societies in Early and Mid-Qing China. The Formation of a Tradition*. Stanford: Stanford University Press, 1996.

Qin Baoqi. *Qing qianqi Tiandihui yanjiu* (Study of the Heaven and Earth Society during the early Qing dynasty). Beijing: Zhongguo Renmin Daxue, Qingshi yanjiu congshu, 1988.

———. "Fujian Yunxiao Gaoxi: Tiandihui de faxiangdi". *Qing shi yanjiu* 3 (1993): 36–46.

Qingchao wenxian tongkao, compiled by Ji Huang et al. In *Shi tong* 十通. Shanghai: Shangwu yinshuguan, 1936.

Qing shi gao, compiled by Zhao Erxun et al. Peking: Zhonghua shuju, 1976–77.

Qing shi liezhuan (1928), edited by Wang Zhonghan. Peking: Zhonghua shuju, 1987.

Shi Yilong. "Mingdai Huidong diqu de haiyang shehui jingji shenghuo ji qi bianqian". *Zhongguo shehui jingji shi yanjiu* 3 (2000): 20–29.

So Billy K. *Prosperity, Region, and Institutions in Maritime China. The South Fukien Pattern, 946–1368*. Cambridge and London: Harvard University Asia Center, 2000.

Wang Mingming. "Place, Administration, and Territorial Cults in Late Imperial China: A Case Study from South Fujian". *Late Imperial China* 16–1: 33–78.

Xiamen zhi (1838), revised by Zhou Gai et al. Taipei: Chengwen chubanshe, Zhongguo fangzhi congshu, Huanan difang 80, 1967.

Xie Jinluan. *Quan Zhang zhifa lun*, 1823.

Yunxiao xianzhi, rev. by Xu Bingwen, 1947.

Zhang Xie. *Dong-Xi Yang kao* (1617). Peking: Zhonghua shuju, Zhongwai jiaotong shiji congkan, 1981.

Zhang Zhenqian. "Yucun tudi wenti de xingzhi ji qi jingying fangshi chutan". In *Ming Qing Fujian shehui yu xiangcun jingji*, edited by Fu Yiling and Yang Guozhen. Xiamen: Xiamen Daxue chubanshe, 1987.

6

Maritime Piracy through a Barbarian Lens: Punishment and Representation (the *S.S. Namoa* Hijack Case [1890–91])

John Kleinen

> Narratives can make us understand. Photographs do something else: they haunt us"
>
> — *Susan Sontag 2002, p. 94*

Introduction

A ghastly photograph haunts the scientific literature about China and Vietnam in the pre-modern period: the execution of Asians somewhere on a beach in the Far East. Triumphant Westerners, this is the impression given, pose relaxed behind a number of decapitated corpses with their severed heads beside them. Readers of Eric Hobsbawm's *Bandits* are familiar with the black-and-white photograph of ten headless corpses triumphed over by eight Caucasians in tropical attire. The caption Hobsbawm accorded to this scene was "(T)he execution of Namoa Pirates, Kowloon 1891, with British sahibs. Namoa, an island off Swatoff, (…) [was] a great centre for piracy and, at this time, the scene of a rebellion. We do not know whether the corpses had been pirates, rebels or both" (1969, pp. 96–97 and 1981, plate 39 between pages 162 and 163).

First published in 1969, *Bandits* belongs to the classical canon of radical British historians chronicling the English transition to modernity, infused with a strong dose on social anthropology.[1] In a journalistic account, *Pirates of the Far East*, published a year after *Bandits*, author Harry Miller, a London editor of *The Straits Times*, identified the photograph as "(P)irates captured by the Chinese government", showing a scene of "a mass execution in one of the South China ports" (1970, illustration 16). Leaving pirates aside, the American historian Richard O'Connor used the same photograph in a pioneering treatise on the Boxer Rebellion. Here the caption indicates the victims as "executed Spirit Soldiers", or Boxer insurgents as they are better known (1973, p. 148).[2] The political dimensions of this image have also not escaped other authors either. In at least two accounts of the Vietnam War, the same photograph is used as evidence of French cruelty to Vietnamese insurgents. "As the peasant's existence worsened", argue two American historians, Edward Doyle and Samuel Lipsman, "many took to banditry or political activity. The French made no distinction — they called them all bandits. Beheading was often their fate" (1981, p. 160). In a similar publication, another historian of the Vietnam War, T.D. Boettcher (1985), underlines this sentiment with a caption which does not beat about the bush: "Frenchmen beheaded Vietnamese who oppressed their rule or who were guilty of crime" (1985, p. 15).[3] Such a catholic interpretation is the outcome of the fact that since no place and year have been given, the origins of the photograph have remained obscure and hence a matter of conjecture. If neither the Boxer Rebellion nor the Vietnamese resistance against the French were the accurate background to the images, what then was the probable answer which Hobsbawm left in the middle? In a major reference book on China dating from 1980, the picture bears the caption "Chinese pirates beheaded in Hong Kong, 1897. The men standing are British government officials" (Buchanan et al. 1980, p. 424). The Hong Kong Museum of History keeps three photographs (sized 20.2 × 24.5 cm) showing the moments before and just after the beheadings. They have two different captions "S.S. Namoa Pirates beheaded on the beach at Kowloon Walled City, 17.4.1891" and "1891 'Namoa' Pirates beheaded at Kowloon City on the Boundary between British and Chinese Kowloon".[4] In one photograph five of the condemned can be seen kneeling on the beach with Chinese soldiers and executioners hovering in the background, waiting for the moment to deliver the deathly blow. Within a slightly different time frame the two other pictures show eight foreigners standing behind the decapitated corpses. The second person from the right is looking at his watch: Is he really checking the time of the day or is he the photographer who has to ensure that his assistant behind the camera is using the right exposure time? This kind of detail is what Roland Barthes called the *punctum*, the thorn in a picture which snags the viewer, in this picture the attitude of the man who is checking his watch. Figure 6.1 is the first of the three images I mentioned here and the most famous.

Maritime Piracy through a Barbarian Lens

FIGURE 6.1

17 April 1891. The "*S.S. Namoa*" Pirates Beheaded. Members of the Chinese Maritime Customs Service as Onlookers

Source: Rijksprenten Kabinet, Leiden. Inventory no. 1505.183.

The narrative of the S.S. *Namoa* piracy case itself is widely known since the registrar of the Supreme Court of Hong Kong, James William Norton-Kyshe, described the events in great detail in his "*The History of Laws and Courts of Hong Kong*" (1898).[5] In more popular accounts of pirates in the Southern China Sea, the *Namoa* case has often been referred to, even at the time at which Hobsbawm published *Bandits* (see for example, A.G. Course in 1966, pp. 194–97). What seems to have been forgotten by contemporary viewers of these photographs are two major aspects: the role and function of maritime piracy in the nineteenth and early twentieth century, and the representation of public punishment and public consumption of it. Whereas Hobsbawm apparently witnessed a maritime variation of social banditry, such other scholars as Antony (2003, p. 171) deny these "'social bandits' robbing the rich to give to the poor or displaying some sort of primitive class-consciousness". The main motivation driving Chinese pirates was not social consciousness, they argue: neither in the high tide of the eighteenth and early nineteenth century, nor in the late nineteenth and early twentieth century.

MARITIME PIRACY AND SOCIAL BANDITRY

In his attack on the "social banditry" thesis, Anton Blok makes a strong case against a model which leans too heavily on folkloric and literary sources. Hobsbawm stressed the tie between peasant and bandit to such an extent that the Robin Hood-dimension, or the social aspects of banditry, overshadowed all other aspects, including the use of indiscriminate violence, and virtually cancelled out any other less flattering interpretations of bandit attributions. Later Blok (2001) repeated in his critique of Hobsbawm: "What animated banditry was the quest for honour and respect. What often motivated it was revenge…" (p. 22). This statement is extremely apt in the case of many pirates, and is equally true of Zhang Yi, the infamous pirate of the 1810s, and in that of Bai Lang, a brigand leader in northern China who sometimes acted as a Robin Hood (Perry 1983). Although Hobsbawm later acknowledged his critics' points, he never surrendered his view that the myths and folkloric sources referred at least to an imagined past.[6] While the general link between banditry and peasantry is contested, that with piracy is never questioned. Fernand Braudel had already underlined the point that pirates and brigands should be understood as products of pre-industrial peasant societies. In a chapter of his magnum opus *La Mediterranée*, entitled

"Misère et Banditisme", Braudel adduced the concept that banditry on land which is the counterpart of piracy at sea is "a long established pattern of behaviour (...). From the time when the sea first harboured coherent societies, banditry appeared, never to be eliminated" (1966 (1972), p. 743). The complexity of the roles of brigands and buccaneers from the perspective of state formation is vividly described in the context of the emergence of Venice in the early sixteenth century. Bandits and pirates were deeply implicated in a process of state centralization: they helped make states, and states made bandits and pirates. These pirates attacked and robbed people outside their own community not only for personal benefit and that of their families, but as it turned out, unconsciously and unintentionally, also for their community at large.

In his treatise on maritime piracy in late imperial South China, Robert J. Antony found that

> Chinese pirates were not Hobsbawmian "social bandits" robbing the rich to give to the poor or displaying some sort of primitive class-consciousness. In this sense they were significantly different from Western pirates. Instead they robbed, kidnapped, and murdered anyone who got in their way. They indiscriminately victimized not only sea captains and rich merchants, but also poor fishermen and sailors (2003, p. 171).

Elisabeth Perry's study (1983) of one of the most famous bandits in Chinese history, the brigand Bai Lang (1873–1914), shows that social banditry is linked by social class and ideology and might come closer to Hobsbawm than to Blok for whom the link with local power holders is more crucial. Chinese pirates often worked hand in glove with local authorities and the shift from what was illegal to what was legal was, as we know from certain careers of pirates, easily made. In incidents in which peasants resorted to banditry, in James Scott's phrase, one of the "weapons of the weak", they did not do so spontaneously, but as instruments of elites and warlords fighting their own wars against other state makers to subdue or overthrow them. Moreover, the history of the South China coast, including that of Macau and Hong Kong, shows that peasants and townspeople actively assisted authorities in arresting pirates. This is a lesson that can be drawn on in finding solutions to the new piracy problems in Southeast Asia.

Moving on from these arguments, there is another angle from which we can observe maritime piracy along the South China coast and that is that the activities of pirates facilitated capitalist penetration. Pirates plundered villages which were hubs of riverside and coastal traffic. It is suggested by Heyman (1999) among others that pirates behaved as military entrepreneurs who connected agriculturists with brigands through a (forced) market mechanism, which consequently led to an increased monetization of the rural economy. In a far more remote past, pirates had already performed the role of merchants, compared with the Uskoks of Segna and Fiume who acted as "*diavoli uniti per rubare*" and against whom "Venice sought to maintain her privileges with compromises and surprises" (Braudel 1966 (1972), pp. 130–31). This is equally apposite when applied to late eighteenth and early nineteenth century piracy in China. And, as I have already suggested, it seems axiomatic that maritime piracy flourished where the state was weak or virtually absent. Gradually it provided the pretext for the state's forcible and ultimately successful intrusion into the countryside of southern China (Heyman 1999, p. 39). In the first half of the twentieth century, pirate gangs once again prowled the waters off the South China coast, but this time they profiteered from the civil strife which plagued the mainland. It is hard to feel convinced that these pirates acted as social or political bandits. The incidents became collectively known as the "Bias Bay piracies" between 1914 and 1931, and echoed the *S.S. Namoa* piracy case of 1890–91. The Hong Kong authorities complained that not many lessons had been learned from the previous century.[7] Obviously the case still remained fresh in official memory.

PIRATES AND PORTS IN THE LATE NINETEENTH AND EARLY TWENTIETH CENTURY

Historically, maritime piracy was synonymous with such criminal acts as armed theft and robbery, but throughout history it has differed in its nature and occurrence. As Antony (2001) has convincingly shown, the nature of piracy in Asia changed as it did in the West: Goethe's Mephistoteles' dictum that war, trade, and piracy are a trinity is an equally apposite definition of the practices current during the Ming and early Qing dynasties. Driven from the lawful pursuit of their livelihood, merchants and seafarers turned to illicit activities, which in a strictly legal definition, transformed them into pirates. Such famous buccaneers as Francis Drake and Henry Morgan had spitting images in Chinese merchant-pirates such as Wang Zhi and Hong Dizhen (see Mote 2004). The period of transition from the Ming to the Qing was likewise a period of great social and economic upheaval, which never really settled in the South. The mid-Qing period towards the end of the eighteenth century and the beginning of the nineteenth century was equally plagued by social upheaval and to add to people's misery, overwhelmed by natural disasters leading to severe food shortages. Between 1790 and 1810, the number of pirates expanded to a formidable force of between 50,000 and 70,000 men and women organized in a Guangdong Pirate Federation. The Federation was divided into six squadrons, each flying separate colours, with Zheng Yi Sao in charge as an admiral or chief over them all (Murray 1987). In a situation in which a coastal zone formed a frontier society, a natural bond rapidly developed between the omnipresent secret societies and pirates (Antony 2003, pp. 135–36). The pirates recruited their members from dispossessed families along the frontier who had connections to such triads as the Tiandihui and the White Lotus. The Vietnamese border town of Giang Binh (Chiang-ping in Chinese) and the island of Hainan off the Chinese and Vietnamese coasts evolved into operational bases which attracted involvement in such political movements as the Tay Son rebellion in Vietnam (1786-1802). The nature of piracy changed from being a forced seaborne trade to an illicit activity where "sharp distinctions were made between legitimate commerce" and robbery at sea (Antony 2003, pp. 52–53).

Most of the pirates were local outcasts, semi-nomadic "water people", referred to as *tanka* or "egg families". Whether they strayed from the straight and narrow coast because they lacked firm roots in communities or simply espoused the role of semi-pirates in the off-fisheries season is still a matter of debate. Antony speaks of an "eclectic demography" of people belonging to such subethnic Han groups as the Hokkien and the Dan (Tanka). At that time the majority of the mariners were Hokkien fishermen, merchants, shipowners, and sailors (2003, p. 9ff). The endemic poverty which afflicted the main coastal populations, the Hokkien and the Dan boat people, provided a natural hotbed for the widespread occurrence of piracy. The weak link between legitimate professions and the piracy of these "water people" was an important factor in the normal state of affairs during the early nineteenth century (Antony 2003, p. 83ff; Lung 2001).

At the end of the nineteenth century piracy still posed a serious threat. Although the tens of thousands of pirates and their suppliers from the hinterlands and even from neighbouring Vietnam had disappeared from the scene, Sino-British relations were still shaped by piracy (Blue 1965).[8] The main reason was political: the first Opium War (1839–42) was concluded with the signing of the Treaty of Nanjing (1842), the first of a number of "unequal treaties" with Western trading nations. The treaty abolished the prevailing licensed monopoly system of trade, opened five ports to British residence and foreign trade and granted British nationals extraterritoriality (exemption from Chinese laws). The subjection to this "national humiliation" as the Chinese referred to it was aggravated by the payment of a large indemnity for the alleged damage suffered by British interests. It was also stipulated that Britain receive "most-favoured-nation" treatment in the trading concessions the Chinese granted the other powers then or later. Other incursions, wars, and treaties brought new, more humiliating concessions in their wake and added new privileges to those foreigners had already garnered after "Nanjing" (Spence 1991, pp. 178–93). The opening of the ports led to an increase in the number of foreign and Chinese vessels, a circumstance which automatically attracted pirates of various sorts. After 1842 the British attempted to suppress them. The Second Opium War broke out in 1858, and using a tactic it had successfully practised in Vietnam by whipping up the killing of Roman Catholic missionaries, France joined Britain in a march on Beijing. For many years, the opening of ten more ports and the legalized treaties served to humiliate China in the eyes of the world. The opium trade and the opening up of China to travellers, traders, and missionaries assumed the shape of a forced modernization. The soft underbelly of the Chinese empire, a frontier in many aspects, heaved and groaned, indelibly linked to crime, vice, and violence.

The Chinese Navy was no match for the numerous pirates who often actually acted semi-legally as privateers. Hong Kong, at the mouth of the Pearl River, once described as the "Ladrone of Piratical islands", served China as a major trading hub, including for illegal opium trafficking, and also became a foster child of the British Navy (Fox 1940, p. 38; quote from Lung 2001, p. 59). The right to capture pirates outside the three-mile limit of the Treaty ports was not included as an article in the Nanjing Treaty and this led to various misunderstandings between the Chinese and British Navies. After several decades, the roughshod gunboat diplomacy of the British and the French eventually led to the Treaty of Tientsin in 1860, which put piracy more clearly on the agenda. In the years immediately after this was signed, between 1861 and 1869, China was forced to negotiate with other Western nations as well (Fox 1940, pp. 106–87). After the last wave of large-scale piracy in the first decade of the nineteenth century, piracy had gradually diminished, but its numbers and strength now recouped once again in response to the growth of foreign trade and the vagaries and social upsets caused by the civil war, articulated by the Taiping Rebellion (1850–64). Piratical raids on the islands off Hong Kong and in the vicinity of Macau gave the British and the Portuguese no option but to mount large-scale patrols along the coasts. Eventually, since such punitive expeditions against pirates hideouts on the coast yielded little satisfactory result, the governor of Hong Kong, Richard Macdonnell, looked for legal measures to drive pirates away from the colony. Between 1868 and 1870, the suppression of piracy was helped by the building of a new Chinese steam fleet which supported the British warships on the China station to police the sea (Fox 1940, pp. 143–87; Lung 2001, p. 293ff). Boxer (1980) has claimed that the ambivalent role of Hong Kong police officials and corruption at all levels led to hand-in-glove activities with leading Cantonese pirates who dominated the waters beyond the perimeters of Hong Kong and the Pearl River. Cantonese pirates preying on shipping in Hong Kong waters posed a constant problem, and not all of these predators were Chinese.

Collusion between Cantonese pirates and Europeans was unequivocally revealed during the trial of the English renegade William Fenton in 1851 and later that of an American pirate Eli Boggs who was tried for murder and piracy in 1857 and deported. In 1863 the Hong Kong magistrate even offered a reward of 1000 dollars for the apprehension of "English and American hands on board" pirate junks (Norton-Kyshe 1898 [II], p. 63). In 1865 four Portuguese and one Spaniard were sentenced to death for murder and piracy (Norton-Kyshe 1898, p. 84).

One favourite tactic deployed by the Cantonese pirates was the hijacking of vessels sailing between Hong Kong and Macau. In 1862, twenty-eight years before the *Namoa* attack, pirates disguised as steerage passengers had already seized the *S.S. Iron Prince*. The attempt failed, but led to a fierce fight between the hijackers and the passengers. Other ships were less lucky. In another case, the killing of three Americans from the clipper the *Lubra* in 1866 provided irrefutable evidence that piracy on high seas posed still a great danger.[9]

The big fleets did finally disappear, but not the pirates themselves. Several villages along the Pearl River, and sheltered coves such as Bias Bay near Hong Kong, and the island of Coloane near Macau, continued to be favourite pirate lairs. Bias Bay (currently known as Daya Wan or Daya Bay) north of Mirs Bay (Tai Pang Wan) and fifty kilometres northeast of Hong Kong Island was a notorious base for operations of Chinese pirates.[10] Around the last quarter of the nineteenth century, Hong Kong achieved the status of a British Crown Colony. The 1880s and 1890s were the heyday of colonialism in Asia and colonial society in Hong Kong perfectly reflected the temper of the times.

Several authors suggest that the seizure of the *S.S. Namoa* was an exception in a period when piracy had virtually died out at the end of the nineteenth century (Miller 1970; Fox 1940). Recent research shows that this was not the case. The putting down of the Taiping Rebellion in 1864 accounted for an increase of cases from thirty-five to fifty-two. Certainly after that year the number declined to twenty-five, even dropping to only fifteen cases of piracy and robbery. The number of cases within a radius of 100 miles of Hong Kong fell from forty-eight in 1865 to eighteen in 1867, and by another three to fifteen in 1869. The 1870s showed a further decline, and this trend did continue into the 1880s (Lung 2001, pp. 293–96). Lung argues that the fact Macau replaced Hong Kong as the main piratical haunt can be attributed to the success of the Chinese Navy. My findings in the Hong Kong archives corroborate this argument. A long series of police reports shows piracy to have been an almost monthly occurrence, with fatal results (see Table 6.1). Two incidents of piracy are reported in 1890 and these resulted in an unknown number of persons being convicted. In the original document, fourteen people are reported arrested and the same

TABLE 6.1

Reports of Piracy Cases between 1883 and 1893 in or Near Hong Kong

Year	Cases	Convictions
1883	13	4
1884	9	16
1885	17	13
1886	10	1
1887	8	18
1888	12	4
1889	4	1
1890	2	n.a.
1891	4	3
1892	3	5
total	82	65

Source: Reports of superior and subordinate courts for 1886 to 1900; Report of the captain superintendent of police for 1892, no. 4/93 <http://www.grs.gov.hk/ws/english> (accessed October 2005).

number discharged. There is reason to believe that in this case the Portuguese and Chinese authorities made the arrests, but the statistics do not mention them. It is also possible that the fourteen suspects were handed over to the magistrate of Canton. More importantly the *Namoa* hijacking did not mark the closure of the period of the "high tide" of maritime piracy, but in the last two decades before the turn of the century the frequency of incidents of piracy did drop slightly.

After the *Namoa* incident, the colonial authorities took suitable precautions aboard ships: coastal steamers were allowed to carry light armaments onboard, though the discussion adopted a similar stance to that taken today where anti-piracy measures are proposed for ocean going ships and for planes. Iron grilles were also inserted between the bridge, the officers' quarters, and the first-class deck, as a shield against a possible attack mounted from the quarterdeck. Armed sailors were also stationed to guard doors. As the heavy hand of authority made itself felt, the pirates' ruses in response grew more ingenious and in later accounts we learn of Chinese pirates who posed as rich, first-class passengers, making any such grille an ineffective oddity.

The end of the Qing dynasty in 1911 and the beginning of Sun Yet Sen's Republic inevitably soon led to civil strife. Local warlords built up private armies the rank and file of which had little or no compunction about embracing robbery and piracy. Even after the transition, piracy continued to infest the waters around the Portuguese and British establishments and along the South China Coast. In 1913, a river passenger steamer, the *S.S. Tai On*, was hijacked in exactly the same circumstances as the *S.S. Namoa*, painfully revealing that the safety measures on board had already become obsolete. Accounts of similar incidents in the 1920s and 1930s demonstrate explicitly that the days of maritime piracy were far from over. In terms of numbers, and possibly heavily under-reported, about eighteen steamers were subjected to similar assaults and in a number of cases led to the killing or wounding of officers and passengers. Constant patrolling by the Royal Navy and the search-and-destroy actions of the Chinese authorities against villages known to be harbouring pirates did nothing to curb maritime piracy along the South China coast. The economic decline after the Japanese Occupation of Hong Kong again resulted in a resurgence of piracy.[11]

Let us now return to the *S.S. Namoa* piracy case, which was not just one case among many for various important reasons. It can be seen not only as a "model" case to which other cases after the turn of the century were referred, but it also stood out because of the amount of attention it received in the contemporary press, its treatment as a judicial case by Hong Kong lawyers and, last but not least, its representation of punishment in Western eyes.

THE *S.S. NAMOA* PIRACY CASE[12]

On 10 December 1890 a band of Chinese pirates launched a violent attack on the *S.S. Namoa*, a coastal steamer of about one thousand tons which ferried goods and passengers between Hong Kong and Swatoff (Shantou) twice a month.[13] The ship, named after the small island of Namoa (or Nan'ao Dao) between Taiwan and mainland, was in the service of the Douglas Steamship Company. It had about 250 returning migrants from San Francisco and coolies from Malacca on board who were going home with their savings in cash from work on plantations and in mines.[14] Five European passengers had taken first-class cabins. At lunch time, a number of Chinese men disguised as soldiers carrying swords and rifles left the position in the waist to which they had been assigned. On the upper deck they fired several shots and threw stinkpots into the salon where the European passengers and the ship's officers were taking their midday meal (*tiffin*).[15] In the ensuing brawl, Captain Thomas Guy Pocock (45) and a Danish lighthouse keeper employed by the Imperial Chinese Maritime Customs Service, a man by the name of Petersen, were mortally wounded.[16] Three Malay quartermasters were fired at and seriously injured. One of them was thrown overboard. Two Chinese cooks also suffered injuries. Another Malay quartermaster later died in hospital, making four deaths in all.[17] After the victims in the salon were robbed of their jewellery, watches, and other valuables, the attackers went on to ransack the cabins and rob the remaining passengers. Another Malay quartermaster was forced to steer the ship to the island of Ping Hoi and a large village at the south-eastern corner of Bias Bay, the notorious pirate lair. At 7.30 a.m. six junks accosted the boat. The pirates, whose number was estimated at between twenty and fifty, handed over the booty which, as it turned out later, was valued at about 55,000 silver dollars. Before leaving at about 9 p.m., the pirates had organized an orgy of drinking and eating on deck and, before quitting the ship, they threw a bag containing about HK$200 into the engine room as a gratuity (in pidgin Chinese called *cum-shaw*) for the stoker who had drawn the engine fires. The officers, engineers, and passengers liberated themselves and managed to return to Hong Kong at 8 o'clock the next morning.

The incident sent shock waves through Hong Kong, which at that time had an estimated population of about 300,000 inhabitants, mostly Chinese. The local English press, represented by *The China Mail*, *The Hong Kong Telegraph*, and the *Hong Kong Daily Press* carried reports about the incident on a daily basis.[18] From his headquarters in Canton, the Chinese Admiral Fong Yao (or Fong Yu) was given the main responsibility for apprehending the suspects. He and the Portuguese authorities in Macau managed to track down twenty-three of them.

Since the principal men accused did not originate from the territory of Hong Kong, the British court was not entitled to try the case, and the trial was placed in the hands of the Qing magistrate of the twin-city of Kowloon. Apparently acts of piracy were seen to fall mainly under the responsibility of the Chinese government. The handing over of the case by the Special Court in Hong Kong was in accordance with stipulations set out in the Treaty of Nanjing and the Treaty of the Bogue (1842). Whereas these treaties stated that any British citizen convicted of crime on Chinese soil would be dealt with in England, a special Ordinance (No. 2) enabled officials on both sides to cooperate closely in the handing over of Chinese fugitives in Hong Kong to Kowloon officials and vice-versa.[19]

In the aftermath of the piracy case, Susan Pocock, the widow of the slain captain, received HK$16,300,000, estimated to be the value of his will (Supreme Court, Hong Kong, 1891, no. 22/92). His son Thomas Guy Pocock was only one year old at that time. His name reappeared on one of the Flanders's fields near Ieper where he died on 3 April 1915 at the age of twenty-five years.[20] Captain Pocock's tomb is now a memorial in the Happy Valley Cemetery in Hong Kong; one which he shares with other pre-World War II Caucasian victims of piracy.[21] The fate of the body of lighthouse keeper Petersen (or Pedersen) remains a mystery, as indeed is the fate of that of Malay quartermaster. But the apparently doomed ship again made headlines in 1897. On the 2 October of that year, she struck a rock and was stranded during a typhoon in the Hai Tan Straits, near Amoy, from where she was outward bound. Out of a total of seventy-seven persons who abandoned ship before she foundered on the beach, eleven lost their lives, all because of an error in judgement by the captain. The rescue boats battled through a huge surf in which seven passengers, the carpenter, and three of the crew drowned. No further details about the rescue of the steamer were given (*The Hong Kong Government Gazette*, 23 October 1897).

The Trial

On 18 February 1891, a special Criminal Sessions opened but was soon adjourned because of the paucity of the evidence and the limited number (2) of the accused charged with piracy on board of the *S.S. Namoa*. In the course of the same month, a number of further arrests were made in Macao, including a man variously named as Mau Lau Yune, or Mau Ayune or Paul Lau Yune, who was seen as the instigator of the attack. He was never brought to trial because, according to *The Herald*, he swallowed poison in his cell. In a related event, the brother of the alleged organizer and financier, Ho Fat To, or Ho Fat Cheong, was intercepted on his junk in the inner harbour of Macau. The Portuguese Water Police discovered that his extended family was on-board. Valuables and money said to have come from the *S.S. Namoa* were found hidden in the stern of the boat. An attempt to arrest Ho Fat To on an island beyond the jurisdiction of the Portuguese authorities failed. The fate of the suspects arrested is unknown, because their names do not figure on the final list of the nineteen death sentences, pronounced by a Chinese court in Canton and later printed in one of the newspapers. It is possible that they were taken to court in Macau and sentenced accordingly. As were the British in 1842, the Portuguese were granted "perpetual occupation and government" in 1887 (see Fei 1996; Gunn 1996). Seventeen accused, among them a man who had spoken pidgin English during the attack and was regarded as the ringleader, the main organizer, and recruiter, heard the death sentence pronounced on them in April 1891. Eight, including a man named Chun Fuk Yin who was identified to have shot the captain, had participated directly in the attack. Eight were onboard the junks which joined the steamer to take on the booty. A certain Low A Wai was found guilty of being one of the financiers behind the operation and he was also found guilty of a similar attack on the *S.S. Greyhound* in 1889.

The Executions

The final sentencing and execution were the responsibility of the Qing magistrates in Canton. With two other condemned criminals arrested on Chinese soil, seventeen "*Namoa* pirates" ended up in Canton where they were kept in custody, awaiting trial under Chinese law. Thirteen of them would be sentenced to decapitation. In the company of six others who had been tried for various offences on Chinese territory, on the afternoon of Friday 17 April 1891, the pirates were transported to the "Walled City of Kowloon" on three gunboats. After disembarking from the boats, the nineteen men who wore their names and their crime — alleged "piracy" — on cangues around their necks were led to the beach. A squad of Chinese soldiers commanded by Colonel Leung Tuow, accompanied by a local magistrate who had descended from his *yamen* (office) in Kowloon, and an executioner with two assistants surrounded them. In a press report the executioner, described as an "excited individual, whose turban proclaimed him a native of Fukhien", aided by two assistants and wielding three heavy iron swords, put an end to the lives of the accused. Reporters from the *Hong Kong Telegraph*, the *China Mail*, and the *Daily Press*, reported the executions of the nineteen men the next day in lurid detail.

Why exactly the British officials were summoned to witness the execution is difficult to assess, but such expeditions were not uncommon in those days. *The Hong Kong Telegraph* described the officials as "brokers and members of the Imperial Maritime Customs". The main reason requiring the attendance of the Customs officials at the execution would undoubtedly have been the murder of Petersen on-board the *S.S. Namoa*. He was a lighthouse keeper, whose duties fell under the jurisdiction of the Chinese Maritime Customs Service. This organization, founded in 1854, was an international, although predominantly British-staffed, bureaucracy under the control of successive Chinese central governments.[22] The Customs Service was labelled "maritime" [*haiguan*] to distinguish it from the inland service and was run principally by Westerners to facilitate international trade. "Contrary to other taxes, the Customs income was paid to the central treasury, hence its importance to the government. Over the years, it came to guarantee loans raised abroad, as well as payment of the successive war indemnities inflicted on China" (Régine Thierrez 1998, p. 69). According to French author, Thierrez (1998) the members of the Service demonstrated a keen intellectual involvement in the study of their host country. Not a few expressed a deep interest in photography, the "modern art of nineteenth century technology", as shown by the impressive images they took of the buildings of the Old Summer Palace. These "Gardens of Perfect Brightness" (Yuanmingyuan) as the palace was called were in 1860 destroyed by British and French troops during the Second Opium War. Drawings and photographs before the destruction show the dimension of the loss. This acknowledged reputation of the Customs Service makes it even more plausible to argue that the anonymous photographer was a member of the group. He checked his watch to control the shutter operated by his assistant since self-timers had not yet been invented in the late 1880s. There is no reason to suppose that he accompanied the reporters of the three Hong Kong newspapers, of whom one dubbed himself "a special horrors monger", since no newspaper published any illustrations at the time (*Hong Kong Telegraph* of 18 April 1891). It is remarkable that a second execution, held on 11 May of that year, of another fifteen prisoners, including six pirates of the *Namoa*, with among them, another leader of the gang named Lai A Tsat, attracted less attention from the non-Chinese residents of Hong Kong. Tsat was identified as the head of the gang which had seized the Europeans on-board, while the rest were occupied with plundering the ship. As far as we know, no photograph of this particular execution exists. Photographs of the 17 April execution found their way into albums and the obvious postcards for a wider mass consumption. Publisher M.Sternberg, a Hong Kong "wholesale and retail postcard dealer at no. 51, Queens Road", was highly instrumental in producing postcards depicting the pirates on the execution ground. His colleague, Graca, produced the picture with the British sahibs, and captioned it " 'Namoa' pirates after the execution". A situation in which foreigners posed behind or next to dead bodies of condemned criminals was not unusual in those days, and pictures of severed heads were produced elsewhere in colonial Indochina, Japan, and British India. Such facetious texts as "a couple of heads looking for their bodies somewhere in China" accompanied the lyrics of a popular song "2 [the two heads] *aint got nobody and nobody cares for me*" were sent to loved ones in Europe and elsewhere. They are, of course, related to what Edwards (1997) has argued is a representation of exoticism, influenced by the tourist gaze, but unquestionably they were also meant to expose the cruelty of a civilization which ignored the rule of law. The fragmented illusions of the executions were created to achieve the idea that these photos were authentic and reproduced the experience of the beholder.

BARBARIAN LENS OR BARBARIAN PRACTICES?

Susan Sontag observes that "photographs taken on the very moment of death (or just minutes before) are highly admired and reproduced many times. (…) More upsetting is the opportunity to look at people who know they have been condemned to die" (2003, p. 60). She argues that such photographs are no longer "a crude statement of fact addressed to the eye". Photographs of executions and slain victims became popular in the second half of the nineteenth century especially as, in contrast to Japan, Qing China was not yet seen as the symbol of a new, modern, and enlightened state (Worswick 1978; Thieriez 1997 and 1998). The rub is that the *Namoa* pictures were not produced for a Chinese public. Here we see a voyeuristic crowd, represented by British *sahibs*, who are observers of cruel Chinese traditions. The picture ambiguously represents modernity mediated by (colonial) capitalism and globalization. The communization of executions by the production of postcards betrays the same trend. They became part of a larger Orientalist discourse which (in the words of Ian Buruma) generated images which had to show that "(B)y the mid-nineteenth century (...) East and West had hardened: the West was virile, dynamic, expansive, disciplined, and the East was indolent, decadent, pleasure-loving, passive" (1996, p. xxi). These images were produced at a time when photo-lithographic printing had been introduced into China, not for mass consumption, but as a means to attract readers and to develop a vehicle for China's visual modernity. The popularity of this process was due to, among various other reasons, the realistic style and new-ness, augmented by the visual displays of Western technology. "Instead of showing a simple direct gaze from China and the West and vice versa", Chinese readers were as curious as Westerners about Chinese traditions (Laikwan Pang 2005, pp. 30–32). The lithographs also reveal the foreigner's fascination with ancient Chinese techniques of punishment, including instruments of torture and executions, ostensibly to help people learn more about the world. By allowing a foreign gaze to light on the cruelty of the traditional world, these lithographs, according to Pang, were used as a "realist desire" combined with an idealistic urge to understand the (modern) world.

    The Dutch anthropologist Anton Blok (1989), following Foucault (1977), regards public executions of (in this case) Dutch brigands as a cross-cultural part of a gradual, long-term transition from corporal (deliberate infliction of power) punishment to confinement. The meaning of a public execution in the European context rested in the deterrent effect executions were supposed to exert on anyone thinking of perpetrating crimes for which capital punishment was deemed the proper sentence. The theatre of the execution played an important role in defining and controlling the social order (R. McGowen 1987). Foucault states that during this time the right to punish was directly linked to the authority of the king. Crimes of the nature of murder were not crimes against the public good, but a personal affront to the king himself. From this he concluded that public displays of torture and execution were public affirmations of the king's authority to rule and punish. Torture and execution belonged to a theatre of punishments in which the body of the condemned criminal participated in the ceremonial of public executions (Foucault 1977, p. 43). The execution of Charles I in 1649 was a perfect combination of politics and theatre in which a reverse role was accorded the king who had betrayed his people. The execution allowed both royalists and parliamentarians to construct their own theatrical and partisan versions of the event with interpretations of every detail of the execution (see for example, Robertson 2005).

French author on traditional Chinese law, Jérôme Bourgon (2005), has discussed the photographs of Chinese executions and states that Western executions differ from their Chinese counterparts in terms of religiosity, in the sense that in the former case, the theatre of executions was chosen to have a redemptive effect on the criminals and the audience, while in the latter case, "punishment fitted the crime as provided in the penal code" (Bourgon 2005, p. 153). While this statement sounds rather tautological, in his treatment of the Chinese (or Oriental) version of public execution, he points out the absence of such spectacular features as a carefully planned stage or show and the aroused activity of the crowds, which made it different from the "*supplice*" (tortured to death) which was carried out in the West until executions became secluded and shielded from the public eye (in 1868 in England, but not in the Commonwealth or the colonies, and in 1938 in France).[23]

The history of corporal and capital punishment in China goes back to the Qin dynasty (259–06 BC), when a number of forms of execution became known. Some were as cruel as those employed under Western *Ancien Regimes*, including drawing and quartering (*chelie*), decapitation (*xiaoshou*), being torn asunder by oxen pulling two carts in opposite directions (*zhe*), and public exhibition of the body (*qishi*). At least one acquired notoriety as the very refinement of cruelty: slicing (*yaozhan* or *lingshi chusi*). In Western eyes, this measure, better known as the "lingering death" or "death by a thousand cuts", was regarded as the most extreme method devised to punish people.[24] Traditionally the victims were the vanquished, traitors, thieves, bandits, highwaymen, raiders of villages, (armed) robbers, and forgers (Dutton 1992, p. 111). Practices differed in the subsequent periods (Dutton 1992, p. 136). Under the Qing, or Manchus (1644–1911), the prison system and disciplinary measures were changed. The emergence of the modern prison in the closing days of the Qing dynasty left local practices untouched (1992, p. 154ff). At the end of the nineteenth century, legal practices in Canton to which the condemned *S.S. Namoa* pirates were subject, still applied sanctions which had been inherited from earlier periods. Death, disfigurement, and banishment were still exercised to punish families. The description of the executions and the way the heads were transported to the *yamen* in Kowloon by the executioner offer enough evidence to conclude that traditional Chinese law was still in use.

The destruction of the body was in violation of the Confucian norm which forbade the mutilation of the (dead) body. Executions were excluded from that norm, because the body was no longer part of a larger whole, that is, the community. Bourgon et al. (2005; 2008) fail to mention that personhood and individuality paled into insignificance compared with severing links with the family and clan.[25] Chinese and Vietnamese believe that the separation of the head from the body prohibits the soul (at least the one out of four, which is thought vital for establishing the link between the living and the dead) to return and condemns the soul to eternal wandering. When such a sentence was passed, the family or lineage was also being punished for the deeds of the accused (Kleinen 1999, pp. 179–83). Dutton argues that "physical punishments (…) were explained not purely as technologies for the maximization of pain but as being materially symbolic because of the relation they established between bodily form, ancestral recognition and lineage continuation" (1992, p. 145). In other words, patriarchal values determined the link between the body and the lineage. Dutton's chronicle of the Chinese prison system deals with the change in corporal punishments. He shows that in a Chinese context, the family and its extension into the community were the pivotal elements of social life. Consequently the public policing of the body extended beyond the individual coercion by the state. Both families and local communities reluctantly accepted the services of the state in administering corporal or capital punishment. Those who are outsiders in every aspect were dealt with by the state and not by the community or the clan. Banishment from the local community was seen as the most serious and dangerous form of punishment for those who had broken off their alliance with family, clan, and community. Execution was the ultimate punishment, and both were seen as "breaking the family tree" and the end of the bond with the ancestors (see Dutton 1992, p. 131ff). This also explains why onlookers and executioners often fail to show any emotion. Bourgon (2005, p. 167ff) wrongly asserts that the apparent apathy of executioners, guards, commoners, even of the victims themselves, is an element of the appositeness of the punishment which eschews theatre and excitement. "The onlookers (…) have not been invited by the protagonists of the execution to display emotion. Chinese executioners never displayed the cruel attitude that their European counterparts were required to show (…)" (Bourgon 2005, p. 162). He argues that this state of affairs reveals the difference between the

Western *supplice* and the East Asian execution.[26] Without denying that differences existed, for example, the role of the victim to display theatrical effects and show repentance, I will argue that the downplaying of feelings and culture complicates the comparison between eastern and western practices.

If we pursue our comparison with the punishment of the family and the lineage yet further, we gain an understanding of the great fear which was inseparable from such an unnatural demise as putting somebody to death. Chinese and Vietnamese funerals are generally characterized by extreme displays of grief, and the absence of this emotion points to a great uncertainty about the fate of the afterlife of the victim, and his lineage. Special ceremonies of "begging the souls to return home" are very sober and introverted. In a revealing essay, Virgil Kit-yiu Ho (2000) has shown that public executions contain all the ingredients of drama, theatre, and use of "a graceful act of justice and of moral triumph" (p. 145), which superficially resemble similar acts in the West. The public execution of the nineteen *Namoa* pirates and others adhered to a scenario which was common in the Canton region: the convicts emerged from the *yamen* prison already as dehumanized bodies, probably underfed, dirty ("thick dirt which coated their faces" wrote an eyewitness), and drugged with opium (which deadened their emotions). One was brought ashore squatting in a big basket normally used for the transport of pigs. The pirates were surprisingly well clad for the occasion: (mourning) white shirts and (auspicious) red and (mandarin) blue trousers of the same style. The presence of the magistrate, in red robes with a scarlet shawl, the soldiers, the executioner with his assistants, all point to a well orchestrated theatre replete with ideological justification and symbolic meaning (*Hongkong Telegraph*, 18 April 1891; see also Ho 2000, pp. 145–53). The presence of the crowd, which surprisingly was not at all silent, the way the heads were disposed of, and even the trading of the executioner's sword (as reported by local newspapers) followed a pattern which was apparently well known and accepted (see for example, Worswick 1978; and Spence 1991).

CONCLUSION

Western and eastern traditions surely overlap in terms of the place of execution as a clearly demarcated location (Blok 1989, p. 46). Located at the outer edge of the jurisdiction of a city or town, execution places required the escorting of the condemned from the place of detention to this liminal location.[27] This reinforced the drama which was an integral part of the theatre of punishments. The condemned had to be watched by everybody to reinforce his humiliation and infamy. The public execution at such a place is not just an act of the restoration of justice and the reinforcement of the law, but also served to restore power relations. This execution took place on the border between British and Chinese Kowloon, at a site nicknamed the Dirty Hollow, used as a garbage dump and brimming over with symbolic meaning. From 1845, public executions in the British part of Hong Kong were carried out on a piece of ground near the old Naval Stores, and were then removed to the north-east corner of the Central Magistracy compound. After 1856, this spot became the Tyburn of Hong Kong.[28] The author of Hong Kong's judicial system, Judge Norton-Kyshe refers to a protest by citizens who complained "on behalf of the ladies and children" that a screen should hide the sight of the "gallows tree" at Caine Road in the Western District (Norton-Kyshe 1898, pp. 385–86 I).[29] Onlookers also attended executions inside the Victoria Goal, before the prison space became so overcrowded that prisoners had to be moved to an island in the harbour and also to a prison hulk. The last recorded public execution took place on 5 April 1894, when a Muslim private in the Hong Kong Regiment, convicted of the murder of a soldier in his regiment, was executed in the presence of twenty privates and four non-commissioned officers (Norton-Kyshe, pp. 451–52).

Chinese and other Asians were not the only people to have been publicly executed; this punishment was also meted out to Caucasians. Death sentences passed on British members of the Royal Marines, who had killed their mates, and executions of Europeans and Americans found guilty of piracy along the Chinese coast, were also carried out during the nineteenth century. Judges wore the prescribed Black Cap when the death sentence was pronounced. Stories of the faulty working of the gallows as a result of poorly tied slipknots or ill-maintained bolts, and deviations from the rule such as conveying European victims to the gaol in a closed sedan chair, suggest that the British authorities wanted public approval of the sentence at any price.[30] In one incident, a large European crowd, instead of what seems to have been the usual group of Chinese onlookers, is mentioned. This happened when an East Indian artillery trooper, by the name of Tik Aram, was hanged on the morning of 5 July of 1882 "in the presence of four of five hundred persons, among whom were a number of Europeans" (Norton-Kyshe 1898, p. 352). The suspect was found guilty of the murder of a young Indian girl called Lachmee.

The way these public executions were carried out in Hong Kong did not differ much from similar practices in the motherland. The "carnival-like processions" with the condemned being taken on a cart still took place during the lifetime of Charles Dickens. The efforts he and other people undertook to ban these practices were ultimately successful in 1868 when these spectacles were finally brought to an end.[31] After that, until the abolition of capital punishment, hangings took place inside the prison. With the formal signing on 27 January 1999 of the 6th Protocol of the European Convention of Human Rights in Strasbourg, Britain abolished the death penalty in the United Kingdom. Although nobody has been hanged on British soil for civil crimes since 1964, high treason and piracy on the high seas still remained capital offences under military law until 1998, but it was extremely unlikely that even if anyone had been convicted of these crimes over the preceding thirty years, they would actually have been executed.

Foucault's argument that torture and public executions disappeared with the *Ancien Regime* and their place was taken by the (modern) prison system is questionable when it is compared with political systems other than that of the *Ancien Regime*, which have allowed and still continue to allow torture and public execution within the prison system. The recent war on terrorism even allows such self-proclaimed democratic governments as that of the United States to employ a system of illicit corporal punishment in the context of an elaborate set of penal sanctions, or to do so with the active support of associated countries where other rules apply. In China the transition from a feudal *Ancien Regime* to a revolutionary State has not altered the regulation and punishment of individuals who are accused of criminal activities. Asia today still tops the list of regions where by far the greatest majority of executions are carried out. The number of executions in China was apparently as high as at least 5,000 in 2005. In 2004 there seems to have been a minimum of 5,403 executions.[32] As Ho says, "(E)xecutions are today no longer, strictly speaking, conducted publicly. However, dramaturchical elements and political symbolisms are still heavily employed in pre-execution trials and parades as well as in the still prevalent practice of letting the victim's family pay for the bullet (2000, p. 158). The execution of the *S.S. Namoa* pirates more than a century ago followed a pattern which did not deviate from what was also being done in the West, nor can it be stigmatized as a pre-modern practice *per se*. Where it did deviate was the way Chinese and Westerners regard so very differently the pain of others.

Notes

1. See also Hobsbawm 1959, 1960, and 1980 for the evolution of the social bandit concept.
2. A German TV documentary about the Boxer Rebellion shown in 1997 used the same picture from a museum in Lausanne. The voice-over commented "Also later attempts to resist economic dictatorship were nipped in the bud by military intervention from European powers."
3. In my 1988 dissertation, I also erroneously used the photograph with the caption "Execution of rebels during pacification, end of 19th century", based on the handwritten caption on the back that read *Indochinois? Decapités et coloniaux vers 1900* (Kleinen 1988; for a correction in print see 1998). A recent misinterpretation of the photograph is shown in <http://turandot.ish-lyon.cnrs.fr/Photographs.php?ID=366> with a clear reference to banditry (re-accessed in March 2009).
4. Depository numbers P.64.58; P.64.60 and P.64.68. The *Rijksprenten Kabinet* of the University of Leiden, an authoritative archive of photographs, keeps a coloured original with a more illuminating caption which reads, "*S.S. Namoa* Pirates beheaded on the beach, between British and Chinese Kowloon, 11 May, 1891, albumine-colored 20,2 x 26,8 cm, anonymous". M.M.1505.183. Inventory I, Rijksprenten Kabinet Leiden. The date is important, because it refers to a second execution of at least six "*Namoa*" pirates, but the picture reveals that 17 April 1891 is meant (see Norton-Kyshe (1898) 1971, p. 428).
5. I was not able to consult the original edition, but the pictures are published in the 1971 reprint.
6. See Anton Blok, 1972, and Pat O'Malley, 1979. Since then a large "revisionist" literature has sprung up dealing with Africa, Republican China, nineteenth-century Corsica, Greece, and Malaysia. For a summary, see Richard W. Slatta, 1987.
7. See HK GRO no. 7/1927. Similar cases, on the same route and the same places occurred in 1921 with the *S.S. Sunning*, and in 1928 with the *S.S. Anking*.
8. See one of the earliest accounts of John C. Dalrymple Hay (1849; published in 1889).
9. Details in HK Public Records Office (PRO). Rf. 06-011 and *The Hongkong Mercury and Shipping Gazette* (25 September 1866).
10. Works of fiction such as Sheridan's *The Shanghai Lily* and such films as the 1935 MGM *China Seas*, caused Bias Bay to be evoked in the imagination of the general public. A more realistic story, but Orientalist in essence, is Lilius, 1930. Nowadays Daya Wan (Ta-Ya Wan) (22°37′N., 114°40′E.) is a large islet-cluttered, deep-water bay and the site of a French-built nuclear power plant, the biggest so far in China, east of Shenzhen, and two to three hours from Hong Kong.

11. *The China Yearbook* published in Tientsin and in Shanghai devoted several articles to security problems. For an Interdepartmental conference on piracy report, see volume 1926–27, pp. 830–36. The editor H.G. Woodhead was once a victim when on-board the *S.S. Tungshaw* between Shanghai and Tientsin in 1925.
12. The details of the case are taken from the following newspapers: *The Hong Kong Telegraph, the China Mail*, and *the Daily Press*. For another detailed report, see, J.W. Norton-Kyshe 1898, pp. 423–29. The newspapers might have been the source of the book *The Mystic Flowery Land* that Charles J.H. Halcombe, a member of the Imperial Maritime Customs, published in 1896 (Luzac & Co, Publishers to the India Office). Chapter 18 is about Amoy and the "Namoa" pirates and two of the three photographs (before and after the execution) are reprinted (between pages 126 and 127, and between 132 and 133). The author also confirms the death of Pedersen.
13. Registration No. 65,090. Registered tonnage 862.73 tons, 130 HP, Schooner, built in Aberdeen, in 1872 (Source: Returns of Superior and subordinate courts for 1886, no. 25/87, page 370, Public Record Office, Hong Kong).
14. Namoa Island (23°26′26″ N and 117°04′07″ E) at the mouth of the Han River adjacent to Swatow was infamous for its opium depots and being an important node in the coolie trade for Latin America (see Arnold J. Meagher, 2008).
    In 1950, the island was the scene of a fierce battle between the Nationalists and Communists.
15. Stinkpots were primitive Molotov cocktails. Made of earthen jars, they contained explosives generating noxious vapours. From 1869 these pots were forbidden on trading vessels.
16. In the database of the Chinese Maritime Customs Project, there is no reference to a Danish or Norwegian Petersen or Pedersen, who died in December 1890, being on the lighthouse-keeper's staff. However, the database is missing an entire year — July 1890–June 1891, which is now being repaired. Dr Robert Bickers from University of Bristol kindly inquired about the missing name in the database. See for example, <http://www.bristol.ac.uk/Depts/History/Customs/> (re-accessed in August 2008). Pedersen is mentioned in a contemporary report (quoted in note 12).
17. The crew was composed of eight European engineers and officers and forty-five Chinese and Malay seamen.
18. A lithographic reproduction was used in a Dutch publication (W. Meischke-Smith 1895, p. 84), and taken from an undated version in the Dutch newspaper *Nieuwe Rotterdamsche Courant*.
19. For background information on Ordinance No. 2 of 1850 which clashed with the doctrine of *piracy jure gentium*, which meant that any state could try and punish a pirate, regardless of whether injury had been caused to such state or its nationals. See Law Lectures for Practitioners, 1993 in <http://sunzi1.lib.hku.

hk/hkjo/article.jsp?book=14&issue=140015> (re-accessed August 2008). For the place and space of Kowloon, see Sinn.
20. <http://1914-1918.invisionzone.com/forums/index.php?showtopic=7235&mode=linear> (accessed 23 December 2006).
21. See <http://www.nmm.ac.uk/memorials/> under M274 (Pocock's tomb) (re-accessed August 2008).
22. See <http://www.bris.ac.uk/Depts/History/Customs/> (re-accessed August 2008).
23. A more elaborate version of this article is found in the book that Bourgon published in 2008 together with Timothy Brook and Gregory Blue. Though the book is well researched, I still keep my doubts about their interpretation of *lingshi* or any public execution as being completely different from Western practices. The book lacks, in my opinion, anthropological studies in which death, pain and suffering in sinocised cultures are analysed (for example, Watson and Rawski 1988; Sutton 2007; Kleinen 1999; Gustafson 2008). Timothy Brook, however, is familiar with funeral practices (1989).
24. Bourgon discusses lingshi in a series of twelve photographs taken in Bejing in 1908 (and not in Canton/Guanchou), with a stereoscopic Verascope camera by a French traveller (Matignon) and reprinted by Louis Carpeaux in Pékin qui s'en va, (Paris: A. Maloine 1913, pp. 188–19). This last known *lingshi* execution on 10 April 1905 is used by Georges Bataille in his *The Tears of Eros*, 1961. For a discussion see <http://turandot.ish-lyon.cnrs.fr/index.php> (accessed December 2006).
25. I do not discuss the punishment of the body as a fundamental method to maintain the body politic in eighteenth-century England, which differs from the Chinese view on family and clan.
26. His website contains references to articles and books which seem to underwrite this proposition: for example, Mrs Archibald Little (aka Alicia Bewicke Little), was witness to a lingshi execution. Her book title is revealing: *In China, We Are Still in the Middle Age* (first published by London: Fisher Unwin, 1905). (See *Note(s):* pp. 243–45). Republished in *Gleanings from Fifty Years in China* (London: Sampson Low, Morston and Co., 1910).
27. In England, the Execution Dock on the Thames was used for seamen, mutineers, or pirates, but it is unclear whether the place was chosen for its liminality or for its nearness to the crime scene. It surely belonged to the architecture of punishment (see in this regard, for example, the excellent work of Gatrell 1996).
28. The Tyburn Gallows, also known as the Tyburn Tree near Marble Arch, was the main place of execution in England for over 600 years, from 1177 until 1783.
29. The site was originally occupied by the first Hong Kong Magistracy, erected around 1847 and later demolished to make way for the present building. Current address is 1 Arbuthnot Road, Central (Hong Kong).

30. Highly placed Chinese convicts were also subjected to the same treat by bringing them in secluded cart to the place of execution.
31. See Charles Dickens letter to the Editor of *The Times*, Letters. 13 November 1849. More letters in <http://home.earthlink.net/~bsabatini/Inimitable-Boz/etexts/dickens_on_capital_punishment.html> (re-accessed August 2008). Dickens, Tolstoy, Turgenev, and Victor Hugo wrote about public executions they had witnessed in France. Hugo's writings are collected in : "Victor Hugo contre la peine de mort" <http://lettres.ac-rouen.fr/francais/dernier/accueil.htm> (accessed August 2008). The use of the guillotine is eloquently analyzed in Daniel Gerould (1992).
32. Chinese use of the death penalty is a state secret. According to the well informed South China Morning Post, the number of executions carried out on the mainland is likely to be about 8000 a year (28 February 2006).

References

Antony, Robert J. "Peasants, Heroes and Brigands. The Problems of Social Banditry in Early Nineteenth Century South China". *Modern China* 15, no. 2 (1989): 128–48.
———. *Like Froth Floating on the Sea. The World of Pirates and Seafarers in Late Imperial South China*. Berkeley: University of California, 2003.
Blok, Anton. "The Peasant and the Brigand: Social Banditry Reconsidered". *Comparative Studies in Society and History* 14, no. 4 (1972): 494-503.
———. "Symbolic Vocabulary of Public Executions". In *History and Power in the Study of Law, New Directions in Legal Anthropology*, edited by June Starr, and Jane F. Collier. Ithaca and London: Cornell University Press, 1989.
———. *Honour and Violence*. Oxford & Cambridge: Polity Press, 2001.
Braudel, Fernand, "Misère et banditisme". *Annales* 2 (1947): 129–43.
———. (1972), *The Mediterranean and the Mediterranean World in the Age of Philip II*. London: William Collins Sons & Co Ltd, 1972.
Boettcher, Thomas D. *Vietnam the Valor and the Sorrow. From the Home Front to the Front Lines in Words and Pictures*. Boston: Little, Brown Company, 1985.
Bourgon, Jérôme. *12 vues stéréo sur plaques de verre*. Fonds du Musée Nicéphore Niépce à Chalon-sur-Saône — CNRS — Institut d'Asie Orientale, Lyon, 2005 [cited. Available from <http://www.museeniepce.com/execution_chinoise/>.
Brook, Timothy, "Funerary Ritual and the Building of Lineages in Late Imperial China". *Harvard Journal of Asiatic Studies* 49, no. 2 (December 1989): 465–99.
Brook, Timothy, Jérôme Bourgon, and Gregory Blue. *Death by a Thousands Cuts*. Cambridge, Massachusetts, and London: Harvard University Press, 2008.
Boxer, C.R. "Piracy in the South China Sea". *History Today* (1980): 40–44.

Buchanan, Keith, Charles P. Fitzgerald, and Colin A. Ronan. *China: The Land and the People*. New York: Crown Publishers, Inc., 1980.

Buruma, Ian. *The Missionary and the Libertine. Love and War in East and West*. New York: Random House, 1996 (2000).

Course, A.G. *Pirates of the Eastern Seas*. London: Frederick Muller, 1966.

Doyle, Edward, and Samuel, Lipsman. *The Vietnam Experience. Setting the Stage*. Boston: MA Boston Publishing Company 1981, 1988.

Dutton, Michael R. *Policing and Punishment in China. From Patriarchy to "The People"*. Cambridge: Cambridge University Press, 1992.

Edwards, Elizabeth. "Postcards: Greetings from Another World". *The Tourist Image*, edited by T. Selwyn. London: Wiley, 1996.

Fei, Chengkang. *Macao 400 Years*. Shanghai: Shanghai Academy of Social Sciences, 1996.

Foucault, Michel. *Discipline and Punish: The Birth of the Prison*. Harmondsworth: Penguin, 1977.

Fox, Grace. *British Admirals and Chinese Pirates 1832–1869*. London: Kegan Paul, Trench, Trubner & Co., LTD., 1940.

Gatrell, V.A.C. *The Hanging Tree: Execution and the English People 1770–1868*. Oxford: Oxford University Press, 1996.

Gerould, Daniel. *Guillotine: Its Legend and Lore*. New York: Blast Books, 1992.

Gunn, G.C. *Encountering Macau: A Portuguese City-State on the Periphery of China, 1557–1999*. Boulder, Colorado: Westview Press, 1996.

Gustafsson, Mai Lan. "The Living and the Lost: War and Possession in Vietnam". *Anthropology of Consciousness* 18, no. 2 (2008): 56–73.

Hacker, Arthur. "The Battle of Bias Bay". *South China Morning Post*, 2 October 1993.

Heyman, J.McC., ed. *States and Illegal Practices*. Oxford and New York: Berg, 1999.

Ho, Virgil Kit-yiu. "Butchering Fish and Executing Criminals: Public Executions and the Meanings of Violence in Late Imperial and Modern China". *Meanings of Violence: A Cross Cultural Perspective*, edited by Göran Aijmer and Jon Abbink. Oxford and New York: Berg, 2000.

Hobsbawm, E. *Primitive Rebels: Studies in Archaic Forms of Social Movement in the 19th and 20th Centuries*. 1959.

———. *Social Bandits and Primitive Rebels*. Glencoe: Free Press, 1960.

———. *Bandits*. London: Liedenfeld and Nicholson, 1969.

———. *Bandits*. Revised edition. New York: Pantheon Books, 1980.

Kleinen, John. "Boeren, Fransen en Rebellen. Een studie van boerenverzet in een Midden-Vietnamese regio, 1880–1940". Ph.D. University of Amsterdam, 1988.

———. "De Kaping van de *Namoa* [The *Namoa* Piracy case]". *Amsterdams Sociologisch Tijdschrift* 25, no. 1 (1998): 99–103.

———. *Facing the Future, Reviving the Past: A study of Social Change in a Northern Vietnamese Village*. Singapore: Institute of Southeast Asian Studies, 2000.

Lilius, Aleko. *I Sailed with Chinese Pirates*. The Mellifont Press, 1930.

Lung, Hong-kay. "Britain and the Suppression of Piracy on the Coast of China with special reference to the vicinity of Hong Kong 1842–1870". M.Phil, University of Hong Kong, 2001.

McGowen, R. "The Body and Punishment in Eighteenth Century England". *Journal of Modern History* 59, no. 4 (1987): 651–97.

Meagher, Arnold J. *The Coolie Trade: The Traffic in Chinese Laborers to Latin America 1847–1874*. Philadelphia: Xlibris, 2008.

Meischke-Smith, W. *Chineesche Karaktertrekken*. Rijk geïllustreerd door J. van Oort naar Schetsen, Photographieën enz. Rotterdam: Nijgh & van Ditmar, 1885.

Mote, F.W. "The Ming Dynasty, 1368–1644". Part 1, edited by F.W. Mote, Denis Twitchett and John K. Fairbank. *The Cambridge History of China*. Vol. 7 of the 14-volume. Cambridge: Cambridge University Press, 2004.

Murray, Dian. *Pirates of the South China Coast, 1790–1810*. Stanford, California: University of California Press, 1989.

Norton-Kyshe, J.W. *The History of the Laws and Courts of Hongkong from the Earliest Period to 1898*. 2 vols. Hong Kong: Vetch and Lee Limited, 1898.

O'Connor, Richard. *The Spirit Soldiers: A Historical Narrative of the Boxer Rebellion*. New York: G.P. Putnam's Sons, 1973.

O'Malley, P. "Social Bandits, Modern Capitalism and the Traditional Peasantry: A Critique of Hobsbawm". *Journal of Peasant Studies*, no. 6 (1979): 489–501.

Pang, Laikwan. "The Pictorial Turn: Realism, Modernity and China's Print Culture in the Late Nineteenth Century." *Visual Studies* 20, no. 1 (2005): 16–36.

Perry, Elizabeth J. "Social Banditry Revisited: The Case of Bai Lang, a Chinese Brigand". *Modern China* 9, no. 3 (1983): 355–82.

Robertson, Geoffrey. *The Tyrannicide Brief. The Story of the Man who sent Charles I to the Scaffold*. New York: Random House, 2005.

Sheridan, Jones, M. *The "Shanghai Lily": A Story of Chinese Pirates in the Notorious Regions of Bias Bay*. n.d.

Sinn, Elisabeth. "The Kowloon Walled City. Its Origin and Early History". *Journal of the Hong Kong Branch of the Royal Asiatic Society* 27 (1987) [1990]: 30–45.

Slatta, R.W. "Eric J. Hobsbawm's Social Bandit: A Critique and Revision". In *Bandidos: The Varieties of Latin American Banditry*, edited by Richard W. Slatta. New York: Greenwood Press, 1987.

Sontag, Susan. *Regarding the Pain of Others*. New York: Picador, 2003.

Spence, Jonathan. *Op zoek naar het moderne China, 1600–1989*. Amsterdam: Agon BV, 1991.

Teitler, Ger. "Piracy in Southeast Asia: A Historical Comparison". *MAST* 1, no. 1 (2002).

Thiriez, Régine. *Barbarian Lens. Western Photographers of the Qianlong Emperor's European Palaces*. Amsterdam: Gordon and Breach Publishers, 1998.

——."Photography and Portraiture in Nineteenth-Century China". *East Asian History*, no. 17/18 (1999): 77–102.

Watson, James and Evelyn S. Rawski, eds., *Death Ritual in Late Imperial and Modern China*. Berkeley: University of California Press, 1988.

Wesley-Smith, P. "Kwok A Song, Sir John Smale and the Macao Coolie Trade". In *Law Lectures for Practitioners*, vol. 1993. Hong Kong: Hong Kong Law Journal Limited, 1993.

Woodhead, H.G. *The China Year Book*. Chicago: The University of Chicago Press, 1926–27.

Worswick, Clark. "Photography in Imperial China". In *Imperial China: Photographs 1850–1912*, edited by Clark Worswick and Jonathan Spence, pp. 134–49. New York: Penwick Publishing, 1978.

Part 3

Southeast Asia

7

Violence and Armed Robbery in Indonesian Seas

Adrian B. Lapian

Theories about piracy can be divided into two main categories, economic and political. H.A. Ormerod, an authority on the history of ancient piracy, sees it as an extended form of the economy of hunters and gatherers. Even after the emergence of agriculture in prehistoric times the life of the hunter persisted, especially where cultivation was difficult and the soil barren. "Where the country is narrow, or game scarce, the primitive inhabitant will take early to the sea" (Ormerod 1978, p. 69). Other writers see brigandage and piracy as a precursor of trade. Only after commerce had organized itself did people see brigandage and piracy as an evil form of trade (Deschamps 1962, p. 11). Indeed, the notion of piracy only emerged when people had abandoned their Hobbesian existence and established themselves in organized political units and states.

    Nicholas Tarling explains the burgeoning of piracy in eighteenth and nineteenth century Southeast Asia as the result of monopolistic trade policies by Western powers, that is, Spanish, Dutch, and British rule (Tarling 1963). Cesar A. Majul, however, sees the piratical raids by the people of the southern Philippine islands as part of the Moro Wars which had been raging since the sixteenth century and which were, in fact — at least from the Spanish point of view — an extension from the battles against the Moros in peninsular Spain (Majul 1973). Against these theories James F. Warren advances a fresh stimulating approach to the booming maritime expeditions of the Sulu sultanate between 1768 and 1898. Rather than looking at it as a desperate manifestation of a decaying state, Warren explained the phenomenon as a dynamic response to the growing external trade opportunities in the region at the time (Warren 1981).

Besides Majul other writers have also related piracy with religion. The Muslim and Christian corsairs of the Mediterranean during the European Middle Ages are seen as part of the religious struggle. Here the Turks make a distinction between *harami* (bandits) and *levend* whose activities had the consent of the government (Villain-Gandossi 1975). The same has been said about the earlier depredations of the Vikings in the North Sea; and in the context of Southeast Asia, P.J. Veth (1870) had also attributed piracy as a special form of a Holy War against infidels.

Religious motivations have certainly played a significant role, but here also political and economic considerations should not be ignored. The Viking attacks on West European coastal settlements and those of the Ilanun in the Philippines were mostly directed against churches and monasteries on which the local people used to lavish their wealth.

Psychological aspects have also been attributed. A spirit of adventure as is implied in the original Greek *peiratès*, but also elements of revenge, were motives that had driven people to resort to piracy.

TYPES OF SEA POWER

This chapter is based on my thesis about the phenomenon of piracy in Southeast Asia which embarks on the Weberian thesis that the State has the monopoly of the means of violence (Lapian 1987). The situation in the area in the nineteenth century was very complicated. First, there were indigenous states of various sizes and various degrees of political and military (naval) power. While contending with one another about supremacy in their respective localities, they also had to face expansionistic ambitions of the colonial powers. The latter had more or less established themselves as effective authorities in the region, each with its own sphere of influence: the Spanish from their capital in Manila since 1571, the Dutch from Batavia since 1619, the British from Penang since 1786 (later moved to Singapore in 1832), and the French from Saigon since 1862. Then there were the marine communities who had no fixed settlements, living outside the jurisdiction of any state.

The absence of definite boundaries, especially at sea where the margins of territorial waters were still in dispute, gave rise to overlapping claims of jurisdiction. In such circumstances conflicting claims appeared about who had the sovereign right to take action against supposed encroachments and to resort to the means of violence at their disposal. Thus in those times "piratical" raids as reported in colonial records should be cautiously scrutinized and not be taken for granted. I, therefore, proposed to make a distinction between three types of sea power: 1] the *Raja Laut* (RL) or sea lords, 2] the *Orang Laut* (OL) or sea people, and 3] the *Bajak Laut* (BL) or sea robbers.

Raja Laut. Literally meaning "sea king", the term is borrowed from the title known in the hierarchy of former kingdoms in the eastern part of Indonesia. It used to be the designation of the commander of the fleet, but even in small kingdoms with hardly any significant maritime power there was an official with the same title. In our typology the RL represents the *legitimate* kind of sea power. And in this context, foreign, that is, Western, naval forces — although initially regarded as unlawful intruders in the region, had eventually developed into virtual RL, and as such, commanded respect from the indigenous RL. At the close of the nineteenth century they had gained a dominant position and became the superpowers in the area, the super-RL. Just like the superpowers of the twentieth century who possessed the monopoly of nuclear technology, these super-RL jealously guarded their hold on steam energy.

The Dutch had their first steamship in the 1820s in the area, but it was only in the next decade that steam vessels were employed against hostile indigenous craft. In 1845, the British started a regular service between Suez and Singapore using steam boats, but steam vessels were already in use for other purposes such as in hydrographic expeditions in 1843 (Belcher 1848). In 1851, the Spanish expedition against Sulu had also the advantage of steam vessels.

Almost all the indigenous RL were not in the position of keeping pace with the new technological developments. Even if they were capable of purchasing steam vessels, they still had to find trained people with sufficient technical know-how to manage the machines and navigate with modern equipment. In the 1870s, the Sultan of Brunei's steamship *Sultana* had a British commander. Earlier, in the mid-1860s, the Annamese King in Hué tried to buy a steamship in Singapore. The movements of the king's agent were stealthily watched by the local French consul who was relieved when he was able to report that the agent's efforts had failed (*Amiraux* 10352, *Archives de France*, Aix-en-Provence). Later, in the 1880s, the king could obtain a small steamboat in Hong Kong with the help of the French, but then French control over Indochina was already firmly established.

Another countermove against the growing power of the super-RL is the case of Berau in East Kalimantan (Borneo). Here in 1862 the sultan appointed a foreigner to the rank of RL, William Lingard — the very model for Conrad's

Lord Jim — with the title of "Pangeran Laut, Kapitan di Berau" [sealord, captain in Berau]. He had been supplying the region with most needed provisions, including guns and ammunition, and had helped them in the war against Bulungan. He proudly called his yacht the "Rajah Laut". Of course, the Dutch government prevented Lingard from assuming real power in the realm (*Kol. Archief*, 30 October 1863, no. 31, The Hague; Lapian 1974).

A similar event happened in Maguindanao in 1855 when a Spanish colonel, Don Romualdo Crespo, was officially installed as "Datto del Mar" (according to the text of the charter "Datu Raja Laut") by the sultan in a ceremony where he was honoured with a salvo of twelve shots. Although he was a colonel of the infantry, the deed should not be regarded as "un vano honor", said the letter reporting the event to the government in Madrid, because as such he would be commanding the "embarcacion mahometana" which, it is hoped, would put an end to the piratical activities of the Maguindanaos. Moreover, Don Romualdo was the son of the governor general in Manila, Don Manuel Crespo. Thus, unlike Berau in East Kalimantan where the office of Raja Laut was given to a British businessman who was opposed to Dutch political expansion in the area, the Maguindanao sultan appeared to be willing to cooperate with the Manila authorities. Surely he had his own designs for doing so (*Ultramar* 1855–56, Legajo 5167, Archivo Histórico Nacional, Madrid; Lapian 1974).

Bajak Laut is used here as the *illegitimate* type of sea power. In daily usage it is the Indonesian equivalent for piracy, that is, every kind of violence committed at sea without the sanction of the local authority. There is, therefore, no distinction between a pirate and a corsair or privateer. Indeed, in actual fact it is hard to make a distinction between the two kinds, for "*il y a eu des corsaires à visage de pirate et des pirates à allure de corsaire*" (Adam 1975, p. 920). Thus the early maritime attacks of European trading companies in the area were actually regarded as BL-type of activities even though the ships carry official charters of their home governments; for example, in Bengal *Olondaz* is an old word for Dutch which means pirate (Schendel 1997, p. 1). In the context of our typology, the privateer occupies an intermediate type between BL and RL.

Other names for pirate in the Indonesian language and vernaculars refer to certain ethnic groups such as Lanun, Mangindano, Tobelo, etc. The first two are from the southern Philpines, the last one from Halmahera in North Maluku. In the seventeenth century the name Papua was also a synonym for pirate in the region of Maluku — in Dutch VOC sources, usually referred to as "Papoesche zeeroovers". Their voyages extended far beyond their own territories and their arrival became a real dread for the local inhabitants. The name Balangingi, also notorious in the nineteenth century, was an island in the Sulu Archipelago which became a sanctuary for professional raiders. "An ethnographic fiction", according to Warren (1981, p. 184), a real multinational organization *avant la lettre*, the Balangingi were a mixture of local people and sailors from elsewhere, including ex-slaves, who had grown as a maritime community mostly committed to *magoorap* (pirating), becoming real rivals of the Taosug (Warren 1981, p. App. Q; Lapian 1978). In old Makassarese "balangingi" meant pirate, today the word refers to a rude person. In Sangirese "malanginging" is the Sasahara word for "mangindano" (pirate). Sasahara is a secret language spoken by Sangirese people when sailing.

During their long-distance operations the BL-fleet used to collaborate with other local BL-groups. For example, Said Hassan Alhabshy reported (1830) that the Ilanun in Pulau Laut, off the South Kalimantan coast, cooperated with Haji Jawa from Kalimantan. They had a fleet of about 90 *perahu*. The report also said that among them were Tobelo's from Halmahera and local Bajau people (Cornets de Groot 1846, p. 23).

Documents also reveal that they used to cooperate with local RL, among others, the Sultan of Riau. An eighteenth-century Malay text, the *Tuhfat al-Nafis*, says that Sultan Mahmud had asked the help of Ilanun sailors to fight the Dutch who tried to monopolize the tin trade in the area:

> ... the Illanun had already entered by the Terusan. A great uproar broke out in Riau, and the Dutch ordered the cannon to be loaded to fire on the Illanun *perahu* while the *penjajab* and the *perahu* in the Riau River were made ready and pretended that they would open fire. The Illanun approached Tanjung Pinang and the *penjajab* fired on them, but only with blanks, so they were able to land and make an assault on Tanjung Pinang. The Dutch put up a strong opposition, and many were killed, but those that were still alive took to their *keci* or *belah semangka* and sailed to Malacca. (Raja Ali Haji 1982, p. 185).

The editors and translators of the text, Virginia Matheson and Barbara W. Andaya, who compared the text with Dutch records, found that the attack occurred in May 1787. The Ilanun indeed offered the Dutch safe passage to Melaka (op. cit., p. 372).

Although operating outside the law (in French *forban*, that is, *hors du ban* or *hors de la loi*), pirates must have links with the legitimate world.

They have to obtain equipment, weapons in particular, sold by special dealers; they also have to sell their catch in the market place. The free port of Singapore was a very convenient place in the nineteenth century to get the necessary supplies. Some fortunate BL did abandon their unlawful activities and turned legitimate as proven by the career of La Ma'dukelleng from South Sulawesi in the eighteenth century who in his younger days made the Strait of Melaka and Makassar unsafe. In the local text he was then called *gora'e* (pirate), but later became Arung Singkang, the ruler of Singkang (Zainal Abidin 1975).

A curious encounter happened in Lampung in southern Sumatra to a Dutch colonial official, M. Francis. He was touring the region in the 1830s and had to stay overnight in a village chief's guest house. Lodged in the same house was Datu Mama, a pirate chief who was also a guest of the local chief. Being guests they had to behave as civilized persons, but, said Datu Mama, if they had met at sea he would certainly have captured the Dutchman (copy of report attached to Francis' letter to Batavia, datelined Padang, 17 October 1837, no. 2520, *Arsip Nasional R.I.*). If that would have happened Mr. Francis most probably would have ended up as a slave. For slaves were a most prized commodity until late in the nineteenth century when the system of hired manpower was not yet commonly practised in the region. Indeed slaves were then much in demand by RL and, therefore, slave-raiding became an important activity of BL. Naturally, for the victims, differentiating between RL or BL would be pointless, also when OL were involved.

Orang Laut is our third type of sea "power". The name is borrowed from a common designation for sea communities in the Strait of Melaka who live(d) on boats. In the eastern part of the Indonesian archipelago they are collectively called Bajau, but they refer to themselves as Orang Sama. Owing to their mobile homes they have no permanent settlements and, therefore, are also called "sea nomads" or "sea gypsies". Nowadays they have been more or less incorporated into the modern states of Southeast Asia. In the nineteenth century, however, they led an independent existence under a loose leadership of their *panglima* or *punggawa*. If the latter's decision in a conflict was against their idea of fairness, they moved their boat and joined another moorage.

It is perhaps not correct to speak of them as a sea power. They did not have a navy and preferred to move to more sheltered places rather than fight an aggressor. But as fishermen they certainly cherished their own fishing ground and would stop any trespasser from poaching in their area. Here we also could apply the Weberian concept of "sovereignty" where they, too, could resort to violent means against unwanted intruders.

In their contacts with the outside world the OL developed trade connections with RL and BL groups. For instance, a report of 1853 said that the Sultan of Gunung Tabur in East Kalimantan used to supply the local Bajau with cloths and other material in exchange for *trepang* (sea cucumbers), bird's nests, turtle shells, etc. (Zwager 1866, p. 249). These connections in due course could grow into a patron-client relationship where the OL could rely on the protection of the RL, while the latter could enjoy the services of the OL, especially as their maritime skills were of great benefit to the ruler. In this context they are also known as *rakyat laut* or simply *rakyat* (sea people, but here *rakyat* is better translated as "subjects" or "followers" — of course, seen from the viewpoint of the RL). An earlier report from the seventeenth century stated that the VOC also used the services of the Bajau in North Sulawesi as they were reliable messengers (Padbrugge 1682, fol. 232–33, Arsip Nasional R.I.).

Some OL had established links with BL fleets. This kind of cooperation made them a sure power to be reckoned with. Perhaps for them there is no distinction between the kinds of power wielded by the RL or BL. Some had already been *rakyat* of the RL before the latter was degraded into the position of BL. Such was the case of Tumenggung Abdul Rahman between 1819 and 1825 when his OL-followers made the sea around Singapore unsafe (Trocki 1979, chapter 2). Their *magosaha* — a Sama Dilaut word for "seeking a livelihood" (Nimmo 2001, p. 1) which is cognate to Indonesian and Malay *mengusaha* (effort, work, act) — had then taken the form of BL-activities. It reminds us of the Greek word *peiratès*, from its root *peiran*, which means "to endeavour" or "to try one's fortune at sea" — the origin of the word "pirate".

COLONIAL CONTINGENCIES

Rivalries among Western powers in the early period, which at times erupted into fierce battles in Southeast Asia, had by the nineteenth century been resolved by negotiated treaties and agreements on spheres of influence. Britain which emerged as the dominant power after the Napoleonic wars allowed the Dutch to return to the Indonesian archipelago and was no longer interested in challenging Dutch monopoly claims of the trade in fine spices as long as her other commercial activities were not obstructed. More important for her was safeguarding her lifeline which in Asia ran from Suez to Hong Kong. Sailing along and around the Strait of Melaka and the South China Sea, however, was still a dangerous venture as various RL, BL, and OL fleets were also active, since there were more prizes to be expected from the increasing traffic of goods.

The Dutch and Spaniards were having similar problems when they were sailing in areas which they considered were within their spheres of influence, in disregard to local notions of territorial waters. It was a time when Western concepts of sovereignty, of law and order, of just and unjust behaviour, were becoming the standard in international relations in Southeast Asia. As for the local RL, they did not have any other options.

Hence the Western concept of piracy was applied to counter all kinds of hostile attacks against colonial shipping. Piracy indeed became a convenient issue to be used as a legal ground for taking action, even though skirmishes occurred on land. That happened in Kedah in 1828 when Tunku Udin and Long with their troops were trying to reconquer the country that was occupied by Siam (Thailand). The British authorities in Penang who were bound by the Burney Treaty of 1826 to assist Siam, used the pretext of piracy to defeat the Malays, despite protests from British businessmen and the London lawyers (Rubin 1974, p. 4ff.). The Dutch by royal decree declared in 1876 that, besides the idea of piracy as specified by international law (viz. acts of violence committed on the high seas), "deeds of violence" committed along the shore, on the sea roads, in ports and estuaries of the Netherlands Indies were also to be considered as acts of piracy. Earlier the Spanish government in the Philippines had proclaimed that all Moro vessels carrying arms would be treated as pirates. But the Sulu government had another view as revealed in a letter to Queen Victoria dated 16 August 1877 (CO 144/148, Labuan, 12755/77, fol. 456–57, Public Record Office):

> When a person takes a thing that does not belong to him, he is looked upon as a thief, or pirate, and men combine together to punish him; if this is so we cannot understand why the Castilians should come and take our country, and fire at our defenceless villages, and kill our people who have not done anything wrong.

The Dutch were troubled by the proximity of a free port in Singapore. It was not only more profitable for ships to bring products there from the "Outer Islands" of Indonesia rather than to Batavia, it was also a place where people could buy arms and ammunition. In fact, resistance forces in Jambi (Sumatra) and Banjarmasin (Kalimantan) in the 1860s were in contact with arms dealers in the free market of Singapore. In the context of combating piracy, the Dutch urged the British government to prohibit the sales of arms there, and indeed in 1863 the local government issued a ban on arms traffic — except for trade with China — with sanctions of heavy fines and hard labour for trespassers. But the authorities in The Hague were surprised to receive a letter from the Dutch vice-consul in Singapore, J. Centers, addressed to the minister of foreign affairs (2 October 1863, no. 365) complaining that the prohibition "has dealt a sensitive blow to our trade" since weapons and ammunition were most important commodities which were sold "to the Chinese and natives of the surrounding islands" and that many Dutch ships "arriving here from Holland, carry big quantities of guns and all kinds of weapons". It would seem that the very guns used by resistance fighters against the colonial government had come from the mother country itself.

An inquiry was soon made and letters sent to the chambers of commerce in Amsterdam, Rotterdam, and Dordrecht for information. They were relieved to know that the goods were trans-shipments from Belgium and Prussia. The export figure for 1862 was a sum total of 195,093 guilders. The Prussian chamber of commerce informed that in 1862 a total of 40,908 guns was exported to British possessions in the East with a value of 86,970 *ropijen*, but there was no specification how much went to the port of Singapore. These, of course, were officially recorded figures. We are not certain whether or not they give the real picture, but the complaint of the vice-consul shows interesting aspects of the network of arms traffic at the time.

Towards the end of the nineteenth century almost all kingdoms in island Southeast Asia had been incorporated into the colonial empires. Only Aceh and Sulu still had their independence. But the Anglo-Dutch treaty of 1871 was a green light for Batavia to expand to the northern tip of Sumatra, one of her arguments being the suppression of piracy. For the Suluanos the signing of the Madrid Protocol of 11 March 1877 between Spain, Britain, and Germany signalled the imminent end of their independence. When the document was carefully read several times by the sultan and his chiefs, they understood that "[their] country is not improved by it" (Treacher to Commander E.I. Church, Sulu, 16 August 1877, CO 144/146, fol. 455, Public Record Office). They realized that the Protocol was for Spain an approval by the two other signatories to step up their attacks on Sulu, which was indeed defeated in July 1878. The colonial war in Aceh lasted until 1904.

PIRACY TODAY

With the abolition of slavery the notorious slaving raids of the Lanun and Mangindano had ceased. Forced labour, however, continued in the form of contract coolies, and the trafficking of human beings, particularly women and children, still exists today. Crime is, indeed, like many other things on earth, "eine alte Geschichte, doch bleibt immer neu" [an old story that is always new]. It is also the case with piracy, especially in places where sea patrols are absent or lax in most frequented sea lanes where a lot of booty is to be expected.

The U.N. Convention on the Law of the Sea (UNCLOS) (1982) defines piracy as acts committed on the high seas, or in places outside the jurisdiction of any state. Under this definition there is actually not much piracy today as many violent acts take place within the territorial waters of a sovereign state. Although legally correct, victims are not much helped by this definition. Therefore, acts of violence against ships, especially those committed in ports or territorial waters, are classified as "armed robbery" which is formulated as follows:

> "Armed robbery against ships" means any unlawful act of violence or detention or any act of depredation or threat thereof, other than an act of piracy, directed against a ship or against persons or property on board such a ship, within a State's jurisdiction over such offences (Resolution A.922(22) Code of Practice for the Investigation of the Crimes of Piracy and Armed Robbery against Ships).

Under this broader definition, piratical actions in modern times, according to Jayant Abhyankar, deputy director of the ICC (International Chamber of Commerce) International Maritime Bureau, can be classified into five types:

(1) The "Asian" type of piracy "where ships are boarded and cash and valuables are stolen from the ship's safe and crew with the minimum of force". Since all the waters are within the territorial jurisdiction of various countries, the attacks are not occurring on the high seas. Most incidents happen in Indonesian waters.

(2) The "South American" or what used to be called the "West African" type. Ships berthed or at anchor are attacked by armed gangs that are "more disposed to be violent than their Asian counterparts". Targets are cash, cargo, personal effects, ship's equipment, in fact, anything which can be moved. Other characteristics are that the total value of goods

stolen per attack are higher than in the "Asian" type, while there are indications of pre-planning. When the ship's equipment are stolen, the safety of the ship is at risk.
(3) Attacks that have a military or political character. The coast of Somalia continues to be prone to piratical attacks until today. Until quite recently the Aceh coast in North Sumatra was also a dangerous zone.
(4) Since the last decade of the twentieth century a violent form of piracy has emerged in Southeast Asia where a ship is hijacked underway, the crew overpowered, and the entire cargo transferred to a barge before the ship is handed back to the crew. In such cases it is not likely that anyone ashore could respond to the attack.
(5) A different type of piracy is where the ship is stolen. The objective is not so much for taking what the ship is carrying, but to use her for cargo frauds by giving it a false identity, turning it into a "phantom ship" (*kapal hantu*). If the crew were thought to be "surplus to requirements", they are set adrift, or thrown overboard, or simply shot dead. This was the case with MV *Tenyu* with her fifteen crew, and MV *Cheung Son* with twenty-three crew who were brutally murdered by pirates in late 1998 (Abhyankar 2002).

In cooperation with a world leading satellite tracking system operator, the International Maritime Bureau (IMB) has developed a device called ShipLoc which can be concealed on board a ship so that owners can locate a ship's position anywhere at sea via the satellite. This new equipment has proved useful when the MT *Selayang* was hijacked on the 21 June 2001, en route from Port Dickson, West Malaysia, to Labuan in East Malaysia. Through this satellite tracking system the whereabouts of the ship could be followed until it was seized on the 27 June off the east coast of Kalimantan near Balikpapan. The ship has meanwhile been repainted and renamed MT *Shan Ho*. The fourteen crew members who were secured in the lowest deck of the vessel were released, while the pirates, ten in number, arrested for further investigation.

Regular meetings, exchanges of information among the region's experts, both governmental and private, have proved effective in a concerted combat against piracy. Participants are countries from South, Southeast, and East Asia. According to an IMB report of July 2005, the number of reported piracy attacks worldwide is down to approximately 30 per cent. Between January and June 2005 a total of 127 acts of piracy were reported, which is a notable decrease from the 182 attacks reported during the same period in 2004. However, Indonesia still recorded the highest number of attacks, accounting for one-third of the global total, with forty-two incidents.

The following is a list of incidents in Indonesian waters as stated in the Weekly Reports of the last five weeks by the ICC Commercial Crime Services (http://www.icc-ccs.org/).

Weekly reports, 27 September – 31 October 2005.

- 28 September 2005 at 05:50 local time at anchor off Balikpapan, East Kalimantan. Two robbers armed with machetes boarded a tanker via the anchor chain and stole the forward life raft. They tried to steal the ship's stores, but were spotted by a duty watchman. The robbers left a machete on board and escaped in a boat waiting with an accomplice.

- 30 September, hijacking of MV *Prima Indah*. The ship departed Bangkal Palam for Singapore on 30 September with a cargo 660 mt tin ingots. At 13:00 UTC (greenwich time) pirates armed with guns hijacked the ship in position 01:28.6 S and 106:41.1 E, in Indonesian waters. The fourteen crew members were sent adrift in a fishing boat and landed safely at an island. The ship and cargo are missing. By now the ship may have changed name and flag and possibly repainted.

- 1 October 2005 at 12:00 local time, position 06:11.4 N and 097:06.3 E near the northern tip of Sumatra, Malacca Strait. Ten persons in a fishing boat chased a supply ship underway The crew activated fire hoses and the master took evasive manoeuvres so the attempted boarding was aborted.

- 4 October at 18:30 UTC in position 00:08.7 N and 117:35.6 E at Bontang anchorage (East Kalimantan. Robbers boarded a tanker. They tied up the duty guard to the anchor cable and stole the ship's stores.

- 13 October at 05:00 local time in the Sunda Straits. An unlit boat chased a bulk carrier underway. The alert crew raised the alarm, directed search lights, and activated the fire hoses. The chase was aborted.

- 13 October at 12:30 local time at the Jakarta anchorage. Six robbers boarded a bulk carrier at the stern. The duty officer raised the alarm, mustered the crew, and the robbers fled. The master contacted a customs patrol boat nearby and the boat chased the robbers for a few minutes and then gave up the chase. Jakarta port authority was informed.

17 October at 03:30 local time in position 06:02.87 S and 106:53.57 E at Jakarta anchorage. Robbers armed with long knives boarded a bulk carrier from an unlit boat. They threatened the crew with knives and stole a life raft. They were in the process of stealing the ship's stores, but the alerted crew thwarted the attempt. The robbers escaped in their boat. The master called port authorities on VHF radio, but received no response.

27 October at 08:36 local time in position 08:41.565 S and 115:43.911 E, in Lombok Strait. Pirates armed with guns in a speedboat fired on a chemical tanker underway. The bridge window was destroyed by gunshots, but there were no injuries to the crew. There were several fishing boats in the vicinity.

27 October between 00:01 and 01:00 local time in position 01:59.6 N and 116.08,7 E off Muara Pantai, East Kalimantan. Robbers boarded a bulk carrier at anchor during cargo operations. They stole the forward life raft and ship's stores, and escaped in their speedboat.

CONTINUITY AND CHANGE

The nineteenth-century pirate chief Dato Mama whom M. Francis met during his visit to Lampung (see p. 4), said that he should not be put on the same level as the *"Rakyat"* (OL)-type, who only attacked and captured fishermen and small trading *perahu*. He himself was only interested in big ships, particularly those with *tiang sambung* (extended masts). Whereas the first type would venture an attack when they met weaker vessels, a genuine pirate, according to Datu Mama, would act "to prove his prowess and valour" (Francis, ibid.).

In today's vocabulary the first type could be included in the "Asian" type of Abhyankar's categorization, while the second one — the rank and file of Dato Mama's – corresponds with the second type, that is, the "South American" type. Both types can again be lumped together in what Perret called *artisanale piracy* (Perret 1998, p. 143), usually involving a prize of a few thousand U.S. dollars while operating in a rather restricted zone.

Recent field work about this "Asian" type of piracy has revealed that Jemaja in the Anambas archipelago in the South China Sea is one of the places where "the pirates lived among local fishermen for a few months, surveying and attacking vessels" (Frécon 205, p. 10). Most curiously, the name Jemaja is also mentioned in an ancient Malay text, the *Hikayat Hang Tuah*, in relation with piratical attacks. "*Nama penghulu kami Aria Negara nama-nya, dan dari Jemaja pun sa-puloh buah hendak merampok ka-tanah Palembang*" (The name of our chief is Aria Negara, and from Jemaja there are ten [vessels] who will go plundering to Palembang) (*Hikayat* 1973, p. 22). This could be the same place as "Jumaia", "near Pahang", which is mentioned in Tomé Pires' *Suma Oriental* as the meeting place of pirates, where they used to gather the captured people to be sold as slaves (Pires 1944, fol. 159 v.).

The politically laden type of attacks are more in line with our RL-kind of typologization. They are challenging the status quo of the present regional political map, and, if successful, will in due time be recognized as a legitimate power.

The fourth and fifth type of piracy of Abhyankar can be grouped in Perret's *la piraterie des réseaux internationaux*. This form does not only need organizational expertise on an international scale, but also involves big capital investments — a true multinational enterprise of the criminal sort. Such a syndicate has to recruit able seamen and daring bandits, work with a network of accomplices, people who supply information on what the ship is carrying, receivers who can take and sell the stolen goods, and, in the case of the hijacking of ships, find collaborators who can give the ship a new identity by providing the necessary "legal" papers. This, of course, must involve working together with corrupt officials in embassies and consulates, and those employed in the law enforcing sector.

Note

This paper was written in Tomohon, November 2005. The author would like to note that now there is a conisderable decline of piratical activities in the region.

References

Abhyankar, Jayant. *Piracy and Armed Robbery against Ships Annual Report.* International Maritime Bureau Barking, Essex, UK, 2002.

Adam, Paul. "Esquisse d'une typologie de la course et de la piraterie". In *Course et piraterie*, vol. 2. Mimeographed. Paris: Commission Internationale d'Histoire Maritime (1975): 917–55.

Cornets de Groot van Kraaijenburg, J.P. "Notices historiques sur les pirateries commises dans l'Archipel indien oriental et sur les mesures prises pour les réprimer par le Gouvernement néerlandais dans les trente dernières années". *Moniteur des Indes*, 1846–48.

Deschamps. Hubert. *Pirates et Flibustiers*. Paris: Presses Universitaires de France, 1952.

Frécon, Eric. "Piracy in the Malacca Straits: Notes from the field". Leiden, *IIAS Newsletter* 36 (2005): 10.

Kasim Ahmad, ed. *Hikayat Hang Tuah: Menurut Naskah Dewan Bahasa dan Pustaka* [The Hikayat Hang Tuah, according to the manuscript kept at the Dewan Bahasa dan Pustaka]. Kuala Lumpur: Dewan Bahasa dan Pustaka, 1973.

Lapian, Adrian B. "Orang Laut, Bajak Laut, Raja Laut: Sejarah Kawasan Laut Sulawesi Abad XIX" (Sea People, Sea Robbers, Sea Lords: A History of the Celebes Sea Region in the Nineteenth Century). Ph.D. dissertation. Gadjah Mada University, Yogyakarta, 1987.

———. "The Road to Balangingi: A Review of 19th-century Slave-raiding Patterns as Reported by Escapd Slaves". Mimeographed. National Seminar on Southeast Asia: "The movement of people in Southeast Asia". HIPIS, Yogyakarta, May 1978.

———. "The Sealords of Berau and Mindanao: Two Responses to the Colonial Challenge". *Masyarakat Indonesia* 1, no. 2 (1974): 143–54.

Majul, Cesar Adib. *Muslims in the Philippines*. Manila: St. Mary's Publishing, 1978.

Nimmo, H. Arlo. *Magosaha: An Ethnography of the Tawi-Tawi Sama Dilaut*. Manila: Ateneo de Manila University Press, 2001.

Ormerod, H.A. *Piracy in the Ancient World*. Liverpool University Press, 1978.

Padbrugge, R. "Berigtinge der jegenwoordige staat, en stand, der Moluccos.... opgesteld door den tegenwoordigen Gouverneurder Moluccos Robbertus Padbrugge, op desselfs vertek over Banda naar Amboina, om tot behulp , en oock wel naar beliefte to narigtinge te mogen dienen, aan desselfs vervanger den Heere Gouverneur Jacob Lops" (Report of the present state and position of Maluku, written by the present governor of Maluku, Robbertus Padbrugge, on his departure via Banda to Ambon, to assist and also to serve as suitable information to his successor, Governor Jacob Lops). Manuscript, Arsip Nasional R.I. Ternate, August 1682.

Perret, Daniel. "Notes sur la piraterie moderne en Méditerranée Sud-Est asiatique". *Archipel* 56 (1998): 121–44.

Pires, Tomé. *The Suma Oriental of Tomé Pires, 1512–15*, edited by Armando Cortesão. 2 vols. London, Hakluyt Society, 1944.

Raja Ali Haji ibn Ahmad. *The Precious Gift (Tuhfat al-Nafis)*. An annotated translation by Virginia Matheson and Barbara Watson Andaya. Kuala Lumpur: Oxford University Press, 1982.

Rubin, Alfred. *Piracy, Paramounrcy, and Protectorates*. Kuala Lumpur: Penerbit Univerisiti Malaya, 1974.

Schendel, Willem van. "Asian Studies in Amsterdam". In *Unsettled Frontiers and Transnational Linkages: New Tasks for the Historian of Modern Asia*, edited by Leo Douw. Amsterdam: VU University Press, 1997.

Tarling, Nicholas. *Piracy and Politics in the Malay World: A Study of British Imperialism in Nineteenth-century South-East Asia*. Melbourne, F.W. Cheshire 1963.

Trocki, Carl A. *Prince of Pirates. The Temenggongs and the development of Johor and Singapore 1784–1885*. Singapore: Singapore University Press, 1979.

Veth, P.J. "De zeerooverij in den Indischen archipel als een bijzondere vorm van de Heilige Oorlog tegen ongeloovigen beschouwd" (Piracy in the Indian archipelago seen as a special form of Holy War against infidels). *Tijdschrift van Nederlandsch-Indië* 1 (1870): 175–76.

Villain-Gandossi, Christiane. "Notes sur la terminologie turque de la course". *Course et piraterie*, I. Paris, Commission internationale d'Histoire Maritime (1975): 137–45.

Warren, James Francis. *The Sulu Zone: The Dynamics of External Trade, Slavery, and Ethnicity in the Transformation of a Southeast Asian Maritime State*. Singapore: Singapore University Press, 1981.

Zainal Abidin Faried, A. "La Ma'dukelleng, Arung Singkang". Mimeographed. Ujung Pandang: IKIP Negeri, 1975.

Zwager, J. "Het rijk van Koetei op de Oostkust van Borneo in het jaar 1853" (The kingdom of Kutei on the east coast of Borneo in 1853). *Tijdschrift voor Nederlandsch-Indië* series IV (1866): 231–66.

8

Robbers and Traders: Papuan Piracy in the Seventeenth Century

Gerrit Knaap

Historically speaking, piracy is a familiar phenomenon in Southeast Asia. The studies of Jim Warren and Adri Lapian testify to this assertion.[1] The island worlds between Sulawesi and New Guinea are no exception to this rule. The "classical" period of piracy here was, as elsewhere in Southeast Asia, the late eighteenth and the beginning of the nineteenth century. Although it is most frequently connected to the figure of the Tidorese prince-rebel Nuku, tradition has it that piracy was already endemic in the region long before this.[2] Early European sources point to the Raja Ampat islands, located at the westernmost tip of New Guinea, as the core area from which all this "evil" emanated. The biggest of the Raja Ampat islands were, from north to south, Waygeo, Batanta, Salawati, and Misool. To provide more data this chapter focuses on the phenomenon of Papuan piracy during the seventeenth century. In reconstructing the facts, ample use will be made of the reports of the headquarters of the three Dutch colonial provinces in the area, namely at the castles Victoria for Amboina, Nassau for Banda, and Oranje for the Moluccas. The label Moluccas is used here in its early modern sense, namely to delineate the archipelago of Halmahera and smaller adjacent islands. Dutch colonial rule in those days was represented by the *Verenigde Oost-Indische Compagnie* (VOC), the Dutch East India Company. The seventeenth-century reports of the VOC are among the first to provide substantial information about what was designated Papuan robbery. The patterns and structures evolving from the analysis of the sources will be considered briefly in the broader framework of violence and trade in the eastern part of island Southeast Asia. The outcome will be to reveal that it is too easy to judge the phenomenon of piracy according to modern-day perspectives as simple forms of "predation" or "macro-parasitism".[3] First, we will take a look at the reports of acts of piracy committed in the VOC provinces of Amboina, Banda, and the Moluccas. Then, conditions in the Raja Ampat islands and their hinterland further east will be reviewed, prior to formulating some conclusions.

RAIDS INTO AMBOINA AND BANDA

By the middle of the seventeenth century, the islands of Amboina were the world's major producer of cloves. This spice had been very much coveted by traders from Asia and Europe. The Dutch, present in the area since 1599, tried to establish a monopoly on the export of cloves. In 1605 they scored their first success when they expelled the Portuguese from the islands. From roughly 1625, many a bloody war was fought between the VOC and those Amboinese intent on resisting the clove monopoly. By 1656, the VOC had won the battle definitively, and subjected the entire core of the Amboina islands to direct rule. To reap the profits from their monopoly, the Dutch exerted every effort to uphold a *Pax Neerlandica*, under which violent actions perpetrated by others, whether they were criminally or politically inspired, were declared illegal. From 1656, the *Pax Neerlandica* was scarcely under threat any longer from within, meaning, by any rebellion from the Amboinese. A similar story could be told for the much smaller archipelago of Banda, south-east of Amboina. From time immemorial these tiny islands were the sole producer of nutmeg and mace. The Dutch also arrived here in 1599, with the aim of establishing a monopoly on the export of these rare commodities. The period of bloody wars was shorter here than in Amboina. In 1622 the Dutch had violently eradicated Bandanese society. It was replaced by a sort of plantation system in which many European or Eurasian owners produced the spices with slave labour.[4] However, in the periphery of the core areas of both the province of Amboina and of Banda, there were still some latent factors liable to disturb the peace. One of these was the menace of "Papuan piracy". The pirates causing the depredations were from the Raja Ampat islands to the north, theoretically under the aegis of another VOC province, namely the Moluccas. The words "Papuan pirates" are misleading. First, the raiders did not always act as aggressive robbers because they sometimes changed their garb for that of a trader. Second, the population of the Raja Ampat was not purely Papuan; it was a mixture of various ethnicities, all of them formally acknowledging the overlordship of the sultan of Tidore.[5]

The area of Amboina province closest to the Papuan heartland was the north coast of Seram. In this area, the alleged pirates often collaborated with local power holders. A good example is the case of Latu Kaysuku, an ambitious leader of the village of Lisabata in the 1660s, who invited pirates to come and attack his rivals over a period of five years. Lisabata was a village composed of several migrant groups, most notably people from Jailolo in Halmahera and from Bacan. Many villages along the northcoast were inclined to enter into agreements with pirates in order to avoid the risk of falling victim themselves. To ward off the danger, they helped the aggressors to rob their neighbours, with whom they often had long-standing histories of conflict. Papuans from Misool, for instance, made slave raids deep into the interior of Seram, with the assistance of the leadership of Muslim coastal villages. The population of the interior was not Muslim, but animist, "pagan" as it was phrased. The captives were then often ransomed in these coastal villages. Besides the kidnapping and trading of captives, the Misoolers also had other business on the north coast, such as extracting flour from the pith of sago palms and exchanging goods with retail traders from the island of Boano to the west of Seram. It was rumoured that the vessels from Misool obtained gunpowder from the sultan of Tidore because the latter was so anxious to have them help substantiate his political claims to the coastal villages in North Seram.[6]

In the first half of the seventeenth century, the Amboina islands had already had a taste of Papuan plunder. In this period it was not only the VOC that had trouble with Papuans. The stadtholder[7] of the Sultan of Ternate in the Amboina islands, who bore the title of *kimelaha*, also had problems with them. Around 1620 two important members of the Tomagola, the clan ruling the area as *kimelaha*, were taken captive; it took two years to set them free. The servants of the VOC soon realized that the people from Lisabata and their associates from the nearby village of Hatuwe played a large hand in stimulating the piratical actions of the Papuan islanders. Men from Lisabata even acted as pilots and guides when the pirates ventured into the realm of the stadtholder of Ternate or the territory of the VOC. The pattern whereby the people taken captive in such raids were ransomed by the Lisabata leadership had already revealed itself. One Dutch governor of Amboina called this "a godless trade with our subjects". The island of Boano, strategically located to the west of North Seram, shared in a tradition of offering hospitality to Papuans. The pirates used Boano as a stepping stone for actions against Buru and the island of Ambon. To make matters worse, Boano itself had a reputation for piracy. Consequently, in 1619 the

Dutch sent a *hongi*, a fleet of *kora-kora* (boats), indigenous galley-like war vessels manned by Amboinese, to punish the population of Boano and to curtail their piratical activities in the future.[8] One year after this expedition the *kimelaha* took the offensive against the Lisabata "intermediaries". Buttressed by his own *hongi*, the *kimelaha* restored Ternatan rule over Lisabata. For about ten years Papuan piracy was reduced to being a low-profile menace to Amboina, but shortly after 1630 there was word of it again, with suspicions of re-emerging assistance from Boano and Lisabata. Now it had the tacit consent of the *kimelaha* because of the heavily strained relations between the latter and the VOC.[9]

In the year 1640, the VOC in Amboina once again assumed a serious stand against incursions by Papuans by forbidding its subjects and allies to entertain any peaceful relations whatsoever with the former. By concluding a treaty, the population of Boano promised no longer to shelter Papuan pirates. A similar sort of anti-Papuan clause was part of the treaty of subjection with the East Seram village of Rarakit in 1650. Rarakit was a marketplace for traders in captives and/or slaves taken by Papuans. To punish the village for this delinquency, as well as for the hospitality it had offered to other VOC enemies, the Amboinese *hongi* had taken the strongholds of Rarakit after some fierce fighting. That same year, 1650, Goram, also in East Seram, followed the example of Rarakit by declaring the Papuans an enemy. By 1650, the then incumbent *kimelaha* in the Ternatan dependencies in Amboina was again assailed by Papuan pirates. He launched an attack on the island of Misool with his own *hongi*.[10] A few years later, in 1653, a part of the Amboinese *hongi* of the VOC, twenty-one *kora-kora* commanded by Simon Cos, made a two-month expedition into the core area of the Papuans, first sailing from North Seram to the eastern tip of Halmahera, where a village was burnt down. The attempt to take the nearby stronghold of Patani proved unsuccessful. From East Halmahera the fleet sailed to Salawati and burnt the very large, but deserted village of that name. From here Cos decided to sail home. Later, we will return to this expedition. Again, that same year, a substantial number of North Seram villages, headed by Hatuwe, promised the VOC not to host Papuans any longer. However, at the time Cos undertook his daring operation, on the orders of the sultan of Tidore, the *raja* of Salawati, the very same whose village was burnt by Cos, prowled around Amboina with a fleet of fifteen vessels effecting extensive damage in Hitu, the northern part of the island of Ambon.[11] Therefore, it should be no surprise that in the 1660s, after the Dutch had won the last Amboinese war, the small, somewhat isolated island of Ambelau still proved easy prey for pirates. At times, the VOC sent its *hongi* on patrol against Papuans, namely to North Seram. The success of these expeditions varied greatly and could not be taken for granted.[12]

A better result in outplaying the Papuans was achieved in 1673, when the Dutch arrested some Misool traders on the north coast of Seram, among them Limau, the brother of the local ruler of Misool, *raja* Mangenane. Limau was only set free on condition that piracy from Misool should be discontinued in the future. This helped, for a while at least. However, if Misool was not active, there was always another group of Papuans willing to step into its place. Towards the end of the 1670s, when the VOC in the Moluccas was at war with the sultan of Ternate, the crown prince of Tidore, against the advice of the sultan of Tidore Sayfudin, joined the anti-VOC camp. As a consequence of his defection, Tidorese subjects started raiding the VOC province of Amboina. In 1678, five vessels sailed through the core area of the province capturing fifty to sixty Amboinese traders and fishermen. Sometime before this incursion, these vessels had tried their luck in Banda, but with little success. Most of the captives from Amboina were ransomed in East Seram for a price of thirty-eight to forty rixdollars per person. The people from East Seram in their turn were only inclined to let the "slaves" go after they had received forty rixdollars in compensation. Of this sum of forty rixdollars, twenty-five were paid by the Company, the rest had to come from the family of the victim.[13]

The 1678 raid greatly alarmed the VOC authorities in Amboina. Thereafter, when rumours of piratical actions surfaced, small squadrons consisting of *kora-kora* and smaller craft called *orembai*, were kept ready at strategic points. In addition, a bounty of 150 rixdollars, plus the prize of the right to keep the vessel, cargo, and crew with the exception of the leaders, was set on the capture of a pirate ship. In 1680 these precautions appear to have had only a limited effect. The biggest blow dealt to the pirates was not meted out by either Dutchmen or the Amboinese from VOC territory. In 1679, in the village of Kwaus, inhabitants gathered from several villages in East Seram attacked four pirate vessels which were trying to sell captured Amboinese. Two of the vessels were taken, whereby sixty-seven pirates were killed and fourteen others taken prisoner. The number of Amboinese set free was twenty-four. The VOC tried to lay hands on some of the imprisoned pirates for a price of thirty to fifty rixdollars. The meagre result was that only three of them were handed over as the East Serammers involved demanded 100 rixdollars per person instead. It transpired that the pirates originated from the small island of Gebe, which fell under the authority of the sultanate of Tidore. The VOC authorities were surprised by the small size of one of the vessels taken: only eighteen–nineteen feet long and five feet in the beam.[14]

After 1680 piracy slowed down a bit. Still spectacular was the destruction of a guard post of the VOC on Boano in 1682. To the southeast, the Aru Islands, nominally part of the province of Banda, fell victim to pillaging by five vessels in 1684. A number of forty-five captives were bought, free in Keffing on East Seram.[15] In 1689, there was a spectacular expedition by twelve *kora-kora* from Patani, Weda, and Maba, villages in the eastern part of Halmahera, against North Seram. In that same year, many *kora-kora*, probably from the same group that harassed North Seram, were active around the Kei Islands, south-east of Banda. This was the last major outburst in the seventeenth century. For a while Papuan piracy in the provinces of Amboina and Banda seemed a thing of the past. By 1699 the Amboina government had even ordered its personnel and subjects to make a clear distinction between traders and raiders among Papuans arriving in North Seram.[16]

THE SITUATION IN THE MOLUCCAS

The Moluccas in the proper sense of the word, namely the area of small islands surrounding Halmahera, was the world's cradle of cloves. It was the area to which the clove tree was indigenous. Consequently, many centuries before the arrival of the Dutch, the islands had already been frequented by traders from abroad seeking the valuable cargo. In the sixteenth century the Portuguese had settled in the Moluccas. As they lacked sufficient naval and military resources, they were never able to establish a complete monopoly on the export of cloves. Their chances to dominate the Moluccas greatly diminished in 1575 when they lost their fortress in Ternate to the sultan of that island. In so far as they were able to maintain their presence in the area, they relied heavily on the alliance with the main contender of Ternate, the sultan of Tidore. The fortress they built on Tidore in 1578 was destroyed by the Dutch in 1605. However, one year after this disaster, in 1606, the Iberian presence in the Moluccas was restored, this time by the Spaniards, who invaded the area from the Philippines. The Spaniards built fortresses on the islands, including Ternate. In response, the Dutch built their own fortresses, the first of which was Oranje, in another part of the island, in 1607. Consequently, the island of Ternate was divided into two parts. Fighting between the Dutch and Ternatans on the one hand, and the Spaniards and the Tidorese on the other, continued from about 1607 until 1648, when the

Netherlands and Spain concluded the Peace of Munster, putting an end to their almost eighty-year conflict. Finally, in 1662–63, the Spaniards evacuated their strongholds in the Moluccas because they needed all their soldiers to defend the Philippines against an imminent Chinese invasion.[17]

It is in the context of the violence of the war between the coalition VOC-Ternate and the coalition Spain-Tidore that most of the seventeenth-century piratical depredations undertaken by Papuans should be seen. When the pirates from Raja Ampat took part in this conflict, they usually joined the Spanish-Tidorese coalition. Because of this their victims were usually Dutch soldiers or subjects, as well as Ternatans and people from Bacan, the latter being the third and smallest of the sultanates in the Moluccas. In the conflict Bacan took the side of the VOC and Ternate.[18] After the Spaniards had left in 1663, establishing peaceful relations with Tidore was a matter of priority for the VOC. In 1667, Sultan Saifudin of Tidore promised to restrain Papuan piracy as far as it was in his power to do so. Any Papuan wanting to set sail to Amboina or Banda was required to obtain a sea pass from the Company. In order to avoid trouble within Raja Ampat itself, no subjects of Amboina and Banda were allowed to trade there. However, the political incentive for piracy flared up again during the conflict between Sultan Sibori, alias Sultan Amsterdam of Ternate, and the Dutch, in which, as said previously, the crown prince of Tidore supported Ternate. He could not be said to have mobilized Papuans in the proper sense of the word as he usually confined his recruitment to inhabitants of Patani, Weda, and Maba in East Halmahera. At the beginning of the 1680s, all this was common knowledge among the Dutch authorities. As a consequence of Maba raiding, many villages in the northern part of Halmahera, an area subject to Ternate, were deserted by their population.[19] But things were set to change again. In 1689, after the crown prince himself was elevated to the throne of Tidore to become Sultan Hamza Fahrudin, he appears to have been quite cooperative in restraining piracy. Signing a treaty with the VOC, he promised to capture and punish some prominent leaders of Patani, Weda, Maba, and Misool, should piracy occur again. Soon afterwards, four of the leaders of the first three villages were sent to the Cape of Good Hope as convict labourers.[20]

Thanks to the restraining policies of Sultan Hamza Fahrudin, piratical acts on the part of the subjects of Tidore declined significantly during the 1690s. In order to keep the status quo and not upset relations, the sultan once more forbade the trading activities in the Raja Ampat area of indigenous and Chinese seafarers from Banda and Amboina. As a reward for his good behaviour, in 1700 the sultan was given authority over the islands off the coast of East Seram, an area which the VOC had never been able to control effectively. Of course, not everybody was overjoyed with the good relations between the court of Tidore and the VOC at castle Oranje. Those from Patani, Weda, and Maba, formerly the staunchest allies of the sultan when he was still the presumptive crown prince, even planned rebellion against their ruler. In the end the rebellion fizzled out like a damp squib and in 1704 one of the leaders of Maba was banned to Ceylon.[21] Relations between Patani, Weda, and Maba on the one hand, and the sultan on the other, deteriorated yet further because the latter assisted the Dutch in their search for clove trees, which after identification had to be cut down. The attempts at extirpating the cultivation of cloves, agreed upon by the sultans, had always been resented by ordinary Moluccans, including those from the villages just mentioned. Fortunately for Sultan Hamza Fahrudin, this resentment did not yet simmer over into an uprising. The long-awaited rebellion in the realm of Tidore, headed by the villages of Patani, Weda and Maba, only broke out after his reign, namely in the second decade of the eighteenth century. At that time the insurgents also claimed that the sultan was raising his demands for tribute to intolerable levels.[22]

In the meantime, the sultan of Bacan played quite another role. As his petty kingdom was running out of subjects, he needed Papuans or any other folk to populate his country. Piratical raids in the sense of kidnapping might be seen as a means to that end. Probably with this purpose in mind, the sultan even married two of his daughters to Papuan leaders. Moreover, he tried to win *raja* Misool over to his side, going as far as to abduct about 150 persons from that island, among other purposes, to populate the uninhabited island of Obi belonging to his realm. Eventually, through the mediation of the VOC a portion of the Misoolers were allowed to stay in the area of Bacan on the condition that the sultan of Bacan paid 400 rixdollars to the sultan of Tidore.[23] Consequently, during the seventeenth century Bacan at times tried to claim Misool, thereby denying the authority of Tidore. It is again in this framework that the efforts of the sultan of Bacan to get his claims to nine villages in North Seram on the agenda should be seen. In 1660 the *kapitan laut*, the admiral as it were, of Bacan had gone as far as taking away some 200 persons from the village of Hatuwe and selling them in the Moluccas. For this daring but illegal action he was later arrested by VOC Amboina and banished to Batavia.[24] In the long run, all the efforts of Bacan to play a role of some significance in the political arena came to nought. After the attempt to populate Obi with "reliable" folk failed, the sultan in 1683 sold his rights to this island to the VOC. The claim to Misool was repeated from 1696–97, but to no avail.[25]

CONDITIONS IN THE RAJA AMPAT ISLANDS

According to Haga, in the sixteenth century the islands of the Raja Ampat, in particular Waygeo, Salawati, and Misool, were still largely independent of the sultanates of the Moluccas, although parts were temporarily claimed by Bacan, Ternate, or Tidore. The Dutch were slow to accumulate information about the area. For a long time, the expedition of the Amboinese *hongi* under Simon Cos in 1653, already mentioned briefly and to which we will return, remained an isolated event. Whereas some parts of the coast of New Guinea, for instance, the area south of the Berau or MacCluer Gulf — more specifically the peninsula known as Onin and Bombarai, were thoroughly investigated in 1678, Raja Ampat did not attract such attention until about 1700. Being a supply area for slave traders, Onin and Bombarai occasionally fell victim to piratical actions from Misool. Towards the end of the seventeenth century, Misool enjoyed the worst reputation as far as piracy was concerned. Not knowing how the area of Raja Ampat was structured politically, the VOC was inclined to see these islands as belonging to Tidore.[26]

One of the facts which inexorably emerges from the sources is that the Moluccas had not always dominated the Raja Ampat islands. The process of state formation resulting in the emergence of the sultanates of Ternate, Tidore, and Bacan was a development in which the Raja Ampat did not play a role. It was only after these sultanates were established that they shifted their gaze to the Raja Ampat. Their subsequent attempts to incorporate the Raja Ampat met with varying success. The process had hardly begun when the Europeans arrived on the scene. In fact, during the seventeenth and eighteenth centuries, the VOC was often called in to help to decide conflicts on matters of authority. In most of these cases the Dutch supported the claims of Tidore. At some point in history, the population of Raja Ampat seems to have recognized Tidore's claims by paying homage to the sultan. Tidore tradition has it that this started sometime in the late fifteenth or early sixteenth century. The links between centre and periphery must, however, have been tenuous at best, as in the 1660s and 1670s, even Sultan Sayfudin of Tidore, to some extent at least, used his good relations with the Dutch to strengthen his grip. Andaya points out that by doing so, the price to be paid was that the sultans had to comply with VOC claims and standards, for instance, by keeping the islands devoid of spice bearing trees and by forbidding the habit of raiding for purposes of revenge and ritual.[27]

The island of Gebe, a sort of a stepping-stone in the sea between Halmahera and New Guinea, being most adjacent to the centre of the realm of Tidore, must have been one of the first to acknowledge a certain degree of Tidore overlordship. The Portuguese had labelled the island of Gebe the seat of one of the four kings or *raja* of the Raja Ampat archipelago. The following data reveal that this was not true. Evidence from the seventeenth century unequivocally states that the most prominent leader on Gebe held the Tidorese rank of a *sengaji*. He functioned as the sultan's of tribute from the islands located east of Halmahera. This coincides with the nineteenth-century impression that the *sengaji* of Gebe ranked higher in the hierarchy of the sultanate than the four *raja* themselves.[28] In the Raja Ampat, using the proper sense of the term, it is generally acknowledged that the highest ranks were indeed those of the *raja*, of whom there should be four. During the seventeenth century, these four were the *raja* of Salawati, Waygeo, Misool, and Waigama, the last being the chief of the village of that name in the western part of the island of Misool. So, the supposition that the leader of Gebe was one of them must have been a result of incomplete information. Under the four *raja* were a *kapitan laut*, a sort of commander of a *hongi*, and a *jojau*, a sort of minister responsible for affairs on land. Towards the end of the seventeenth and at the beginning of the eighteenth century, the leaders from Patani, Weda, and Maba also functioned as intermediaries between the Raja Ampat and the court in Tidore. On studying the relations in the Raja Ampat, Andaya draws what would appear to be the right conclusion when he says that the four *raja* of the area never functioned as a unit in the organizational structure of the sultanate. The concept of four leaders was a Moluccan rather than a Papuan "invention".[29]

Although the people of the Raja Ampat gradually acknowledged the overlordship of Tidore, it is difficult to see how they were actually integrated into the state apparatus. The concept of the area being ruled by the number four *raja* is a strong clue to the involvement of Tidore. Legend has it that before this involvement, there was only one king in the Raja Ampat, whose centre of power was in the eastern part of Waygeo. By 1500 the area had begun to experience migrations of Papuans from the island of Biak, farther east. According to their own stories, the Biakkers mixed with the local population and put an end to the domination of recent intruders from Halmahera. One of the leaders of the migrant Biakkers of Waygeo, the legendary hero Sekfamneri alias Gurabesi, assisted the sultan of Tidore in a war against Jailolo in Halmahera. The legend goes on to say that the hero was given a princess of Tidore as a bride as his reward and that the sultan expected him to be a subject of and tributary to Tidore. Unfortunately, the couple had no children of their own. The legend recounts how they adopted four boys, born from eggs found on the beach. These sons became the first four *raja*, but because they quarrelled so much, they split up and dispersed themselves throughout the islands. In 1534 the sultans of the Moluccas seem to have requested the four *raja* to help them fight the Portuguese.[30]

Referring to the period after 1500, Andaya relates stories about visits of the Raja Ampat leadership to the court of Tidore, the ceremonies, and the handing over of tribute and the reciprocal gifts received in return. Unfortunately, the frequency of such visits for the seventeenth century is difficult to establish. We know little detail about the obligation to pay tribute or to deliver manpower for compulsory service and/or the *hongi*. On the other hand, small *hongi* seem to have been sent out regularly, probably on an annual basis, from Tidore to the Raja Ampat to collect tribute. Valentijn records such *hongi* were eighteen to twenty *kora-kora* strong. They were probably manned by subjects from Halmahera. The tribute consisted of slaves, ambergris, wax, and pearls. The quantities of these products are unknown. It should be stressed that during the seventeenth century the Raja Ampat was not yet a source of supply of the internationally important product of *trepang* (sea cucumber).[31]

On the basis of nineteenth-century information, Kamma concludes that the tribute the Raja Ampat had to hand over to Tidore was not really impressive. In fact, it was not the tribute that was the problem. The biggest hurdle was the obligation to hand it over personally to the court. Because of the difficulty and the length of the journey to and from Tidore, quite a number of men were required to be absent from home for a long period. No wonder that this obligation was often not met. Nineteenth-century evidence reveals that in reality tribute was not handed over annually, but usually at intervals of up to five years. As was just mentioned, ostensibly the primary function of the *hongi* sent from Tidore and Halmahera was the collection of tribute, but those manning the *hongi* soon turned their attentions to plunder. As a precautionary measure the population of entire villages moved inland at the approach of a *hongi* from Tidore, only to show up again when the coast was literally clear. As a matter of fact, such a reaction was no different to what happened in certain parts of Seram when the *hongi* of VOC Amboina was in sight. Kamma was the first to claim that from the viewpoint of the cruelly misused victims there was no difference between a Tidore *hongi* and a Papuan *rak*, a head-hunting expedition. A Tidore *hongi* often returned with many Papuans as slaves. Information from the nineteenth century further reveals that Tidorese *hongi* were only sent on an occasional basis and not annually. An ordinary *hongi* to the periphery of the realm in the east seemed to have consisted of a few small-size *kora-kora* from Tidore itself, supplemented by about five *kora-kora* from Patani, Maba, and Weda, one or two from Gebe, and another five from the Raja Ampat. In such a fleet, totalling twelve to thirteen vessels, not all the *kora-kora* of the Raja Ampat were mobilized at the same time. Sometimes those from Waygeo stayed home, another time those from Misool did not participate, and so on.[32]

How far the authority of the four *raja* stretched presents a pretty insuperable difficulty. The information from the middle of the nineteenth century tends to be obscure on this point. It is even more problematic to try to translate what little is known of earlier periods. It appears that besides the four *raja*, there were also nine *sengaji* who each ruled nine separate villages. These *sengaji* had to hand over tribute directly to the sultan. Apparently, they were not included in the territory or the hierarchy of the *raja*. Kamma claims that we should not expect that either the *raja* or the *sengaji* were able to exert much authority among their followers. They were only a sort of "first among equals". When the old *raja* or *sengaji* died, the lesser chiefs of the area selected three candidates for the succession, not necessarily according to primogeniture, leaving the sultan to decide who the successful candidate would be.[33]

Recently Arfan summarized the political geography of the Raja Ampat. From him we learn that the *raja* of Waygeo had his seat at Mumus, at the entrance to the inlet called Mayalibit Bay, from where he claimed to rule almost the entire island. The *raja* of Salawati governed from Samate on the north-east corner of the island of Salawati. He claimed the northern part of that island, a few places in West Waygeo, the eastern part of Batanta, and the nearby coast of the Kepala Burung or Bird's Head peninsula. On the west coast of Salawati, there was a *kapitan laut*, who resided in Sailolof. His area included the southern part of the island of Salawati, the western part of Batanta, some adjacent areas on Kepala Burung, and the small archipelago of Kofiau. It seems that the lineages of the *raja* and of the *kapitan laut* frequently intermarried. The *raja* of Misool resided in Lilinta on the south coast of the island of Misool. The fourth *raja*, that of Waigama, had his seat in the village of that name in the western part of Misool. The *raja* of Waigama is sometimes seen as not genuine. In fact, the fourth *raja* was supposed to be resident in Kilmuri, a place in East

Seram. At some point, the sultan of Tidore had him replaced as the fourth *raja* by Waigama. Cogently, Arfan mentions no *sengaji*.[34] Arfan's political geography is certainly valid for the twentieth century. Its general outline is confirmed by the observations of Dutch civil servants, albeit that they also included a few *sengaji* in their descriptions.[35]

THE FIRST EXPEDITION REPORTS ON RAJA AMPAT

The first historical written account offering some details about the Raja Ampat goes back to the late sixteenth century. It is the short report by the Portuguese Miguel Roxo de Brito of a voyage in 1581–82, unique of its sort. It seems that Misool and Waygeo, and probably also Salawati, were visited by De Brito. It is explicitly stated that the *raja* of Misool and his subjects, numbering about 4,000 to 5,000 men, were in the habit of regularly raiding neighbours, in particular those of Seramlaut in East Seram, to obtain prisoners who were released for gold, gongs, and cloth. It is said that the number of *kora-kora* of Misool was about thirty to forty and the annual number of hostages taken on the raids seventy to eighty. The *raja* of Waygeo, who showed himself very inclined to subject himself to the Iberians, accompanied De Brito to the Onin area with a fleet. Onin was a place for supplying slaves to the market in East Seram.[36] In the seventeenth century, the Onin area was paid further attention in reports from Johannes Keyts and Georgius Rumphius, writing in 1678 and 1684, respectively.[37]

The only seventeenth-century account of a journey to the Raja Ampat is that of Simon Cos, who has already been mentioned. He sailed with a part of the Amboinese *hongi* from the eastern tip of Halmahera to Salawati via Gebe in 1653. On his trip, he saw hardly a living soul because on his appearance everybody had retreated into the jungle. The only occupation of his men was looting and burning villages. On the journey they also reached the village of Salawati, probably Sailolof. Cos describes the village as lying behind a long stretch of muddy water, impossible for relatively large *kora-kora* to cross. The beach was protected by a defence work of stockades. At some point, between a river and a swamp, there was a wall, nine feet high and ten feet thick, with a rounded bastion. Cos said that if his men had had to storm the place, they might have had a very tough job. Luckily for him, the defensive works, which were constructed only on the seaside, as well as the village itself, were totally deserted. There was not a single sign of the inhabitants or of the twelve to thirteen *kora-kora* this place was supposed to have. At the departure of the *hongi* the village was burnt and the gardens in its environs laid waste.[38] The information supplied by Cos leads to the conclusion that at some point in this remote island-world of inaccessible jungles, swamps, and creeks, there were pockets of habitation displaying signs of a high degree of social organization. Nine years later, in 1662, when Cos wrote his memoir of transfer for his successor as governor of the Moluccas, he was still not able to supply any new information. He only claimed that the sultan of Tidore had the area inspected on a regular basis, up to twice a year, and obtained considerable tribute from it. Sultan Saifudin was fairly popular because he himself was generous in distributing presents. Cos ends with the obvious conclusion that a part of the population in these peripheral districts made a living from slave raiding.[39]

It was only after the end of the seventeenth and the beginning of the eighteenth century that the Dutch renewed their interest in the Raja Ampat. In 1706 Governor of the Moluccas Pieter Rooselaar summarized what the Dutch knew in an appendix to his memoir of transfer to his successor. The political geography then was as follows. On the eastern side of Misool, both the *raja* and the *kapitan laut* of Misool had their own village. The number of able-bodied men was about 3000. In former times on the north-west side of the island of Misool, but now on the south-west, was the village of the *raja* and *kapitan laut* of Waigama. The number of able-bodied men was 500 to 600. The island of Salawati was described as rather well populated, although numbers were not mentioned. Most of the population lived in temporary settlements in the interior. A nomadic way of life also seems to have been the case in adjacent Batanta. The most important village on the island of Salawati was the settlement of the same name, where both the *raja* and the *kapitan laut* were residing. This village lay on a river in the south-west, obviously Sailolof. The *raja* of Waygeo was said to reside at the end of the long inlet, accessible from the south coast, in a village called Kabilolo. Again there is no mention of the number of able-bodied men. The Papuans in general were described by Rooselaar as almost naked and rather simple-minded. They were heathens. The chiefs, however, most of whom originated from Tidore and Seram, dressed like Muslims. Raiding was an important source of income. In the case of Misool, it is said that slaves were obtained by raiding other areas and through buying in Salawati. Papuans were good sailors and their long and narrow rowing vessels were hard to overtake. Their weapons consisted of bows and arrows, shields, and swords, as well as javelins.[40]

Rooselaar could count on recent information supplied by some expeditions to the Raja Ampat. The renewed interest of the Dutch had to do with two preoccupations. First, the Dutch feared that other Europeans, and they had in mind the Spaniards or the French, two nations with which the Dutch were at war at that time, or again the English, might show up in this area. There was a rumour that the English "adventurer" William Dampier had been sighted in New Guinea. Second, there was a suspicion that spice bearing trees were growing in the Raja Ampat, which might become a threat to the VOC monopolies. Such trees, if found, should be eradicated. William Dampier was indeed in the area. Towards the end of 1705, he reported himself with the remainder of the crew loyal to him at castle Oranje, after a long and adventurous journey across the Pacific. A few months later he sailed to Batavia with Rooselaar.[41]

Before Rooselaar sent expeditions to the Raja Ampat, in 1702 the VOC authorities in castle Nassau on Banda had dispatched two ships under the command of bookkeeper Jan van Benthem. Leupe published a summary version of the report of this journey in the nineteenth century.[42] Van Benthem's guide and intermediary was *orangkaya* Maba of the village of Keffing in East Seram. The voyage finally took them all the way to Halmahera, although it was a small miracle that they actually reached that island because sometimes the Dutch did not have the slightest idea of where they were. In Misool the people had fled their villages at the sighting of the ships. In Salawati, now called Sailolof, two *kora-kora*, one of which flew a Dutch flag, were seen. This vessel was from the sultan of Tidore, carrying one of his interpreters who showed himself inclined to come on board after the Dutch had fired a one-cannon shot salute to mark the meeting officially. However, after the firing of the shot, the two *kora-kora* sailed away. An attempt to go ashore peacefully was also aborted because people greeted the Dutch shouting: "Come over here, then we will cut you to pieces." On another island a hail of arrows welcomed the commissioners and it was explicitly stated that Hollanders were not appreciated on their land.[43]

Prompted by rumours about the presence of other Europeans and spice bearing trees, the VOC in 1704 and 1705 sent two expeditions from castle Oranje consisting of three to four small vessels to the island of Misool. One constant factor in these expeditions was sergeant, later ensign, Adolph Johan van der Laan, who compiled the reports. The reports were published in summary by Leupe in the nineteenth century.[44] Both expeditions proved to be very time-consuming as the winds and the currents in this island-world were not favourable to sailing vessels. Sometimes, it was necessary to wait for days on end before progress could be made in the desired direction. Because of these nautical problems, it was not uncommon that the vessels in one expedition completely lost track of one another. Another constant factor was that expeditions to the Raja Ampat first called at Tidore to inform the sultan of the plans and to take on board envoys, usually two, to join the voyage and to serve as intermediaries. Compared with the bad experiences of Van Benthem, the expeditions of Van der Laan were a success. When Van der Laan first met the *raja* of Misool and his counterpart of Waigama in August 1704, local leaders from Misool declared that they were astonished to see envoys of the sultan on board a VOC vessel. Van der Laan explained that this should be seen as a sign of the unity between Tidore and the Company. The local leaders said that envoys of the sultan had already informed them beforehand of the prospect of the arrival of VOC vessels. This advance information was the sole reason the population had not fled to the jungle, the usual reaction to the appearance of Western ships. During Van der Laan's stay, relations between all parties proved to be fairly peaceful, in spite of the fact that the local authorities had to deliver quite a number of men to join in the search for spice bearing trees in the interior. Although Van der Laan had serious trouble in recruiting enough men to do this job, the search went on. However, no such trees were found. Van der Laan himself was cordially received by the *raja* of Misool in "the king's palace" which, according to the former, looked like "a half-demolished farm-shed" rather than the house of a grandee.[45]

More interesting than Van der Laan's endeavours was the expedition of lieutenant Pieter Lijn and junior merchant Jacob van Gijn, the latter in the role of a reporter, with three vessels, the most important of which was the *Oostvoorn*, to Salawati and Waygeo in 1705. The nineteenth-century historiographer of early modern Dutch exploratory expeditions, Leupe, has published an extract of the report. Andaya has a short summary of it.[46] The principal reason for the undertaking of the expedition of Lijn and Van Gijn was the message, conveyed through Tidore, that seven unknown European vessels had been sighted off the coast of Waygeo. In Tidore, the Dutch took two Tidorese envoys on board. The sultan had already sent some of his servants to the islands in advance to notify them of the imminent arrival of the expedition. In addition to the ships and their crew, Lijn and Van Gijn were accompanied by fifteen military men and one interpreter. The latter was recruited from the community of foreign Asians living around castle Oranje. Victuals for a period of five months were taken on board. Besides these, a considerable quantity of alcoholic drinks were carried to give the meetings with the local grandees some extra flavour. On top of this, some pieces of Indian cloth were to be presented to the local grandees as tokens of gratitude for the hospitality and hoped-for assistance.[47]

When Lijn and Van Gijn visited the sultan of Tidore, the latter told them that on their arrival in a place they always had to send his envoys ashore first, in order to make contact. Lijn and Van Gijn promised to do so. After a slow journey of forty-five days and having lost sight of the two accompanying vessels, Lijn and Van Gijn reached the village of Salawati, now called Sailolof. With their ship moored quite a distance from the shore, they disembarked with the soldiers and were lodged in a house in the village, just opposite the residence of the *raja*, whose name was Foukere. Apparently, in the seventeenth century the *raja* of Salawati lived in Sailolof and not in Samate, on the other side of the island which seems to have been the case in the nineteenth century. At the time of the visit of Lijn and Van Gijn, there was no mention of a wall or the defensive works reported by Cos. When the local grandees came to escort the Dutchmen from their ship, it appeared that, besides its local crew, the *kora-kora* had on board two Tidorese with muskets. On another Salawati vessel, notably the one which served the *raja* on his longer voyages, there seems to have been a swivel gun. The local government appeared to consist of the *raja*, the *kapitan laut*, a *gogugu*, and a *hukum*. A *gogugu* or *jojau* is sometimes portrayed as a "grand-vizier", a *hukum* indicated a "judge". As said previously, a *kapitan laut* was a sort of "commander-at-sea". During their stay in Salawati, which lasted eighteen days, Lijn and Van Gijn also met the *raja* of Misool, named Bulan, and his *kapitan laut*, who had come, among other intentions, to hand over part of the annual tribute they owed to the sultan to the Tidorese envoys. This tribute appeared to consist of three slaves. Lijn and Van Gijn tried to get as much information as possible about the European ships, the number of which appeared to be not seven, but three. They were sighted mainly off the coast of Sorong on Kepala Burung peninsula and near Waygeo. As there were no Tidorese envoys on board these ships, at their appearance, the population of the villages usually retreated inland. Lijn and Van Gijn also tried to find out whether there were spice bearing trees on Salawati and Batanta. On leaving the village of Salawati the Dutch, assisted by local grandees, men and vessels, spent more than a week searching the interior of north-west Salawati and a part of Batanta for trees. None was found.[48]

During the time they spent at Batanta, one of the two Tidorese envoys, *ngofamaniera* Mustapha, was sent with a rowing vessel of Salawati to search for the European ships. He returned after only one day having had a bad encounter with a European shallop near the small island of Jefmaan, located between the island of Salawati and Sorong. The shallop flew a Dutch flag, but when the envoy made himself known by shouting that he was Tidorese, muskets and cannon fire greeted on the rowing vessel, killing one person. All persons on board, except for the envoy himself, jumped into the water, which proved to be not much help as subsequently two more were shot. The envoy begged his people to come on board again and flee with him. Finally, with sixteen out of twenty-eight of the original crew, the envoy was able to get away under cover of darkness. After hearing this story Lijn and Van Gijn decided to board the *Oostvoorn* and sail to the area where the incident had taken place. Consequently, they also encountered the shallop, which transpired to be the VOC vessel *Nova Guinea*. This vessel, in the company of two others, had departed from Batavia half a year earlier to survey the coast of New Guinea. Those on the *Nova Guinea* declared they had fired on the vessel from Salawati, once they heard the word "Tidore" because earlier on during their expedition it appeared that they had been attacked by 43 vessels, which had initially made themselves known under the name of Tidore. Suddenly, it became clear to everybody that all rumours about foreign European vessels were, in fact, caused by the three VOC ships from Batavia engaged in this survey. It all turned out to be one great misunderstanding, caused by the fact that there had not been enough communication between Batavia and the Moluccas.[49]

A further two-day sail brought Lijn and Van Gijn to Waygeo, where they were offered hospitality in the village Wayamerok, the residence of the *kapitan laut* located on the south-coast at the entrance of the inlet Mayalibit Bay. With the exception of two, they remained here for a period of thirty-eight days. The two days were spent to row through the inlet to pay a visit to Kabilolo, the village of the *raja*. During their stay they had regular contact with the *raja*, whose name was never mentioned, the *kapitan laut*, the *gugugu* for Waygeo as a whole, and with some lower-ranking leaders of less important villages with titles of *sengaji*, *kimelaha*, or *marinyu*. It is important to note that the *raja*'s residence was then at a place other than its location in the middle of the nineteenth century. Lijn, in particular, made many tours with search parties for spice trees, although nothing was found. Finally, in the company of other Europeans on board among many whom were sick, Lijn and Van Gijn sailed back to castle Oranje. This journey took them another sixteen days. By the time they reached Oranje, Pieter Lijn's health was in a perilous condition. Nevertheless, thanks was offered to God for the "undeserved mercy" of bringing the expedition home again. Fortunately, Lijn recovered to live for a few more years.[50]

The *Nova Guinea*, mentioned above, had been part of a surveying fleet party under the command of skipper Jacob Weyland, consisting of three vessels, the most important of which was the *Geelvinck*. Unfortunately, the original report by Weyland himself has been lost. In so far as there is any information about the adventures of the expedition, it is second-hand. The vessels had left Batavia towards the end of January 1705. After a short stay in Banda, four interpreters from East Seram were taken on board to facilitate communications with the people they expected to meet on the coast of New Guinea. During the voyage the three vessels lost sight of one another. In August and September 1705, they appeared again in Amboina and Banda, having lost many crew members through disease and subsequent death. The most important result of the expedition was that it discovered and mapped most of the Cendrawasih or Geelvinck Bay. The encounters with the local population were often violent. At times the ships of the VOC were fiercely attacked by twenty to forty vessels. Going ashore was perilous as ambushes posed a constant threat. The interpreters from East Seram proved useless on the north coast of New Guinea. Only in the Bombarai area, a part of the south coast, were the interpreters able to establish some real communication with a particular village. The people here said that they were subjects of the sultan of Tidore, to whom they had recently presented some slaves as tribute. Sometimes they also sold slaves to Waygeo.[51] Weyland's expedition did not provide any new information about the society and political conditions of the Raja Ampat in the proper sense of the word.

THE PROVISION OF SLAVES IN RAJA AMPAT

During the expeditions of Adolph Johan van der Laan to Misool and the one of Pieter Lijn and Jacob van Gijn to Salawati and Waygeo, nothing of a society in the grip of "lawlessness" in our sense of the word, that is, characterized by piracy and slave raiding, was encountered. Thanks to the intermediairy services of the envoys of Tidore, relations between the VOC servants and the local Papuan elite were harmonious in the extreme. The people accompanied the Dutch for weeks on end along the coasts, either in rowing vessels or searching the jungle for non-existent spice bearing trees. There appears to have been a surprising degree of cooperation on the part of a population which had the reputation of being violent and warlike. It was a far cry from the evasion discovered by Simon Cos some half a century before. All was quiet and peaceful. Nevertheless, the phenomenon of slavery was part of reality, in the sense that slaves were used as a tribute to the sultan. How were these slaves "produced", if there was no raiding from the Raja Ampat to the west, the Moluccas, or the south, namely Amboina and Banda? Both the Raja Ampat itself as well as its eastern hinterland, in particular the Kepala Burung peninsula, the adjacent coasts in the Cendrawasih Bay, and the Bombarai peninsula might be considered candidates for the provision of slaves. So far, there is no information that the Raja Ampat society itself was a source of slaves. Consequently, somehow the solution has to be found in the hinterland.

This draws the spotlight to the so-called *kain timur* system. This phenomenon has been the object of anthropological study. *Kain timur* means "eastern cloth" and indicates the import trade into Kepala Burung of cloths in exchange for slaves or kidnapped persons. In the peninsula itself, the *kain timur* were used as the bride price for obtaining women for marriage into a man's tribe.[52] It seems that this exchange of slaves-for-cloth, a sort of a chain of raiding and trading, was kept going not so much through the Raja Ampat, but rather propelled through Onin, the western tip of Bombarai, a place traditionally dominated by navigators from East Seram. Goodman has given a description of the trade relations of East Seram with the most prominent Onin *raja* and the periphery of the latter consisting of sea bays and river estuaries reaching far inland.[53]

Returning to the hinterland in a more narrow sense of the word, and to the Kepala Burung peninsula in particular, we note that Miedema has claimed that the north coast of the latter was less involved in the slave trade than the southcoast. Hence, the tribes characterized by the *kain timur* system of exchange were those of the southern and central part of the peninsula. Not all regions here proved to be equally "cloth-oriented". There were also areas which used other trade items, such as plates and chinaware to make up the bride price or to buy slaves. Recent research posits the beginning of the *kain timur* system in the sixteenth century. Indian cloth immediately springs to mind. However, it may well be that here we are not dealing with a kind of luxury textile, but rather with a Southeast Asian product, which was usually much cheaper. The raiding and kidnapping itself led to fierce fighting among the local tribes. It seems that the Maybrat people near Ayumara produced the most feared "big men" or war leaders.[54] The oral tradition of the tribes located between Ayumaru and the western part of the south coast of Kepala Burung recollects that slaves were not only carried away by people from Onin, but also by those from the Raja Ampat. The *Raja* of Salawati's sphere of influence seems to have stretched as far east as the Kaibus estuary near present-day Teminabuan. Recently, Timmer has coined the term "merchant rulers" for the *raja* of Salawati and of Onin, who combined raiding and trading with the collection of tribute. Moreover, in an earlier publication, on the grounds of historical sources for the eighteenth century, Miedema also mentions Salawati among the slave raiders on the north coast.[55]

Cendrawasih Bay, farther east along the north coast of New Guinea than the Kepala Burung peninsula, enjoys a historical reputation of slave taking and headhunting, both facilitated by raiding expeditions called *rak*. The anthropologist Held left us some interesting information about this phenomenon. The radius of such expeditions was fairly circumscribed by the problem of providing the crews with enough food. Chiefs of clans usually took the initiative and bought one or more vessels, if the expeditions had to be seaborne. The fates of captives, held for ransom, were at the hands of the clan leadership. Taking a captive or "slave" earned the perpetrator prestige. This was particularly important to the chiefs. In a raid, young men could prove that they had entered the ranks of the "courageous", the males who mattered in their village. Once captives had been taken to the village of the raiders, there was great feasting. The captives were kept in the clan houses and their escape was prevented by shackling one of their legs to a wooden block. Besides living booty, the raiding parties also brought back the decapitated heads of slain enemies. The skulls were often given a ceremonial place near the house poles, in particular the central pillar, of a clan house. Hence, they might be seen as an offering to the ancestors. The reasons for staging a *rak* were manifold, and not limited only to the kidnapping of persons or the taking of heads as such. Among the motives might also have been revenge for manslaughter in the sense of "blood for blood" or for incest and other violations of customary law. As far as the captives were concerned, the clan leaders seem to have been prepared to free and return them to their village when a good ransom, consisting of textiles, ceramics, and so forth, was paid. This was the "economic element" running parallel to the state of endemic warfare which dominated the area. Were a prisoner so unlucky as not to have relatives or friends capable or prepared to pay the ransom, he or she was degraded to a status of permanent slavery, which could entail being sold to traders from outside. Held postulated the gradual introduction of a profit-incentive during the course of history, which relegated the headhunting motive to the background. In this way raiding and trading became complementary activities.[56]

Concluding Remarks

At regular intervals the seventeenth century saw piratical expeditions to the region west of New Guinea, especially the Dutch colonial provinces in Amboina, Banda, and the Moluccas. Many of these attacks originated from Misool and Salawati, two of the Raja Ampat islands. On closer examination, it appears that the most daring raids were not launched by seafarers from the Raja Ampat entirely on their own initiative, but undertaken in cooperation with people from the Moluccas or Amboina itself. In times of political instability local leaders, whether from Tidore, Bacan, Maba, Weda, Patani, the northern part of Seram, or the island of Boano, used the "fierce Papuans" against enemies or competitors to strengthen their own prestige and authority. They manipulated the pirates — who probably would not have come as far west if they had had to undertake it all by themselves — in their own political games. Similar political mechanisms were prevalent in many other parts of Southeast Asia, especially where centre-periphery relations were at certain stages of development.[57] When the political situation stabilized these piratical forays grew less frequent. This was particularly so when the VOC managed to exert its dominance to an increasing extent and was accepted by the indigenous ruling castes of Amboina and the Moluccas. It should be stressed that the geographical range of the expeditions from the Raja Ampat was much smaller than that of the well known pirates from Sulu in a later era.[58]

Whereas at the end of the seventeenth and the beginning of the eighteenth century the islanders of the Raja Ampat still bore the reputation of being merciless pirates, the reports of the VOC expeditions of 1704 and 1705 to the islands revealed fairly peaceful conditions. That was the situation as long as the expeditions were carried out under the joint banner of the VOC-Tidore alliance. It is obvious that the overlordship of Tidore in the Raja Ampat was an effective means to free the core areas of VOC rule in this part of the world from the threat of attack. The leading circles at the court of Tidore apparently subscribed to the view of the VOC that raiding expeditions had to be stamped as piracy and, hence, forbidden. However, whenever the relations between the court and its intermediaries for the Raja Ampat, such as the heads from Weda, Maba, and Patani in the eastern part of Halmahera, became troubled, the Papuans could prove a persistent menace. The court of Tidore on the other hand also capitalized on its good relations with the VOC. The latter helped the court to tighten its reins of authority, which in its turn resulted in a more or less regular flow of tribute from the Raja

Ampat. In fact, it broadened and strengthened the relatively small range of the original Tidore state. Consequently, the rhythm of piracy was heavily orchestrated by interstate political factors.

Many authors have already stressed that there is also an incontrovertibly economic aspect to piracy.[59] In this particular case, the economic factor was slaves. The slave trade was an important element, although we should not overestimate its extent. The scant information we have about the number of slaves taken in raids suggests an annual turnover of hundreds rather than thousands. Thus, from the viewpoint of numbers, the slave trade of the Papuan islanders is hardly comparable to the situation in nineteenth-century Sulu.[60] With raiding in a westward direction only taking place in unruly times and at long intervals, the Raja Ampat islanders and their allies had to look for other supply areas to keep the trade going. Small-scale warfare might have been a source for obtaining slaves. However, the Raja Ampat itself, although not a political unity, does not seem to have been a theatre of intense internal conflict, at least not to the degree encountered in Amboina and Seram before colonial rule.[61] So far, sources generally have not shown us a typical pattern of particularistic rivalry, leading to endless raiding parties on land or along the coasts.

With the Raja Ampat itself not generating many slaves, the supply had to come from the hinterland, namely the Kepala Burung peninsula and adjacent areas as far east as Cendrawasih Bay. In this hinterland, the evidence to sustain a conclusion that small-scale tribal warfare was a way to generate captives is plentiful. In the early modern period this phenomenon was also found in other parts of East Indonesia.[62] Those captives, who were not ransomed by their clans or villages, were most likely traded in a westerly direction in exchange for cloth, ironware, and other valuable commodities. In such circumstances, small-scale warfare, originally intended as retaliation for offences and to obtain status, loot, or the trophy of cut-off heads essential to the socio-religious system, intertwined with commercial trade relations. As the Papuan hinterland had, economically speaking, not much to offer to the more "developed" parts of Southeast Asia, somehow it is not surprising that human beings gradually became a prominent export item. Therefore, robbery and barter were two complementary sides of one activity. For a long time, this activity was intrinsic to the political economy of the area. In such a construct violence was never far away. Those persons acting as pirates, the aggressors as it were, were certainly not part of a marginal criminal group on the fringes of society. On the contrary, the phenomenon was taken for granted and the elite was often heavily involved.

Notes

Gerrit Knaap is programme director in the Institute for Netherlands History (ING) in The Hague. He has published extensively about the early modern and the maritime history of Indonesia. He wishes to express his gratitude to Rosemary Robson-MacKillop for looking at his English. He can be contacted at gerrit.knaap@inghist.nl.

1. J.F. Warren, *The Sulu Zone, 1768–1898: The Dynamics of External Trade, Slavery, and Ethnicity in the Transformation of a Southeast Asian Maritime State* (Singapore: Singapore University Press, 1981); J.F. Warren, *Iranun and Balangingi: Globalization, Maritime Raiding and the Birth of Ethnicity* (Singapore: Singapore University Press, 2002); A.B. Lapian, *Orang Laut, Bajak Laut, Raja Laut: Sejarah Kawasan Laut Sulawesi pada Abad XIX* (Ph.D. dissertation, Universitas Gadjah Mada, 1987).
2. E. Katoppo, *Nuku, Sultan Saidul Jehad Muhamad El Mabus Amirudin Syah, Kaicil Paparangan, Sultan Tidore: Riwayat Perjuangan Kemerdekaan Indonesia di Maluku Utara 1780–1805* (Jakarta: Sinar Harapan, 1984); L.Y. Andaya, *The World of Maluku: Eastern Indonesia in the Early Modern Period* (Honolulu: University of Hawaii Press, 1993); M.S. Widjojo, *Cross-Cultural Alliance-making and Local Resistance in the Moluccas during the Revolt of Prince Nuku, c. 1780–1810: A Historical-Anthropological Study into the Resistance of the Moluccan vis-à-vis Western Strive for Hegemony and Domination* (Leiden: Brill, forthcoming).
3. J.L. Anderson, "Piracy and World History: An Economic Perspective on Maritime Predation", *Journal of World History* 6 (1995): 175–76.
4. W.A. Hanna, *Indonesian Banda; Colonialism and its Aftermath in the Nutmeg Islands* (Philadelphia: ISHI, 1978), pp. 11, 25–30, 38–41, 49–61; G.J. Knaap, *Kruidnagelen en Christenen; De Verenigde Oost-Indische Compagnie en de bevolking van Ambon 1656–1696* (Leiden: KITLV Press, second revised imprint, 2004), pp. 20–30.
5. Knaap, *Kruidnagelen*, pp. 65, 67, 73.
6. W. Buijze, *De generale lant-beschrijvinge van het Ambonse gouverment ... door G.E. Rumphius* (Den Haag: n.p., 2001), pp. 85–87; Knaap, *Kruidnagelen*, p. 73.
7. Dutch term to designate a sort of governor.
8. P.A. Tiele, *Bouwstoffen voor de geschiedenis der Nederlanders in den Maleischen archipel*, vol. 1 ('s-Gravenhage: Nijhoff, 1886), pp. 304, 331; G.E. Rumphius, "De Ambonse historie behelsende een kort verhaal der gedenkwaardigste geschiedenissen zo in vreede als oorlog [...]", *Bijdragen tot*

       de Taal-, Land- en Volkenkunde 64 (1910) 1, p. 38; Buijze, *Lant-beschrijvinge*, pp. 87, 117.
9. Rumphius, "Ambonse historie" 1, pp. 43, 87.
10. J.E. Heeres, "Corpus Diplomaticum Neerlando-Indicum", vol. 1, *Bijdragen tot de Taal-, Land- en Volkenkunde* 57 (1907), pp. 336, 535; J.E. Heeres, "Corpus Diplomaticum Neerlando-Indicum", vol. 2, *Bijdragen tot de Taal-, Land- en Volkenkunde* 87 (1931), pp. 6, 72; Rumphius, "Ambonse historie", vol. 1, pp. 282–83, 292, 297.
11. National Archives, VOC 1205: pp. 803v–810r; Rumphius, "Ambonse historie", 2, pp. 64–66; Heeres. "Corpus Diplomaticum", vol. 2, p. 72.
12. Knaap, *Kruidnagelen*, p. 74.
13. W.Ph. Coolhaas, *Generale missiven van gouverneurs-generaal en raden aan Heren XVII der Verenigde Oostindische Compagnie*, vol. 4, pp. 242–43; Knaap, *Kruidnagelen*, pp. 74–75.
14. Coolhaas, *Generale missiven*, vol. 4, pp. 405–06; Knaap, *Kruidnagelen*, pp. 75–76.
15. Coolhaas, *Generale missiven*, vol. 4, pp. 604, 713; Knaap, *Kruidnagelen*, p. 76.
16. P.A. Leupe, "De reizen der Nederlanders naar Nieuw-Guinea en de Papoesche eilanden in de 17ᵉ en 18ᵉ eeuw", *Bijdragen tot de Taal-, Land- en Volkenkunde* (1875), p. 104; F.W. Stapel, "Corpus Diplomaticum Neerlando-Indicum", vol. 4, *Bijdragen tot de Taal-, Land- en Volkenkunde* 93 (1935), p. 184; Coolhaas, *Generale Missiven*, vol. 6, p. 105.
17. Andaya, *World of Maluku*, pp. 117, 132–34, 138–43, 152–60.
18. P.A. Tiele and J.E. Heeres, *Bouwstoffen voor de geschiedenis der Nederlanders in den Maleischen archipel*, vol. 2 ('s-Gravenhage: Nijhoff, 1890), pp. 6, 8.
19. Heeres, "Corpus Diplomaticum", vol. 2, pp. 352–53; F.W. Stapel, *Pieter van Dam, Beschrijvinge van de Oostindische Compagnie*, vol. 2-1 ('s-Gravenhage: Nijhoff, 1931), pp. 43, 111; Knaap, *Kruidnagelen*, p. 75.
20. F.W. Stapel, "Corpus Diplomaticum Neerlando-Indicum", vol. 3, *Bijdragen tot de Taal-, Land- en Volkenkunde* 91 (1934), p. 502; Coolhaas, *Generale missiven*, vol. 5, pp. 448, 495.
21. Stapel, "Corpus Diplomaticum", vol. 4, p. 184; W.Ph. Coolhaas, *Generale missiven*, vol. 6, pp. 96, 119, 295.
22. Andaya, *World of Maluku*, pp. 99–100, 192–201.
23. Coolhaas, *Generale missiven*, vol. 5, pp. 394, 448, 585; Coolhaas, *Generale missiven*, vol. 6, p. 672.
24. Rumphius, "Ambonse historie" 2, p. 133; Buijze, *Lant-beschrijvinge*, pp. 89–90.
25. A. Haga, *Nederlandsch Nieuw Guinea en de Papoesche eilanden; Historische bijdrage, ±1500–1883*, vol. 1 (Batavia/'s-Gravenhage: Bruining/Nijhoff, 1884), pp. 135–36.

26. Haga, *Nieuw Guinea*, pp. 17, 65–67, 99, 102–20, 133, 139–40, 176.
27. F.C. Kamma, *Koreri; Messianic Movements in the Biak-Numfor Culture Area* (The Hague: Nijhoff, 1972), pp. 215–17; Andaya, *World of Maluku*, pp. 55–59, 66, 69, 104–06, 172–73, 242–43.
28. Andaya, *World of Maluku*, p. 99; F. Huizinga, "Relations between Tidore and the North Coast of New Guinea in the Nineteenth Century", in J. Miedema, C. Odé, R.A.C. Dam, eds., *Perspectives on the Bird's Head of Irian Jaya, Indonesia (Proceedings of the Conference, Leiden, 13–17 October 1997)* (Amsterdam: Rodopi, 1998), p. 393.
29. Andaya, *World of Maluku*, pp. 101, 107.
30. F.C. Kamma, "De verhouding tussen Tidore en de Papoese eilanden in legende en historie", *Indonesië* 1 (1948), number 4, pp. 364–70, number 6, pp. 536–41, 545; H. Arfan, "Peranan pemerintah tradisional kepulauan Raja Ampat waktu dulu", in E.K.M. Masinambow, ed., *Halmahera dan Raja Ampat sebagai kesatuan majemuk; Studi-studi terhadap suatu daerah transisi* (Jakarta: LEKNAS/LIPI, 1987), pp. 210–11.
31. F. Valentijn, "Beschrijving der Moluccos", *Oud en Nieuw Oost-Indiën*, vol. 1. (Dordrecht/Amsterdam: Van Braam/Onder de Linden, 1724), p. 248; Andaya, *World of Maluku*, pp. 106, 108; R.Z. Leirissa, *Halmahera Timur dan Raja Jailolo; Pergolakan sekitar Laut Seram awal abad 19* (Jakarta: Balai Pustaka, 1996), pp. 107–08, 137.
32. Kamma, "Tidore en de Papoese eilanden", *Indonesië* 2 (1948), number 2, pp. 184–85, number 3, pp. 259–61, 265–68; Huizinga, "Relations", pp. 402–05; Knaap, *Kruidnagelen*, pp. 200–01.
33. Kamma, "Tidore en de Papoese eilanden", *Indonesië* 2 (1948), number 2, pp. 180–83.
34. Arfan, "Pemerintah tradisional", pp. 211–14.
35. J. Miedema and W.A.L. Stokhof, *Memories van overgave van de afdeling West Nieuw-Guinea*, vol. 2 (Leiden: DSALCUL/IRIS, 1993), pp. 322–31.
36. C.R. Boxer and P.-Y. Manguin, "Miguel Roxo de Brito's Narrative of his Voyage to the Raja Empat, May 1581–November 1582", *Archipel* 18 (1979), pp. 177–94; J.H.F. Sollewijn Gelpke, "The Report of Miguel Roxo de Brito of his Voyage in 1581–1582 to the Raja Ampat, the MacCluer Gulf and Seram", *Bijdragen tot de Taal-, Land- en Volkenkunde* 150 (1994), pp. 127–45.
37. P.A. Leupe, "Reizen der Nederlanders", pp. 115–57; G.P. Rouffaer, "De Javaansche naam 'Seran' van Z.W. Nieuw-Guinea vóór 1545; en een rapport van Rumphius over die kust van 1684", *Tijdschrift van het Koninklijk Nederlandsch Aardrijkskundig Genootschap* 25 (1908), pp. 316–25.
38. VOC 1205, pp. 806v–08v.
39. VOC 1240, p. 795.
40. VOC 8075, pp. 880–85.
41. Coolhaas, *Generale missiven*, vol. 6, pp. 329, 386, 387, 414.

42. Leupe, "Reizen der Nederlanders", pp. 212–17.
43. VOC 1662, pp. 133–40.
44. Leupe, "Reizen der Nederlanders", pp. 220–23, 240–47.
45. VOC 8074, pp. 557–60, 583–84; VOC 8075, pp. 636, 648, 656.
46. Leupe, "Reizen der Nederlanders", pp. 223–40; Andaya, *World of Maluku*, pp. 101-02.
47. VOC 8074, pp. 628–29, 631–35, 643, 648–49.
48. VOC 8075, pp. 416–18, 450–65, 496–98, 511–21; F.S.A de Clerq, "Het gebied der kalana fat of vier radja's in westelijk Nieuw-Guinea", *De Indische Gids* 11 (1889), pp. 1312–13.
49. VOC 8075, pp. 527–30, 533–35, 540–43.
50. VOC 8075, pp. 545–48, 557–65, 572, 585, 597, 601, 605; De Clerq, "Kalana fat", p. 106.
51. A. Haga, "Het rapport van H. Zwaardecroon en C. Chasteleijn betreffende de reis naar Nieuw Guinea in 1705 ondernomen door Jacob Weyland", *Tijdschrift voor Indische Taal-, Land- en Volkenkunde* 30 (1885), pp. 236–37, 245–58.
52. J. Miedema and G. Reesink, *One Head, Many Faces; New Perspectives on the Bird's Head Peninsula of New Guinea* (Leiden: KITLV Press, 2004), p. 62.
53. T. Goodman, "The Sosolot Exchange Network of Eastern Indonesia during the Seventeenth and Eighteenth Centuries", in J. Miedema, C. Odé, R.A.C. Dam, eds., *Perspectives on the Bird's Head of Irian Jaya, Indonesia (Proceedings of the Conference, Leiden, 13–17 October 1997)* (Amsterdam: Rodopi, 1998), pp. 430–34, 436–40.
54. J. Miedema, "Trade, Migration, and Exchange; The Bird's Head Peninsula of Irian Jaya in a Comparative Perspective", in A.J. Strathern and G. Stürzenhofecker, eds., *Migration and Transformations: Regional Perspectives on New Guinea* (Pittsburgh: University of Pittsburgh Press, 1994), pp. 123–24, 133; Miedema and Reesink, *One Head*, pp. 63–68, 116, 183.
55. J. Miedema, *De Kebar 1855–1980; Sociale structuur en religie in de Vogelkop van West-Nieuw-Guinea* (Dordrecht: Foris, 1984), pp. 5–6; J. Timmer, *Living with Intricate Futures: Order and Confusion in Imyan Worlds, Irian Jaya, Indonesia* (Nijmegen: Centre for Pacific and Asian Studies, 2000), pp. 66, 119–22, 167.
56. G.J. Held, *The Papuas of Waropen* (The Hague: Nijhoff, 1957), pp. 198, 200–03, 207–10, 213–16, 223–26, 229–31.
57. E. Velthoen, "'Wanderers, Robbers and Bad Folk': The Politics of Violence, Protection and Trade in Eastern Sulawesi 1750–1850", in A. Reid, ed., *The Last Stand of Asian Autonomies: Responses to Modernity in the Diverse States of Southeast Asia and Korea, 1750–1900* (London/New York: MacMillan/St. Martins, 1997), pp. 368–69.
58. Warren, *Sulu Zone*, pp. 146, 167.

59. Anderson, "Piracy", pp. 177–80; J.N.F.M. à Campo, "Zeeroof, bestuurlijke beeldvorming en beleid", in G. Teitler, A.M.C. van Dissel and J.N.F.M. à Campo, eds., *Zeeroof en zeeroofbestrijding in de Indische archipel (19de eeuw)* (Amsterdam: Bataafsche Leeuw, 2005), pp. 119–22.
60. Warren, *Sulu Zone*, pp. 207–08.
61. Knaap, *Kruidnagelen*, pp. 14–15, 76–79.
62. Velthoen, "Wanderers", p. 370; G.J. Knaap, "Kora-kora en kruitdamp; De Verenigde Oost-Indische Compagnie in oorlog en vrede in Ambon", in G. Knaap and G. Teitler, eds., *De Verenigde Oost-Indische Compagnie tussen oorlog en diplomatie* (Leiden: KITLV Press, 2002), pp. 259–63.

References

Archival sources

National Archives, The Hague.
———. VOC 1205: 803v–10r. Summary report of the journey of Simon Cos to the Papuan Islands, in Arnold de Vlaming van Oudshoorn's journal dated 30 December 1653.
———. VOC 1240: 775–826. Memoir of transfer of office of Simon Cos, 23 May 1662.
———. VOC 1662: 132–45. Report of Jan van Benthem and Frans Ernst of an expedition to the Papuan Islands, 17 August 1702.
———. VOC 8074: 534–99. Journal of Pieter Kleijn and Adolph Johan van der Laan of an expedition to the Papuan Islands, 9 October 1704.
———. VOC 8074: 627–59. Instruction for Pieter Lijn and Jacob van Gijn for an expedition to the Papuan Islands, 30 May 1705.
———. VOC 8075: 414–605. Journal of Pieter Lijn and Jacob van Gijn of an expedition to the Papuan Islands, 7 June 1706.
———. VOC 8075: 605–72. Journal of Adolph Johan van der Laan of an expedition to the Papuan Islands, 3 November 1705.
———. VOC 8075: 846–99. Short description of the Moluccas by Pieter Rooselaar, 1 March 1706.

Printed sources and literature

Andaya, L.Y. *The World of Maluku; Eastern Indonesia in the Early Modern Period.* Honolulu: University of Hawaii Press, 1993.
Anderson, J.L. "Piracy and World History: An Economic Perspective on Maritime Predation". *Journal of World History* 6 (1995): 175–99.
Arfan, H. "Peranan pemerintah tradisional kepulauan Raja Ampat waktu dulu". In *Halmahera dan Raja Ampat sebagai kesatuan majemuk: Studi-studi terhadap*

suatu daerah transisi, edited by E.K.M. Masinambow. Jakarta: LEKNAS/LIPI, 1987, pp. 209–16.

Boxer, C.R. and P.-Y. Manguin. "Miguel Roxo de Brito's Narrative of his Voyage to the Raja Empat, May 1581–November 1582". *Archipel* 18 (1979): 175–94.

Buijze, W. *De generale lant-beschrijvinge van het Ambonse gouvernment ... door G.E. Rumphius.* 's-Gravenhage: n.p., 2001.

Campo, J.N.F.M. à. "Zeeroof, bestuurlijke beeldvorming en beleid". In *Zeeroof en zeeroofbestrijding in de Indische archipel (19de eeuw)*, edited by G. Teitler, A.M.C. van Dissel, and J.N.F.M. à Campo. Amsterdam: Bataafsche Leeuw, 2005, pp. 25–133.

Clercq, F.S.A. de. "Het gebied der kalana fat of vier radja's in westelijk Nieuw-Guinea". *De Indische Gids* 11 (1889): 1297–351.

Coolhaas, W.Ph. *Generale missiven van gouverneurs-generaal en raden aan Heren XVII der Verenigde Oostindische Compagnie.* 's-Gravenhage: Nijhoff, 1960–79. 7 vols. Rijks Geschiedkundige Publicatiën, 104, 112, 125, 134, 150, 159, 164.

Goodman, T. "The Sosolot Exchange Network of Eastern Indonesia during the Seventeenth and Eighteenth Centuries". In *Perspectives on the Bird's Head of Irian Jaya, Indonesia: Proceedings of the Conference, Leiden, 13–17 October 1997*, edited by J. Miedema, C. Odé, R.A.C. Dam. Amsterdam: Rodopi, 1998, pp. 421–54.

Haga, A. *Nederlandsch Nieuw Guinea en de Papoesche eilanden; Historische bijdrage, ±1500–1883.* vol. 1. Batavia/'s-Gravenhage: Bruining/Nijhoff, 1884.

———. "Het rapport van H. Zwaardecroon en C. Chasteleijn betreffende de reis naar Nieuw Guinea in 1705 ondernomen door Jacob Weyland". *Tijdschrift voor Indische Taal-, Land- en Volkenkunde* 30 (1885): 235–58.

Hanna, W.A. *Indonesian Banda; Colonialism and its Aftermath in the Nutmeg Islands.* Philadelphia: ISHI, 1978.

Heeres, J.E. *Bouwstoffen voor de geschiedenis der Nederlanders in den Maleischen archipel.* vol. 3. 's-Gravenhage: Nijhoff, 1895.

———. "Corpus Diplomaticum Neerlando-Indicum". vol. 1. *Bijdragen tot de Taal-, Land- en Volkenkunde* 57 (1907).

———. "Corpus Diplomaticum Neerlando-Indicum". vol. 2. *Bijdragen tot de Taal-, Land- en Volkenkunde* 87 (1931).

Held, G.J. *The Papuas of Waropen.* The Hague: Nijhoff, 1957. Koninklijk Instituut voor Taal-, Land- en Volkenkunde, Translation Series 2.

Huizinga, F. "Relations between Tidore and the North Coast of New Guinea in the Nineteenth Century". In *Perspectives on the Bird's Head of Irian Jaya, Indonesia: Proceedings of the Conference, Leiden, 13–17 October 1997*, edited by J. Miedema, C. Odé, and R.A.C. Dam. Amsterdam: Rodopi, 1998, pp. 385–419.

Kamma, F.C. "De verhouding tussen Tidore en de Papoese eilanden in legende en historie", *Indonesië* 1 (1948), number 4, 361–70, number 6, 536–59; 2 (1948), number 2, 177–87, number 3, 256–75.

———. *Koreri; Messianic Movements in the Biak-Numfor Culture Area*. The Hague: Nijhoff, 1972. Koninklijk Instituut voor Taal-, Land- en Volkenkunde, Translation Series 15.

Katoppo, E. *Nuku, Sultan Saidul Jehad Muhamad El Mabus Amirudin Syah, kaicil paparangan, Sultan Tidore: Riwayat perjuangan kemerdekaan Indonesia di Maluku Utara 1780–1805*. Jakarta: Sinar Harapan, 1984.

Knaap, G.J. "Kora-kora en kruitdamp; De Verenigde Oost-Indische Compagnie in oorlog en vrede in Ambon". In *De Verenigde Oost-Indische Compagnie tussen oorlog en diplomatie*, edited by G. Knaap and G. Teitler. Leiden: KITLV Press, 2002, pp. 257–81. Verhandelingen Koninklijk Instituut voor Taal-, Land- en Volkenkunde 197.

———. *Kruidnagelen en Christenen: De Verenigde Oost-Indische Compagnie en de bevolking van Ambon 1656–1696*. Leiden: KITLV Press, second revised imprint, 2004. Verhandelingen Koninklijk Instituut voor Taal-, Land- en Volkenkunde 212.

Lapian, A.B. *Orang laut, bajak laut, raja laut; Sejarah kawasan Laut Sulawesi pada abad XIX*. Yogyakarta: Ph.D. dissertation Universitas Gadjah Mada, 1987.

Leeden, A.C. van der. "The Raja Ampat Islands: A mythological interpretation". In *Halmahera dan Raja Ampat sebagai kesatuan majemuk: Studi-studi terhadap suatu daerah transisi*, edited by E.K.M. Masinambow. Jakarta: LEKNAS/LIPI, 1987, pp. 217–44.

Leirissa, R.Z. *Halmahera Timur dan Raja Jailolo: Pergolakan sekitar Laut Seram awal abad 19*. Jakarta: Balai Pustaka, 1996.

Leupe, P.A. "De reizen der Nederlanders naar Nieuw-Guinea en de Papoesche eilanden in de 17[e] en 18[e] eeuw". *Bijdragen tot de Taal-, Land- en Volkenkunde* 22 (1875): 1–162, 175–307.

Miedema, J. *De Kebar 1855–1980: Sociale structuur en religie in de Vogelkop van West-Nieuw-Guinea*. Dordrecht: Foris, 1984. Verhandelingen Koninklijk Instituut voor Taal-, Land- en Volkenkunde 105.

———. "Trade, Migration, and Exchange: The Bird's Head Peninsula of Irian Jaya in a Comparative Perspective". In *Migration and Transformations: Regional Perspectives on New Guinea*, edited by A.J. Strathern and G. Stürzenhofecker. Pittsburgh: University of Pittsburgh Press, 1994, pp. 121–54.

Miedema, J. and G. Reesink. *One Head, Many Faces; New Perspectives on the Bird's Head Peninsula of New Guinea*. Leiden: KITLV Press, 2004. Verhandelingen Koninklijk Instituut voor Taal-, Land- en Volkenkunde 219.

Miedema, J. and W.A.L. Stokhof. *Memories van overgave van de afdeling West Nieuw-Guinea*. vol. 2. Leiden: DSALCUL/IRIS, 1993. Irian Jaya Source Materials 6.

Rouffaer, G.P. "De Javaansche naam 'Seran' van Z.W. Nieuw-Guinea vóór 1545: en een rapport van Rumphius over die kust van 1684". *Tijdschrift van het Koninklijk Nederlandsch Aardrijkskundig Genootschap* 25 (1908): 308–47.

Rumphius, G.E. "De Ambonse historie behelsende een kort verhaal der gedenkwaardigste geschiedenissen zo in vreede als oorlog [...]". Two parts in one volume. *Bijdragen tot de Taal-, Land- en Volkenkunde* 64 (1910).

Sollewijn Gelpke, J.H.F. "The Report of Miguel Roxo de Brito of his Voyage in 1581–1582 to the Raja Ampat, the MacCluer Gulf and Seram". *Bijdragen tot de Taal-, Land- en Volkenkunde* 150 (1994): 123–45.

Stapel, F.W. *Pieter van Dam, Beschrijvinge van de Oostindische Compagnie*, vol. 2-1. 's-Gravenhage: Nijhoff, 1931. Rijks Geschiedkundige Publicatiën 74.

———. "Corpus Diplomaticum Neerlando-Indicum". Volume 3. *Bijdragen tot de Taal-, Land- en Volkenkunde* 91 (1934).

———. "Corpus Diplomaticum Neerlando-Indicum". Volume 4. *Bijdragen tot de Taal-, Land- en Volkenkunde* 93 (1935).

Tiele, P.A. *Bouwstoffen voor de geschiedenis der Nederlanders in den Maleischen archipel*. Volume 1. 's-Gravenhage: Nijhoff, 1886.

Tiele, P.A. and J.E. Heeres. *Bouwstoffen voor de geschiedenis der Nederlanders in den Maleischen archipel*. Volume 2. 's-Gravenhage: Nijhoff, 1890.

Timmer, J. *Living with Intricate Futures: Order and Confusion in Imyan Worlds, Irian Jaya, Indonesia*. Nijmegen: Centre for Pacific and Asian Studies, 2000.

Valentijn, F. *Oud en Nieuw Oost-Indiën*. Volume 1. "Beschrijving der Moluccos". Dordrecht/Amsterdam: Van Braam/Onder de Linden, 1724.

Velthoen, E.J. "Wanderers, Robbers and Bad Folk: The Politics of Violence, Protection and Trade in Eastern Sulawesi 1750–1850". In *The Last Stand of Asian Autonomies; Responses to Modernity in the Diverse States of Southeast Asia and Korea, 1750–1900*, edited by A. Reid. London/New York: MacMillan/St. Martins, 1997, pp. 367–88.

Warren, J.F. *The Sulu Zone, 1768–1898; The Dynamics of External Trade, Slavery, and Ethnicity in the Transformation of a Southeast Asian Maritime State*. Singapore: Singapore University Press, 1981.

———. *Iranun and Balangingi; Globalization, Maritime Raiding and the Birth of Ethnicity*. Singapore: Singapore University Press, 2002.

Widjojo, M.S. *Cross-Cultural Alliance-making and Local Resistance in the Moluccas during the Revolt of Prince Nuku, c. 1780–1810: A Historical-Anthropological Study into the Resistance of the Moluccan vis-à-vis Western Strive for Hegemony and Domination*. Leiden: Brill, forthcoming.

9

The Port of Jolo: International Trade and Slave Raiding

James Warren

The impact of the West's commercial intrusion in China at the end of the eighteenth century had significant bearing on the growth of the slave trade in Southeast Asia. It led to the establishment of permanent slave traffic around organized markets and ports in the Sulu Zone. Jolo island with its port(s), as the centre of a redistributive network encompassing the Sulu Zone, became one of the most important slaving centres by 1800.[1] For several centuries, the Sulu-Mindanao region had been known for "piracy", and slavery. However, by the early nineteenth century, entire ethnic groups — Iranun and Balangingi — had specialized in state sanctioned maritime slave raiding, attacking Southeast Asian coastal settlements and trading vessels bound for the Spice Islands, or for Singapore, Manila, and Batavia. Consequently, much of eastern Indonesia was to be scoured clean of labour power. At this critical juncture in the political and economic development of the Sulu sultanate, Iranun and Balangingi slaving and raiding evolved into large-scale operations and massive raids were conducted throughout the Philippines. Jolo was described by one British emissary as, "the greatest slave mart and thieves market in the whole of the East Indian Islands. The pirate fleets return here after their long cruise to sell their slaves and booty and buy supplies from the Chinese and Bugis merchants".[2]

A key factor in Jolo's ascendancy as a slaving port, seat of the sultanate, and regional entrepot, was Europe's globalizing trade with China. The West's search for suitable local commodities to exchange for Chinese tea is certainly the most convincing explanation of the origin of the Sulu sultanate's startling regional expansion to the west and south.[3] Here the broad backdrop of the Sulu Zone provides the setting to enquire into the struggles and misunderstandings that linked patterns of consumption and

FIGURE 9.1
Late Eighteenth-century *Joanga*

Source: A late eighteenth century *joanga* (*lanong*), an Iranun maritime raider, with three banks of oars, under full sail. Upward of 100 feet long, these vessels were provided with large bamboo outriggers, both sides were rowed and paddled by more than 150 men. The biggest Iranun raids were directed against the Philippines, especially southern Luzon. (Courtesy Museo Naval, Rafael Mouleon, Construccion Navales)

"frontiers" of desire in Europe, China, and Southeast Asia with particular entangled commodities, maritime spaces, and cultural geographies.

The insatiable demands of the sultanate for labour to harvest and procure exotic natural commodities reached a peak in the first half of the nineteenth century as the China trade flourished. For the sultan with his port-capital, the entrepot and neighbouring areas incorporated a set of cultural-institutional practices, typical of centralized trading states, based on redistribution for the production and acquisition of trade goods on the one hand, and kinship, warfare, slavery, and other forms of organization and culture on the other. Within the Sulu zone, centres of distribution and exchange developed and, in association with the development of larger interregional markets, capital flows, and technology transfers, international trade increased and the sultanate established itself as a major regional entrepot and slave emporium. When notable English country traders first came to Sulu in the 1760s they had already recognized its potential as an inexhaustible source of exotic natural commodities for the China trade.[4] The steady influx of captives and slaves to collect and process these commodities for the thriving Canton trade made the Sulu sultanate one of the most strategic cultural crossroads to conduct global-local commerce in insular Southeast Asia.

By the nineteenth century, the population of the Sulu sultanate was heterogeneous and changing socially, economically, and ethnically, as a direct result of external trade. The populating of the Sulu Zone by captives and slaves from the Philippines and various parts of the Malay world, and their role in the redistributional economy centred at Jolo, was not fully understood by the colonial powers at the time. In the eyes of European observers Sulu was regarded as hostile to their interests — an Islamic world whose activities centred about slavery and piracy.

One feature of the global interconnections between Sulu slavery and the advent of the capitalist world economy was the rapid, systematic movement of maritime slave raiding across the entire region, as one Southeast Asian coastal population after another was hunted down. From 1768 to 1848, Southeast Asia felt the full force of the slave raiders of the Sulu Sultanate. During this period, Sulu became known as a "pirate and slave state", in the minds of early nineteenth century Europeans and Jolo as the nerve centre for the coordination of slave raiding and marketing. One of the earliest published references to Jolo at this time was from French navigator Pierre Sonnerat. He states: "… the harbour serves as a retreat for the moors, who roam over the seas as pirates, molesting the navigation of the Spaniards, and sometimes carry off with them the people of the colonies, in their incursions, whom they make slaves".⁵ In return for providing security, equipment, vessels, and sometimes crew to the Iranun and Balangingi, the Taosug dato received in exchange wealth in the form of exotic natural commodities and slaves as physical labour power. Slavery and slave raiding had become fundamental to the state.

KNOW YOUR ENEMY: SOURCES OF INTELLIGENCE ON THE SULU SLAVE TRADE

Spain chose to wage a defensive "sea war" in Philippine waters against the Iranun and Balangingi by creating deterrents to raiding such as cruising, construction of coastal defences, and building *vinta* and *barangyan*.⁶ These methods were preferred over a pre-emptive strategy against the principal centres of Iranun and Balangingi, raiding, and the occupation of the port of Jolo. Such a strategy was not in the best interests of the Manila administration which was in the ironic position of developing regional trade with Sulu, a trade that was inadvertently predicated on the slaving and piracy it so religiously decried.

In the eyes of the Dutch and British the Iranun and Balangingi were considered the scourge of the seas from Papua to the Strait of Malacca. The Dutch and British realized that if they ignored them they would become bigger, more dangerous, and equipped with ever more sophisticated raiding technology. In the first half of the nineteenth century, Philippine and eastern Indonesian waters had the highest risk of coastal and maritime attack with cases increasing every year. At that time, the total number of Iranun sea raiders conservatively numbered between 10,000–15,000. J. Hunt, an East India company servant, was dispatched to the Sulu archipelago, shortly after the occupation of Java in 1811. Hunt identified twelve piratical establishments belonging to Sulu, of which the total fleet was estimated at 200 *perahu*, and above 8,000 slave raiders.⁷

In Hunt's account of Sulu he charged the sultan with participating in the profits of the "pirates" of the Sulu-Mindano region. Some of the Iranun and Balangingi prisoners who, after an 1838 trial in Singapore, were brought once again before the Admiralty Court, corroborated Hunt's statement maintaining that "to this day the sultan still continues to receive a certain portion of the plunder from the boats on their return to Sooloo".⁸ When Captain Belcher visited Jolo in the mid-1840s, he was repeatedly reassured by leading Taosug dato that they had no connection whatsoever with these maritime raiders who preferred "self destruction to submitting to capture".⁹

But during his stay in Jolo, several Balangingi *perahu* arrived and he was informed that slaves captured in the Philippines by these vessels were exchanged in the local market. In Belcher's mind, this "event" was proof of the fact that the sultan and *dato* had created a complex interdependent political and economic system to regulate the slave trade and the activities of slave raiding ships based in the Sulu zone.

During the 1830s and 1840s handpicked colonial naval commanders were dispatched in the struggle to rid the region of slaving and raiding. They exchanged intelligence and published warnings about arms trading and its links to Iranun-Balangingi raiding,[10] and were also in charge of surveillance operations, cruising, and search and destroy missions. However, during this period these measures proved fruitless and regional-wide sightings of heavily armed "Illanoon" expeditions and attacks on settlements and coastal shipping rose steadily.

To the Spanish, the Iranun and Balangingi, were the arch-enemy.[11] A Spanish writer described the misery inflicted by them on the inhabitants of the archipelago over an eighty-six year period as a chapter in the history of Spain and the Philippines "written in blood and tears and nourished in pain and suffering".[12] The Iranun and Balangingi raids were persistent, well-organized, on a huge scale, and almost always launched from the sea.[13]

Friars, in beleaguered towns and villages on Luzon, Cebu, Bohol, Leyte, and Samar, depicted the Iranun raiders as savages and plunderers. Their accounts may have been exaggerated, due to the fear and horror of a Muslim enemy. Generally, however, their information corresponds closely with other accounts of Iranun slave raids written by merchant traders such as Thomas Forrest in the very different cultural atmosphere of cosmopolitan Jolo and neighbouring Malayo-Muslim states.

The naval authorities recognized that the accounts of merchant traders, friars, and the intelligence provided by fugitive captives and captured slavers, allowed them to comprehend better the forces that shaped the way of life of the Iranun and Balangingi. Most statements and captivity narratives have a first person observer-narrator — an authentic voice of experience attempting to present a testimony or narrative that usually contains similarities with other accounts dealing with the same subjects. The statements contain data on the social status of slaves, their occupations, and roles on board the slaving vessels. Given that Spanish and Dutch strategic interests required information on the social organization of maritime slave raiding and ethnic interrelations, it follows that evidence given in interrogations revolved around these issues.

AN 1845 REPORT ON SLAVE MARKETING IN JOLO

In an effort to understand the wide ranging activities of these slave raiders, and to unravel the structural basis of the system of socio-political organization which united them, it was necessary also to gather vital intelligence about their way of life from European traders travelling between Manila and Jolo. In the twenty years after 1807, the number of Spanish vessels involved in the trade doubled. Native sailing craft were replaced by brigantines and frigates as Spanish vessels in increasing numbers visited Sulu. Rare fragments of evidence suggest that occasionally Spanish captains who entered the port of Jolo maintained a confidential log of occurrences during their stay, replete with observations on current political developments, the number of slaving vessels entering the bay and harbour, and estimates on the numbers captured and brought to be sold.[14] One such individual was the Spanish merchant captain, Juan Bautista Barrera. Barrera moored in Jolo from May to September 1845, during which time many fugitive captives escaped to his vessel. He comments in his daily log:

> Regarding several captives who have escaped from this evil town several days ago, there is a rumor (circulating) amongst these moros that I have a boatload of captives from Jolo (sad to say this is not true). However, my local agent and go-between, as well as myself, have already told these swine that they can come on board whenever they wished to do so. On the 19th September, at 10 o'clock in the evening, about 18 moros went to the house of my agent, telling him that they knew that I had hidden many captives, men and women (it is a fact that I indeed had some on board, but all of them were from distant towns) and if none of them were given up, they would kill me, or any my crew that they could catch.[15]

Barrera also noted that almost all the Iranun and Balangingi slaving commanders who visited Jolo to trade did so without any interference from the sultan.[16] He soon discovered too that the Taosug merchants, or "rogues and riff-raff of this wretched town", when they did not have sufficient goods to meet their outstanding obligations, also visited Balangingi where they were given captives on credit to be trafficked to Borneo and exchanged for *trepang*, and birds nests.[17] By September, the scale of the slaving activity led the Spanish captain to note in his log on 15 September: "This afternoon, 5 *pancos* anchored carrying forty captives." He then added in brackets "(at this moment in time life seems have dealt us a mortal blow!)"[18]

Nonetheless, from the late 1830s until the mid 1850s, one trader in particular was to supply vital inside information about the slave trade at the port of Jolo. This information would enable English and Spanish naval intelligence to conduct field operations against the Iranun and Balangingi in a more lethal manner. William Wyndham had firmly established Sulu's trade link with Singapore by the early 1840s.[19] By 1842 the self-educated merchant adventurer had settled at Jolo and owned his own schooner, the *Velocipede*. From his commercial establishment in Jolo's Chinese quarter, he frequented the Aru Islands to procure tortoise shell and mother of pearl for customers in Singapore. Married to a *mestiza* from Iloilo, Wyndham spoke fluent Taosug and Visayan and had acquired considerable status and authority in Jolo. In 1848, Spencer St. John described him as being "dressed in Malay costume and from long residence among them, he assumed much of both the appearance and manner of a native".[20] Not surprisingly, many Manila-based Spanish captains who traded at Jolo repeatedly accused him of trafficking with the Taosug and Iranun in munitions, saltpetre, and opium.

Wyndham possessed great influence with the Taosug, who made him a *datu*. He ransomed dozens of captives from his trading base at Jolo and acted as intermediary on behalf of others in their ransom dealings and negotiations with Spanish captains.[21] In September 1845, Barrera described Wyndham's efforts to ransom and free captives, in the aftermath of the punitive expedition of the Spanish warship *Esperanza*, in the following manner:

> Don Guillermo, as well as his brother-in-law, is admired by the many captives whom they have brought and are bringing since the departure of the war frigate from this port. He says that in the eighteen or twenty years of travelling to this infamous port, he has never seen so many captives being trafficked, and that the atrocities committed by the pirates in the Visayas and the provinces to the North are a great shame.[22]

After the expedition, the Spanish governor general left an advance column of troops and engineers behind to establish a small fort on the island of Basilan. The small, well fortified outpost, flying the Spanish flag in the heartland of the sultanate attracted immediate Taosug attention. Barrera's log notes that on 18 August, five Iranun vessels from Basilan entered the port, reporting to the sultan that the governor of Zamboanga had established a fort on the island. The Sultan organized an Iranun flotilla giving them cannon and other equipment either to drive out, or destroy the governor's representative and his garrison on Basilan. If they did not leave peaceably, the Iranun were either to kill him, or imprison him and his men, in order to "send a message about the temertiy of the Spaniards, wishing to govern in a domain that does not belong to them".[23] Wyndham and the Spanish merchant both got wind of the planned expedition and attempted to warn the governor of Zamboanga, but the sultan set up a zone of interdiction for all vessels entering and leaving the port of Jolo.[24]

Fearing possible English or Dutch intrusion in the Sulu archipelago, Spain had adopted a hard line along the borders of its southern frontier and had attempted to destroy the Samal "pirate nests" on Balangingi with a major military expedition in 1845. This initial offensive shook the confidence of the Taosug and convinced them of the necessity for English friendship and trade. The sultanate severed its well established commercial tie with Manila and welcomed the assistance of James Brooke, the ambitious governor of Labuan, who sought to protect Sulu from the Spanish embrace while destroying the Iranun stranglehold on the trade and traffic of north Borneo. However, by the mid-1840s the Spanish had formulated a strategic plan of occupying key positions in the Iranun-Balangingi heartlands. The theory now expressed by Spanish naval experts, was to control Iranun and Balangingi "piracy" at the source by establishing forward bases for naval operations and as places of refuge for victims of Iranun and Balangingi aggression. A Spanish naval officer, reconnoitring Balangingi in a disguised sailing craft in 1842, had already described the Sulu sultanate's key raiding base, slowly but surely improving Manila's naval intelligence about this island bastion.

On the basis of such intelligence, Governor Claveria, to protect Spain's claim to sovereignty over the Sulu archipelago, established the fort on Basilan and authorized a major expedition against the Balangingi in 1845. Although the expedition had been ill-prepared and ultimately failed, the Spanish managed for the first time to completely reconnoitre the Samalese group, and formed a detailed picture of the topography, defences, and population of Balangingi.[25] Armed with this information, Claveria devoted several years to organizing a far more formidable expedition. Claveria understood that control of Balangingi would cut the Sulu archipelago in two and largely curtail slave raiding in the Philippines.

Barrera wrote in his log on 29 July 1845 that the sultan, still smarting from the Spanish attack against Balangingi, had ordered that no more Iranun and Balangingi slaving *perahu* were to enter the port of Jolo because he realized that their movements were now being monitored and reported to the government of Manila by individuals such as Wyndham and Barrera. The Spanish captain then concludes: "The Sultan does not want it to be said (in government circles) that Jolo is the major emporium for captives and slaves, as he is afraid that some heavily armed vessels will come to initiate a war against them".[26] Less than a month later, this concern to placate the

Spanish did not prevent the sultan from planning with his Iranun allies to destroy the newly established Spanish outpost on Basilan and block all trade between there and Zamboanga.[27]

The growth of the sultanate's population had not kept pace with its expanding globalized economy. The West's desire for natural commodities acceptable in Chinese markets promoted an intensification of Taosug sponsored Iranun-Samal slaving expeditions to seize captives to work in the fisheries and forests of the sultanate's domain. These captives procured commodities such as *trepang*, mother of pearl, and tortoise shell which European traders used to barter for tea in China. The gunpowder and firearms supplied by these same merchants allowed the coastal dwelling Taosug to promote maritime slave raiding on a hitherto unprecedented scale and kept the Sulu-Mindanao region free of neighbouring competitors and colonial intruders until the late 1840s.

THE WORKINGS OF A SLAVE PORT

It is difficult to estimate the annual number of Filipinos lost to maritime slave raiding through captivity and death at the end of the eighteenth century. In 1761, the bishop of Nueva Caceres, southern Luzon, was unable to provide an overall figure for the decline in the population of his provinces, but conservatively estimated the loss in Camarines alone between 1759–60 to be 800 people.[28] In 1817, more than half a century later, the bishop estimated that raiders captured more than 1,500 people, predominately boys and girls from the *cabeceras* and *visitas* of Albay, Camarines and Tayabas.[29] By 1830, the intensity of Balangingi slave-raiding supports an estimate that 750–1,500 Filipinos were carried off or killed from Nueva Caceres alone, annually. Furthermore, the cumulative totals rose in the first half of the nineteenth century at an annual rate that was greater than in the last quarter of the eighteenth century. However, losses from slave raids varied considerably in different parts of the archipelago. Cruikshank conservatively estimates that 100 inhabitants of Samar were either captured or killed each year between 1768 and 1858.[30]

The Balangingi slavers were forced to rely on the Taosug credit system to sustain their food supply. Rice was either brought directly to the Samal islands in Taosug trading *perahu* or obtained in Jolo at the advanced rate of thirty cavans per slave in 1836. The extent to which the Balangingi were at the mercy of their environment is reflected in the annual turnover of large numbers of captives and slaves by the Samal raiders to the Taosug for advances (or payment of previous advances) of rice and war stores. In 1836, Mariano Sevilla estimated that the Balangingi had seized more than a thousand captives from the Philippines by September, of which two-thirds had already been taken to Jolo.[31] Nine years later, Barrera's daily log, tracking the number of Balangingi *garay*[32] entering Jolo, and the numbers captured and brought to be sold in the port, indicates that the slave trade had continued to escalate. His invaluable register begins on 24 May, noting the arrival at three o'clock in the afternoon of three Balangingi vessels with forty-five captives; four days later, at ten in the morning, two slaving vessels came into the port with twenty captives. Five entries appear in the log for June, suggesting that the slave raiders tended to maintain a weekly cycle and never arrived with more than four large vessels at any one time; 3 June, five o'clock in the afternoon, a single large vessel with eight captives; a week later, four large *garay* anchored with twenty-eight captives; 15 June, three *garay* anchored with two raiding canoes which carried eighteen captives, amongst them men, women, and children; at midday a week later, two *garay* arrived with eighteen captives; the last entry for the month, 30 June, saw four *garay* arrive, with thirty-two captives; amongst them seven women and five boys and girls.[33]

The log also records on 13 July disturbing news about the magnitude of the traffic. Wyndham and Barrera had learned from the Balangingi commander of a slave raider that between two and three thousand Visayans had already been enslaved by July of that year. In addition, they discovered that the Balangingi had sent out no fewer than eighty *garay* to avenge the damage wrought by the Spanish war frigate, *Esperanza,* against their island stronghold. Five days later on 18 July Barrera wrote: "From a pirate vessel that has just arrived, I have learned that 20 days ago, more than 120 Visayans had been captured in Romblon, Mindoro, Surigao and Panay. This vessel brought ten captives."[34] There are six entries for the month of July, indicating that the slavers tended to visit the Jolo port on a weekly basis. Barrera found out from their crew that the eighty slave raiders sent out the previous month had already captured more than 250 people.[35]

In early August, eight smaller slaving vessels arrived and anchored, bringing thirty captives. Barrera notes that the sultan had "turned a blind eye" to these vessels. Then completing his entry for 2 August, he implicates the sultan in the slave trade.

> To this I say: in my view of these events, and from the things that I have found out from these Joloanos, the Balangingi will never stop bringing

captives, being encouraged to do so by the Sultan right down to the last vile datu. They are the ones who provide the pirates with all kinds of warstores, to such a great extent that the above mentioned William Wyndham as well as the three of us Spaniards who are involved in this(trade), realize that everyone from the Sultan on down, are knaves. If we were to write down everything that has happened since the departure from here of the frigate *Esperanza,* a hundred reams of paper would not suffice.[36]

The human traffic continued throughout August with the confidential log listing five visits to the port between the second and eighteenth of the month. Large numbers of captives and slaves were being brought to Jolo on a weekly basis; the entry for 15 August reads as follows: "Eight vintas came in with 35 captives. They say they still have to bring in 100 more captives."[37] Three days later mention is made for the first time that the *dato* also travelled directly to Balangingi, where they obtained captives on credit to be taken to Borneo to be exchanged for birds' nests and sea cucumber.[38] Between 3 and 23 September when Barrera wrote his last entry in the log, there were nine separate occasions when groups of two to five large slaving vessels arrived bringing captives. Again, the scale and intensity of the slave raiding taking place in late 1845 was reflected upon by Wyndham and Barrera on 6 September: "4 garay arrived; with 35 captives captured 25 days ago in Panay and Mindoro. From the 20th of August up to the 4th of September, they have captured about 210 captives, according to information from these same pirates."[39] In other words, the Balangingi were seizing about a 100 captives a week, just in the central Visayas. Six days later, the daily log lists three very big *garay* anchoring at ten o'clock in the morning, with forty captives who had been seized thirty-five days previously in Masbate, Romblon, and Panay. Barrera then penned the following ominous observation in brackets: "…(if at this stage they go out slave raiding again right away (*pronto*) in the Visayas, some provinces will become totally uninhabited)".[40]

INDIVIDUAL FATES

Based on the intelligence gathered with the assistance of Wyndham and his brother-in-law, glimpses of the experience of the captives from the time of their seizure to their arrival and exchange in Jolo, emerge from anonymity in the weekly entries in Captain Barrera's daily confidential log. This information throws light on the internal workings of the slave trade and its conduct in the bay of Jolo in the middle of the nineteenth century. In Jolo many factors were taken into consideration when determining the value of individual slaves in the market. The prices varied with sex, age, ethnicity, and personal condition, as well as demand. The highest prices were reserved for young women (who could be offered as wives and concubines to recruit warriors to a *dato*'s retinue) and adolescents and children (who were considered malleable and more readily incorporated into Taosug or Samal society).[41] There appears to have been a standard schedule of prices for various categories of slaves, but the basic price level varied according to Sulu's political, economic, and demographic situation. In 1726, the value of a slave in Jolo was as follows: "a man or woman in excellent health, forty pesos; a man or woman with a weak constitution, 30 pesos; boys and girls, twenty pesos; and small children, ten pesos".[42] By the beginning of the nineteenth century, due to ethnic and social transformation in the Sulu Zone, the price of female slaves was now much higher than male slaves, indicating the important role they played both biologically and socially in the reproductive and recruitment process. In general, the price of a male slave varied according to his age and qualifications from twenty to thirty pesos; the price of a female slave now ranged from between sixty to one hundred pesos and occasionally more, her value more than doubling in some instances depending on her age and ability to work and bear children, while small children were estimated to be worth half the price of a man.[43]

Taosug *dato*, European traders, Chinese merchants, Visayan renegades, and tribal chiefs from Borneo all gathered in Jolo's market to purchase slaves and captives from the Iranun and Balangingi.[44] As early as 1774, Colonel Juan Cencilli noted in a confidential report that Jolo's slave market operated on a preferential basis, with the Iranun reserving all Spaniards and friars for the Taosug, who also had their pick of the Filipinos before the Chinese and other prospective customers were allowed to purchase their human cargoes.[45] The Taosug *dato* involved in global-local trading, procurement activities, and rice cultivation would dominate the purchase of slaves in Sulu throughout the first half of the nineteenth century as well.

The experience of women as slaves in the Sulu Zone differed for both biological reasons, because of their sexual and reproductive use, and for socio-cultural reasons related to the gender division of labour. In his log Barrera recorded four entries in June when Balangingi slaving vessels arrived with cargoes of women; on 3 June one *garay* arrived in the afternoon with three captive women on board; on 10 June, four slaving vessels arrived and dropped anchor, amongst the twenty-eight captives were six women and four children aged between six and ten years old, who had been caught three weeks earlier in the Camarines; on 15 June, informants told Barrera that there were women and children on board the three *garay* that had arrived that day; and, at the end of the month, the Spanish captain learned that four *garay* had arrived on 30 June, carrying thirty-two captives; amongst them seven women and five children, boys and girls, some as young as two years old.[46] The entry for 6 August states, "at eight o'clock this morning, a woman — who was captured last year, in April — was rescued". This woman stated that she had been on board a trading vessel of the Alcalde of Batangas which transported tobacco to Manila. She told Barerra that her companions on the ill-fated voyage were two women and three men.[47] Then almost three weeks later on 26 August, the largest slaving flotilla to enter the port during Barrera's stay, anchored. At six in the afternoon, eight *garay* along with four *vinta*, brought almost 100 captives to the Jolo market, amongst them twenty-five women, and twelve young children who had been caught while either on a government coast guard vessel bound for Manila, or on board several small defenceless coasting *perahu* that had originated from Surigao.[48]

Captives, ransomed by Wyndham and the merchant captains of Spanish trading vessels, were a key source of intelligence providing information about the traditional Taosug social system and everyday life in the slaving port. From the statements of fugitive captives it is clear that women were less likely to attempt escape in the face of violence and domination, and more apt to be resigned to their fate. But in the 1840s, the increased prospect of ransom by a Manila based trader readily crossed the minds of some female captives, especially among the newly enslaved, who were not yet reconciled to their fate. Barrera's log lists the dates and cases of those "unfortunates" whom he was able to ransom and others either ransomed or brought to him by Wyndham and his brother-in-law. His log notes the arrival on 5 July of seven *vinta*, with seventeen captives. It then states, "On this same day, an unfortunate woman was ransomed." She had been captured in March of the previous year while leaving Sorsogon with some relatives and friends to attend a *fiesta* in a neighbouring town. Her ransom was set at 22 pesos fuertes. Barrera closed the entry as follows: "At the same time, I ransomed two men — who arrived with her. These men cost me 12 pesos." The price set for the ransom of this woman, which was double the amount paid for the two male captives who had been brought with her to be exchanged for either cash or kind, signified the high value and status of female slaves in Jolo in the mid 1840s.[49] One of the longest entries in the log recounts the plight of a woman of some means and her family who were bound from Surigao to Manila on a *falua*, a government coast guard vessel, that was attacked.

Wyndham ransomed her on arrival in Jolo. Barrera carefully recorded the circumstances of what happened on 26 August, as eight Balangingi *garay* anchored along with four *vinta*, carrying about 100 captives:

> On it (the *falua*) was a married couple, and their three children, two of whom were aged between 10 and 12 years old. The poor mother, inconsolable, has been ransomed by William Wyndham, at the value of sixty four pesos fuertes. She asked the said gentleman to ransom the rest of the family, for the value of five hundred pesos.[50]

The woman told Wyndham and Barrera that, including herself, the Balangingi on her vessel had caught about thirty captives. Apart from this, the raiding squadron had "plundered" the town of Surigao, and devastated a part of the province of Caraga. The number of captives rose to 250 and more than three thousand pesos in cash was lost as well as goods of lesser value.[51]

To be ransomed either for cash or kind it was necessary for the captives to have a witness from the same town or province vouch for them, in order to make sure that the "fortunate" individual would repay the debt in due course. Barrera explained how the credit and debt aspects of the ransom system worked for most Filipinos: "If an unfortunate captive begs him for mercy, to free him, he is not told no. However, if he is automatically told yes, then his ransom was set at 40 pesos in pearl shell, or goods of another kind."[52] But if a far greater amount was demanded and the captive was unable to promise to pay the amount requested for their ransom they had to have witnesses who could act as guarantors against the amount of the ransom. Barrera wrote in the log that without such a guarantor:

> The unfortunate ones are left without receiving any charity from a good heart. Thus, if this is done by Christians to other Christians, what would the Moros do under such circumstances? In such a context, each person fashions their own luck, but now there is a saying here that 'God does not reserve anything for anybody'.[53]

Barrera closed this late August entry in his log on a note of anger, as well as a feeling of helplessness and frustration, regarding the plight of such captives, especially women and mothers:

> I myself have been speaking with these pirates, and I have been extremely irritated by the insolence and effrontery with which they have spoken to me. However, at the same time, I had to control myself and conceal my feelings so as to avoid personal danger, and other possible outcomes.

The feeling of witnessing the personal outpouring of the unfortunate Mother pleading for her sons, and them for her swayed my emotions even more.[54]

It was the fate of other less fortunate captives to be taken across the zone to the coast of east Borneo for sale. Riverine tribes on the Kinabatangan, Sambakong, Bulungun, and Berau rivers were involved in the slave trade with Taosug merchants, who had gained a permanent foothold on the east Bornean coast. These Taosug middlemen acquired bird's nest and wax for the external trade at Jolo in return for the captives. The traditional mortuary ceremony held among the headhunting Ida'an, Kenyah, and Kayan, referred to by European observers of the late eighteenth and nineteenth centuries as *surmungup* — a ritual sacrifice — accounted for much of the demand for captives by these interior tribes. These swidden cultivators were among the most ardent headhunters in Borneo. The veneration of heads was central to their way of life. Fresh heads were required for *mamat*, recurrent head feasts, which accompanied purification, funeral, and initiation ceremonies.[55] Traditionally, small parties led by war chiefs participated in organized raids against rival longhouse groups and neighbouring tribes for this purpose. The intrusive effects of external trade from Jolo were felt among these tribes, for whom bird's nest became the key to acquiring the slaves (an alternative source of heads), cloth, and salt offered by the Taosug traders of Jolo.[56] Barrera notes that Wyndham had informed him, based on reliable intelligence from his brother-in-law, that the Balangingi lent Taosug *nakodahs* captives on credit to be taken to the Borneo coast to be "exchanged for sea cucumber and bird's nest (that is to say, they use Christians for purposes of trade)".[57] On 6 September, the entry in Barrera's log verifies the extent to which long distance trade and slavery had modified the traditional culture of these vigorous predatory slash-and-burn agriculturalists, especially on the Sibuco and Sambakong rivers. The entry begins by noting that four *garay* anchored, carrying thirty-five captives from Mindoro and Panay. This information was followed by a stunning disclosure:

> Today William (Don Guillermo) ransomed a captive whose own master told us that if he was not ransomed, he would have been brought to a port in Borneo, where the entire esteem and wealth of a person there is measured in terms of owning as many heads of captives as possible, and an individual who has many heads hanging in his house, is one who is considered to be one of the bravest and most powerful amongst them.[58]

COUNTING THE VICTIMS OF THE TRAFFIC

There are no statistics on the overall number of slaves imported into Jolo between 1768-1848, except the estimates of European observers and local informants. These range from 750 to as high as 4,000 captives per year for the Philippines alone from 1775 to 1848.[59] However, it is possible to reconstruct a clearer picture of the pattern of slave imports to the port of Jolo and the Sulu sultanate on the basis of the captive's statements, Barrera's 1845 log of slaving vessels entering the port of Jolo, and from other sources. By using a comparative sample of boatloads of slaves from these sources to determine the average number carried by an individual *perahu*, and multiplying this figure by the number of raiding *perahu* possessed by Balangingi and Iranun groups, one can establish an estimate of the overall number of slaves imported during a particular period. From 1770–1835, the slave raiding communities had 100–50 *perahu*; from 1836 to 1848, 150–200 *perahu*; and from 1852–78, 60–100 prahus.[60] On the basis of the statements of slaves seized between 1826 and 1847, an average of twenty-one captives were carried in the middle passage on a slaving vessel. This sample supports St. John's calculation of twenty slaves per *perahu* in 1849.[61] However, Barrera's daily log suggests that the Iranun and Balangingi tended to carry fewer captives and slaves on board when they came to Jolo to market them. Barrera's informants were able to provide information over four months about the arrivals of thirty-six *garay*, bringing 473 captives to sell or exchange, which meant an average of thirteen captives per *garay*.[62] Clearly this was only a small proportion of the slave imports taking place both at Jolo and Balangingi, as well as elsewhere in the zone. In, *The Sulu Zone*, I have argued that slave imports to the Sulu sultanate during the first sixty- five years probably averaged between 2,000 to 3,000 a year. The steepest rise in the number of slaves brought annually to Sulu, between 3,000 and 4,000, occurred in the period 1836–48 and slackened considerably in the next several decades, with imports ranging between 1,200 and 2,000 slaves a year until the trade collapsed in the 1870s.[63] Interestingly, Barrera's 1845 "census" of the Sulu slave trade suggests the figure on the annual number of slaves imported into Jolo in the second quarter of the nineteenth century needs to be revised upward. The total number of captives who had been brought to be exchanged or sold by the Balangingi during Barrera's stay in the port of Jolo, between the third week of May and the third week of September, 1845, had reached nearly a thousand. But the Spanish captain was sure that during the period of his four-month stay, the

Balangingi had enslaved more than two thousand people from the Visayas alone,[64] besides an estimated two to three thousand Visayans whom he was told had already been seized prior to July 1845! In fact, Barrera's confidential log or "census" suggests that between 4,000–6,000 Visayans alone were being enslaved on an annual basis by the Balangingi by 1845.[65]

The major determinants of the composition of the slave intake were external forces affecting raiding patterns. Until 1848 a larger percentage of the captives (perhaps as high as 65 per cent) were from the Philippines, particularly southern Luzon and the central Visayas, while the rest came from various parts of the Malay world — the great majority from Celebes and the Moluccas.[66] According to Hunt, slaves constituted the bulk of the port-town's population in 1814.[67] Commenting on the influx of captives at Jolo and their incorporation into Taosug society, Juan de los Santos stated:

> The Taosug do not participate in slave raids but the people from Balangingi, Tunkil and the other islands in the Samalese group as well as the Iranun come to Jolo to barter large numbers of Christian captives annually. At present in Jolo there are more captives than Taosugs with whom they are easily confused. Many of them have intermarried with the Taosug.[68]

Francisco Feliz, another captive, confirmed his observation: "... presently (1836) the number of Christian captives in Jolo is at least twice as great as the Taosug population, the vast majority being Visayan."[69] By 1843, Jolo's population had risen to ten thousand, but there were other settlements that were as large, notably Parang.

From the intelligence provided by fugitive captives and the confidential reports of merchants it seems clear that before 1850 the size of the slave population was several times larger than that of the dominant society. The remaining slaves were being incorporated into the population of the Sulu sultanate which included perhaps a half a million people by mid-century.[70] It was a dynamic process and manumitted slaves and their descendants were continually being redefined according to the ethnicity of their host communities. After 1850, the ethnic class structure would become more stable, and the proportion of locally born slaves increased every year as slave raiding declined. According to the intelligence of these traders and captives, slaves also appear as an important commodity and form of common purpose currency in Sulu's thriving cross-cultural market. The most unfortunate — the elderly and infirm — were shipped to Borneo. Those left behind were absorbed into Sulu society for work in the fisheries and fields. Sulu chiefs involved in trading, slave raiding, and procurement activities came to depend on their own household slaves and were reluctant to give them away. The astonishing fact, however, is that captives or their descendants came to constitute fifty per cent or more of the population of the Sulu archipelago by 1850.

The beginning of the end of Iranun and Balangingi slave raiding, and the slave market at Jolo, came in 1848. A Spanish fleet, including three steam gunboats, bombarded the fortress at Balangingi, forcing the slave raiders to abandon their stronghold and disperse across the archipelago. When, in that fateful year, the Spanish, with the aid of steam warships, successfully destroyed the fortified strongholds in the Balangingi cluster and deported hundreds of Samal maritime people — men, women, and children — to the distant mountain valleys of north central Luzon to become tobacco and corn farmers, the Balangingi slave raiders were dealt a crippling blow from which they would never fully recover.

Prior to 1848, Spanish policy against the Iranun and Balangingi was based on principles of containment; periodic naval expeditions were sent to destroy the shipping and communities of the slave raiders and their Taosug patrons. However, by mid-nineteenth century, the Spanish authorities had decided to annex a number of the Muslim sultanates in the south, including Sulu. The major shift in strategic thinking and foreign policy was primarily meant to prevent the British and Dutch from expanding their colonial spheres of interest and territorial ambitions in the Philippine archipelago and adjacent areas. The slave raiding activities of the Balangingi would be severely curtailed by the advent of steam gunboats. But in 1848 the Spanish also attempted to use the crusade against slaving and the destruction of the slaver's forts on Balangingi as a pretext to declare war on the Taosug. This was aimed at forcing the sultan of Sulu over the next several decades to close down the slave market in his port and sign a treaty acknowledging Spanish sovereignty.[71]

Notes

1. Tomas de Comyn, *State of the Philippines in 1810, Being an Historical, Statistical and Descriptive Account of the Interesting Portion on the Indian Archipelago*, trans. with notes and a preliminary discourse by William Walton (Manila: Filipininiana Book Guild, 1969), pp. 123–24.
2. J. Hunt, "Some Particulars Relating to Sulo in the Archipelago of Felicia", in *Notices of the Indian Archipelago and Adjacent Countries*, edited by J.H. Moor (London: Cass, 1967), p. 5.

3. James Francis Warren, *The Sulu Zone The World Capitalist Economy and the Historical Imagination* (Amsterdam: VU University Press/CASA, 1998), pp. 9–10.
4. Alexander Dalyrmple, *Oriental Repertory*, 2 vols. (London: 1808); James Rennell, *Journal of a Voyage to the Sooloo Islands and the Northwest Coast of Borneo, from and to Madras with description of the Islands, 1762–1763* (London: British Museum); Thomas Forrest, *A Voyage to New Guinea and the Moluccas from Balambanga: Including an Account of Maguindanao, Sooloo and Other Islands* (London: C. Scott, 1779).
5. Pierre Sonnerat, *A Voyage to the East Indies and China Performed by Order of Louis XV between the Years 1774 and 1781*, 3 vols., translated by Francis Magnus (Calcutta: Stuart & Cooper, 1788), vol. 3, p. 131.
6. *Vinta* is an outrigger sailing vessel of the Philippines, varying in length from 15 to upward of 50 feet. *Barangyan* is a Philippine sailing vessel up to 55 feet in length carrying two masts and worked by oars as well as by sails.
7. Hunt, op. cit., pp. 50–51, 57–60.
8. Statements of Balangingi prisoners, 1838 in Bonham to Maitland, 28 June 1838, Public Records Office (PRO), Admiralty, 125/133; *Singapore Free Press*, 28 June 1838.
9. Edward Belcher, *Narrative of the Voyage of H.M.S. Samarang, during the Years 1843–1846*, 2 vols. (London: Reeve, Benham and Reeve, 1848), vol. 2, pp. 208–09.
10. Ibid., pp. 208–09; D.H. Kolf, *Voyages of the Dutch Brig of War Dourga, through the Southern and Little Known Parts of the Moluccan Archipelago and the Previously Unknown Southern Coast of New Guinea Performed during the years 1825 and 1826*, translated by George Windsor Earl (London: James Madden, 1840); Ms.211.Diario de Navegacion del Capitan de Frigata de la Real Armada D. Jose Maria Halcon en su Navegacion de Manila a Jolo con la Galeota de S.M. 'La Olosea' y una division de Faluas Comprende desde 10 Junio de 1836 y abraza noticias peculiares a comision extraordinaria que en calidadde plenipotenciario desenipeno cerca del Sultan de Jolo, Madrid Coleccion de Guillen, Museo Naval.
11. See James Francis Warren, "Moro", in *Encyclopedia of Asian History*, vol. 3, edited by Ainslie T. Embree (New York: Charles Scribner's Sons, 1988), p. 39; Charles O. Frake, "The Genesis of Kinds of People in the Sulu Archiplego", in *Language and Cultural Description* (Stanford: Stanford University Press, 1980), pp. 314–18; Francisco Mallari, S.J., "Muslim Raids in Bicol, 1580–1792", *Philippine Studies* 34 (1986), p. 257.
12. Pablo Fernaddez O.P., *History of the Church in the Philippines, 1521–1898* (Manila: National Book Store, 1979), p. 203.
13. James Francis Warren, *Iranun and Balangingi: Globalization, Maritime Raiding and the Birth of Ethnicity* (Singapore: Singapore University Press, 2002), p. 72.

14. Diario de los Pancos Piratas que han entrado mi residencia en el Puerto de Jolo, y de los pobres que han cautivado, y traido para vender; dando principio el de dia que al margen expresa y Mayo de 1845, Juan Bautista Barrera, 25 September 1845, Archivo — Museo Don Alavaro de Bazan.El Viso Del Marques, legajo, 1176/262.
15. Ibid., p. 9.
16. Ibid., p.10.
17. Ibid., p. 6.
18. Ibid., p. 8.
19. No. 293,Gobierno Militar de la Plaza de Zamboanga a GCG, 23 August 1847, Philippine National Archive, unclassified legajo (bundle) Mindanoa/Sulu.
20. Spencer St. John, *Life in the Forests of the Far East*, 2 vols. (London: Smith Elder & Company, 1862), vol. 2, p. 203.
21. Nicholas Loney, *A Britisher in the Philippines or the Letters of Nicholas Loney* (Manila: n.p., 1964), p. 64.
22. Diario de los Pancos Piratas que han entrado mi residencia en el Puerto de Jolo, Juan Bautista Barrera, 25 September 1845, Archivo — Museo Don Alavaro de Bazan, legajo, 1176/262, p. 8.
23. Ibid., p. 4.
24. Ibid., p. 4.
25. Warren, *The Sulu Zone The World Capitalist Economy and the Historical Imagination*, op. cit., p. 191.
26. Ibid., p. 3.
27. Ibid., p. 4.
28. El Arzobispo de Manila a Nuestra Majestad, 31 June 1761, AGI, Filipinas 603; No. 46, 17 August 1770, AGI. Filipinas 490, p. 11.
29. El Obispo de Nueva Caceres a Nuestraa Majestad, 14 May 1817, AGI, Ultramar 684. *Cabeceras* are settlements or neighbourhoods (*barangays*) regrouped into towns during Spanish rule and *visitas* are Catholic missions or settlements.
30. Bruce Cruikshank, *Samar 1768–1898* (Manila: Historical Conservation Society, 1985), pp. 99–100.
31. Statements of Mariano Sevilla, Domingo Candelario, Augistin Juan, and Juan Santiago in Expediente No. 12, 4 October 1836, PNA, Mindanao/Sulu, 1803–90; *Expediente* No. 2, El Gobierno Politico y Militar de Zamboanga a GCG, 30 May 1842, PNA, Mindano/Sulu 1838–85.
32. *Garay* is Balanginni maritime vessel of the nineteenth century.
33. Diario de los Pancos Piratas que han entrado mi residencia en el Puerto de Jolo, Juan Bautista Barrera, 25 September 1845, Archivo — Museo Don Alavaro de Bazan, legajo, 1176/262, p. 1.
34. Ibid., p. 2.
35. Ibid., p. 3.

36. Ibid., p. 3.
37. Ibid., p. 4.
38. Ibid., p. 6.
39. Ibid., p. 7.
40. Ibid., p. 8.
41. Extract from the *Singapore Free Press*, 6 April 1847, PRO Admiralty 125/133.
42. No. 7, GCG a Senor Secretario de estado, 4 June 1806, AGI, Filipinas 510, p. 27.
43. Extract from the *Singapore Free Press*, op. cit., 125/133.
44. Warren, *The Sulu Zone The World Capitalist Economy and the Historical Imagination*, op. cit., p. 206.
45. Colonel Juan Cencilli A Senor Conde Aranda, 16 April 1774, Archivo Historico Nacional (AHN), Estado 2845, caja 2.
46. Diario de los Pancos Piratas que han entrado mi residencia en el Puerto de Jolo, Juan Bautista Barrera, 25 September 1845, Archivo — Museo Don Alavaro de Bazan., legajo, 1176/262, p. 1.
47. Ibid., p. 4.
48. Ibid., p. 5.
49. Ibid., pp. 1–2.
50. Ibid., p. 5.
51. Ibid., p. 5.
52. Ibid., p. 6.
53. Ibid., p. 7.
54. Ibid., p. 5.
55. Frank M. Le Bar, ed., *Ethnic Groups of Insular Southeast Asia*, vol. 1 (New Haven: Human Relations Area Files Press, 1972), pp. 170, 172.
56. H. Van Dewall, "Aanteekeningen omtrent de Noordoorkust van Borneo", *Tijdschrift voor Indische Taal-Land-en Volkenkunde, uitgegeven door het (Koninklijk) Bataaviaasch Kunsten en Wetenschappen* 4 (1885), p. 450.
57. Diario de los Pancos Piratas que han entrado mi residencia en el Puerto de Jolo, Juan Bautista Barrera, 25 September 1845, Archivo — Museo Don Alavaro de Bazan, legajo, 1176/262, p. 6.
58. Ibid., p. 7.
59. Many of the estimates conservatively ranged from 750–1,500 captives a year. See No. 9 El Consejo de las Indias, 19 December 1775, AGI, Fiipinas 359; Farren to the Earl of Aberdeen, 20 January 1846, PRO, Foreign Office (FO) 72/708; Webb to Lord Russel, 24 October 1864, FO, 71/1; Hunt, "Some Particulars Relating to Sulo", op. cit., pp. 551–62; Bernaldez, *Guerra al Sur*, p. 147.
60. El Gobernador Politico y Militar de Zamboanga a GCG, 30 May 1842, PNA, Mindanoa/Sulu 1838–85; *Expediente* 12 sobre haber salido la expedicion contra Balangingi, 17 February 1845, PNA , Mindanoa/Sulu 1836–97;

information obtained by Charles Grey in Singapore from Wyndham relating to Sulo, 24 February 1847, PRO Admiralty 125/133.
61. Spencer St. John, "Piracy in the Indian Archipelago", *Journal of the Indian Archipelago and Eastern Asia* 3 (1849): 258.
62. Diario de los Pancos Piratas que han entrado mi residencia en el Puerto de Jolo, Juan Bautista Barrera, 25 September 1845, Archivo — Museo Don Alavaro de Bazan, legajo, 1176/262.
63. Farren to Palmerston, 16 March 1851, Colonial Office 144/8; for a precise calculation on slave imports to the Sulu Zone and the port of Jolo, between 1770 and 1870, I have used the figure of 20.5 slaves per boat in middle passage, based on the statements of the slaves seized between 1826 and 1847, minus 4,800 to 8,000 slaves (1,200 to 2,000 per year) for the period 1848–52. From the calculation it therefore follows that the number of slaves imported over the period 1770–1870 varied from a low estimate of 201, 350 to a high estimate of 302, 575.
64. Diario de los Pancos Piratas que han entrado mi residencia en el Puerto de Jolo, Juan Bautista Barrera, 25 September 1845, Archivo — Museo Don Alavaro de Bazan, legajo, 1176/262, p. 11.
65. Ibid., p. 11.
66. *Expediente* 12, 4 October, 1836, PNA, Mindanao /Sulu 1803–1890. See statements of Evaristo Pinto and Francisco Xavier.
67. Hunt, "Some Particulars Relating to Sulo", op. cit., p. 50.
68. Statement of Juan de los Santos in *Expediente* 12, 4 October 1836, PNA, Mindanao/Sulu 1803–90.
69. Ibid.
70. James Francis Warren, *The Sulu Zone 1768–1898: The Dynamics of External Trade, Slavery, and Ethnicity in the Transformation of a Southeast Asian Maritime State* (Singapore: Singapore University Press, 1981) p. 210.
71. Ibid., pp. 105–06.

10

Pirates in the Periphery: Eastern Sulawesi 1820–1905

Esther Velthoen

In the first decade of the twentieth century, the colonial crusade against piracy in the Indonesian archipelago ended. Throughout most of the nineteenth century it had been a central concern in the erratic process of colonial maritime expansion that took place in the eastern archipelago. The takeover of indigenous ports signalled the end of this process and the transition of the colonial state from a predominantly maritime power in the eastern archipelago to a territorial one, a state in which mobile populations were seen as anomalies, subjects that needed to be transformed into sedentary, more controllable populations.[1]

The central question in this chapter is how piracy related to the indigenous political system in eastern Sulawesi[2] and how this came to change with the pressures put to bear by the colonial state in its pursuit of "security". The time span dealt with is ca. 1820–1900, the period in which eastern Sulawesi was transformed from an area with relatively autonomous small-scale polities into a periphery of a colonial state. Piracy had occurred in eastern Sulawesi as part of local and regional warfare. In the late eighteenth and nineteenth centuries, this coastline was also targeted by slave raiders from the southern Philippines and eastern Indonesia. As a result of anti-piracy campaigns, certain groups of pirates took refuge in eastern Sulawesi, thus heightening raiding activity in the middle of the nineteenth century.

It would be a mistake to examine piracy separately from the political and economic context in which it occurred. It was one aspect of a decentralized political system in which mobile populations were key elements. It was through diasporas of traders, adventurers, aristocrats, and appointed officials that political spheres of influence were created and maintained. These diasporas were only in a very limited way orchestrated by the centres of power with which they were associated. Bugis traders, for instance, who originated from South Sulawesi, but were active in eastern Sulawesi, claimed allegiance to the South Sulawesi ruler of Bone, even if their actions there were not necessary known or approved of by him.

In eastern Sulawesi, the Tobelo, originally from Maluku, and the Bugis, originally from South Sulawesi, played important roles as raiders, traders, and settlers. Their presence points to the "diasporic" process through which fluid regional spheres of influence were formed over long distances by the migration of traders, raiders, adventurous aristocrats, and appointed officials. Being located between two major indigenous spheres of influence of Bone and Ternate, eastern Sulawesi felt any upset in the regional balance of power keenly and this was so too during this period of expanding colonial maritime power. Not only did the colonial government endeavour to undermine the indigenous political system of which raiding was a part, it also worked with Ternate and actively tried to undermine Bone.

The colonial state undermined piracy directly through its campaigns of warships. However, it intended to bring about a much greater change by curtailing or, at least, controlling mobility in general by restricting movement and cutting ties between rulers and chiefs with migrant populations living away from their homeland. In the case of piracy, the colonial state was reasonably successful. Tobelo raiders, originally from Halmahera (Maluku), who were dispersed throughout the eastern archipelago, were in the end "transformed". Most returned to Maluku, and abandoned raiding. Magindanao raiders, too, were not heard of again in eastern Sulawesi.

In other respects, the mobility of populations continued to pose a challenge. Whereas the overtly political dimension of diasporas declined, mobility and diasporas, remained an important feature of indigenous societies. Ironically, the safer conditions created by the colonial state encouraged the migration of Bugis to frontier areas where they were often able to build a dominant position *vis-à-vis* the original population.

EASTERN SULAWESI: THE MAKING OF A COLONIAL PERIPHERY

Eastern Sulawesi consisted of numerous small chiefdoms or petty states that remained beyond Dutch control until the beginning of the twentieth century. The best known and most important ones were the maritime oriented Buton, Tobungku, and Banggai. These polities enjoyed a high level of autonomy while also being part of regional tributary and trading networks. At different times, coastal polities were in alliance with either Ternate, to the east, or Bone to the west. Despite the importance of regional networks, contact was more frequent with neighbouring polities in and near eastern Sulawesi.

Eastern Sulawesi in the mid-nineteenth century was one of the few unpatrolled parts of the archipelago. It thus became one of those "interstitial seams between the 'sinews' of the state power" where pirates took refuge from the unremitting anti-piracy campaigns of Dutch warships.[3] Raiders from other parts of the eastern archipelago responded to the threat of Dutch warships by changing their routes and retreating. A different response was to relocate their communities to areas that were acknowledged as allies of the Dutch, and thus safe from attacks. As Banggai and Tobungku, both on Sulawesi's east coast, were known to be tributaries of Ternate, they were deemed to be safe from attacks from the Dutch, because Ternate was a close ally of the Dutch.

In Dutch archival sources eastern Sulawesi does not figure prominently until the middle of the nineteenth century when it is mentioned regularly under the subheading of "piracy". The increase of reports on piracy in eastern Sulawesi in the second half of the nineteenth century was a side effect of the colonial state's maritime expansion in which eastern Sulawesi, a largely ignored coastline, was now transformed into a colonial frontier.

The suppression of piracy in eastern Sulawesi was not the only reason eastern Sulawesi started to feature on the colonial map. Of great concern to the Dutch in Sulawesi was Bone,[4] the most powerful Bugis state in the southern peninsula that had cooperated closely with the VOC in the late seventeenth century, but on the return of the Dutch to the archipelago, resisted signing a new treaty in 1825. The concern was not so much with Bone itself, but the status and influence it had far beyond what the Dutch perceived as its legitimate borders, through the flow of traders, migrants, and ambitious chiefs who continued to acknowledge Bone's overlordship in their new places of abode. This "diasporic" nature of Bone was not unusual. The regional political system that included trade, tributary relations, warfare, and migration was held together by mobile populations.

Eastern Sulawesi had been a Bugis frontier since Bone rose to power at the end of the seventeenth century. Bugis traders controlled most of the trade in valuable commodities such as *trepang* (sea-cucumbers) and pearl shell, and (often) mobile Bugis chiefs and their armed followings were a factor to be reckoned with. Its polities, Banggai, Tobungku, and Buton, had however, also had contact with Ternate, a sultanate on one of the so-called spice islands in Maluku. By the middle of the nineteenth century, Banggai and Tobungku were clearly in the Bugis sphere of influence, but were being claimed by Ternate, which was in turn supported by the Dutch. This gave rise to tension that led to local conflicts in which raiders played an important role.

Colonial expansion was clearly not the sole cause of local conflict in eastern Sulawesi. Dutch sources, though sparse, do list regular conflicts between polities in eastern Sulawesi and also their attempts to involve outside forces in these conflicts. In the 1820s, a Bugis chief named Arung Bakung resided in Kendari Bay with his following and engaged in *trepang* trade. There was obviously rivalry between him and the sultan of Buton, whose trade was threatened by Arung Bakung's presence, even if Buton made no direct claim to Kendari at this time. In the resulting conflict, Arung Bakung requested the help of Magindanao raiders who were based in north Sulawesi, and had close ties to the Sulu sultanate in the southern Philippines. They did indeed assist Arung Bakung, until they themselves were attacked and defeated by the Dutch in 1822 as part of their campaign against piracy.[5] This was the first known effect of the suppression of piracy in eastern Sulawesi.

The main way in which the Dutch endeavoured to expand their influence into eastern Sulawesi was through "indirect rule", through supporting its vassal Ternate[6] and assisting in the expansion of its sphere of influence so as to counter Bone's claims to this coastline. Though less associated with trading networks, the Ternaten sphere of influence was equally dispersed and dependent on the same mechanisms as the Bugis one. The colonial states use of such an ally was naturally fraught, as the Ternaten sultan did not have the kind of control over his subjects desired by the Dutch. The outcome of this process was mixed in the sense that the actions taken on Ternate's periphery were inspired by Dutch notions of peace and order, but carried out with substantial aid from Ternate and through the placement of Ternaten officials in Tobungku and Banggai. These two east coast polities officially had been tributary to Ternate since the late seventeenth century, but their relationship with Ternate was patchy, and contact, intermittent. The Dutch were interested in Ternate consolidating its influence in this outlying periphery to counteract Bone's influence, and also to extend their own into this area.

COLONIAL ATTEMPTS TO TRANSFORM RAIDERS: INCORPORATION AND SEDENTARIZATION C. 1820–40

The increase in raiding in the Indonesian and Philippine archipelago in the late eighteen century as documented by Warren also affected eastern Sulawesi, though it is poorly documented because the VOC retreated as a result of raiding attacks. Patchy evidence suggests that local raiding continued unabated and followed a similar pattern to conflicts documented for the late seventeenth century. Raiding had been very much an aspect of the political system, and this continued to be the case after the increase of the late eighteen century. The two main raiding networks that affected eastern Sulawesi were both affiliated with political centres. The raiders emanating from the Sulu archipelago were affiliated with this sultanate, and the Tobelo raiders that operated in eastern Indonesia on a much smaller scale had been affiliated with the rebellious Tidorese Nuku in the late eighteen century. In this section I will discuss three attempts of the colonial state to incorporate Tobelo raiders through treaties and sedentarization.

The Tobelo[7] originated from Halmahera, but had been displaced during the war of 1780–1800 against the VOC led by the Tidoren Prince Nuku, whose claims to the Tidore throne were not recognized by the Dutch. The Tobelo diaspora that came about during this war stretched from eastern Sulawesi to Nusa Tenggara. As early as the 1820s, many Tobelo had formed alliances with Magindanao raiders, and were, therefore, under threat from Dutch warships for providing shelter and food to these raiders. Several attempts were made to draw them away from raiding and transform them into peaceful peasants and fishers.

RAJA JAILOLO

The most elaborate case that intended to "sedentarize" an entire raiding polity was that of Raja Jailolo, the successor of Prince Nuku of Tidore, who used the north coast of Seram as a major base. Just as Nuku had done in the late eighteenth century, Raja Jailolo too made claims to the Tidore sultanate, but he too had no chance of being acknowledged by the Dutch.[8] In 1822, Raja Jailolo's subjects on the north coast of Seram numbered more than 8,000, not counting those who were at sea or settled elsewhere. Dutch-Ternaten anti-piracy measures directed at populations suspected of supporting or carrying out maritime raiding inadvertently increased Raja Jailolo's numbers.[9] In 1822, a large number of refugees from Halmahera who had been punished by Ternaten *hongi*[10] because of their suspected participation in maritime raiding joined his ranks. Raja Jailolo and his disaffected followers in turn attacked areas that were directly or indirectly allied to the Dutch.[11] The Dutch concern about the swelling ranks of Raja Jailolo's followers led to the first experiment of resettling the "pirates", and in this manner incorporating them into the colonial state system. Raja Jailolo used his personal control over maritime raiding groups as his main bargaining chip to obtain formal recognition of his claim to the throne of Tidore. This was out of the question for the Dutch, but they did grant him the north-coast of Seram and nullified Tidore's claims to this area. Raja Jailolo's followers then agreed to establish villages there as long as they did not have to go to Tidore.

The attempt to transform a diasporic, raiding polity into a land-based polity populated by peasants and fishers failed for a number of reasons. The location was not suitable for supporting a large concentration of people who depended almost entirely on agriculture. The coast was too swampy, and too much labour was required to cut down the forests. Local sago forests did not provide enough food to support the population. More importantly, Raja Jailolo's power still depended on his alliances with maritime raiding groups who continued to bring him tribute. The new sultan was soon accused of supporting raiding, receiving gifts from raiders, and being addicted to opium, whereas the Dutch expected him to encourage his subjects to settle permanently, open new fields and grow food crops. More and more chiefs and their followers moved away, mostly offshore to the nearby island of Obi that had served as a forward base for the Tobelo for decades. Semi-sedentary communities consisting of women and slaves were left behind when the men went on annual raiding expeditions throughout the eastern archipelago. In 1833, Raja Jailolo requested permission to move to Obi as well, where his subjects were better able to feed and clothe themselves. The Dutch refused his request, removed him from his position, and abandoned the project. The remaining chiefs from Maba, Patani and Weda, who together had 1,300 subjects, then returned to their original homelands. But the Tobelo and Galela continued to live on the north coast of Seram and on Obi.[12]

DAENG MAGASSING

During the same years of the experiment with Raja Jailolo and his followers, the colonial government undertook two other similar projects to transform the Tobelo and Iranun around Flores into peaceful subjects of the colonial state, through negotiation and resettlement. The first was carried out by Daeng Magassing, an aristocrat from Bonerate, a small island to the south of Sulawesi with long-standing connections to maritime raiders. He was to use his "local" knowledge and status to form alliances with the raiding groups and resettle them on Tanah Jampea. This tiny island to the south of Selayar had in the past been tributary to Bonerate, but because of frequent attacks by raiders had become depopulated. Here, the resettled raiders would be able grow their own food and live in peace under the protection of the colonial government. In 1830, fifteen Tobelo chiefs signed a peace treaty with Daeng Magassing, which was reinforced by swearing an oath. Towards the end of that year, Daeng Magassing left for Bima and Tana Jampea with his recently acquired following that numbered about 300 people.[13] But three years later, it was evident to the Dutch that this project had failed. Daeng Magassing himself was suspected of committing acts of piracy, and orders were issued to confiscate his ship. Five years later, a Dutch government official was told in Kendari that Daeng Magassing "served the Dutch government in appearance only", and that arms and ammunition supplied by the Dutch were used to raid and pillage. The booty was subsequently sold in Kalengsusu, a settlement that had been captured by Raja Jailolo and the Iranun in 1822, on the northeast coast of Buton.[14] The connections between Bonerate and Iranun raiders continued: in the 1850s Iranun ships were frequently reported to take in water and supplies in Bonerate. In that period, the son of Daeng Magassing sailed in a fleet of raiding *perahu* of Iranun and other raiders.[15]

KENDARI BAY: TAMING THE TOBELO

Kendari Bay, located on the southern part of Sulawesi's east coast, was the location of a failed experiment by a Dutch adventurer and trader, J.N. Vosmaer, who tried to convert Tobelo pirates into peaceful fisher folk by offering them a secure place to live under his protection. This experiment was in itself not of great import, but is significant because of the strong reactions it provoked from both neighbouring Buton, and the regional power of Bone. Vosmaer's ability to create alliances with Bajo[16] fisherfolk and Tobelo raiders and the possibility of him founding a lucrative trading settlement supported by the colonial government had the potential to upset both local and regional balances of power. Buton's attempt to employ raiders against Vosmaer also illustrates how raiding was used as a weapon against political opponents.

Vosmaer had obtained permission from the colonial government to open a trading post in what was — according to the information he gathered during his first visit in the 1830s — an extremely promising location. There was an abundance of the much sought after *trepang* and the presence of Bajo fisher folk. It was, in fact, the repeated request for protection by Bajo that gave rise to the idea of founding a trading settlement in Kendari Bay. More importantly, he had been able to create alliances with semi-nomadic Tobelo chiefs who engaged in raiding and fishing. His plan was to resettle them, and by giving them an honest means to procure a livelihood, he was sure they would forego raiding.

Before arriving in the Netherlands-Indies, Vosmaer had sailed around the world and visited his brother, who was a colonial official in South Sulawesi. Fascinated by the indigenous trading vessels arriving from different parts of the archipelago, he learned to speak both Bugis and Makassarese and befriended Makassarese chiefs and maritime traders. Through these personal contacts and the patronage of the chief, Tuanna-I-Dondang, also known as Sarib Ali, he was able to travel safely to the east coast.[17] In October 1830 he bought a brig in Batavia with his business partner Brouwers Holtius, which he baptized *Celebes*. Exactly a year later, he completed his first trading voyage to the Gulf of Bone, Buton, and up the east coast as far as Tobungku. Unfortunately he suffered shipwreck on the return journey near Selayar, and lost all the notes he had taken. On this journey he "discovered" Kendari Bay which he then named after himself, calling it the Vosmaerbaai.[18] He also encountered a booming *trepang* trade, with Tobungku as the most important centre on the east coast. Vosmaer immediately saw an opportunity to open a trading settlement that could double as a government outpost in Kendari Bay. He convinced the struggling colonial government to support his bold plan on the grounds that he would be able to transform "robbers" into "honest and decent people" and resettle them in Kendari Bay. From Batavia's distant standpoint, it was a matter of taking specific advantage of Vosmaer's local knowledge and skills, which he had obtained through extensive contact with Makassarese and Bugis chiefs and traders. Batavia's support was reluctant.

Vosmaer entered into alliances with a number of Tobelo chiefs whom Daeng Magassing had also listed as his new followers. He was able to win the confidence of these raiders through the patronage and protection offered by Tuanna-I-Dondang, thus operating in the same manner and regional network as the Bugis aristocrat Arung Bakung, who preceded him as a key patron of the *trepang* trade in Kendari Bay in the 1820s.[19] Besides resettling maritime raiders, Vosmaer argued that a Dutch outpost in Kendari Bay would attract some of the indigenous trade on the east coast that had thus far evaded ports under Dutch control. But in the aftermath of the failure of Daeng Magassing's venture, the idea of resettling "pirates" was not greeted with great enthusiasm.[20] Furthermore, the colonial government could not authorize opening new government posts without consulting with the Netherlands. Hence, Vosmaer was appointed resident of Gorontalo (North Sulawesi), from where he could travel to the east coast. It was hoped that he would gather further knowledge about the various peoples who inhabited this coast still virtually unknown to the Dutch, and establish good relations with them, at little cost to the colonial government. Batavia granted Vosmaer permission to conduct trade, but refused his request for a personal advance of f25.000, so as to not subsidize private trading schemes.[21]

Kendari Bay is a long, narrow bay with an entrance that is so well concealed that even from close proximity it is invisible.[22] For this reason, according to Vosmaer, Bugis traders in the early decades of the nineteenth century frequently passed it by and anchored at Bokori, a small island near the entrance of the bay. Coastal Tolaki[23] travelled there from the mainland to meet the Bugis traders.[24] However, in the first part of the nineteenth century the bay was sought out by the nomadic Bajo, who were attracted there by its sheltered anchorage, abundance of food, fresh water, and wood to repair their boats.[25] It was Vosmaer's encounters with Bajo fisherfolk that initially drew his attention to Kendari. Under the patronage of the Bugis aristocrat Arung Bakung, Kendari had become a prosperous trading settlement with a large number of semi-nomadic Bajo and traders frequenting the bay in the late 1820s. Tebau, the Tolaki chief who had invited Arung Bakung, also benefited greatly from the trade. When Arung Bakung left Kendari with his following, the Bajo stopped visiting Kendari in large numbers, and so did the traders, thus depriving Tebau and the coastal Tolaki of their principal source of wealth. Vosmaer was introduced to Tebau by a younger relative of Tuanna-I-Dondang when they visited Kendari. Just as Tebau had requested Arung Bakung to take up residence, he was now eager for Vosmaer to settle there too.

Laiwui was a coastal realm that was part of a loose federation of Tolaki chiefs often referred to as Konawe, after its most prominent realm in the hinterland of Kendari Bay. One of Kendari's advantages was that it could not be cut off from food supplies in the hinterland by a siege, as was the case with Ambon and Banda, and it was easy to defend because of the narrow entrance to the bay. The disadvantage of proximity to its hinterland was that Kendari was not easy to defend from headhunting expeditions from the interior. The population of Laiwui was estimated at approximately 7,000 in 1837.[26] In the 1830s, Laiwui extended northwards along the coast as far as Matarape, which later became part of Tobungku, and southwards to Rumbia, inhabited by the ToMoronene, which in later decades was claimed by Buton. Buton claimed suzerainty over Kendari, and Butonese influence was noticeable in the rank titles of Lakina and Sapati, which were borrowed from Buton. Tebau's clever alliances with Arung Bakung and then Vosmaer enabled him to elevate his status and ignore Buton's claims of dominance.

By the beginning of 1836, Vosmaer had met with Tobelo raiding chiefs on Selayar, including the prominent Tobelo chief kapitan Tobungku, and notified Batavia that eighty *perahu* would "go over" to the Dutch side.[27] Vosmaer played down the extent to which he himself now depended on the protection of these raiding chiefs, and that the future success of his trading post also possibly depended on these somewhat dubious connections. The former governor of Makassar, D.W. Pietermaat, who had spoken to Vosmaer in 1832 and 1833 about his plans to open a trading post in Kendari Bay, was pessimistic about its chances of success because of objections coming from Buton, Luwu, and "Bone Bugis", all of whom made some claim on Kendari.

Vosmaer indeed complained bitterly about the Ssultan of Buton's attempts to undermine his trading post. The sultan claimed Kendari as his tributary, and tried to employ Tobelo raiding groups to attack the new settlement.[28] News reached Makassar that he had posted a reward of one hundred slaves for the persons who managed to kill Vosmaer. He went so far as to grant certain Tobelo raiding chiefs permission to settle in Kalengsusu on north Buton on condition that they attacked Vosmaer's trading post in Kendari. Interestingly, he made a point of forewarning the Bajo in Kendari in case of an attack so that the *trepang* trade would not be harmed. However, because of their good relations with Vosmaer, the raiding chiefs Dagi-Dagi and Tobungku rejected the sultan's offer.

Besides employing local raiders to attack Kendari, Buton also made a formal complaint to the governor of Makassar about Vosmaer's plans to resettle raiding groups, in the Bay — ironically, the very same groups he wanted to employ to attack Kendari, reportedly because he worried that these raiders would then attack Buton.[29] Buton depended on Kendari for agricultural imports, but also demanded duties from traders who went there to collect *trepang* from Bajo fishers. The sultan's claims were flatly denied by the Tolaki chief Tebau, who admitted only to having formal trade relations with Buton.

Vosmaer did die on Buton in 1836, not as a result of violence or murder, but of a fever that started on a journey between Selayar and Buton on board his own ship.[30] Tebau wrote a letter to Makassar pleading to maintain the post in Kendari. Based on an 1837 report by Budi Bastiaanse, who was sent to Buton and Kendari on a fact finding mission, the governor of Makassar decided to continue the post at Kendari. According to his report, Vosmaer's plans for a colonial trading post had been realistic.[31] A Bajo chief informed Bastiaanse that the day before his arrival, the former chief of Kalengsusu passed through Kendari on his way from Buton to Tobungku, north of Kendari, with three armed *kora-kora* (boats). His aim was to persuade Tobungku to join him in a combined attack on Kendari. The presence of the Dutch post between Buton and Tobungku may have temporarily united the traditional enemies in a common purpose to destroy the Kendari Bay settlement. Whether Tobungku's support eventuated is not known, but raiders from Kalengsusu regularly attacked Kendari, while the sultan of Buton denied having any knowledge of these attacks. At this time, Kalengsusu was a market for stolen goods and captives, frequented by the likes of Daeng Magassing and Tobelo raiders.

The Bajo chiefs implored Bastiaanse to maintain the government post, so that they would be able to leave their women and children behind in safety when they went fishing and trading. For the time being, Cornelius, Vosmaer's trusted underling, was considered the most capable person to run the trading post. When the post was not closed down despite Vosmaer's death, the sultan of Buton threatened that the Dutch presence there would eventually lead to problems with Bone. The Bugis claim over Kendari Bay in the 1830s was not voiced directly to the colonial government, nor was it based on outright territorial claims. Rather, it was based on the widespread presence of Bajo fishers in the bay who sold their produce to Bugis traders.[32] In Kendari, people were aware of Bone's claims, but stated that they were in no way dependent on Bone, nor were they worried because Bone was too preoccupied with its own internal conflicts to concern itself with them.[33] Towards the end of 1840, Cornelius arrived in Makassar with unsettling news that a severe smallpox epidemic had killed most of the population of Kendari Bay, including the Tolaki chief Tebau, and that the rest of the population had fled deep into the interior.

Consequently, Cornelius was forced to abandon the depopulated settlement in Kendari Bay.[34]

Soon thereafter, a group of Tobelo raiders used the bay as an anchorage and started to build houses, taking advantage of this sheltered bay once it was vacated. Before returning to Makassar, Cornelius spent four months on Buton and maintained good relations with the sultan. During his stay, the sultan mounted an expedition of fifteen large perahu with 1,000 men and succeeded in defeating the raiders who had settled in Kendari Bay. If these were the very same raiders whom the sultan had earlier encouraged to raid Kendari Bay, they were not shown any mercy in the presence of a Dutch government official. Interestingly, three of the five captured chiefs were Tobelo, while one was a cousin of the Butonese sultan, and the fifth a Makassarese, once again underlining the symbiotic ties between local elites and the Tobelo raiders. They were all beheaded in Buton.[35] Thus, initially encouraging Tobelo raiders to attack the budding Dutch trading post in Kendari, the sultan of Buton later mounted an armed expedition to defeat Tobelo raiders who had occupied Kendari Bay.

Vosmaer's idea of settling maritime raiders and transforming them into "peaceful subjects" did not end with his death. In 1837, the governor of Makassar organized for Tobelo chiefs and four hundred of their people to be settled on Tombolangan, a small island near Selayar, possibly some of the same chiefs Daeng Magassing and Vosmaer dealt with earlier. This project would prove successful and their descendents can still be found there today.[36] The Tobelo turned to fishing for their livelihood.[37] Vosmaer's experiment ended abruptly, but it had drawn the attention of the colonial government to the east coast. The sultan of Buton proved to be right concerning Bone's claim. Ten years after Cornelius left Kendari Bay, a new Bugis settlement had arisen, with the *syabandar* Latumana or Latimammang (harbour master) as its head, who collected taxes on behalf of the ruler of Bone.

The episode of Vosmaer's trading post is of interest for two reasons. First, how local raiding affected the safety of the coastal and maritime population such as the Bajo, who were actively in search of a new patron once Arung Bakung had left Kendari Bay. Second, these patrons needed to be integrated in some way into wider regional networks in order to provide protection and trading connections. Arung Bakung was part of Bone's sphere of influence, but was also directly allied to Magindanao raiders. Vosmaer was tied into the same regional raiding and trading network, but obviously also enjoyed patronage from the colonial government. How these regional alliances manifested themselves on a local level could vary:

Arung Bakung waged war on Buton with the aid of Magindanao raiders. The sultan of Buton made use of Tobelo raiders to attack Vosmaer's settlement while at the same time being an ally of the colonial government. The antagonism between Arung Bakung and Buton is but one of many examples of how raiding and local warfare shaded into each other and were intertwined with regional networks at the same time.

Finally, as a result of the attempted trading post and plans to transform Tobelo raiders, the Kendari Bay that fell within the area claimed by Bone became a focal point for Bone's attention. The posting of a Bugis *syabandar* in Kendari, thus formally staking out Bone's sphere of influence, was a response the creeping influence of the colonial state into eastern Sulawesi. In a period of thirty years, the bay was occupied by a Bugis chief (Arung Bakung), a Dutch trader and adventurer (Vosmaer), Tobelo raiders who had been used by Buton to attack the settlement, and finally in 1850, by a Bugis *syabandar*.

NEW ALLIANCES: MIGRATING RAIDERS AND LOCAL ELITES IN THE COLONIAL PERIPHERY 1850–1905

By the middle of the nineteenth century, the situation in eastern Sulawesi had changed. The campaign against piracy had been stepped up, and the tension between Bone and the Dutch was mounting. The Bugis diaspora in eastern Sulawesi and the political power of Bugis chiefs there were a thorn in the side of the Dutch, as it was supposedly illegitimate since Bone's claims were dismissed as invalid. Latumana, the Bugis *syabandar* in Kendari in 1850, was one of several Bugis harbour masters and chiefs active in eastern Sulawesi. These men were not raiders, but they could muster a fleet of armed ships on short notice, as was evident during the war on Banggai between the Bugis supported Raja Agama, and the Ternatens in 1846 and 1848. Correspondence between the ruler of Bone and the Sultan of Buton intercepted by the Dutch revealed that the fugitive Raja Agama from Banggai and his followers were given protection by the ruler of Bone.

The expedition against Banggai and the defeat of Raja Agama indirectly led to local raiding sponsored by Ternaten chiefs who had won the war over Banggai. The immediate result of the campaign was the collapse of trade in Banggai that was carried on by the Bugis from the nearby island of Togean. These Bugis traders had also assisted Raja Agama in the war and helped him flee. In 1846, just as this conflict was taking place, three Tobelo chiefs and their followers arrived from Kalatoa after having been attacked by Dutch warships.[38] They were immediately enlisted as allies on the Ternaten side. After the war, Sorani, one of these chiefs, was allowed to settle on one of the small islands of the Banggai archipelago and raid the coastlines under the auspices of two Ternaten officials in Banggai. The looted goods were brought to market in Banggai and the profit pocketed by a prominent Ternaten official.

Inadvertently, Dutch attempts to stamp out illegitimate Bugis activity and raiding had given rise to a situation where local raiding was the only way in which the Ternaten officials could support themselves after the Bugis trade networks collapsed. Sorani and his men were warned in advance in the event of Dutch warships arriving on the east coast, so that they were not caught. Complaints eventually led to the discovery of the Ternaten-sponsored raiding in Banggai and to outrage on the part of Dutch officials, as Ternatens were meant to be the principal allies in the struggle against piracy in the eastern archipelago.

INDIGENOUS ALLIES IN ANTI-PIRACY CAMPAIGNS

Piracy in eastern Sulawesi was, just like its polities, small-scale and decentralized. Guns and warships were not sufficiently effective when it came to eradicating this kind of piracy, not only because large warships were unable to follow raiders into shallow waters and inlets, but also because of continuing support by local elites and communities. The strategy of the Dutch redirected itself towards breaking the alliances between local elites and maritime raiders. Instead of force, the colonial state pressured local chiefs and rulers into pledging their support in the fight against piracy and slavery and, in no circumstances, to provide raiders with shelter and food. But, without closer surveillance by the Dutch, little changed. Thwarting the alliances between raiding groups and indigenous rulers in eastern Sulawesi would prove a more difficult task than disrupting raiding routes and dispersing large raiding fleets.

By the mid-1860s, large raiding vessels had become rare in the seas of the Netherlands-Indies, and this was attributed to persistent patrolling and use of force by the Dutch and Spanish navies. Warships as a means of suppressing maritime raiding had been criticized in the late 1850s for being too expensive and ineffective in pursuit of raiding *perahu*, both large and small. As even larger *perahu* were relatively low in the water, they often discovered Dutch steamships before they were spotted themselves. They were also fast enough to move way in time. Small vessels readily disappeared into creeks and sailed into shallow water inaccessible to warships. Bombing campaigns against pirate settlements by warships dealt a major blow to large-scale regional raiding networks, but did not lead to their immediate demise. As regional networks broke down, a multitude of smaller, more localized raiding groups came into being.

Situations such as Banggai, where new alliances were formed with Tobelo raiders, occurred elsewhere as well, drawing more land-based communities into maritime raiding than had been the case previously. A further problem with small-scale raiding fleets and boats was that they were difficult to detect, because they often doubled as fishing *perahu*, and were furnished with legitimate passes. Severing alliances between such raiders and local elites was seen as the key to solving the "problem" of raiding, but could only be effectively accomplished with more frequent surveillance.[39] The colonial state sought the answer to this problem in the time-honoured custom of actively involving indigenous allies. Regular expeditions in Maluku caused a new wave of Tobelo migration from Halmahera and Bacan. This time moving to eastern Sulawesi did not give much respite, since Dutch patrols responded promptly by moving eastwards to the Sula — and Banggai archipelagos in their pursuit of Tobelo raiders. As Dutch naval power and frequent indigenous patrols were extended into eastern Sulawesi, the threat of sanctions for protecting raiders became far greater than the fear of retaliation from raiders.

At this time, Tobelo vessels had crews of approximately ten men, and expeditions were carried out with four or five boats. For larger, more important expeditions, several smaller flotillas banded together to form a larger fleet under the command of a chief who was chosen by the lesser chiefs. The largest documented fleet of Tobelo *perahu* in the 1870s was forty-eight vessels in the years 1872/73 in the Gulf of Tomini.[40] From there, the fleet divided into smaller raiding groups that spread along the east coast of Sulawesi. The extent of small-scale raiding on the east coast is apparent from the Italian Beccari's reports on his experiences in Kendari Bay in 1874.[41] He wrote very little about the plants he set out to collect, but a great deal about the constant threat of attacks by maritime raiders.

By 1878, the Tobelo and other raiders in the eastern archipelago no longer dared to raid openly. The alliances between raiding chiefs and land-based elites broke down under the same pressure as the alliances had between Tobelo and Magindanao several decades earlier. The more extensive patrolling by Dutch warships made it difficult for local chiefs to maintain their relations with Tobelo and protect them. For the same reason, there was less fear of retaliation by Tobelo raiders if chiefs and rulers did not cooperate with them as they had done in the past. At this time, more Tobelo chiefs surrendered voluntarily to the Dutch. One of these was Medom, or Medomo, who was among the most notorious and influential of the Tobelo leaders. In 1879, continuous patrols and expeditions were carried out against the "alfurs" in the waters around Banggai and Sula. Local chiefs and groups of Bajo who were former allies of the Tobelo were pressured into participating.[42] The Dutch then decided to contact the remaining Tobelo chiefs through their former chief and friend Medom. These Tobelo were to resettle the island of Obi, which had served as a base for the Tobelo for several decades. After four months in Banggai, Medom only succeeded in bringing back seven men, three women, and eight children to his village.[43] They were made to swear an oath never again to commit acts of piracy. Medom's settlement expanded; by the end of 1879 more than forty former raiders and their families had come voluntarily to settle under his leadership. He also convinced three other famed Tobelo chiefs and their followers to surrender to the Dutch resident in Ternate, after they had been pursued in vain by the Ternaten Said Mohammad Said's *hongi* in 1878. These headmen had been living deep in the interior of Obi with sixty men, women, and children for fear of the Ternaten *hongi*. The last Tobelo chief in eastern Sulawesi, Tofor, was tracked down and defeated on a tiny island south-east of Banggai with the help of Tobelo informants.[44] In eastern Sulawesi, no descendants of Tobelo raiders are to be found, since the movement back to Halmahera in the latter part of the nineteenth century included their local affines. The collective memory that remains of the Tobelo in eastern Sulawesi is of their reputation as dangerous raiders, who occupied themselves solely with murdering and capturing people.

Despite the occurence of occasional coastal raiding after 1880, colonial efforts to stem maritime raiding had rendered the coasts safer. Security and prosperity no longer depended on access to guns and alliances that guaranteed protection, so more people now could take part freely in the new cash crop economy. Between 1880 and 1890 patterns of trade in Banggai responded to the changed regional environment. A greater part of the population now took part in collecting rattan and damar, which made imported commodities such as cloth more accessible.

The worldwide demand for damar, rattan, and copra opened a new resource frontier on the east coast, which set in motion a new flow of people in search of wealth and commodities. Chinese traders arrived on the coasts of eastern Sulawesi to set up trading posts; Bugis repopulated stretches of abandoned shorelines and ventured inland as produce traders. And finally, groups of men from other parts of inland central and south-east Sulawesi covered long distances in search of forest products. Islam also travelled on the wave of economic expansion beyond its traditional boundaries that confined it to coastal areas, thus providing a new religious and social framework in the face of sweeping changes.

IMPACT OF COLONIAL MARITIME EXPANSION

This chapter deals with the period 1820–1905, during which raiding decreased and raiding networks fragmented and disintegrated. The colonial campaign against piracy in the eastern archipelago was part of the larger project of colonial expansion that culminated in taking control of indigenous ports and setting up a land-based administration in the beginning of the twentieth century. By the end of the nineteenth century, eastern Sulawesi was no longer situated between two political centres, but occupied an ambiguous position on the periphery of the expanding colonial state. Raiding was integrated into the political system as part of warfare and as a lucrative economic activity. Both aspects of raiding came under pressure as a result of the maritime expansion of the colonial state.

Relations between small-scale polities with the colonial state had changed radically. Mutual raiding no longer occurred, and local elites had to forego alliances with maritime raiding groups. However, local conflict continued on a smaller scale as a result of competition for control of the new economic resources. In the last decade of the nineteenth century, the reports of violence that reached colonial officials were not of mutual raiding, but of the several instances Chinese traders trading in forest products who were killed, supposedly by Bugis whose position was threatened by these new traders.

Finally, as the political dimension of previous diasporas was systematically undermined, new economic diasporas emerged, equally uncontrollable by the colonial state. The irony of the continuing Bugis diaspora was that as Bone declined as a political force, the Bugis colonization of coastal strips meant that, inadvertently, an enormous territorial expansion took place, one that would prove impossible for the Dutch to reverse. In the 1990s, coastal inhabitants of eastern Sulawesi invariably said they had been subjects of Bone, rather than of a local ruler, let alone the Netherlands-Indies government.

A new constellation of power came into place that favoured men who were able to move on two fronts simultaneously: they could speak Malay and negotiate with the colonial state, and had "traditional" authority and the network to support their authority. In this new situation, a new kind of alliance could occur, such as that between Hadji Taata and the Tolaki ruler Sao-sao, one was maritime, Islamic, commanded authority, had a reputation for black magic, the other was acknowledged by the colonial power.

The advent of the colonial state to areas such as eastern Sulawesi, which had been the last refuge for raiders, was by no mean the end of piracy. For the time being however, the Tobelo had returned to Maluku, and warfare between local rulers and chiefs with their maritime allies was replaced by a tenuous Pax Neerlandica.

Notes

This chapter is based on parts of my Ph.D. dissertation: "Contested Coastlines; Diasporas, Trade and Colonial Expansion 1680–1905" (Ph.D. dissertation, Murdoch University, 2003).

1. See also James C. Scott, *Seeing Like a State, How Certain Schemes to Improve the Human Condition Have Failed* (Yale University Press, New Haven and London, 1998), on the tendency of states to strive towards the sedentarization of populations within their boundaries.
2. Eastern Sulawesi comprises the entire east coast of Sulawesi starting from Balantak, the Banggai Archipelago, Tobungku, Kendari, down to Buton and Muna. This area of research is not based on contemporary or Dutch administrative divisions, but on the fact that these polities were historically closely connected through trade, warfare, cultural similarities, and kinship relations, and secondly, because they shared a similar positioning between South Sulawesi and Maluku.
3. Eric Tagliacozzo, "Kettle on a Slow Boil: Batavia's Threat Perceptions in the Indies Outer Islands, 1870–1910", *Journal of Southeast Asian Studies* 31, no. 1 (March 2000): 74, as quoted in Adam Young, "Roots of Contemporary Maritime Piracy in Southeast Asia", in *Piracy in Southeast Asia: Status, Issues, and Responses*, edited by Derek Johnson and Mark Valencia (IIAS/ISEAS Series on Maritime Issues and Piracy in Asia, Singapore, 2005), p. 15.
4. Bone had fought on the side of the VOC in order to defeat its arch enemy Makassar in the 1660s, and in that capacity of main ally of the VOC, its famed ruler Arung Palaka built up the power of Bone to unknown heights.
5. A. Ligtvoet, "Beschrijving en Geschiedenis van Boeton", *Bijdragen tot de Taal-, Land- en Volkenkunde van Nederlandsch-Indië*, II, (1878): 1–112; J.N. Vosmaer, "Korte beschrijving Korte beschrijving van het Zuid-Oostelijk-Schiereiland van Celebes", *Verhandelingen van het Bataviaasch Genootschap van Kunsten en Wetenschappen*, 17 (1839): 129, 130.

6. Since the rebellion against the VOC led by Ternate was put down in 1682, the status of Ternate changed from "ally" to "vassal", the consequences of which were not that apparent to most at that stage. When the Dutch re-established themselves in the archipelago in the second quarter of the nineteenth century, they justified their actions by referring to treaties that had been concluded during the VOC period. In this manner, Ternate was automatically accorded the status of "vassal". For a more elaborate account, see Leonard Y. Andaya, *The World of Maluku: Eastern Indonesia in the Early Modern Period* (Honolulu: University of Honolulu Press, 1993).
7. In Dutch sources the Galela are often mentioned in one breath with the Tobelo. The Galela also originated from Halmahera and participated in the raiding networks.
8. H.C. van Eibergen, "Geschiedkundige Aantekeningen omtrent de Noordkust van Ceram, vanaf het jaar 1816 tot 1832", *Tijdschrift voor Indische Taal-, Land- en Volkenkunde*, 1910, p. 489.
9. The reasons people gave for leaving their homes and joining Raja Jailolo provide an interesting insight into the role of violence in the political system. According to Dutch reports, people left their homes to avoid oppression by the Ternaten and Tidorese sultanates, particularly the former. The *hongi*, raiding expeditions operating under the auspices of elites, followed people wherever they moved with demands for tribute. They became so desperate they would give their children away instead of being killed. The pressure was so great that they were willing to participate in maritime raiding rather than being victimized themselves. Since the Dutch could not provide protection against the small-scale raiding that took place in Maluku, joining Raja Jailolo who had some control over these raiders was a more attractive choice. His reputation as an even-handed and fair minded ruler spread throughout the islands and he was said to be more popular than either of the sultans of Ternate or Tidore. Ibid., p. 498.
10. A *hongi* was an expedition from Ternate to its tributaries, for the eradication of spices, for levying tribute, or for disciplining tributaries. Often Tobelo from Halmahera were included in this expeditions.
11. The chief of Sawai on the north coast of Seram was held hostage for three months by Raja Jailolo because he had allowed a Dutch steamship to anchor near his village. This provoked retaliation from the Dutch resident Merkus, who was the first official to begin to re-establishing Dutch authority in Maluku. The Dutch and Ternaten forces took the fortress and burned over eighty boats. Ibid., p. 493.
12. Ibid., p. 503.
13. ANRI Resolutie, 12 November 1833 No. 3.
14. ANRI Besluit, 31 March 1837 No. 3, p. 17.
15. "Berigten omtrent den Zeeroof in den Nederlandsch-Indischen Archipel, 1858", *Tijdschrift voor Indische Taal-, Land- en Volkenkunde*, 1873, p. 307. After

Daeng Magassing was dismissed from the government's service and his boats confiscated, he was also banned from visiting or living anywhere under Dutch rule. This ban was lifted after he assisted the captains of a Dutch schooner that had been attacked by their own crew in 1841. His father, who was the *bonto* (equivalent to ruler) of Bonerate, ordered him to take the Dutchmen to Bima, the closest Dutch post. ANRI Makassar 7 & 7A, "Beknopt Overzigt der Stukken en Aangelegenheden rakende de Regten welke Boni zich heeft aangematigd over de Landen gelegen in de Tomini-Baai".

16. Bajo were mostly nomadic fisherfolk spread along the Gulf of Bone, eastern Sulawesi, and the Gulf of Tomini. They were sought after as allies because of their knowledge of the sea and their ability to collect pearls, *trepang* and tortoise shell.
17. ARA Vosmaer Collectie 548, 153, Letter by J.N. Vosmaer to his brother J. Vosmaer, Batavia, 29 August 1829.
18. Ibid., Letter to J. Vosmaer, 31 October 1830, Surabaya 16 October 1831.
19. Nicholas J. Vosmaer, "Korte beschrijving", 1839, pp. 63–184; ANRI Resolutie 7 May 1835, No. 2; Resolutie 2 June 1836, No. 11.
20. ANRI Resolutie 7 May 1835 No. 2; Makassar to Batavia, 21 February 1835, p. 1d.
21. ANRI Resolutie 12 January 1835, No. 16; Resolutie 7 May 1835, No. 2; Resolutie 7 May 1835, No. 2, Batavia to Makassar, 19 March 1835.
22. It is so well concealed that when entering the bay by ship, it seems as if the ship is heading straight into the rocky coastline but then a sharp turn suddenly reveals the entrance and a view of Kendari Bay.
23. The Tolaki are an ethnic group who inhabits the eastern part south-east Sulawesi. They were swidden agriculturalists. Coastal Tolaki at this time adhered to a syncretic version of Islam, whereas their inland kin did not, and continued to practise headhunting. They lived in kinship groups under the leadership of chiefs who were loosely united in the chiefdom of Konawe.
24. J.N. Vosmaer, *Korte Beschrijving*, 1839, p. 78.
25. See previous chapter for a discussion of Bajo migration and the *trepang* trade.
26. ANRI Besluit 31 March 1837, No. 3.
27. ANRI Resolutie 2 June 1836, No. 11.
28. Ibid., letter from former governor of Makassar, D.W. Pietermaat, to Batavia, 21 April 1836.
29. Ibid., letter from sultan of Buton to governor of Makassar, 4 April 1836.
30. "Het Eiland Celebes volgens de togten en ontdekkingen van Jacques Nicholas Vosmaer", *Koloniaal Tijdschrift*, 1862, p. 335.
31. ANRI Besluit 31/3 1837, No. 3, "Advies van de raad van Indië", 6 March 1837.
32. Ibid., On board of HM Schooner *Krokodil*, 31 October 1836.

33. ANRI Besluit 31 March 1837, No. 3, p. 21.
34. ANRI Resolutie 13 May 1836, No. 12, "Post te Kendari ingetrokken", p. 2.
35. Ibid., pp. 5, 6.
36. Oral communication from Christiaan Heersink.
37. J.H.P.E Kniphorst, "Historische schets van den Zeeroof in den Oost-Indischen Archipel. — Middelen, ook aanverwante, ter bestrijding", *Tijdschrift voor Nederlandsch Indië*, 1st vol. (1882): 241–93.
38. ANRI Ternate 180, p. 21a.
39. See references to raiding in the 1850s: "Berigten omtrent den Zeeroof in den Nederlandsch-Indischen Archipel", *Tijdschrift voor Indische Taal-, Land- en Volkenkunde*. It may not be a coincidence that these elaborate retrospective accounts of the anti-piracy campaigns started to be published just as the anti-piracy campaigns were criticized for being ineffective.
40. "Memorie van Overgave van het bestuur der Residentie Ternate door den aftredenden Resident S.C.I.W. van Musschenbroek aan den benoemde resident, 1875".
41. Guido Cora, "Viaggio di O. Beccari nel Sud-est di Celebes", *Cosmos*, II (1874): 200–02; O. Beccari, "Recenti Spediziono ala Nuova Guinea", *Cosmos*, II (1874): 203–08.
42. *Koloniaal Verslag*, 1879, p. 28.
43. Ibid., 1880, p. 22.
44. A. Hueting, "De Tobeloreezen in hun denken en doen", *Bijdragen tot de Taal-, Land- en Volkenkunde van Nederlandsch-Indië* 78 (1922): 22. In 1902, the young Christian congregation of Wari on Halmahera was joined by a small group of Muslims who had been taken back by Medom because they were related to Tobelo raiders.

References

Andaya, Leonard Y. *The World of Maluku: Eastern Indonesia in the Early Modern Period*. Honolulu: University of Honolulu Press, 1993.

"Berigten omtrent den Zeeroof in den Nederlandsch-Indischen Archipel, 1858". *Tijdschrift voor Indische Taal-, Land- en Volkenkunde* (1873): 350–78.

Eibergen, H.C. van. "Geschiedkundige Aantekeningen omtrent de Noordkust van Ceram, vanaf het jaar 1816 tot 1832". *Tijdschrift voor Indische Taal-, Land- en Volkenkunde* (1910): 489–504.

Kniphorst, J.H.P.E. "Historische schets van den Zeeroof in den Oost-Indischen Archipel. — Middelen, ook aanverwante, ter bestrijding". *Tijdschrift voor Nederlandsch Indië*, I (1882): 241–93.

Ligtvoet, A. "Beschrijving en Geschiedenis van Boeton". *Bijdragen tot de Taal-, Land- en Volkenkunde van Nederlandsch-Indië*, II (1878): 1–112.

Scott, James C. *Seeing Like a State: How Certain Schemes to Improve the Human Condition Have Failed*. New Haven and London: Yale University Press, 1998.

Tarling, Nicholas. *Piracy and Politics in the Malay World: A Study of British Imperialism in Nineteenth-century South-East Asia*. Melbourne, Canberra, Sydney: F. Cheshire, 1963.

Vosmaer, J.N. "Korte Beschrijving van het Zuid-Oostelijk Schiereiland van Celebes". *Verhandelingen van het Bataviaasch Genootschap van Kunsten en Wetenschappen* 17 (1839): 63–184.

———. "Het Eiland Celebes volgens de Togten en Ontdekkingen van Jacques Nicholas Vosmaer". *Koloniaal Tijdschrift* 2 (1862): 321–42.

Warren, James Francis. *The Sulu Zone, 1768–1898, The Dynamics of External Trade, Slavery, and Ethnicity in the Transformation of a Southeast Asian Maritime State*. Singapore University Press, 1981.

Young, Adam J. "Roots of Maritime Piracy in Southeast Asia". In *Piracy in Southeast Asia, Status, Issues, and Responses*, edited by Derek Johnson and Mark Valencia. Singapore: IIAS/ISEAS Series on Maritime Issues and Piracy in Asia, 2005.

11

Suppressing Piracy in Asia: Decolonization and International Relations in a Maritime Border Region (the Sulu Sea), 1959–63

Stefan Eklöf Amirell

INTRODUCTION

In the 1990s and early 2000s Southeast Asia was frequently referred to as one of the most piracy-prone regions in the world. However, in spite of the great attention given to piracy in the Malacca Strait, the most pirate infested part of the region were and are the waters of the southern Philippines and eastern Malaysia. Between 1993 and 2004, the Philippine authorities have recorded over 1,300 cases of piracy and armed robbery against vessels, mainly in the southern parts of the country, and several hundred cases were recorded by Malaysian authorities in the waters off Sabah. In the Philippines alone, 431 people were killed, and 426 people were reported missing as a result of the raids.[1]

The problem is by no means new. At least since the early nineteenth century, observers of the region have described the so-called "Moros", the Muslim peoples of the southern Philippines, as prone to piracy and maritime raiding. From the late eighteenth century up to the mid-nineteenth century, the famous "pirate wind", annual slave raids by Illanun and other Sulu pirates, struck fear in the coastal populations throughout Southeast Asia.[2] Consequently, European observers came to regard piracy as endemic among the populations of the southern Philippines, and the inclination to piracy was even taken as a marker of ethnic identity with all Muslim groups in the area being lumped together as *Piratenstämme*.[3]

Culture in itself, however, cannot explain historical developments. The fact that piracy, among some of the ethnic groups in the region, seems to be a legitimate and even high status practice, does not in itself explain why piracy is endemic in the region — especially after more than 200 years of serious effort to eradicate it by colonial and post-colonial governments. On the contrary, this circumstance in itself needs to be explained. Why has the seemingly anachronistic practice of piracy not come to an end, or, at least, been relatively efficiently suppressed, in the Sulu region as it has in other formerly pirate infested waters, such as the east and south coasts of China, the Mediterranean, and the Caribbean?[4] In order to understand this, we need to look not only at the economic and cultural aspects of the problem, but also — and above all — the political aspects, especially in relation to private maritime trade. Why do certain national and international political contexts seem to favour piratical activity?

Anne Pérotin-Dumon has in a thought provoking article argued that the classic age of the European pirates — from about 1520 to 1750 — was conditioned by the commercial policies of the major political empires, first Spain and Portugal, then England and France:

> Thus, ironically, the hegemonic nature of some merchant empires did much to keep piracy alive. As long as monopolies went along with commercial wars, piracy simply fluctuated according to the degree of a state's authority at sea. It was the linkage between trade, war, and hegemonic policies that engendered a cycle in which smuggling and piracy alternated. [...] To eliminate piracy as a phenomenon, however, trade monopoly had to be given up altogether. This was a policy toward which England, France, and Spain only gradually moved till the second half of the eighteenth century.[5]

Piracy — whether in the sixteenth-century Mediterranean, seventeenth-century China or eighteenth-century Caribbean — occurred on the margins of territorially based merchant empires with hegemonic policies. These were empires that were primarily concerned with asserting their political and military hegemony over other states, and in the mercantilist ideology of the age, trade was seen as a means of acquiring the economic means for the expansion of state power. In trying — albeit unsuccessfully — to control and monopolize maritime commerce, the states created the favourable conditions in which piracy and smuggling could flourish.

With Pérotin-Dumon's argument as inspiration, the purpose of the present chapter is to explore the ways in which piratical activity was fuelled by state policies and international relations in the Sulu region in the late 1950s and early 1960s.

THE RETURN OF PIRACY

As the title of this chapter indicates, piracy in the Sulu region was actually rather efficiently suppressed for a period, that of the late colonial era from about 1915 to 1941. With the aid of steam gunboats, the Spanish, Dutch, and British navies managed to put an end to the large-scale raiding of the Sulu pirates already in the second half of the nineteenth century, but they never managed to suppress piracy and coastal raiding on a smaller, but still frequent, scale. Spain never gained control of the southern parts of the Philippine archipelago and Dutch control of the waters of eastern Indonesia was incomplete. In Sabah, the British North Borneo Company was administratively and financially weak and unable to prevent piracy and raiding by Sulus along its coast right up until the end of the nineteenth century.[6]

It was only after Spain ceded its Philippine colony to the United States in 1898 that Sulu piracy was efficiently suppressed. After a surge in piratical activity in the first decade of the twentieth century, the Americans resumed anti-piracy patrols in the area and through the deployment of gunboats, Sulu piracy was promptly eradicated.[7] In the subsequent years, the American "pacification" campaign brought the southern Philippines under central government control, and some 7,000 firearms were collected from outlaw elements.[8] The task of maintaining law and order in the region was delegated to the Philippine constabulary, a police force which had been set up by the Americans in 1901. The outcome was that law and order was successfully maintained in the region until the outbreak of the war with Japan in 1941.

After the Philippines gained independence in 1946, however, it seems that law and order was less efficiently upheld in the region than during the pre-war years. Two immediate legacies of the war again made piracy and maritime raiding a viable occupation for Sulu outlaws. One was the proliferation of large numbers of modern firearms after the war, and the other was the motorization of sea travel due to the widespread availability of inexpensive U.S. military surplus engines.[9] Compared with the pre-war era, these legacies of the war gave the pirates a relative advantage — in firepower and velocity — over the authorities that were charged with the task of upholding law and order on the sea.

At the end of 1949 the British authorities in North Borneo arrested thirty-three suspected Filipino pirates in North Borneo waters, all of whom subsequently were convicted and sentenced to between five and seven years imprisonment for "dacoity" and related offences.[10] In relation to the sentences, a despatch from the British Legation in Manila to London said:

> Piracy was the traditional means of livelihood of the Sulu Moros in the nineteenth century. With the advent of the Americans in the Philippines at the end of the century conditions improved considerably. A group of American officers organised the Philippine Constabulary which was very successful in maintaining law and order in Sulu up to the outbreak of war with Japan. But now the American officers are gone and the Philippine authorities have not hitherto shown themselves capable of maintaining the constabulary at its old standards. The result among the Moros is, I fear, that they are reverting to type and are again finding in piracy and smuggling an easy way of making a living.[11]

After a particularly serious raid on the East Borneo town of Semporna in 1954, however, the British set up an armed force of marine police which in subsequent years reportedly developed into a "very efficient body".[12] The marine police thus seems to have been capable of upholding law and order in North Borneo waters between 1954 and 1958.

In May 1959, however, a surge in piratical attacks in North Borneo led the colonial government to request the assistance of the Royal Navy to combat the problem. In the twelve months between November 1958 and October 1959, the North Borneo police recorded fifty-four piratical attacks, although it was noted that the real number was probably much higher due to the reluctance on the part of many victims to report attacks to the authorities in order to avoid delays consequent on police interrogation. Rumours, moreover, circulated in the port of Tawau, close to Sabah's Indonesian border, of sinkings and gun battles at sea in which convoys of traders had fought off would-be pirates.[13]

Most of the reported attacks, 83 per cent, took place between May and August 1959, a period of fair weather in the Sulu region. Most occurred in an area east of, or close to, the island of Si-Amil near the Indonesian-North Borneo maritime boundary, and in all cases the perpetrators were Sulus from the southern Philippines. The pirates used motor *kumpits* (wooden boats), often powered by one or more outboard engines, and in most cases they were armed with firearms or explosives, including shotguns, Garand (semiautomatic) rifles, carbines, Sten (submachine) guns, Bren (light machine) guns, pistols, and fishing bombs. In fourteen of the attacks, firearms or bombs were used, but there were no reports of casualties among the victims.[14]

TRADERS, SMUGGLERS AND RAIDERS

All the victims were Indonesian vessels, mostly originating from various ports in Celebes (Sulawesi), Indonesia, on their way to Tawau with cargoes of copra (coconut). The great majority of the victims were relatively small sailing craft engaged in the intensive barter trade in the region. In this trade, based on traditional trading networks of the region, copra from the Philippines and Indonesia — mainly Celebes — was exported to North Borneo and exchanged for consumer goods, such as cigarettes, engines, textiles, and clothing. The *kumpit*s carrying the trade were operated by Filipino and Indonesian crews, but some of them were owned and financed by North Borneo businessmen.[15]

From the Indonesian point of view, most of the trade seems to have been illegal, but the central government was unable to control it. Copra traders were required to obtain export licences at their port of origin, but as there was no proper organization for issuing them, exporters instead reportedly bribed local officials to see through their fingers. The Indonesian navy tried to stop the trade by intercepting trading craft, often confiscating both cargo and vessel.[16] The navy, however, lacked the capacity to enforce the export regulations efficiently; at one time it was reported that Indonesia had only one operating naval patrol vessel in the region.[17]

As regards the relation between the Philippines and North Borneo, the trade was more or less straightforward from the end of World War II until 1956. North Borneo was a natural market for copra producers in the southern Philippines (as well as Celebes), and exporters were attracted to the British colony by the "law and order of our institutions and by a copra price which includes no element of levy imposed officially (or unofficially by officials)", as put by the North Borneo governor in 1959.[18] The copra — without any money actually changing place although accounts were kept in Straits dollars — was exchanged for limited amounts of consumer goods that were imported to the Philippines.

From 1956, however, the barter trade came to be seen as problematic by the Philippine government, as large quantities of consumer goods — especially cigarettes — were being imported to North Borneo from Hong Kong and then re-exported to the Philippines in exchange for copra thus evading licensing and foreign exchange restrictions imposed by the Philippine government.[19] The trade was still perfectly legal from the point of view of the North Borneo government, but as the scale increased during the second half of the 1950s the Philippine government's stance went from unclear to outright condemning. In the mid-1950s, an inconsistently applied rule of dubious legal status seemed to give southern Filipinos the right to barter their produce for household goods up to a value of 1,000 pesos per person. President Ramon Magsaysay apparently favoured the arrangement and intended to issue a special directive regulating the barter trade when he was tragically killed in a plane crash in 1957. The barter trade was thus left without a proper legal framework, and the Philippine customs authorities instead began to apply an extensive list, issued by the Central Bank, of items banned to the trade.[20] In January 1959, Magsaysay's successor, President Carlos Garcia, moreover, issued a ban on exporting copra to North Borneo, apparently in an attempt to curb the smuggling of cigarettes and counterfeit pesos into the Philippines.[21] The ban, together with intensified naval patrolling and efforts to regulate the barter trade, initially had the effect of bringing the trade to a virtual standstill, but it gradually revived again in 1959 as the Philippine authorities were unable to uphold the ban.[22]

The British were not only concerned that the Philippine efforts to quench the barter trade would have negative consequences for the trade and economy of North Borneo, but also feared that it might bring about an increase in piratical activity as Sulu barter traders — or "smugglers" as seen from the Philippine perspective — were deprived of their livelihood and thus might revert to "their traditional occupation of piracy".[23] The problem did indeed continue in spite of the efforts of the British authorities, and in 1960, forty-two piracies were reported to the British authorities. In the following year, the marauding reached a post-war record of ninety-seven attacks with eight people killed and forty-five wounded or missing. In 1962, the number of reported piracies declined to thirty-nine with four people killed and three wounded, but on the other hand, there was a sharp increase in the number of armed raids on coastal settlements in North Borneo. There were twenty armed raids in 1962, resulting in the killing of at least eight people.[24] The most serious raid took place on 20 July at Kunak, a timber camp on the east coast of North Borneo:

> The raid began about 1740 hours [...] when a vessel (technically a "kumpit", but more like a Chinese launch in appearance and about 24 feet long) approached Kunak from the Semporna Channel. It had a "kajang" covering, badly maintained. At the time the government launch "Rusakan" was alongside the steps of the wharf, and the British Borneo Timber Company log towing boat, "Darvel Bay", was alongside the longest part of the wharf. As the "kumpit" came alongside the "Rusakan", the muzzles of four rifles appeared over its side. The occupants of the "kumpit" opened fire and in the first burst killed the Engineer of the "Rusakan", who was sitting on the forward deck, and wounded two children also on deck. The two sailors, the Engineer's wife and one of the sailor's wives jumped into the sea. The serang (skipper) was wounded in the left arm as he also jumped for the sea. The kumpit then pulled up to the wharf. Four raiders ran across the wharf to the "Darvel Bay", which had its engine running, shot four members of the crew and did some damage to the engine. One man returned to the "Rusakan", smashed the copper pipes of the engine, tore out the radio and transferred it and the "Rusakan's" binoculars to the kumpit. While one raider stayed in the kumpit, the rest, some seven in number, advanced from the wharf, with two firing up the road, while others entered the shops near the wharf and forced local people to carry goods and money back to the kumpit. The telephone-line was cut and an attempt was made to launch the Mostyn Estates launch "Lucinda". This was unsuccessful, as it was locked up. The raiders then stove in the boat and damaged the engine. [...]
>
> After the raiders had loaded their boat, they saw a Chinese launch coming in round the coral. They intercepted it, tied up their own boat to it, told the passengers to jump into the sea and ordered the skipper and engineer, named Kamaludin, to tow the kumpit out.[25]

For the British, the armed raids on the coast were even more serious than the pirate attacks. Whereas the latter mainly affected Indonesian barter traders, the former directly affected the population of North Borneo. Moreover, the raids were a serious shock to morale all along the east coast of the colony, causing local labourers to drift away. This in turn could have serious implications for the whole economy of North Borneo.[26]

The British were apparently unable to protect the trade and coast of its colony from the raiding activities of the Sulu pirates. In the period 1959–62, sixty-one Filipino nationals were convicted of piracy in North Borneo courts, and another twenty-seven of lesser crimes related to acts of piracy, but this apparently did little to stop the raids.[27] The authorities also took a range of measures to improve security, including the strengthening of police patrols and posts along the coast, constructing watch towers and forts in vulnerable places, improving radio communications between outlying settlements and police posts, temporarily providing military garrisons, and increasing naval patrolling. The main purpose of these measures, however, as the British were well aware, was to boost the morale of the population, as there was very little chance of the authorities actually apprehending the pirates.[28]

INTERNATIONAL COOPERATION AND PRIORITIES

The British realized that the only way to rid its waters and coast of the pirates was to deal with the pirates on their land bases. These were located in the southern Philippines, mainly in the Tawi-Tawi group of islands, some forty nautical miles east of the eastern tip of North Borneo, and any chance of dealing effectively with the pirates thus required the cooperation of the Philippine authorities. Cooperation with Indonesia, meanwhile, was out of the question because of its objection to the plan, set for 31 August 1963, of forming Malaysia through the merger of Malaya with the British colonies in north Borneo and Singapore.[29] At the beginning of 1963, Indonesia even declared a policy of Confrontation (*Konfrontasi*) against Malaysia, involving armed incursions along the British and later Malaysian border in north Borneo.

Even though British-Philippine relations in principle were friendly in the years leading up to the forming of Malaysia, the possibilities for naval cooperation between the two countries were hampered by two major unresolved sovereignty issues. One was the Philippine claim that its territorial waters, in agreement with the 1898 Spanish-American Treaty of Paris, encompassed most of the Sulu Sea. The British, by contrast, only recognized the much smaller territorial waters set down in the 1958 United Nations Convention on the Law of the Sea (UNCLOS), which the United Kingdom had ratified, but not the Philippines.[30]

The other dispute concerned the territory of British North Borneo itself. In June 1962, as preparations for the transfer of sovereignty of North Borneo to Malaysia in the following year were underway, Philippine President Diosdado Macapagal unexpectedly announced his country's claim to the territory.[31] These unresolved territorial disputes made naval cooperation difficult, as Great Britain was careful not to enter into any operational or other agreements that might be interpreted as a tacit recognition of the Philippine claims.

Aside from the territorial disputes, the two countries also had fundamentally different views on what constituted the main problems of maritime law enforcement in the Sulu region. In order to combat the pirates, the British worked to establish cordial, informal relations with the Philippine police and naval officers in the region, but wished to avoid, at all costs, the signing of any formal agreement for naval cooperation with the Philippines.[32] The Philippines, on their part, proposed a formal agreement between Great Britain and the Philippines, similar to the one which the country had signed with Indonesia in 1960 — or, alternatively, expanding that agreement to a trilateral agreement. The purposes of the Indonesian-Philippine agreement was to eradicate piracy, offences against the security of the state, all forms of smuggling (including the barter trade), and illegal entry. According to the British, however, the focus in implementing the agreement was all on the smuggling problem:

> The Philippine Navy, in conjunction with the Indonesian authorities, are active in harassing barter traders, and display a comprehensive knowledge of trading craft. However, the take little interest in other unlawful pursuits entailing loss of life and property and show an ignorance of raiders.[33]

The British, therefore, were of the opinion that such an agreement would be more to the detriment of the traders than to the pirates and raiders. They, moreover, foresaw operational problems with joint patrolling stemming from different perceptions of the local craft that would be stopped. The Filipinos were likely to insist that the crews were smugglers who should be shot, whereas the British were likely to insist that they were traders who should be released.[34]

In mid-March 1963, a group of North Borneo government officials and British naval officers visited the Philippines for exploratory talks on Anglo-Philippine naval cooperation, but still with the aim of avoiding any formal agreement or additional commitments. It was clear from the talks that the problem of cigarette smuggling and its detrimental effect on the national economy was the main priority for the Filipinos. Although the talks reportedly were conducted in a constructive and friendly atmosphere, the British realized that unless they showed their willingness to cooperate in controlling the cigarette smuggling, they could expect no cooperation from the Filipinos in the prevention of piracy and armed raids on the coasts of North Borneo, which in Philippine eyes was a "comparatively minor issue".[35]

Following the talks, the Philippine authorities did take some measures to curb piratical activity, including increased patrol activity in the Tawi-Tawi area and, notably, the killing of one of the principal gang leaders, Amak, a fearful, one-eyed outlaw who had been involved in several of the armed raids on the coast of North Borneo. The campaign, however, was not primarily carried out in order to appease the British, even though the Filipinos apparently tried to use the clean-up as a bargaining chip in order to gain more cooperation in controlling the cigarette smuggling. Rather, it seems that a tour by British and Philippine officers of the Sulu region in March 1963 prompted the Filipinos to try to curb the lawlessness and prevalent corruption in the local constabulary forces.[36] The Philippine action contributed to a decline in piratical activity, and especially armed raids, in North Borneo, but piracies nevertheless continued right up until the end of British rule in the territory in August 1963.

Conclusion

After having been relatively successfully suppressed during the period of American colonialism in the Philippines, piracy and maritime raiding returned to the Sulu region in the years following World War II and Philippine independence in 1946. The situation grew increasingly serious towards the end of the 1950s and early 1960s when Sulu pirates attacked numerous local traders, mainly from Indonesia, and coastal villages and settlements on the coasts and islands of British North Borneo.

With the raiders, heavily armed and equipped with fast motor boats, coming from the Philippines, there was little that the British — who were genuinely concerned about the problem — could do to uphold law and order on the seas. The main priority for the British colonial government was to guarantee security in its territorial waters in order that free trade could flourish and bring economic prosperity to the colony. Free trade, however, largely meant importing copra from Indonesia and the Philippines, in contravention of the (inefficiently implemented) export regulations of those countries, and exporting cigarettes, an activity which was seen as smuggling from the Philippine perspective. For the Indonesian and Philippine governments, the main issue was to control the illegal trade and impose taxes and licences on the import and export of goods in and out of their respective countries. The British colonial government, by contrast, only imposed minor fees on the trade and rejected any suggestions that they cooperate with their neighbours — particularly the Philippines — in curbing the smuggling.

In general terms, the failure to achieve efficient naval and police cooperation in order to curb piracy was due to a clash between what may be termed the British "trading state" on the one side, and the Indonesian and Philippine "political states" on the other.[37] The former saw free trade as the key to national advancement and the government's role, in that context, was to provide the institutions which allowed free trade to flourish — including to maintain law and order on the sea in order to secure the free passage of traders and goods. For Indonesia and the Philippines, by contrast, the main priority was to strengthen authority of the central government and to assert its control over the vast territories and territorial waters of their respective country. In the immediate postcolonial period, moreover, free trade was viewed by the latter countries with suspicion because of its association with predatory capitalism and Western imperialism. For Indonesia, the British commercial policy in North Borneo seemed designed to maintain the uninterrupted supply of cheap raw materials, whereas smuggling of cigarettes from the territory to the Philippines deprived the government there of considerable incomes. For both Indonesia and the Philippines, therefore, the main priority was to safeguard their borders and suppress the trading activities which the British encouraged and thrived on.

International relations were further complicated by the Philippine claim to Sabah, by different conflicting maritime border claims and Indonesia's policy of Confrontation against Malaysia. These issues also illustrated the Indonesian and Philippine concerns with issues of national sovereignty and territorial integrity rather than free trade and economic development.

Just as in previous instances of piratical activity during the last 500 years, piracy in the Sulu region re-emerged in the mid-twentieth century as a result of the different political economies of the states involved. In the clash between free trade and hegemonic trading policies of certain states, the roots of piracy — at least in one of its major forms — can be found. As long as the differences in policies and priorities between trading states and political states persist, piracy is likely to persist.

Notes

An earlier version of this chapter appeared in Working Paper No. 15, 2005 of the series Working Papers in Contemporary Asian Studies of the University of Lund. Stefan Eklöf, "The Return of Piracy: Decolonization and International Relations in a Maritime Border Region (the Sulu Sea), 1959–63" // ISBN 91-975726-4-0.

1. Santos (2006, p. 40), citing unpublished reports by the Philippine Coast Guard and Navy, and Sazlan (2002, p. 3) citing unpublished reports by Malaysia's Maritime Enforcement Co-ordination Centre. By comparison, the International Maritime Bureau, a unit of the International Chamber of Commerce, reported 189 attacks (actual as well as attempted) in the Malacca Strait during the same period; see ICC — International Maritime Bureau (2005, p. 4). Armed raids against ships will, for the present purposes, be designated as "piracy" regardless of whether they take place on the high seas or in the territorial waters of a state. See ibid. (2005, p. 3) for the major current definitions of piracy and armed robbery. The present discussion, however, excludes cases of petty theft against ships at berth or anchor, many of which are included in the IMB's reports.
2. See Warren (2002).
3. Blumentritt (1882).
4. In 2004, the IMB recorded one attack against a ship underway in Chinese (Hong Kong) waters and no acts of piracy in the Mediterranean. The Caribbean was identified as a piracy prone area, but there were only five reported cases of piracy against vessels outside of port areas; see ICC — International Maritime Bureau (2005, pp. 44 and 49–54). Even if this figure is doubled to account for underreporting, it is far below the ninety-six cases recorded by Philippine authorities for the first seven months of the year.
5. Pérotin-Dumon (2001, p. 48).
6. Warren (2002, pp. 379–85).
7. Hurley (1997, ch. 23).
8. Hurley (1997, ch. 25). See also Russel (1981) for the American campaign.
9. Kiefer (1972, p. 4) and Sidel (1995, p. 155). See also Hedman & Sidel (2000).
10. "Persons, Stated to be from Sitangkai'", enclosure to letter from British Legation in Manila to the secretary of state for Foreign Affairs, 24 March 1950, FO 371/84337.
11. British Legation in Manila to the minister of state for Foreign Affairs, 24 July 1950, FO 371/84337.
12. Acting governor of North Borneo to the secretary of state for the Colonies, 23 May 1957, FO 371/129539.
13. Governor of North Borneo to the commissioner general for the United Kingdom in Southeast Asia, 13 November 1959, CO 1030/752. The original request for naval assistance was made by the acting chief secretary (of the Government of North Borneo) to the commander-in chief, Far East Station on 22 May 1959.
14. "Notes on Piracies", October 1959, CO 1030/752.

15. "The Barter Trade", Annex C to "Report on the Visit of the Philippine Mission to North Borneo to Look into the Barter Trade, July 3–11, 1958", undated, CO 1030/752.
16. R.G. Symons to J.E. Cable, 16 March 1962, DO 169/31, and "Indonesian Naval Activity", letter from the governor of North Borneo to the commissioner general for the United Kingdom in South East Asia, Singapore, 12 June 1963, FO 371/169741.
17. Governor of North Borneo to the commissioner general for the United Kingdom in Southeast Asia, 13 November 1959, CO 1030/752
18. Ibid.
19. "Anglo/Philippine talks: Economic Aspects of Philippine Interests in North Borneo", undated, DO 169/32.
20. "The Barter Trade", Annex C to "Report on the Visit of the Philippine Mission to North Borneo to Look into the Barter Trade, July 3–11, 1958", undated, CO 1030/752.
21. "From Manila to Foreign Office", 23 September 1959, CO 1030/752.
22. "Extract from Monthly Intelligence Report — February, 1959", undated, CO 1030/752.
23. "Extract from Monthly Intelligence Report for January, 1959 — North Borneo", undated, CO 1030/752.
24. "Piracies and Armed Raids", note attached to letter from the governor of North Borneo to the secretary of state for the Colonies, 8 January 1963, CO 1030/1660.
25. "Armed raids along the Coastline of North Borneo", letter from the acting governor of North Borneo to the commander-in-chief, Far East Station, 30 July 1962, DO 169/31.
26. Ibid. and Commander-in-Chief, Far East Station to Admiralty, 8 August 1962, DO 169/31.
27. "Piracies and Armed Raids", 1963.
28. Governor of North Borneo to the secretary of state for the Colonies, 8 January 1963, CO 1030/1660, and North Borneo to the secretary of state for the Colonies, 9 January 1963, FO 371/169740.
29. North or northern Borneo is Sabah and Sarawak; north Borneo was a British Colony, Sabah.
30. "Advice to Flag Officer Commanding in Chief Far East Fleet in connection with Station Orders in Territorial Limits and the Protection of Merchant Shipping", undated, FO 371/169740.
31. See Noble (1977).
32. Governor of North Borneo to the secretary of state for the Colonies, 1963.
33. "Piracies and Armed Raids", 1963.
34. F.A. Warner to T. Peters, 12 June 1963, DO 169/33.

35. "Anglo-Philippine Naval Cooperation. Report of a Meeting Held at Philippine Naval Headquarters, Manila, 15th March, 1963", Annex B to "Report by Lieutenant Commander P.A. Woollings R.N. on his visit to the Philippines 11th–22nd March 1963", undated, CO 1030/1660.
36. "Anglo-Philippine Talks Concerning Piracy and Other Activities in The Sulu Area", letter from Lieutenant Commander P.A. Woollings to the Flag Officer Commanding-in-Chief, Far Eastern Fleet, 30 July 1963, DO 169/33.
37. Cf. Rosecrance (1986).

References

Archival Sources — British National Archives, Kew

Records of the Colonial Office, Commonwealth and Foreign and Commonwealth Offices, Empire Marketing Board, and related bodies, 1570–1990 (CO).

Records created or inherited by the Dominions Office, and of the Commonwealth Relations and Foreign and Commonwealth Offices, 1843–1990 (DO).

Records created and inherited by the Foreign Office, 1567–2003 (FO).

Literature

Blumentritt, Ferd. *Versuch einer Ethnographie der Philippinen*. Gotha, Germany, 1882.

Hedman, Eva-Lotta and John T. Sidel. "The Sulu Zone Revisited: The Philippines in Southeast Asia". In *Philippine Politics and Society in the Twentieth Century: Colonial Legacies, Post-colonial Trajectories*, edited by Eva-Lotta Hedman and John T. Sidel. London and New York: Routledge, 2000.

Hurley, Vic. *Swish of the Kris*. 1997 (1936). Republished as e-book at the Internet web page <http://www.bakbakan.com/swishkb.html>, version current at 21 June 2005.

ICC — International Maritime Bureau. "Piracy and Armed Robbery against Ships: Annual Report 1st January–31st December 2004". Barking, Essex: ICC — International Maritime Bureau, 2005.

Kiefer, Thomas M. *The Tausug: Violence and Law in a Philippine Moslem Society*. New York etc.: Holt, Rinehart and Winston, 1972.

Noble, Lela Garner. *Philippine Policy toward Sabah: A Claim to Independence*. Tucson, Arizona: The University of Arizona Press, 1977.

Pérotin-Dumon, Anne. "The Pirate and the Emperor: Power and the Law on the Seas, 1450–1850". In *Bandits at Sea: A Pirates Reader*, edited by C. R. Pennel. New York and London: New York University Press, 2001, pp. 25–54.

Rosecrance, Richard. *The Rise of the Trading State: Commerce and Conquest in the Modern World*. New York: Basic Books, 1986.

Russel, Roth. *Muddy Glory: America's "Indian Wars" in the Philippines, 1899–1935*.W. Hanover, Mass: Christopher Pub. House, 1981.

Santos, Eduardo Ma. R. "Piracy and Armed Robbery against Ships in the Philippines". In Piracy, Maritime Terrorism and Securing the Malacca Straits, edited by Graham Gerard Ong-Webb. Singapore: Institute of Southeast Asian Studies, 2006.

Sazlan, Iskandar. "Incidents at Sea: Shipjacking, Maritime Muggings and Thefts in Southeast Asia". Unpublished paper presented at the Intercargo Roundtable Discussion on Piracy, Singapore, 4 February 2002.

Sidel, John T. *Coercion, Capital, and the Post-colonial State: Bossism in the Philippines*. Stanford, Ca., and Cambridge: Stanford University Press and Cambridge University Press, 1995.

Warren, James Francis. *Iranun and Balangingi: Globalization, Maritime Raiding and the Birth of Ethnicity*. Singapore: Singapore University Press, 2002.

12

Contemporary Maritime Piracy in the Waters off Semporna, Sabah

Carolin Liss

Introduction

The town of Semporna, located on the southeastern coast of Sabah, Malaysia, has long been associated with smuggling and piratical activities. Semporna is situated near the border with Kalimantan, Indonesia, and is only a short distance across the Sulu Sea from the southern Philippines. The waters off Semporna are plied by a large number of small and medium sized vessels commuting between these countries and the countless islands in between, transporting goods or passengers. Semporna is also home to a large number of traditional fishing vessels and modern mechanized fishing trawlers.

As the town has no port for merchant vessels, most pirates in the waters off Semporna have in recent years targeted small craft, particularly fishing vessels of all types.[1] The occurrence of these assaults, as well as attacks by separatist and terrorist movements based in the southern Philippines, particularly the kidnapping of tourists and resort workers from the island of Sipadan in 2000, have prompted the Malaysian government to respond and have resulted in increased Marine Police and Navy presence in the waters off Semporna. This chapter aims to give an insight into the nature of piracy in the waters off Semporna and to discuss the political, economic, and social factors which shape and influence the character of attacks in the area, including the armed conflict in the southern Philippines. The chapter then explores how increased patrols by the Malaysian Marine Police, and to a lesser extent the Royal Malaysian Navy, have affected maritime security in the waters off Semporna.

The first part of the chapter offers a brief introduction to the town of Semporna, the local population, and the surrounding area. The following parts then provide an overview of contemporary piracy in Malaysian waters off Semporna, and discuss the characteristics and nature of attacks on small craft since the early 1990s. The next section briefly traces the history of separatist and terrorist groups in the southern Philippines before discussing the kidnapping of foreign holidaymakers and resort workers from a dive resort on the island of Sipadan by the Abu Sayyaf. It examines the role of this kidnapping in the substantial increase of security personnel stationed in and near Semporna. The chapter then looks at the consequences and impact of these improved security arrangements in regard to pirate attacks in the waters off Semporna, suggesting that the actual number of pirate attacks in Malaysian waters near Semporna has declined. However, this section will also demonstrate that due to corruption within local law enforcement agencies, a number of new problems have surfaced for the local population. The chapter concludes with the suggestion that until the conflict in the southern Philippines is solved, it will be difficult to eradicate piracy in the waters off Semporna, and that if internal problems, such as corruption, within Malaysian local authorities are not dealt with, the situation will not substantially improve for local people.

SEMPORNA AND THE SURROUNDING AREA

The East Malaysian state of Sabah occupies the north-eastern part of the island of Borneo. The close geographical proximity and the historical links of Sabah to Indonesia and, maybe even more so, the southern Philippines, has shaped the social, political, and economic features of Sabah over past centuries. The state is home to a large number — between half a million and 800,000[2] — of legal and illegal immigrants from the Philippines, and trade between the southern Philippines, Indonesia, and Sabah is a vital source of income for parts of the local population. The timber trade and, increasingly, palm plantations, are the mainstays of the economy in Sabah. The beautiful beaches, national parks, and the rich wildlife also attract a rising number of Malaysian and international tourists. Tourism has, therefore, in recent years become an important part of the economy, with a record high of 1,773,271 tourists visiting Sabah in 2004.[3] Many of the holidaymakers travelling to Sabah also visit the district of Semporna, with its world famous diving sites and magnificent islands.

Situated on the south-eastern coast of Sabah, the district of Semporna (meaning, a place of rest) is part of the Tawau Division and encompasses 1,145 sq km. With a population of more than 110,000, the district of

FIGURE 12.1
Police Boats, Semporna

Source: Author's photo

Semporna is one of the most densely populated in Sabah.[4] Three-quarters of the district area is located on the mainland of Borneo and the remaining area is comprised of forty-nine islands of varying sizes.[5]

The town of Semporna itself has a population of well over 40,000 (43,311 according to the 2000 census)[6] inhabitants. For outsiders, Semporna is difficult to distinguish from the many surrounding villages and settlements that merge with the town. As the principal town of the district, Semporna is the seat of the local government, and home of the district court rooms, hospital, library and law enforcement agencies, including the Marine Police and of late, the Royal Malaysian Navy. Semporna town is also a busy commercial centre with formal and informal wet and dry markets and shops of all kinds, including internet cafes, supermarkets and travel agencies, as well as more traditional shops and restaurants.

The population of the district of Semporna is comprised of a large variety of ethnic groups,[7] but the majority of the population today is ethnic Bajau[8]. Most Bajau people are Muslim and Semporna has a large mosque near the town centre. Several smaller mosques and prayer rooms (*surau*) are located in adjoining settlements. Due to its proximity to Indonesia and the Philippines, Semporna is home to many legal and illegal immigrants, especially from the southern Philippines. Many of the immigrants from the Philippines are Sama-Bajau speakers and blend in with the Bajau majority and are part of the local economy. Many goods and fruits in the local markets are, for example, imported from the Philippines and sold by Filipinos.

While many of the buildings in the centre of Semporna are made of concrete and built on land, parts of the town and many of the surrounding settlements consist of wooden, often simply constructed, stilt houses built along the shore line or over the sea.[9] Some of the houses are large and well equipped with modern furnishings, such as TVs and refrigerators, but a large number of the stilt houses reflect the poverty and simple lifestyle of their inhabitants. However, although most of the buildings in the area around the town of Semporna have electricity and access to fresh water, other basic facilities such as domestic sewage systems are rare in the stilt houses — and their inhabitants rely on the sea to clear away raw sewage. Large quantities of rubbish, which increasingly consists of plastic, are also regularly thrown into the sea. While the outgoing tide takes out some of the litter, the incoming tide brings much of it back, leaving the waters and coast of Semporna, as well as the outlying islands, polluted. The ever present rubbish and lack of sound basic facilities are conducive to the spread of illnesses such as cholera, malaria, tuberculosis, and typhoid. Semporna compares unfavourably with many other rural Malaysian communities in regard to health issues,[10] with the latest outbreak of Cholera occurring in the first half of 2005.[11] Indeed, walking through Semporna today the visitor often encounters visibly ill people.

The district of Semporna is still in the process of economic development, and according to local politicians the lack of profitable jobs and business opportunities and prospects for the local population remains a major concern in the area.[12] To create employment opportunities, the government has in recent years initiated agricultural and aquaculture projects, trade and business programmes, and has promoted deep-sea fishing and seaweed farming.[13] While some of these programmes have been delayed or are slow to develop, some, such as the farming of seaweed, are at least partially successful, with a rising number of seaweed plantations now in business off the coast of Semporna.

Another industry that has developed in Semporna since the early 1990s is the tourism sector. The geographical features of the district with its forty-nine beautiful islands and their surrounding reefs seem predestined for tourist development. Diving enthusiasts from all around the world have begun to travel to Semporna to dive in the internationally renowned national parks near the island of Sipadan. To accommodate the tourists, a number of hotels have opened in the town of Semporna.[14] The majority of visitors, however, only pass through the town and stay in diving resorts[15] on islands, such as Pulau Mabul, and until recently, the island of Sipadan.[16]

The geographical features of Semporna have also shaped the local economy. Fishing and the collection of marine produce has always been an important part of life and a major economic activity in Semporna, and marine products,[17] such as fish and seaweed, are still the main sources of livelihood for the local population. At present, nearly 2,000 people in the district of Semporna are working as full-time fishermen on traditional fishing vessels and mechanized trawlers, hauling in a catch of about 12,000 metric tons of various species of fish per year.[18]

In 2002, of 1,992 full-time fishers active in the district, only 119 worked on fishing trawlers. Most fishers operating in the area, therefore, still use traditional fishing methods and equipment, with 1,004 fishers using regular nets, and the remaining 869 fishers using tools such as fishing rods. These more traditional fishers work mainly in the shallow waters, not too far off the coast or near islands. Other methods still used by fishers in Semporna include the now illegal use of explosives and poisonous substances, which damage and destroy the environment, particularly the reefs and corals, which are the breeding grounds and habitat of marine fish.[19]

The traditional fishers based in Semporna mostly use their own small boats to fish. Life can be difficult for these fishers, with some earning less than RM300 per month (US$78.90). Fishing trawlers are often owned by businessmen or other local people with access to funds, as the purchase and ownership of these vessels requires substantial capital investment. There are around seventy wooden hulled mechanized trawlers based in Semporna at present. The smaller trawlers carry a crew of ten to twelve people, medium sized trawlers, a crew of seventeen to twenty-one, and the largest, around thirty fishers. The crew members are predominantly from Sabah or the southern Philippines. The vessels vary in value, with a medium-sized boat worth around RM400,000 and the larger trawlers valued at between RM800,000 and RM1 million.[20] With all these different types of fishing vessels and the large number of other small vessels commuting within Malaysian waters or between Malaysia, Kalimantan, and the southern Philippines, transporting goods and/or passengers, the waters off Semporna are busy and offer tempting targets for pirates operating in the area.

THE WATERS OFF SEMPORNA: PIRACY 1990 TO THE EARLY 21ST CENTURY

The economic, social, and geographical features of the district of Semporna, as well as its proximity to Indonesia and the southern Philippines, where government forces and insurgents are engaged in violent conflict, make the waters off Semporna prone to a variety of illicit activities, such as smuggling and piracy, which pose a severe challenge for local law enforcement agencies.

The coast of Sabah is notorious for smuggling activities from neighbouring countries, particularly Indonesia and the Philippines. Within Sabah, the districts of Tawau, located north of Semporna, and Semporna itself are renowned entry points for smuggled goods. In recent years, cigarettes, mostly from Indonesia, followed by liquor, are the goods most commonly brought into Sabah illegally. Other favoured smuggled items include forged currency, rice, timber, VCDs, firecrackers, and drugs. Furthermore, people without proper entry visas are also often brought to Sabah illegally.[21] In the district of Semporna the authorities have in recent years mounted successful operations against smugglers. In June 2003, for example, a marine security patrol seized 45,470 cartons of cigarettes near Semporna. In the event, the authorities spotted a suspicious looking longboat with a 200 horsepower outboard engine late one evening. Noticing the approaching patrol vessel, the perpetrators attempted to flee, but the authorities were able to capture the longboat after a fifteen minute chase in which shots were fired at the smugglers.[22] As in this case, many goods smuggled into Semporna, and other parts of Sabah, are brought in via the ocean by fast boats, such as longboats or *kumpits*, equipped with powerful outboard engines. These smuggling boats, loaded with valuable cargo, are tempting targets for another group of perpetrators of illegal activities in the waters off Semporna — pirates and sea robbers.

The waters off Sabah have a long history of piracy and the local population is, therefore, no stranger to it.[23] The state has until the 1990s been subject to a "special" type of "pirate" attack, in which gunmen arriving in fast vessels raided towns, villages, and islands. One of the last attacks of this kind occurred in Semporna in early 1996, when six "pirates" threw bombs used for fishing into the police station and stole jewellery from a goldsmith.[24] These attacks are, however, not pirate attacks in the more common interpretation, which only considers attacks against vessels as acts of piracy. The International Maritime Bureau (IMB), for example, defines piracy as any "act of boarding any vessel with the intent to commit theft or any other crime and with the intent or capability to use force in the furtherance of that act", which excludes raids of towns. For the purpose of this chapter the IMB's definition of piracy will be adopted with the proviso that those acts have to be committed for private — as opposed to political — ends.

The actual number of attacks occurring in this area since the 1990s is difficult to estimate as attacks are seldom reported to local authorities or the IMB, either out of ignorance, fear of revenge by the pirates, or because the victims believe that reporting an attack would be of no advantage to them. Also, fishermen may be reluctant to report an attack that occurred in waters where they were not allowed to fish, such as national parks or a foreign country's Exclusive Economic Zone (EEZ) or territorial waters. Nonetheless, the Malaysian Enforcement Coordination Centre and the IMB regularly publish statistics of piracy attacks in Sabah waters, as shown in Table 12.1.

TABLE 12.1
Attacks in Sabah

	93	94	95	96	97	98	99	00	01	02	03	04
MECC	37	34	57	42	20	17	5	18	9	9	12	NA
IMB	3	3	0	0	2	5	0	9	14	5	2	4

Source: IMB, MECC

TABLE 12.2
Attacks in Sabah Waters by Vessel Type

	2001	2002	2003
Fishing Boat	9	9	12
Merchant Ship	1	0	0
Total	10	9	12

Source: Malaysian Marine Police

While these statistics include attacks on all types of vessels, most attacks in these waters target small vessels, including fishing vessels of all types and sizes, as demonstrated in Table 12.2.

Table 12.2 indicates that, at least for 2001, 2002, and 2003, the great majority of attacks listed for Sabah are attacks on fishing vessels. Furthermore, a report by the Malaysian Marine Police Sabah Division compiled in November 1996 lists outboard engines, fishing vessels (for ransom), valuables (cash, watches, gold, and jewellery), communication radio sets, and "other equipment on board i.e. fishing gears, fuel, fishes and others" as items sought after by contemporary pirates in the area:[25] This list indicates that fishing vessels and other small craft have at the time already been preferred targets of pirates operating in Sabah waters.

This focus on fishing (and other small) vessels can at least in part be explained by the fact that Semporna does not have a port suitable for merchant ships. Indeed, piracy has been a concern for operators of small vessels and has affected businesses in the region. In the late 1990s, for example, an operator of a small fish processing plant near Semporna relocated his business to Labuan due, in part, to the constant pirate attacks on his transport and fishing vessels, in which the perpetrators regularly stole the engines of his vessels. The owner himself was attacked once by Filipino pirates. The pirate vessel approached his boat and the pirates, who possessed good local knowledge, recognized who the victim was, treated him with respect, and even shared some food with him. Nonetheless, the perpetrators took his boat engine and loaded it onto their vessel, which was already carrying other stolen motors.[26]

All types of vessels based in Semporna are subject to pirate attacks or other forms of extortion at sea. The crews on-board the larger trawlers, for example, face a number of problems at sea. The vessels go further out to sea than the traditional fishing vessels and usually fish for twelve to twenty-four hours before returning to Semporna with their catch. According to local fishers, fish stock in Malaysian waters off Semporna is declining, due to the large number of trawlers based in the area and the destruction of reefs as a result of fishing with dynamite. The fishers, therefore, occasionally fish in Indonesian waters, where more fish can still be caught. The waters of the Philippines are generally avoided by Malaysian trawlers because these waters are known to be the hunting ground of pirates and terrorists.[27] While the Indonesian waters are generally safer, the boats fishing in or near Indonesian waters are occasionally approached by the Indonesian authorities, who threaten to confiscate the fishing vessels and tow them to Indonesia, if the crew does not pay a "fee". Trawlers therefore carry cash when fishing in Indonesian waters in case they have to pay the "fee" to the authorities.

Most of the more conventional pirate attacks target smaller vessels such as traditional fishing boats, transport or smuggling vessels. Three different types of pirates operated in the waters off Semporna throughout the 1990s. The first type of pirate ("the borrower") operated from a small fishing boat, with usually two or three pirates on-board. The local fishermen, often local Bajau, usually allowed these pirate vessels to approach as they believed they were fishers who needed water or other assistance. The pirates were armed with guns or rifles and target the vessels to steal outboard engines and other small valuables onboard. They were generally friendly and only harmed their victims when met with resistance. Resistance, however, was rare, as Malay fishers were not armed with firearms. Nonetheless, in some cases, the victims were forced to jump overboard and their vessel was taken over by the pirates and left at some distance from the swimming fishers.[28]

The identity of these perpetrators is contested. The 1996 Marine Police Sabah Division report concludes that the sea robbers who pose as local fishers operate from a base in the southern Philippines.[29] According to fishers from Semporna, the pirates often spoke Malay and are thought to live in Sabah. The booty, however, was mostly sold in the southern Philippines, on islands such as Sitangkai, which is still notorious for its market of stolen goods. The local fishermen also believe that some of these attacks were conducted by members of the Malaysian Marine Police in their time off work. They used fishing boats and wore masks during the attacks, but as they lived and worked locally, the fishers knew who they were, and in some cases even exchanged pleasantries with the culprits. The perpetrators of these attacks are evidently aware of the patrol schedules of the Marine Police and could, therefore, easily avoid patrol vessels.[30]

The second type of pirate attacked boats which they suspected — or knew — to carry either large amounts of cash or other valuable goods. Therefore, boats used for smuggling between the Philippines, Indonesia and Sabah were often targeted. Yet, if fishing vessels crossed the perpetrator's path, they were also occasionally attacked. The pirates in these cases stole the engine or the entire vessel and were more likely to use violence than the "borrowers" and occasionally killed fishers or other victims. The culprits were believed to be Filipinos with good knowledge about the geographical features of Sabah and the legal and illegal trade conducted between Malaysia and the Philippines. The perpetrators had access to this information either from informers or because they had lived in Malaysia for a period of time.

The third type of pirate robbed vessels and took crew members hostage. The perpetrators were Filipinos and relied on information from informants in Malaysia. These attacks could be violent and were, like all other attacks discussed above, seldom reported to the authorities. The victims were often Filipinos living in Sabah, without valid documents or Malaysian identity cards. Some of the kidnapped victims were believed to be targeted because they were wanted in the Philippines, with some, for example, being alleged terrorists or criminals who could also be "sold" to interested parties in the Philippines.[31]

SHAPING PIRACY

A range of local political, social, economic, and geographical circumstances and conditions are conducive to the occurrence of pirate attacks in this area, and determine the nature and characteristics of attacks in the waters off Semporna. Geography, for example, plays a crucial role, with the sea between Semporna and the southern Philippines dotted with numerous islands that offer ample opportunities for pirates to hide. Furthermore, the proximity of the southern Philippines to Semporna (a fast boat needs less than half an hour to get from the town of Semporna to the Philippines) allows pirates to commute between the two countries, and offers refuge for pirates across a national border. Indeed, the majority of attacks off the coast of Semporna are conducted by perpetrators originally from the southern

Philippines. Also, the geographical features ensure the abundance of target vessels as well as access to fast, mostly unregistered, vessels suitable for pirate attacks. Growing up in the region, the perpetrators naturally also have the required maritime experience and knowledge to conduct pirate attacks. The poverty of parts of the population and the lack of economic opportunities in Semporna, and even more so in the southern Philippines, is another factor contributing to the occurrence of piracy. For the disillusioned and the more desperate of the poor population in the area, piracy may be one way to earn a living. However, most of those living in economic hardship do not engage in piracy or other illegal activities and pirates are by no means only those left with no other opportunities. Indeed, piracy in the waters off Semporna may in part simply have occurred in the 1990s because the opportunities were there, the profits considerable, and the risk of being caught moderate.

The Royal Malaysian Marine Police and, to a lesser extent, the Royal Malaysian Navy were, throughout the 1990s, responsible for securing the Malaysian waters off Semporna. The resources and abilities of these law enforcement agencies were, at least to some extent, favourable to the occurrence of pirate attacks in these waters. Given the geographical features, securing the waters off Semporna is not an easy task at the best of times, and the limited resources and equipment of local law enforcement agencies made the mission considerably more challenging in the 1990s. By 1996, the Sabah Marine Police had a fleet of sixty-two patrol boats of different classes and types to safeguard the inshore and offshore waters of the entire state. Forty to sixty per cent of the vessels were normally operational, with the remaining vessels being out of service due to maintenance or repair work. Furthermore, to operate these vessels and attend to other security concerns, the Marine Police were scheduled to employ about 800 personnel, but only 650 policemen (and woman) were stationed in Sabah. In 1996, an assessment of the resources of the police from within their own ranks came to the conclusion that despite the fact that new, faster patrol vessels were purchased in the first half of the 1990s, the number of vessels and personnel remains insufficient to combat piracy and other illegal activities in Sabah waters. Despite this acknowledgement, the resources of the Marine Police were not significantly improved until 2000.

To prevent attacks on villages, the Marine Police cooperated with the Police Field Force which is stationed at strategic locations in coastal villages and on islands throughout Sabah.[32] In addition to the efforts by the

Marine Police, the presence of the Malaysian Navy in Sabah was increased throughout the 1990s in order to strengthen security in East Malaysian waters. Yet, while plans to build additional naval bases in Sabah had already been made in the late 1980s, it was not until late 1996 that the Malaysian government proceeded with the development of a major naval base in Sandakan, on the north-eastern coast of Sabah.[33] Plans to build an additional naval base near Semporna, were, however, further delayed.

Patrolling the waters off Semporna by all law enforcement personnel is made difficult by the proximity of Malaysia to Indonesia and the Philippines. Not only can pirates slip across national boundaries, but the borders between these countries are also contested, with all interested parties claiming ownership of various resource and oil rich waters and islands situated between the three countries.[34] A long standing dispute about the islands of Sipadan and Ligitan between Indonesia and Malaysia,[35] has, for example, only recently been settled by the International Court of Justice in The Hague. The case was transferred to the court in 1996 and was eventually resolved in 2002, with the court announcing the islands part of Malaysia.[36] Such overlapping claims pose an obstacle for law enforcement agencies from all countries concerned and make agreements of maritime security cooperation between the nations exceedingly difficult to reach.

In addition to the factors discussed above, there are other conditions that have shaped piracy in the region. Pirate attacks in this area involved in many cases a high level of violence. For example, this may partly be explained by the fact that the perpetrators predominantly attack small craft. Unlike attacks on merchant vessels, pirates attacking small craft necessarily come face to face with their victims, which increases the likelihood of conflict and injury. Another reason is that the perpetrators operating in these waters are comparatively well equipped with small arms and light weapons. In the southern Philippines a great number of armed groups exist, including bandit gangs, civilian militia, "private armies" of politicians, Christian cultists and vigilante groups, and government forces. Weapons are, therefore, widely distributed in the area and are easy to obtain by pirates. The availability of these weapons in the area is also a legacy of the ongoing conflict between the government and separatist and terrorist movements in the southern Philippines. People living in a place such as the southern Philippines, where violence and the use of weapons are the order of the day, may also turn more easily to activities such as piracy and show less scruple in using violence. Also, the lawless state of parts of the southern Philippines offers the perpetrators safe places to sell their stolen goods.

Furthermore, some insurgent groups based in the southern Philippines are also believed to have conducted pirate attacks to raise funds for their struggle.

The following part of the chapter provides a brief overview of separatist and terrorist movements in the southern Philippines because the conflict in the southern Philippines shaped and influenced the occurrence and nature of piracy in the waters off Semporna in the past and at present. Furthermore, it was an attack by a Muslim Filipino terrorist group, the Abu Sayyaf, that was responsible for the substantial increase in maritime security measures in Semporna in 2000.

THE SIPADAN KIDNAPPING AND ITS IMPACT

In the early 1970s, broad-based separatist movements began to emerge in the southern Philippines as a result of the political, social, and economic marginalization of the Muslim population of Mindanao and Sulu. As Muslims in a Christian dominated state, Islam has been an important ideological-cultural aspect of the separatist struggle[37] in the southern Philippines.[38] Increased globalization and, with it, the rapid exchange of money, goods and ideas, including the dissemination of radical ideologies and political tactics, as well as the increased travel of Muslims between the Middle East and the southern Philippines also played a pivotal role.[39] The first major group to emerge in 1971 was the Moro National Liberation Front (MNLF) led by Nur Misuari. The initial aim of the groups was to establish a separate Moro homeland with "a democratic system of government which (does) not allow or tolerate any form of exploitation and oppression[40] of any human being by another or of one nation by another",[41] and the preservation of Islamic and indigenous culture.[42] However, internal fighting divided the group from the outset and over the years a number of factions split from the MNLF,[43] including the Moro Islamic Liberation Front (MILF), identified with the Islamic scholar Hashim Salamat, which separated from the MNLF in 1984. The MILF broke away from the MNLF stressing the ideological importance of Islamic renewal as part of the struggle for Muslim self-determination.[44]

Like separatist movements in other parts of the world, the MILF and MNLF chose armed struggle to further their aims and successive Philippine governments answered in kind, with some presidents opting for extreme forms of violence, including the use of napalm,[45] against the local population in the south. Over the years the ongoing conflict between these groups and the successive Philippine governments resulted in the considerable destruction of villages and towns in the area and the displacement of the local population, including Christians, Muslims, and Bajau. Many of the Muslims and Bajau[46] fleeing the conflict in their home country moved to Sabah to escape the violence and to find work.

Guerrilla warfare was the predominant pattern of armed struggle used by the MNLF and the MILF,[47] with MNLF and MILF troops controlling parts of the countryside and establishing fixed bases in the southern Philippines. However, in both organizations individual leaders and their idiosyncratic tactics constantly caused problems. Rogue elements within both the MNLF and MILF were accused of being responsible for kidnappings, extortion, and robberies in the Philippines and occasional pirate attacks off the country's coast. It remains difficult to establish whether these rogue elements acted outside or within the MNLF and MILF structure.[48] However, to conduct their operations, both groups needed outside financial support and weapons. Considerable assistance for the MNLF came from Tun Mustapha, the Tausug chief minister of Sabah, who reportedly granted the MNLF sanctuary for training, regional communication, and supply. In the early to mid-1970s, Sabah became the principal stabling point and supply depot for the MNLF, where weapons and other supplies from foreign supporters were received before being trans-shipped to Sulu and Mindanao.[49] When Tun Mustapha was defeated in the 1976 elections, Sabah ceased to provide sympathetic patronage and a safe haven.[50] Nonetheless, the ties between Sabah and insurgent movements operating in the southern Philippines were never fully cut, with members and former members of the MNLF, MILF and other organizations still commuting between the two areas. Furthermore, until recently, at least some of the weapons destined for separatist movements were channelled through Sabah.

Since the 1970s, attempts have been made by the MNLF, MILF and the Philippine government to end the conflict in the south. In 1996, after decades of negotiations, the MNLF signed a peace agreement with the Philippine government. Throughout the negotiation process many dissatisfied MNLF members defected to the MILF, particularly after 1996, due to their frustration over the outcome of the peace agreement. Therefore, by 1996 (if not earlier) the MILF became the most powerful insurgent movement in the southern Philippines. The Philippine government recognised the importance and influence of the MILF early on and in 1992 began negotiations with the MILF. While a number of agreements and ceasefires could be reached over the years, the situation still remains volatile. Dissatisfaction with the MILF and MNLF and the failure of the Philippine government to solve the Mindanao-Sulu problem either politically, or truly abide by the tenets of the various peace agreements reached with the MNLF and MILF, enhanced the radicalization of some young Muslims. This radicalizing process and political frustration on the part of Muslim youth was demonstrated by the emergence and rise of the extremely militant group, Abu Sayyaf.

The Abu Sayyaf was founded in the early 1990s by a former MNLF member, Abdurajak Janjalani. A charismatic leader and an eloquent speaker, Janjalani was also a committed Muslim scholar who had studied in, among other places, Mecca and Libya. After his return to the Philippines from the Middle East, Janjalani broke with the MNLF, as he, unlike the MNLF leadership, remained committed to the notion of *jihad* for an independent Islamic state, and founded his own organization — the Abu Sayyaf.[51]

Since the early 1990s the Abu Sayyaf is believed to be responsible for a spate of attacks and robberies in the southern Philippines, including bombings, extortion, raids of villages, attacks on military posts, and kidnappings. The military blamed the Abu Sayyaf for committing 102 "terrorist" acts between 1991 and 1995 alone, and claimed it amassed twenty million Pesos through kidnapping in that period.[52] The government reacted in force against the Abu Sayyaf and by the mid-1990s, the sporadic battles between the Abu Sayyaf and the Armed Forces of the Philippines (AFP) were severely affecting the civilian population on the island of Basilan, the stronghold of the Abu Sayyaf,[53] as well as on surrounding islands, resulting in the displacement of thousands of people in the area.[54]

In 1998 Abdurajak Janjalani was killed in a gun battle with the police and the organizational and ideological structure of the Abu Sayyaf changed. After considerable internal struggle within the Abu Sayyaf, Abdurajak Janjalani was succeeded by his brother Khaddafy Janjalani, who lacked the ideological and religious moorings of Abdurajak.[55] Not all commanders and fighters of the Abu Sayyaf accepted Khaddafy as their new leader, and the group developed into an even more radical movement consisting of several loosely connected factions, without a clear set of doctrines and principles.[56]

However, even before Abdurajak Janjalani's death, the Philippine government repeatedly characterised the Abu Sayyaf as a group of bandits with no political agenda, profiting from the general state of lawlessness on the edge of the frontier in the southern Philippines. Indeed, it often appears difficult to draw a clear line dividing political aims from criminal purposes in regard to the Abu Sayyaf, and, therefore, classify them as a terrorist group or a criminal gang. What distinguishes the terrorist from an ordinary criminal (or a pirate) is his motive. While the ordinary criminal/pirate is acting primarily for selfish, personal reasons, the terrorist believes that he is serving a "good" cause, designed to achieve a higher good for a wider constituency. The terrorist's action is, therefore, designed to have political and social consequences or create psychological repercussions beyond the sheer act of violence itself. Unlike the ordinary criminal (or pirate), the terrorist aims at conveying a fundamental message — often political or religious — through an act of violence.[57] Thus, the rationale behind terrorist acts is not simply the destruction or the killing itself, but such acts are designed as an extreme communication strategy; a political approach and form of weapon, which has become increasingly effective with recent advances in satellite communication technology. As the principal conduit of information about terrorist acts, the modern news media play a vital role in the terrorist's calculations and operational strategy. While the distinction between terrorism and criminal activities, including piracy, may seem irrelevant or purely "academic" for some observers, these distinctions are important as they determine the modus operandi of perpetrators as well as the character and outcome of an attack.

In the case of the Abu Sayyaf there is no doubt that kidnapping and ransom have played an important part in the group's strategy and tactics. However, the group's basic aim in the past was clearly defined as the establishment of an independent Islamic state in the southern Philippines. Judging by demands made during kidnapping incidents throughout the 1990s, other, maybe more realistic, aims were also of critical importance to the group. These included the exclusion of undesirable foreign influences, such as Christian missionaries from the southern Philippines, the banning of foreign fishing boats and fishermen from the waters of the Sulu and Celebes seas, and the teaching of Islam in Philippine schools.[58] These demands indicate that the group is not just "in it for the money", but has been fighting for fundamental political and economic objectives and changes. However, as indicated above, after the death of Abdurajak Janjalani, the group's aims, tactics, and operations became less clearly defined.

While the Abu Sayyaf contributed significantly to creating a milieu of unrest and terror in the southern Philippines, the group, just like the MNLF and MILF, had, until 2000, always strictly confined their operations, including kidnappings, to the southern Philippines.[59] In late April 2000, however, the Abu Sayyaf's strategy changed with the audacious kidnapping of international tourists and resort workers from the Malaysian resort island of Sipadan. In the course of the daring event, members of an Abu Sayyaf faction led by Ghalib Andang, alias Commander Robot, entered Malaysian waters in two small vessels, raided a diving resort on the island of Sipadan, and escaped with twenty-one hostages. The captives, who included seven resort employees from Malaysia and the Philippines, four members of the Malaysian Wildlife Department, two South Africans, a Lebanese, two Finns, a French couple, and a German couple and their adult son, were taken to the southern Philippine island of Jolo, where they were held captive for several months, while political and financial demands for their freedom were negotiated. The Sipadan hostages were eventually released in small groups after the kidnappers accepted the promise of major "developmental projects" to be implemented in the Sulu-Mindanao region, and substantial ransoms were paid in exchange for the hostages.

The kidnapping event attracted the attention of media representatives from around the world, particularly from the hostages' home countries. Many international journalists and television crews travelled to Jolo to cover the kidnapping and in the process actually entered into and changed the course of the event itself, as some of them were themselves abducted and held hostage for various lengths of time. The kidnapping was singularly attractive for the media not only because of the involvement of a large number of "innocent" international holidaymakers, but also because the Abu Sayyaf gave the journalists an unprecedented opportunity. For more than a month, the kidnappers opened the hostage camps to global media representatives, allowing them to interview, film, and photograph the hostages on a regular basis. With up to 200 journalists on the small island of Jolo directly involved in the event, the kidnapping was transformed into a major media spectacle.[60] Hence, it received extensive news coverage, which focused world attention on a region — the southern Philippines — and a cultural group of people — the Muslim Filipinos — that had rarely received any prior international media coverage.[61] The media coverage, however, also drew the world's attention to Malaysia, or more precisely, the lack of security for foreigners, and to lesser extent, locals in Sabah and Semporna. The coverage put considerable international pressure on the Malaysian government to ensure the safety of foreign tourists and Malaysians in its territory. Furthermore, as tourism is a major source of income in Semporna, concern arose that holidaymakers would travel to other destinations out of consideration for their safety.[62] This fear was further increased when on 10 September 2000, only one day after the last of the tourists kidnapped from Sipadan were released, an Abu Sayyaf faction raided yet another Malaysian resort on Padanan Island, abducting three Malaysian citizens. [63]

The Malaysian government responded promptly to the kidnappings and increased security in the waters off Semporna. While the Sipadan hostages were still held in the Philippines, Malaysian government representatives announced that a major new naval base would be built in Semporna and that patrols by the Marine Police would be increased immediately.[64] Following these announcements, an action plan and programme of surveillance were prepared by the state government, the Malaysian Defence Ministry, and the Malaysian Royal Police, which put heavy emphasis on increased patrols in Malaysian waters near the border to the Philippines and Indonesia. The number of Marine Police officers was increased and new equipment, including eleven speed boats and "blitz" boats, was supplied for the district of Semporna. Additional police booths were also established at strategic points and in villages exposed to the sea. Furthermore, teams consisting of members of the Police General Action Group were placed on "vulnerable" islands, including Sipadan and the neighbouring holiday island of Mabul.[65] Within the town of Semporna a major new building was erected for the Semporna District Police Administration, which includes living quarters for 270 policemen and their families. The number of Malaysian Navy personnel was also increased considerably in the district. A navy vessel with a crew of 200 officers was brought to Semporna, as were five additional specialized boats to patrol the waters in this area. Additionally, special army teams were placed on selected islands, including the islands of Sipadan and Pandanan.[66] The teams worked under the command of the Sri Wangsa Camp in Semporna, which housed 200 army personnel.[67] In accordance with the announcement made during the Sipadan kidnapping, construction began on a naval base which was officially opened in July 2005. The facilities of the new base include a swimming pool and new security-relevant equipment such as high-powered vessels and patrol boats.[68]

THE IMPACT OF THE SECURITY IMPROVEMENTS

The Malaysian authorities responded to the Abu Sayyaf attack in the traditional manner by increasing maritime patrols and the number of law enforcement agents in the area. However, realizing that large patrol vessels are of limited use in the waters off Semporna, smaller faster vessels were also introduced. Following the Sipadan kidnapping, the government also issued a ban on the use of pump boats in Malaysian waters. The ban was, however, short-lived as it was difficult to enforce, particularly because local Malaysians also use this type of boat for their day to day business.[69]

The improved security arrangements in the area had considerable impact in the waters off Semporna. While tourist bookings initially declined after the kidnapping incident, continuous publicity campaigns by local authorities to regain the confidence of overseas scuba divers have succeeded in bringing back tourists to Sipadan and the surrounding islands.[70] Indeed, despite the incident, Sipadan was voted the world's "Top Dive Destination" together with two other diving sites by some 6,000 of the world's most avid diving enthusiasts in late 2000.[71]

The increased presence of Malaysian Marine Police patrol boats off Semporna also had a substantial impact on piracy in the area. While the waters of the Philippines and Indonesia remain trouble spots for Malaysian fishermen, the number of pirate attacks on fishing vessels and other small craft has declined considerably in Malaysian waters near Semporna.[72] Due to the increased patrols by the local law enforcement agencies, it seems comparatively more difficult for Malaysian pirates to operate in the area and for Filipino pirates to enter and leave Malaysian waters unnoticed. These developments indicate that the argument that increased patrols can reduce the number of pirate attacks may prove correct to some extent in this area. Nonetheless, the increased presence of law enforcement personnel in the area could not eradicate piracy, and pirate attacks still occasionally take place in the Malaysian waters off Semporna. This, however, is understandable as many of the conditions conducive for piracy discussed earlier in the chapter still exist. These include the economic hardship of parts of the population in Semporna and the Philippines, as well as the conflict in the southern Philippines. Furthermore, having received millions of U.S. dollars in ransom for the tourists abducted from Sipadan, the Abu Sayyaf emerged from the event strengthened and the highly successful kidnapping itself has been an incentive for similar attacks. Consequently, a number of abductions conducted by a variety of perpetrators occurred in the following years in Sabah waters, including in and near the district of Semporna. In 2001, for example, fifteen Malaysians were abducted from six fishing vessels in two separate incidents between Sabah and the Philippines. Jalaludin Abdul Rahman, deputy commander of Malaysia's Marine Police, stated in a newspaper interview that the kidnappers had no links to the

Abu Sayyaf, but that "they were obviously influenced" by the successful Sipadan kidnapping.[73] In 2003 ten gunmen raided the Borneo Paradise Resort near Kunak, north of Semporna, and abducted six workers when no tourists could be found.[74] The victims were believed to be held in the Philippines by an Abu Sayyaf faction, which demanded ransom money in exchange for the captives. Reports about the whereabouts of the hostages remained contradictory, but five of the kidnap victims were allegedly killed in the Philippines.[75] Also, in March 2005, yet another abduction took place in the waters off Semporna. Near the island of Mataking, five pirates abducted three Indonesian crew members of a Malaysian tug towing a barge from Indonesia to Sandakan. The pirates, armed with M16 and AK47 assault rifles, approached the slow moving vessels as they were entering Malaysian waters around 11 a.m. The perpetrators fired warning shots and boarded the vessel. They stole the communication set and several hand phones before fleeing towards the Philippines with the hostages.[76]

The increased presence of law enforcement personnel could not prevent these recent attacks and abductions in Malaysian waters, indicating that further, and maybe different, measures are needed to secure the waters off Semporna. Furthermore, the increased presence of Marine Police officers also did not improve the overall situation for all parts of the population in Semporna and, in fact, created additional problems for local residents. According to local sources, a number of officers from the Marine Police continue to be involved in sea robberies, targeting small fishing vessels and other small craft. Also, small fishing vessels are regularly forced to hand over some of the most valuable fish they catch to Marine Police officers at sea. Part of the fish given to the police is then sold on the local market. Trawler owners, in contrast, have to pay substantial amounts of "protection money" to Marine Police officers upfront. The payments, in cash or occasionally in kind, are mostly arranged by phone, or trawler owners receive notes detailing the demands. The "fee" for a three months "fishing licence" for a large trawler (worth between RM600,000 to RM800,000) lies between RM10,000 and RM14,000. The owners of smaller trawlers pay a lesser amount of between RM2,000 and RM5,000. When trawler owners refuse to pay, problems are created for the crew of the vessel or the boat itself. Some of the crew members on trawlers based in Semporna are from the Philippines and not all have valid working documentation allowing them to work on Malaysian vessels. In cases in which all crew members do have valid papers, other faults or problems can easily be found or created, preventing the vessel from going out to fish. While protection money had been paid even before the Abu Sayyaf kidnapping, the increased number of Marine Police patrols and officers stationed in Semporna raised the power, influence, and demands of the members of the Marine Police engaged in the protection racket. However, it remains open whether the Marine Police as an institution is involved in these illegal activities, or if the extortion is conducted solely by rogue officers. Either way, the involvement of Marine Police personnel in these activities explains the reluctance of local fishers to report pirate attacks to the Marine Police. Interestingly, trawler owners seem to welcome the growing presence of Navy vessels in the region, as the Navy is not involved in any of the illegal activities discussed above and local trawler owners believe that the Navy's presence will ultimately weaken the influence and power of the Marine Police in Semporna.[77]

Conclusion

The occurrence of pirate attacks in the waters off Semporna is not a new development, and different types of pirate attacks took place throughout the 1990s. However, it was the kidnapping of tourists from the island of Sipadan that prompted the Malaysian government to increase security in Malaysian waters off Semporna substantially. As a result, the overall number of pirate attacks declined in this area. Yet, piracy in these waters still exists, with attacks today including simple hit-and-run robberies at sea, as well as abduction of sailors and fishermen. Further steps are therefore planned for the future to improve security in Malaysian waters and to combat piracy and other illicit activities such as smuggling and illegal fishing. These measures include the formation of a special tactical team under the Marine Police to counter crime at sea in Sabah, and the establishment of the Malaysian Maritime Enforcement Agency.[78] Both these measures will have an impact on the security in the waters off Semporna.

So far, most attempts to counter piracy and other illegal activities in Semporna have been in the form of increased numbers of law enforcement personnel and patrol vessels patrolling the area. A more comprehensive approach, including, for example, the eradication of poverty and the creation of business opportunities in the district of Semporna, could perhaps deter locals from turning to piracy to supplement their income. However, the fact that many perpetrators (originally) come from the Philippines complicates the matter. The unsolved conflict in the southern Philippines, paired with poverty and the availability of weapons in the area, remains conducive to piracy. Evidently, the Malaysian authorities cannot solve the conflict in the Philippines, which requires genuine efforts on the part of the Philippine government and the separatist and terrorist movements operating in the southern part of the country. However, in the short run, Malaysian authorities could improve the situation for their own people considerably by eradicating corruption within the Marine Police and halting all illegal activities conducted by its personnel. This way, law enforcement agencies would not only combat the threat of piracy, but also increase the well-being of the local population, create an atmosphere in which businesses can prosper unhindered, and provide a crucial service for local people.

Notes

1. The information about piracy in this chapter is in part based on interviews which the author conducted in Semporna in November 2004, April 2005, and November 2005. For reasons which will become clear, the names of the author's informers will not be given.
2. As many Filipinos enter Sabah illegally, the actual number is difficult to establish. "Philippines: More Filipinos deported from Sabah", *Asian Labour News*, 2 July 2004 <http://www.asianlabour.org/archives/002033.php> (accessed 27 September 2005). Maita Santiago, "Filipino Refugees from Sabah: Trapped in an Endless Journey", *Bulatlat.com*, November 2002 <http://www.bulatlat.com/news/2-41/2-41-refugees.html> (accessed 27 September 2005).
3. This is an increase of 42 per cent compared with the previous year. According to the Sabah Tourism Board this "translates into a preliminary tourism receipt of over RM2 billion for Sabah". For more statistics on tourism in Sabah see: Sabah Tourism Board, "Statistics", Sabah Tourism Board <http://sabahtourism.com/statistic.php> (accessed 28 September 2005).
4. According to the 2000 census, 114,989 people live in the district of Semporna. "Statistical Data on Sabah's Population" <http://www.ids.org.my/stats/Population/> (accessed 1 October 2005).
5. Hj Chacho Hj Bulah, "Towards Enhancing the Economy and Improving the Society's Quality of Living in the Semporna District through the Management and the Implementation of the Development Programmes/Projects under the National Public Policies — it's Challenges and Prospects", Ph.D. thesis, Irish International University of Europe <http://www.iiuedu.ie/view.php?v=Graduates_Thesis> (accessed 14 October 2005), p. 1.
6. Clifford Sather, *The Bajau Laut. Adaption, History, and Fate in a Maritime Fishing Society of South-eastern Sabah* (Oxford: Oxford University Press, 1997).

7. According to the 2000 consensus, the composition of ethnic groups in Semporna District is: (a) Bajaus (the local Malays): 63,008; (b) Malays: 3,562; (c) Chinese: 1,049; (d) Kadazans: 604; (e) Muruts: 43; (f) Other Natives: 7,237; (g) Non-Natives: 2,725; (h) Others: 35,761. Hj Chacho Hj Bulah, op. cit, p. 2. For an overview of the 1991 Semporna population statistics see: "General Information: Main Towns" <http://www.sabah.com.my/borneotrade/a9town05.htm> (accessed 10 May 2005).
8. The Bajau are divided into numerous subgroups. For a study of ethnic identity in Semporna see, Wilfredo Magno Torres III, "Voyages and Ethnicity across Reordered Frontiers: Conflict Resolution and Leadership in the Dynamics of Ethnic Identity Formation among the Sama Dilaut of Semporna" (Paper presented at the "Ateneo Center for Asian Studies Conference", Ateneo de Manila University, 2005). Or for a more historical approach, see Carol Warren, *Bajau Consciousness in Social Change: The Transformation of a Malaysian Minority Community* (Townsville: James Cook University of Northern Queensland, 1983). Or, Sather, op. cit.
9. It was only since the 1950s that the Bajau Laut started to settle on land. Before, they lived as boat — dwelling people entirely afloat. See, Sather, op. cit., pp. 1, 63–68. Warren, op. cit.
10. Sather, op. cit., pp. 74–75.
11. "Cholera outbreak was only in Semporna", *ASEAN Disease Surveillance Net*, 16 May 2005 <http://www.asean-disease-surveillance.net/ASNNews_Detail.asp?ID=2930>.
12. Author's interviews in Semporna.
13. Hj Chacho Hj Bulah, op. cit., pp. 16–17.
14. The town of Semporna and its hotels are, however, a busy tourist destination during festivals, such as the annual traditional boat festival. See, Ahmad Fauzi Mustafa, "Lepa Bajau Semporna tidak pernah karam" <http://www.bharian.com.mym/BHarian/Sunday/Dekor/20050409135331/Article/> (accessed 26 September 2005).
15. A large number of these resorts and dive companies, however, seem to be owned in conjunction with, and operated by, foreigners.
16. In early 2005 the owners of resorts on Sipadan were asked by the government to vacate the island. It remains to be seen what will develop on the island in the future. The evacuation of Sipadan is just one indicator of the many difficulties that are inherent in the development of the tourism industry in the area. The continuous change of policies is just one among many obstacles. A serious problem is also the lack of ecological awareness that seems necessary to preserve the reefs and the beauty of the landscape.
17. Sather, op. cit., p. 28.
18. For information about the amount and types of fish caught in Sabah and Semporna see the informative webpage of the Sabah Fisheries Department.

"Department of Fisheries, Sabah", Department of Fisheries, Sabah <http://www.fishdept.sabah.gov.my/> (accessed 2 October 2005).
19. Hj Chacho Hj Bulah, op. cit., pp. 74–83.
20. Author's interviews in Semporna.
21. "Cigarettes smuggling tops list", *Daily Express*, 14 November 2004 <http://www.dailyexpress.com.my/print.cfm?NewsID=22914> (accessed 27 September 2005). "Smuggling of 300 logs into Sabah foiled", *Daily Express*, 7 May 2005 <http://www.dailyexpress.cim.my/print.cfm?NewsID=34344> (accessed 29 September 2005). "Lahad Datu Customs up checks on smuggling of firecrackers", *Daily Express*, 5 November 2003 <http://www.dailyexpress.com.my/print.cfm?NewsID=22701> (accessed 29 September 2005).
22. "Security patrol foils smuggling attempt", *Daily Express*, 30 June 2003 <http://dailyexpress.com.my/print.cfm?NewsID=19870> (accessed 27 September 2005).
23. See James Francis Warren, *Iranun and Balangingi. Globalization, Maritime Raiding and the Birth of Ethnicity* (Quezon City: New Day Publishers, 2002); James Francis Warren, "A Tale of Two Centuries: The Globalisation of Maritime Raiding and Piracy in Southeast Asia at the end of the Eighteenth and Twentieth Centuries" (Long version of paper presented) (Paper presented at the "KITLV Jubilee Workshop", Leiden, 14–16 June 2001). James Francis Warren, *The Sulu Zone, 1768–1898: The Dynamics of External Trade, Slavery, and Ethnicity in the Transformation of a Southeast Asian Maritime State* (Singapore: Singapore University Press, 1981).
24. Diana Peters and Maureen De Silva, "Piracy in Sabah" <http://www.ums.edu.my/sss/bm/poster_diana&maureen.htm> (accessed 11 June 2005).
25. Marine Police Sabah Division, "Sea Robberies in Sabah" (Paper presented at the Persidangan Maritim Malaysia '96, Kuala Lumpur, 16–19 December 1996).
26. Author's interviews in Semporna.
27. The IMB reports covering the years 1995 to 2005 list fewer than ten attacks on fishing vessels in the southern Philippines. However, even though the number of attacks included in the report is small, all of the attacks listed are violent in nature and often involve the killing of fishermen.
28. Author's interviews in Semporna.
29. Marine Police Sabah Division, op. cit.
30. Author's interviews in Semporna.
31. Author's interviews in Semporna.
32. Marine Police Sabah Division, op. cit.
33. Robert Karniol, "Malaysians Boost Naval Power in South China Sea", *Jane's Defence Weekly*, 9 October 1996, p. 18.
34. For a map showing the contested area, see George Kent and Mark J. Valencia, eds., *Marine Policy in Southeast Asia* (Berkeley: University of California Press, 1985), pp. 64–65. There are also a number of other contested claims between

Malaysia and other countries in the region, such as the ongoing disputes over the Spratly Islands. Furthermore, there still exists a never fully resolved controversy between the Philippines and Malaysia over the "ownership" of the state of Sabah itself.

35. The Philippines also entered the debate at a later stage.
36. International Court of Justice, "Sovereignty over Pulau Ligitan and Pulau Sipadan (Indonesia/Malaysia)", 2002 <http://www.icj-cij.org/icjwww/ipresscom/ipress2002/ipresscom2002-39_inma_20021217.htm> (accessed 4 October 2005).
37. W.K. Che Man, *Muslim Separatism. The Moros of Southern Philippines and the Malays of Southern Thailand* (Singapore: Oxford University Press, 1998) p. 12.
38. It is important to note that efforts were also made by Muslims to solve their problems and maintain their identity by peaceful means. One example is the Bangsa Moro Liberation Organisation (BMLO), which split from the MNLF in the 1970s. See Rainer Werning, "Wer sind die Moros?", *Philippinen Forum*, Doppelnummer 39/40 (July 1995), p. 7; Macapado Abaton Muslim, *The Moro Armed Struggle in the Philippines: The Nonviolent Autonomy Alternative* (Marawi City: Mindanao State University, 1994); Thomas M. McKenna, *Muslim Rulers and Rebels. Everyday Politics and Armed Separatism in the Southern Philippines* (Berkley: University of California Press, 1998), pp. 197–233.
39. There are other factors that also played a role, such as the education of individual Muslims in Manila and the Middle East and the ensuing lack of upward motilities in Filipino society for the beneficiaries of these education programmes. Other factors include political developments in the Philippines, such as the declaration of martial law by President Marcos, which cannot be discussed here.
40. The argument against oppression and exploitation was not only aimed at the Philippine government, but also against the United States, whose involvement in the Philippines was seen as neo-colonial and imperialistic.
41. Nur Misuari, quoted in Man, op. cit., p. 87.
42. McKenna, op. cit, pp. 163–64.
43. A number of other groups split from the MNLF over the years, but in regard to the armed struggle, the MNLF and the MILF played the most prominent roles.
44. Anthony Davis, "Evolution in the Philippine War" *Jane's Intelligence Review*, July 2000, p. 29; Rainer Werning, "Viel Widerstand, wenig Anpassung", *Südostasien*, Jg. 16, Nr. 3 (September 2000), p. 70.
45. Rainer Werning, *US-Imperialismus auf den Philippinen. Der Mindanao Konflikt* (Muenster: Wurf Verlag, 1983), pp. 89–91.
46. Many of the Bajaus (or Sama Dilaut) fleeing the conflict were Muslims, especially in the earlier years of the conflict. See Torres III, op. cit., pp. 14–16.

47. Some argue, however, that the MNLF initially employed mostly conventional warfare tactics. It was only after the increased government effort to crush the movement militarily and the destruction of Jolo in 1974 that the MNLF resorted to guerrilla warfare. See Werning, *US-Imperialismus auf den Philippinen. Der Mindanao Konflikt*, p. 90.
48. Lela Garner Noble, "The Moro National Liberation Front in the Philippines", *Pacific Affairs* 49, no. 3 (Fall 1976), pp. 412–18.
49. Samuel K. Tan, *Internationalization of the Bangsamoro Struggle* (Quezon City: University of the Philippines Press, 1993), pp. 77–78; Man, op. cit., pp. 83, 138–41.
50. Ronald J. May, "The Religious Factor in Three Minority Movements: The Moro of the Philippines, the Malays of Thailand, and Indonesia's West Papuans", *Contemporary Southeast Asia* 13, no. 4 (March 1992), p. 400.
51. Christos Iacovou, "From MNLF to Abu Sayyaf: The Radicalization of Islam in the Philippines", 11 July 2000 <http://www.ict.org.il/articles/articledet.cfm?articleid=116> (accessed 24 January 2001); Marites Danguilan Vitug and Glenda M. Gloria, *Under the Crescent Moon* (Quezon City: Ateneo Centre for Social Policy and Public Affairs, Institute for Popular Democracy, 2000). p. 211.
52. Vitug and Gloria, op. cit., pp. 219–20.
53. It remains difficult to establish the approximate number of persons who belong to the group. Estimates vary widely, from around one hundred to one thousand armed men. Some observers believe the Abu Sayyaf swelled from an initial band of twenty to a group of 600 between 1992 and 1998, before rapidly declining to about 200 members. However, it seems possible that the Abu Sayyaf has never numbered more than 300 armed men. Nonetheless, in addition to the fighting core, the group has an unknown number of active civilian supporters alleged to engage in recruiting, training and other non-combat activities, as well as an unascertained number of local-regional sympathizers. Mark Turner, "Terrorism and Secession in the Southern Philippines: The Rise of the Abu Sayyaf", *Contemporary Southeast Asia* 17, no. 1 (June 1995), p.15; "A Past Traced in Terror — Abu Sayyaf's Short but Violent History, part of: "The Koenighsa Assignment". (ASG)-(Part 2), *The Global Spy Magazine*, 2001 <http://www.spynews.net/AbuSayyafGroup-2.html> (accessed 21 April 2001).
54. Turner, op. cit., pp. 7–8.
55. "Bearer of the Sword. The Abu Sayyaf Has Nebulous Beginnings and Incoherent Aims, Part of: The Koenighsa Assignment". (ASG)-(Part 2), *The Global Spy Magazine*, 2001 <http://www.spynews.net/AbuSayyafGroup-2.html> (accessed 21 April 2001).
56. Haikal Mohamed Isa, "Govt Negotiators Pocketed Ransom Money, Abu Sayyaf Claims", *Bernama* <http://global.umi.com/pqdweb?TS=9907845...

Fmt=3&Sid=4&Idx=26&Deli=1&RQT=309&Dtp=1> (accessed 25 May 2001). "Military Sees Diminished Threat from Extremist Group", *Businessworld Manila*, 7 May 1999 <http://global.umi.com/pqdweb?TS=9907885...mt=3&Sid=5&Idx=387&Deli=1&RQT=309&Dtp=1> (accessed 25 May 2001). See also Rommel Banlaoi, "Leadership Dynamics in Terrorist Organisations in Southeast Asia: The Abu Sayyaf Case" (Paper presented at International Symposium: The Dynamics and Structures of Terrorist Threats in Southeast Asia, 2005).

57. Bruce Hoffman, *Inside Terrorism* (London: Victor Gollancz, 1998), pp. 41–42.
58. Turner, op. cit., p. 15.
59. The Abu Sayyaf did kidnap foreigners, often priests or nuns, but until 2000, this occurred only within the Philippines.
60. Realizing the impact of the media coverage, the Philippine government restricted the involvement of journalists in later kidnappings.
61. See Carolin Liss, "The Sipadan Kidnapping 'Drama' (April–September 2000). The Rise of the Abu Sayyaf, International Terrorism, and the Global Media" (BA Honours Thesis, Murdoch University, 2001).
62. "Possible Location of Hostages Still Unconfirmed", *e-Borneo.com*, 2000 <http://www.e-borneo.com/news/s22.html> (accessed 9 June 2005).
63. "Malaysian Authorities Search for Gunmen, Hostages Following Weekend Attack", *CNN.com*, 12 September 2000 <http://archives.cnn.com/2000/ASIANOW/southeast/09/11/malaysia.raid.02.ap/> (accessed 8 October 2005).
64. Arjuna Ranawana, "The Malaysian View", *Asiaweek.com*, 19 May 2000 <http://www.asiaweek.com/asiaweek/magazine/2000/0519/nat.phil.malaysia.html> (accessed 11 May 2005); "Remain Calm, Give Info, Shafie Advises Seporna People", *e-Borneo.com*, 25 April 2000 <http://www.e-borneo.com/news/s16.html> (accessed 4 October 2005).
65. Other islands are: Mataking, Kalapuan, Bohey Dulang, Bum-Bum (Hampalan Village), Siamil, Kapalai, Omadal islands, and around the area of the Tanjung Kapor Village at Manis Beach, Pokas Village, Adau Island, Timbun Mata Island, Gading-Gading Village, and Lihak-Lihak Village.
66. Other islands are Kapalai, Menampilik, Boheyan, Sibuan, and Denawan Island, and on Roach Reef.
67. Hj Chacho Hj Bulah, op. cit., pp. 156–65.
68. "Semporna RMN Base Opens", *Daily Express*, 13 July 2005 <http://www.dailyexpress.com.my/print.cfm?NewsID=35748> (accessed 27 September 2005).
69. Mark Bruyneel, "Reports in 2002: April–June", 10 July 2002 <http://home.wanadoo.nl/m.bruyneel/archive/modern/2k2repb.htm> (accessed 25 August 2005).
70. After the attack, thirteen soldiers, four policemen, and two secret service agents guarded the island on an around the clock basis. Additionally, extra Malaysian marine patrol boats keep watch along the east Malaysian coastline.

71. Catharine Goh, "Sipadan voted world´s top dive site", *Borneo Bulletin*, 31 March 2001, p. 36.
72. Author's interviews in Semporna.
73. "Sulu Sea Sees Pirate Hostage Takers", *CNN*, 15 June 2001 <http://www.cnn/2001/WORLD/asiapcf/southeast/06/15/malaysia.kidnap/index.html> (accessed 20 February 2004).
74. The tourists had in this case left the resort earlier than expected. "Pirates split into three groups", *Daily Express*, 7 October 2003 <http://www.dailyexpress.com.my/print.cfm?NewsID=22095> (accessed 27 September 2005).
75. Al Jacinto, "Sabah Hostages Now in Abu Sayyaf Hands", *Arab News*, 22 October 2003 <http://www.arabnews.com/?page=4&section=0&article=33993&d=22&m=10&y=2003&pix=world.jpg&category=World> (accessed 9 October 2005); Georg Mischuk, "Ostmalaysia. Piraten Schmuggler, Terroristen", *Marine Forum*, Jg. 79, 2004, pp. 25–26. It is not unusual in the southern Philippines for diverse groups to sell or exchange kidnap victims among each other.
76. "Pirates abduct Indons of Mataking", *Daily Express*, 31 March 2005 <http://www.dailyexpress.com.my/print.cfm?NewsID=33590> (accessed 27 September 2005).
77. Author's interviews in Semporna.
78. "Marine Police Will Not Be Disbanded", *New Straits Times*, 16 May 2005; "Special Team for Sabah Soon to Fight Sea Crime", *Daily Express*, 16 July 2005 <http://www.dailyexpress.com.my/news.cfm?NewsID=35798> (accessed 16 July 2005).

References

"Bearer of the Sword. The Abu Sayyaf Has Nebulous Beginnings and Incoherent Aims, Part of: The Koenighsa Assignment" (ASG)-(Part 2). *The Global Spy Magazine*, 2001 <http://www.spynews.net/AbuSayyafGroup-2.html> (accessed 21 April 2001).

"Cholera Outbreak Was only in Semporna". *ASEAN Disease Surveillance Net*, 16 May 2005 <http://www.asean-disease-surveillance.net/ASNNews_Detail.asp?ID=2930>.

"Cigarettes Smuggling Tops List". *Daily Express*, 14 November 2004 <http://www.dailyexpress.com.my/print.cfm?NewsID=22914> (accessed 27 September 2005).

Department of Fisheries, Sabah. <http://www.fishdept.sabah.gov.my/> (accessed 2 October 2005).

"General Information: Main Towns". <http://www.sabah.com.my/borneotrade/a9town05.htm> (accessed 10 May 2005).

"Lahad Datu Customs Up Checks on Smuggling of Firecrackers", *Daily Express*, 5 November 2003 <http://www.dailyexpress.com.my/print.cfm?NewsID=22701> (accessed 29 September 2005).

"Malaysian Authorities Search for Gunmen, Hostages Following Weekend Attack", *CNN.com*, 12 September 2000 <http://archives.cnn.com/2000/ASIANOW/ southeast/09/11/malaysia.raid.02.ap/> (accessed 8 October 2005).

"Marine Police Will Not Be Disbanded". *New Straits Times*, 16 May 2005.

"Military sees Diminished Threat from Extremist Group". *Businessworld Manila*, 7 May 1999 <http://global.umi.com/pqdweb?TS=9907885...mt=3&Sid=5&Idx =387&Deli=1&RQT=309&Dtp=1> (accessed 25 May 2001).

"A Past Traced in Terror — Abu Sayyaf's Short but Violent History, Part of. "The Koenighsa Assignment (ASG)-(Part 2)". *The Global Spy Magazine*, 2001 <http:// www.spynews.net/AbuSayyafGroup-2.html> (accessed 21 April 2001).

"Philippines: More Filipinos deported from Sabah". *Asian Labour News*, 2 July 2004 <http://www.asianlabour.org/archives/002033.php> (accessed 27 September 2005).

"Pirates Abduct Indons of Mataking". *Daily Express*, 31 March 2005 <http://www. dailyexpress.com.my/print.cfm?NewsID=33590> (accessed 27 September 2005).

"Pirates Split into Three Groups". *Daily Express*, 7 October 2003 <http://www. dailyexpress.com.my/print.cfm?NewsID=22095> (accessed 27 September 2005).

"Possible Location of Hostages Still Unconfirmed". *e-Borneo.com*, 2000 <http//www. e-borneo.com/news/s22.html> (accessed 9 June 2005).

"Remain Calm, Give Info, Shafie Advises Seporna People". *e-Borneo.com*, 25 April 2000 <http://www.e-borneo.com/news/s16.html> (accessed 4 October 2005).

"Security Patrol Foils Smuggling Attempt". *Daily Express*, 30 June 2003 <http:// dailyexpress.com.my/print.cfm?NewsID=19870> (accessed 27 September 2005).

"Semporna RMN Base Opens". *Daily Express*, 13 July 2005 <http://www. dailyexpress.com.my/print.cfm?NewsID=35748> (accessed 27 September 2005).

"Smuggling of 300 Logs into Sabah Foiled". *Daily Express*, 7 May 2005 <http:// www.dailyexpress.cim.my/print.cfm?NewsID=34344> (accessed 29 September 2005).

"Special Team for Sabah Soon to Fight Sea Crime". *Daily Express*, 16 July 2005 <http://www.dailyexpress.com.my/news.cfm?NewsID=35798> (accessed 16 July 2005).

"Statistical Data on Sabah's Population". <http://www.ids.org.my/stats/Population/> (accessed 1 October 2005).

"Sulu Sea Sees Pirate Hostage Takers". *CNN*, 15 June 2001 <http://www.cnn/2001/ WORLD/asiapcf/southeast/06/15/malaysia.kidnap/index.html> (accessed 20 February 2004).

Ahmad Fauzi Mustafa. "Lepa Bajau Semporna tidak pernah karam". <http://www. bharian.com.mym/BHarian/Sunday/Dekor/20050409135331/Article/> (accessed 26 September 2005).

Al Jacinto. "Sabah Hostages Now in Abu Sayyaf Hands". *Arab News*, 22 October 2003 <http://www.arabnews.com/?page=4&section=0&article=33993&d=22& m=10&y=2003&pix=world.jpg&category=World> (accessed 9 October 2005).

Arjuna Ranawana. "The Malaysian View". *Asiaweek.com*, 19 May 2000 <http://www.asiaweek.com/asiaweek/magazine/2000/0519/nat.phil.malaysia.html> (accessed 11 May 2005).

Banlaoi, Rommel. "Leadership Dynamics in Terrorist Organisations in Southeast Asia: The Abu Sayyaf Case". Paper presented at International Symposium: The Dynamics and Structures of Terrorist Threats in Southeast Asia, 2005.

Bruyneel, Mark. "Reports in 2002: April–June". 10 July 2002 <http://home.wanadoo.nl/m.bruyneel/archive/modern/2k2repb.htm> (accessed 25 August 2005).

Davis, Anthony. "Evolution in the Philippine War". *Jane's Intelligence Review* (July 2000): 28–33.

Goh, Catharine. "Sipadan Voted World's Top Dive Site". *Borneo Bulletin* (31 March 2001): 36.

Haikal Mohamed Isa. "Govt Negotiators pocketed Ransom Money, Abu Sayyaf claims". *Bernama* <http://global.umi.com/pqdweb?TS=9907845...Fmt=3&Sid=4&Idx=26&Deli=1&RQT=309&Dtp=1> (accessed 25 May 2001).

Hj Chacho Hj Bulah. "Towards Enhancing the Economy and Improving the Society's Quality of Living in the Semporna District through the Management and the Implementation of the Development Programmes/Projects Under the National Public Policies — Its Challenges and Prospects". Ph.D. dissertation, Irish International University of Europe <http://www.iiuedu.ie/view.php?v=Graduates_Thesis> (accessed 14 October 2005).

Hoffman, Bruce. *Inside Terrorism*. London: Victor Gollancz, 1998.

Iacovou, Christos. "From MNLF to Abu Sayyaf: The Radicalization of Islam in the Philippines". 11 July 2000 <http://www.ict.org.il/articles/articledet.cfm?articleid=116> (accessed 24 January 2001).

International Court of Justice. "Sovereignty over Pulau Ligitan and Pulau Sipadan (Indonesia/Malaysia)". 2002 <http://www.icj-cij.org/icjwww/ipresscom/ipress2002/ipresscom2002-39_inma_20021217.htm> (accessed 4 October 2005).

Karniol, Robert. "Malaysians Boost Naval Power in South China Sea". *Jane's Defence Weekly* (9 October 1996): 18.

Kent, George and Mark J. Valencia, eds. *Marine Policy in Southeast Asia*. Berkeley: University of California Press, 1985.

Liss, Carolin. "The Sipadan Kidnapping 'Drama' (April–September 2000). The Rise of the Abu Sayyaf, International Terrorism, and the Global Media". BA Honours thesis, Department of Asian Studies, Murdoch University, 2001.

Man, W.K. Che. *Muslim Separatism. The Moros of Southern Philippines and the Malays of Southern Thailand*. Singapore: Oxford University Press, 1998.

Marine Police Sabah Division. "Sea Robberies in Sabah". Paper presented at the Persidangan Maritim Malaysia "96, Kuala Lumpur, 16–19 December 1996.

May, Ronald J. "The Religious Factor in Three Minority Movements: The Moro of the Philippines, the Malays of Thailand, and Indonesia's West Papuans". *Contemporary Southeast Asia* 13, no. 4 (March 1992): 396–414.

McKenna, Thomas M. *Muslim Rulers and Rebels. Everyday Politics and Armed Separatism in the Southern Philippines.* Berkley: University of California Press, 1998.

Mischuk, Georg. "Ostmalaysia. Piraten Schmuggler, Terroristen". *Marine Forum*, Jg. 79 (2004): 25–26.

Muslim, Macapado Abaton. *The Moro Armed Struggle in the Philippines: The Nonviolent Autonomy Alternative.* Marawi City: Mindanao State University, 1994.

Noble, Lela Garner. "The Moro National Liberation Front in the Philippines". *Pacific Affairs* 49, no. 3 (Fall 1976): 405–24.

Peters, Diana and Maureen De Silva. "Piracy in Sabah" <http://www.ums.edu.my/sss/bm/poster_diana&maureen.htm> (accessed 11 June 2005).

Sabah Tourism Board, "Statistics", Sabah Tourism Board, <http://sabahtourism.com/statistic.php> (accessed 28 September 2005).

Santiago, Maita. "Filipino Refugees from Sabah: Trapped in an Endless Journey". *Bulatlat.com*, November 2002 <http://www.bulatlat.com/news/2-41/2-41-refugees.html> (accessed 27 September 2005).

Sather, Clifford. *The Bajau Laut. Adaption, History, and Fate in a Maritime Fishing Society of South-eastern Sabah.* Oxford: Oxford University Press, 1997.

Tan, Samuel K. *Internationalization of the Bangsamoro Struggle.* Quezon City: University of the Philippines Press, 1993.

Torres III, Wilfredo Magno. "Voyages and Ethnicity across Reordered Frontiers: Conflict Resolution and Leadership in the Dynamics of Ethnic Identity Formation among the Sama Dilaut of Semporna". Paper presented at the "Ateneo Center for Asian Studies Conference", Ateneo de Manila University, 2005.

Turner, Mark. "Terrorism and Secession in the Southern Philippines: The Rise of the Abu Sayyaf". *Contemporary Southeast Asia* 17, no. 1 (June 1995): 1–19.

Vitug, Marites Danguilan and Glenda M. Gloria. *Under the Crescent Moon.* Quezon City: Ateneo Centre for Social Policy and Public Affairs, Institute for Popular Democracy, 2000.

Warren, Carol. *Bajau Consciousness in Social Change: The Transformation of a Malaysian Minority Community.* Townsville: James Cook University of Northern Queensland, 1983.

Warren, James Francis. *Iranun and Balangingi. Globalization, Maritime Raiding and the Birth of Ethnicity.* Quezon City: New Day Publishers, 2002.

———. *The Sulu Zone, 1768–1898: The Dynamics of External Trade, Slavery, and Ethnicity in the Transformation of a Southeast Asian Maritime State.* Singapore: Singapore University Press, 1981.

———. "A Tale of Two Centuries: The Globalisation of Maritime Raiding and Piracy in Southeast Asia at the end of the Eighteenth and Twentieth Centuries"

(Long version of paper presented). Paper presented at the "KITLV Jubilee Workshop", Leiden, 14–16 June 2001.

Werning, Rainer. *US-Imperialismus auf den Philippinen. Der Mindanao Konflikt.* Muenster: Wurf Verlag, 1983.

———. "Viel Widerstand, wenig Anpassung". *Südostasien*, Jg.16, Nr.3 (September 2000): 69–71.

———. "Wer sind die Moros?". *Philippinen Forum*, Doppelnummer 39/40 (July 1995): 4–8.

13

Piracy in Contemporary Sulu: An Ethnographical Case Study

Ikuya Tokoro

Introduction

The Sulu Archipelago is placed in the southernmost part of the Philippines. It is a typical border zone, with both geographical proximity and the cultural affinity to nearby Malaysia and Indonesia. Geographically, the Sulu Archipelago is positioned at the crossroads of three large island-areas of maritime Southeast Asia: Mindanao, Borneo, and Sulawesi Islands. As historians have discovered, violent maritime activities which are generally called "piracy" by western observers have a long historical antecedent in the Sulu Archipelago and its adjacent areas. What had been called "piracy" in the Sulu area during the period from the late eighteenth century to the mid-nineteenth century was, in reality, "slave raiding" which was strongly related to the long-distance maritime trade of the Sulu sultanate.[1] As we will refer to later, the dynamic nature and intricacies of the complex interplay of maritime trade, slave raiding, and the emergence of ethnic stratification are vividly described and explained by the monumental works by James Warren.[2]

Compared with the detailed historical studies on piracy in Sulu during pre-colonial period, an ethnographical (or anthropological) study on piracy in Sulu of more recent days, especially that of the contemporary period is relatively missing.[3] This chapter tries to fill the gap and its main purpose is to give a brief picture of piracy in contemporary Sulu. It is mainly based on the ethnographic data and case studies obtained during my field research among the local maritime folk in the Sulu Archipelago.[4]

Methodologically, the main part of this chapter adopts an ethnographical or anthropological approach. By "ethnographical/anthropological approach",

I mean that, firstly, the research is aimed at describing the nuanced local, socio-cultural context wherein any local social practice, including piracy, is embedded. For this purpose, I have acquired the language competence of the local dialect (in this case, "Sinama" or the Sama dialect) which is necessary for any substantial field research within the local society. The fieldwork was conducted by me in the Tawi Tawi province, which is the southern half of the same archipelago (1992–95). Secondly, I have conducted several direct interviews with (ex-) pirates during the fieldwork. The purpose of these interviews is to get first-hand information on the identities and social backgrounds of each (ex-) pirate. I had then examined each narrative, including their personal life histories and living memories of piracy or piracy-related acts they carried out.

By introducing these unique and singular narratives, this chapter tries to figure out the relevant factors, including socio-cultural and even "religious" or so-called "folk-Islamic" elements relating to piracy or piratical acts, mainly from the "ethnographical" or anthropological point of view. The advantage of adopting ethnographical or anthropological methods is that in doing so one can obtain both first-hand/direct data and in-depth analysis of the piracy and socio-cultural setting of the piratical activities. It enables the researchers to understand this phenomenon not only from ready-made viewpoints or categories imposed by outside observers, but also from local and indigenous meanings, significances, interpretations, views, motivations, etc. of the piracy within the local society which would contain the very actors who commit piracy or piracy-related activities (such as smuggling). In other words, this chapter aims to present a culturally nuanced description of the intersubjective meaning of the world of pirates in contemporary Sulu.[5]

In contemporary Sulu society, piracy and various piracy-linked acts such as smuggling are related, not only to its economic and political (under)development at the national and international level, but also to the social and cultural contexts intrinsic to the local maritime societies as well. But before going straight to the socio-cultural aspects of piracy, we will touch, though briefly, on the more general geographical and historical background information of the Sulu area.

GEOGRAPHICAL AND HISTORICAL BACKGROUND

The Sulu Archipelago lies at the southern periphery of the Philippines, adjoining both the Malaysian and Indonesian borders. In a sense, it is a "contact zone" of different state powers, nations, ethnic groups, traditions, and cultures. Geographically, the Sulu Archipelago is connected by the Sulu Sea to Sabah (Malaysia), and by Celebes Sea to Kalimantan (Indonesian Part of Borneo) and to Sulawesi Island (Indonesia). Between Sulu and its adjoining areas, various border crossing activities such as fishing voyages, migration, smuggling, and piracy or various piratical acts have been quite common and active up to today.

In pre-colonial times, Sulu was one of the emporiums in the maritime world of Southeast Asia. Its political and economical centre was Jolo Island where the capital of the Sulu sultanate was placed. The trading zone of the Sulu sultanate extended far beyond the Sulu Archipelago itself. The trade was systematically incorporated by the transnational long distance trade between the maritime world of Southeast Asia and China. In the eighteenth to nineteenth centuries, the sphere of influence of the Sulu sultanate reached northeast coast of Borneo, some part of Celebes, and Palawan island.[6]

The main commodities of this transregional trade were mostly marine products such as sea cucumbers, shark fins, pearls, tortoise shells, and edible birds nests. For supplying the labour power needed for collecting these marine products, the Sulu *datos* (aristocrats) engaged in "slave raiding" in almost all the coastal areas within maritime Southeast Asia.[7] In the eighteenth to nineteenth century, the sphere of influence of the Sulu sultanate reached the northern and eastern coasts of Borneo, some parts of Celebes, and Palawan island. A lot of mostly maritime ethnic groups engaged in the complex political and/or economical network of Sulu. These groups included the Tausug, Sama Dea, Sama Dilaut, Iranun, Balangingi (Warren 2002). In the latter half of the nineteenth century, a Spanish military outpost was constructed on Jolo Island. In 1898, the United States engaged in a war with Spain resulting from rivalry over Cuba. The United States won the war and, as a consequence, took possession of the entire Philippine Archipelago, including Sulu. It was only after the colonization of the entire Philippine archipelago by the United States that the sultanate of Sulu was finally brought to an end.

CONTEMPORARY SULU AS A MARITIME SOCIETY

The end of the Sulu sultanate does not necessarily mean that the maritime activities have disappeared in Sulu. Quite the contrary. Even after the colonization and decolonization of the region, various maritime activities, including fishery, maritime trade (both legitimate ones and "smuggling"), piracy, and piratical acts have been quite active up to this day. For example, during my fieldwork in Sulu in the 1990s, it was not difficult for me to find one of these "smugglers" or illegal cross-border traders in the local villages. Though goods and articles of the trade are due to time and route, various marine products, manufactured foods and clothing are typical items. As it is a kind of informal economy, exact statistical data on the cross-border trade do not exist. However, we can see that even today this cross-border trade plays a significant role in the local economy in and around the border zone of Sulu. Generally speaking, it can be recognized that the cross-border trade is more active in the border area between Sabah and Sulu, than that between Sulu and Indonesia. This might be because of the difference in the strength of border controls and also that of the economic conditions between Indonesia and Malaysia.

According to the locals, until the first half of the 1960s, the border between Indonesia and the Philippines was more porous than today. Due to this fact, there are many local veterans in Sulu who participated in the cross-border trade or smuggling between Sulu and Indonesia from the 1950s to the 1960s. Various marine products such as sea-cucumbers and shark fins were important commodities since the pre-colonial days up to the present. Now, many sea products are exported to different sides of the border depending on the relative market price. Highly dependent on changeable weather and other natural and/or socio-economic conditions, the prices of these marine products constantly fluctuate on both sides of the border. For fish brokers and traders, the difference in market prices of any sea products between the national borders could give them a great business opportunity. Besides collecting relatively "traditional" marine products such as sea-cucumber and shark fins, contemporary maritime folk in Sulu cultivate relatively novel products such as *agar-agar* or seaweeds which are mainly exported to foreign countries for use as raw material in processed goods.

In terms of ethnic composition, contemporary Sulu society is not a monolithic society, but a highly heterogeneous, multi-ethnic society composed of several different ethnic groups. Generally speaking, there are two major dominant ethno-linguistic groups in contemporary Sulu. The first group is the Tausug speaking group. In terms of inhabitation, they are centred on Jolo Island, the capital city of the Sulu province. During the pre-colonial period, the *datos* (aristocrat class) of the Tausug had engaged quite actively in the maritime trade of the Sulu sultanate. The second major groups speak Sama. These Sama speaking groups are sometimes called "Bajau" ("Badjao") especially in the Malay-Indonesian world. Traditionally, the

Tausug are more concentrated around Jolo Island, while the Sama live more in the southern half of the Sulu Arhipelago, especially in the Tawi Tawi groups of islands. Among the Sama speaking groups, one can also discern roughly two distinct sub groups, namely, the land-oriented Sama (the so-called "Sama Dea" in some parts of Sulu, especially the Sama on Sibutu Island and so on) and the sea-oriented group, which are called "Sama Dilaut (or "Bajau laut"). While the Sama Dea engage in various economic activities including agriculture, trading, fishery etc., the Sama Dilaut overwhelmingly engage in maritime fishery, including collecting sea-cucumbers (*trepangs*), shark fins, and the agar-agar cultivation.[8]

PROBLEM OF DEFINITION: CONCEPT OF "PIRACY" IN CONTEMPORARY SULU

As has been frequently pointed out by many researchers on piracy, defining the very concept of "piracy" is a troublesome task. The term "piracy" derives from ancient Greek and Roman concepts, but it has transformed its definitions and connotations quite substantially through the history of legal and political systems in the Western societies.[9] As is well known, even among the contemporary international organizations coordinating maritime security issues, there are two distinct definitions of "piracy". One, the definition adopted by the IMO (International Maritime Organization) and that by the IMB (International Maritime). Though both IMO and IMB define "piracy" as criminal acts committed in sea, the IMO defines "piracy" in relatively narrow ways; an act committed in the high seas, for private gains an attack by ship on other ships, etc. in accordance with the 1982 United Nations Convention on the Laws of the Sea. On the other hand, IMB defines "piracy" as a relatively broader and encompassing concept such as "an act of boarding, or attempting to board any ship with the intent to commit theft or any crime and with the attempt or capability to use force in furtherance of that act".[10]

In the Southeast Asian context too, the concept of piracy changes in different time and places, and it especially differs from the Western one. According to Young (Young 2005), "The intricacies of raiding, its important role in those societies, and the widespread nature of similar traditions suggest that it was a practice of great diversity and depth in the region. Traditionally, piracy/raiding in Southeast Asia served a variety of socially constructive purposes. Unlike European piracy, Southeast Asian piracy/raiding did not generally involve "criminal" elements." (Young 2005,

p. 9). Thus, the Western definitions and understandings of piracy "do not entirely fit the reality of piracy. They do not take into account the local context in maritime Southeast Asia, and thus create a conceptual gap in our understanding of the phenomena" (Young 2005, p. 11). It is precisely in this context, that we should pay more attentions to the local definitions, understandings, connotation of "piracy" in the society under discussion, in this case the concept of piracy in Sulu.

However, this time again we might face some difficulty because there are several different local words and terms, which are more or less referring to "piracy" or piracy-related acts in contemporary Sulu. Therefore we should now examine closely the connotations of each term and understand how there terms/concepts are classified in the local contexts. Firstly, the most commonly used word relating to piracy in contemporary Sulu is *mundu*. This term is a highly generic term for pirates, used in various forms, depending on the context. Usually, *mundu* refers to a person who commits piratical acts. The act of piracy itself is called *pagmundu*. It is a broad term which can cover from petty robbery against small fishermen's boat to relatively well organized maritime raiding voyages. It does not necessarily correspond to either the IMO or IMB definitions of "piracy" because in a few cases, robbery or attack on coastal houses, villages, or even bank robberies could be covered, though not always, under *(pag-)mundu*. Also, sometimes the term *mundu* has a connotation of "outlaw(s)". But, unlike IMO's definition of "piracy", it does not necessarily mean that all *mundu* are criminals for private gains, for the members of anti-governmental, secessionist armed groups for either political and/or religious causes such as MNLF, MILF or the Abu-Sayyaf Group, could be referred by this term in certain circumstances.

Besides *mundu*, one can discern several other different terms relating to piratical activities in contemporary Sulu. While the term *mundu* is a very broad and general term/concept encompassing a broad spectrum of acts which are loosely related to piracy or piratical acts, *(pag-)salsu* is a relatively narrow term that refers to maritime raiding on coastal villages for acquiring of hostages or slaves. Quite often, *(pag-)salasu* refers to traditional slave raiding during pre-colonial times, which is more commonly called *pangayau*. Another important term is *(pag-)kulukulu*. *Pagkulukulu* roughly means attacks on ship in the high sea or seas relatively far from the coast, or land. Attacks on ships in the Celebes Seas from the 1950s to the early 1960s is especially a typical referent of the term *kulukulu*.

PATTERNS OF PIRATICAL ACTS IN CONTEMPORARY SULU

Here, we would describe typical patterns of actual piratical acts in contemporary Sulu, and try to figure out some notable characteristics among these acts. Though *kulukulu* or piratical attacks on ships in the high seas (such as Celebes Seas) has become relatively fewer compared with the 1950s or the early 1960s, more small-scale attacks or robbery against small fishermen's boats or petty trader's vessels are quite rampant in the Sulu Sea area, especially within the territorial waters of the Philippines. The main purpose of these attacks is mostly to get engines, or other valuables, cargoes, and personal belongings of the target boats. It is very hard to know the exact number or frequencies of these relatively small piratical attacks on fishermen/trader's boat/vessels because most victims are reluctant, or even fear to report to the local authorities either because it is a time-consuming process and they feel the fruitlessness of such reporting, or even distrust local security authority.

The second pattern of piracy in contemporary Sulu involves attacks on sea shore villages, towns, and other coastal installations, etc. Though less frequent than the first pattern of attacks on small fishing boat/trading boat, this second pattern is usually more well-organized, sometimes planned carefully before the actual attack, and quite often more harmful to the victims in terms of damages. It might be arguable if this pattern of attack on seashore communities, villages, or towns is conceptualized as "piracy" in the Western definition of the term. However, this act of raid on coastal areas has been traditionally the most common practices in this part of maritime Southeast Asia since pre-colonial times. And, as will be shown by narratives from (ex-) pirates themselves in the following section, it did not end even after the decolonization period. Usually, the purpose of this type of attack is to rob money and other valuables, though hostage taking could be another possible purpose.

Compared with traditional large-scale, long-distance slave raiding of the Sulu sultanate in the eighteenth and the nineteenth centuries, contemporary piracy is a small-scale activity, in terms of the geographical distance of raiding, mobilization, or number of participants. In pre-colonial times, the slave raiding expeditions organized by the *datos* (aristocrats) of the Sulu sultanate could reach as far as Sumatra, Luzon, Papua New Guinea, etc., and involve expedition fleets composed of hundreds, or sometimes even thousands, of participants (Warren 1982). In contrast to this, most of the petty piratical raids today are committed within relatively short distances in and around the Sulu Archipelago and the neighbouring north-east coast of Sabah, Malaysia. And the number of participants is small; let's say the majority of piracy is committed by fewer than ten people per one raid in present day.

Another distinctive feature of contemporary piracy in Sulu is that there is a strong, and seemingly paradoxical juxtaposition, or coexistence of modern technologies and traditional, mystical beliefs and rituals among the contemporary pirates. By this "juxtaposition," I mean the following phenomenon: On the one hand, contemporary pirates in Sulu are quite actively appropriating modern technologies such as high-speed outboard engines, automatic rifles, grenades, radio talkies etc. So, in terms of material culture, pirates are pretty well adapted to modern technologies and innovations of Western origin. However, at the same time, these same pirates usually have strong beliefs in traditional, or so-called "folk-Islamic" rituals and ideas, such as *ilmu, duwaa salamat*, and so on. We will examine these beliefs and/or rituals, again from concrete case studies of narratives and/or life histories of (ex-)pirates in the following sections.

Case Study: A Life History of Retired (ex-) Pirates in Tawi Tawi

Here we examine the socio-cultural composition of piracy in more detail through personal life histories, and narratives of each (ex-) pirate in contemporary Sulu. The first example is that of Usman (pseudonym). When I conducted the interview with Usman in May 1993, he was sixty-five years old. At that time, he was already "retired" from piracy. He had stopped joining any piratical acts because of his age, namely he had become an ex-pirate in that sense. Usman's birth place is B-village (pseudonym) not far from Bongao, Tawi Tawi Island (located in the southern part of the Sulu Archipelago). Usman speaks several local dialects including Sama, Tausug, and Malay. A brief abstract of his life history is as follows; since the 1950s, Usman had engaged in *pagmundu* (piracy in general) for more than two decades. If he had been an active especially participant in *pagkulukulu* (attacks on ship in the Celebes Sea) from the 1950s to the early days of the 1960s. At the same time, he was also conducting long-distance trading to Indonesia and sometimes engaged in fishing voyages to

Palawan, too. Thus Usman was not a "full-time pirate" in its narrow sense, but selectively engaged and participated in piracy depending on appropriate conditions, opportunities, expected returns and risks, and so on (Interview by the author, May 1993, Bongao).

Voyage of Piracy (Pagkulukulu) by Usman

Here, we examine the details of typical piratical voyages for *pagkulukulu* (attacks on ships in the Celebes Sea) conducted by Usman and his fellow pirates. According to him, vessels for this piratical voyages were relatively small, usually loaded with rice, sugar, etc. These boats were not necessarily equipped with engines. As a matter of fact, even during the 1950s, it was not unusual for Usman to use sailing boats for piratical voyages. In any piratical voyage, Usman and his followers used several kinds of lethal weapons such as rifles, guns, knives, etc. The main targets of *pagkulukulu* were sailing trading ships (which were called *parangkang* by the pirates) in the Celebes Sea. These trading ships were operated by the Bugis merchants from Celebes (Sulawesi) for the copra trade.

The *modus operandi* for *pagkulukulu* was as follows: firstly Usman and his fellow pirates went on a piratical voyage in the Celebes Sea in one of their boats. There, they stood by for several days in the high sea, waiting for any Bugis trading ship. When they found a target ship, they would approach the boat by pretending they were fellow traders. Then, if the target ship was unarmed or poorly armed, the pirates would rob the goods (mostly copra) of the ship, or do forced exchange (*pagsambi*) at an exploitable rate. On the contrary, if pirates noticed that the Bugis ship was strong enough to resist the attack, they just aborted the attack plan and waited for other, easier targets.

From these narratives by Usman, we can easily notice that there existed a close relationship between trading and piracy during the 1950s. As a matter of fact, the sudden emergence of the *pagkulukulu* (piratical voyages) during the 1950s was strongly connected to the fundamental economical situation at that time. It was the rise of active copra trading. This copra trade involved very brisk activities between Celebes (Sulawesi) and British North Borneo (present-day Sabah, Malaysia) during the 1950s and up to the early days of the 1960s. And ironically, many pirates such as Usman were traders (smugglers) themselves. Piracy voyages (*pagkulukulu*) would turn to become trading voyages, depending on the situation.

Attack on Coastal Villages in North Borneo/Sabah, Malaysia by Usman

The second pattern of piracy by Usman was the attack on seashore villages and other coastal targets. According to him, he had attacked several coastal villages in North Borneo/ Sabah, during the 1960s. For example, he attacked a village in Kinabatangan area (in the Sandakan district, British North Borneo) together with his fellow pirates in the early days in the 1960s (exact date unknown). In that attack, Usman's group used a one engine boat with ten crew members, armed with M1 Garland rifle and other guns and *barong* (native swords).

Usually, before committing this kind of attack on the coastal targets, Usman had conducted detailed planning and preparations for the piratical attack, (at least one month) before the actual attack. As part of this preparation, one of Usman's followers would do a reconnaissance or spying survey before the attack. The purpose of this reconnaissance or spying was to gather information on the population, number of houses, location of main buildings, distance to the local police, location of houses which have valuables in the target village, etc. After getting enough information on the target village, Usman would carefully decide the landing point on the beach, entry and escape route, etc. for the attack.

Usman usually recruited fellow participants for each piratical raid: mostly relatives in same village. Before the piratical voyage, the *nakula* or the leader of pirates has to prepare/provide guns, ammunitions, food, etc. in advance. Surprisingly, Usman tells us that he sometimes borrowed guns from relatives, friends, and even the police or military personnel! After the piratical voyage/raid, Usman gave some share of the booty to those relatives, friends, police and military personnel.

After each successful piratical raid/voyage, the *nakula* had to distribute the booty of the piratical raid/voyage. An example of the distribution of the booty of the piratical voyage by Usman was follows. In the cases of *pagkulu-kulu* during the 1950s, the booty was mostly copra or coconuts. After the raids, these copra or coconuts were brought to Tawao (a southeastern city in North Borneo) and sold there. Then, the amount was distributed according to the contribution for the piratical voyage. From the total amount of the booty, about 30 per cent went to the *nakula*. From this 30 per cent, the *nakula* had to pay the debt for the cost of engines, gasoline, food, etc. About 10 per cent of the total booty was the share of those who provided guns and ammunitions (sometimes including policemen and military personnel). The rest went to all other participants and was to be divided equally.

Another interesting aspect of contemporary piracy in Sulu is its ambivalent and sometime contradictory relationship with rebels and government. After 1972, Usman became a member of ICHDF (Integrated Civilian Home Defence Force: a government sanctioned vigilante group in the Philippines). At the same time, he was a sympathizer of MNLF (Moro National Liberation Front: Muslim secessionist group). As a sympathizer, he smuggled a lot of MNLF guerillas to Tawi Tawi from Sabah, Malaysia, in the 1970s. In this way, we can notice Usman's ambivalent and sometimes contradictory relationship to the government and rebels.

"INNER" (SUBJECTIVE) WORLD OF PIRATES: TRADITIONAL BELIEFS AND RITUALS OF MUNDU"

We now will examine another undeniable feature relating to contemporary piracy in Sulu, namely, an act of piracy strongly connected to traditional, mystical beliefs, and the "folk Islamic" rituals of *mundu*. For example, during my interview with Usman about his engagement in piracy, he told me *"Mbal aku ata'u magmundu, karna taga-ilmu aku* (I am not afraid when I commit piracy, because I have *ilmu*)." This word *ilmu* is originally an Arabic word referring to "knowledge" in general. But in contemporary Sulu, the word *ilmu* has a special connotation for specific kinds of esoteric knowledge and/or magical spells and its power, etc. Without exception, pirates in Sulu have strong belief in these *ilmu*. Another example of traditional belief is the belief in *ajji matt* or *anting-anting* (amulets).

Rituals before piratical voyage/raids are also practised among pirates in Sulu. The *tinagu inyawa* ritual is a typical example of such rituals relating to piratical activities. Basically, this is a ritual divination before a piratical voyage. The word *tinagu inyawa* means "to keep breath" in the local Sama dialect. Before a piratical voyage, the leader (*nakula*) of the voyage will gather his followers beside him and swallow his saliva or rub his own hair very rapidly. And if every member can hear the sound of these acts, they will come back safely from the voyage. If not, it is inauspicious and the member who could not hear the sound cannot go on the trip. Thus this *tinagu inyawa* has symbolically preguaranteed the safety of each piratical voyage.

Another example of *ilmu* is a belief in imaginary "twins." Pirates believe everybody has invisible, imaginary "twins" (*kambal*) since the time of his birth. Before going on a piratical voyage, he has to give offerings (food) to this "twin". During the piratical voyage/raids, this "twin" would predict (*alamat*) and inform him (pirate) of every danger beforehand. As another example of *ilmu*, we can look at *ajji matt* or *anting-anting*, the amulets. Spells or incantations in both local dialects (Sama and Tausug) and Arabic are also very common among the local pirates. These amulets and spells have a variety of types, depending on the purposes. For example, there is an amulet and spell for becoming invulnerable against bullets, or becoming invisible in the enemy's eye, or calming strong winds and waves, etc.

The *duwaa salamat* ritual is also quite common in Sulu. This is a so-called "folk Islamic" ritual relating to piracy. *Duwaa salamat* basically means "praying for safety/security". As a matter of fact, this is a quite common ritual among local Muslims in general. Usually, this ritual consists of some formalized acts such as reciting Arabic words, spells (including *jikils*) by the participants. In the case of *mundu* (pirates), the ritual is highly esoteric and closed. Before and after piratical voyage, pirates perform this ritual both to pray for and acknowledge the success of the piratical voyage.

Blurred Line: Case of Dato Hassan Brothers: Muslim Rebels Turned Pirates

Another concrete case study of pirates in contemporary Sulu is Dato Hassan (pseudonym), who had been a famous pirate in Tawi Tawi, together with his six brothers. His birth place is L village (pseudonym) in the Tawi Tawi province.

An abstract of his life history is follows: He was born as a descendant of a famous *datu* (traditional aristocratic) family. From the 1970s to the 1980s, he and his six siblings were famous MNLF commanders who had substantially controlled many areas of Tawi Tawi. In the so-called "amnesty" programme, they surrendered to the Philippine government. However, even after the amnesty, they still held a lot of guns and followers as members of ICHDF. In the early 1990s, they committed *pagmundu* (piratical acts) such as attacking fishing vessels. In 1994, Dato Hassan was shot dead during a family feud.

From this brief life history of Dato Hassan, we will notice another distinctive nature of contemporary piracy in Sulu, namely, sometimes the distinction between "pirates" and "rebels" and between "governmental-" and "anti-governmental-" agencies is very much blurred, as is clearly shown in the cases of Usman and Dato Hassan. We can also notice the ambiguity of vigilante groups such as the ICHDF. Even in the case of the notorious Abu Sayaff Group, there is a similar feature of ambiguity. Firstly, the Abu Sayyaf Group is a Muslim insurgent group who claims to fight for secession of the Muslim dwelling area in the Southern Philippines. However, in reality, Abu Sayyaf Group has strong affinity to *mundu* like activities such as cross-border attack and hostage-taking for ransom money. Recently, in Sitangkai (Tawi Tawi), many Sama Dilaut fishermen were assaulted by these Abu Sayyaf members. According to my own observation, because of rampant piratical activities by Abu Sayyaf, a lot of Sama Dilaut fishermen have migrated from Tawi Tawi to Semporna (Sabah) these days.

RESURGENCE OF PIRACY AND SMUGGLE IN CONTEMPORARY SULU

Finally, we examine, the background and factors relating to the resurgence of piracy and piracy-related activities, which have so far been described mainly in the cultural context, from the general politico-economical contexts also.

After colonization by the United States, both the maritime trading network of Sulu and the sultanate itself, which depended on it, were forcefully abolished. However, another kind of cross-border trade and the flow of people in and around Sulu had been established, up to now. Even after the introduction of modern nation states, various cross-border activities such as cross-border fishing voyage, "smuggling", and rampant cross-border migration have been flourishing very actively between Sulu and Sabah, Malaysia.

For example, inter-island migration has been quite common in this region. The reasons for migration vary; including seeking for good fishing grounds, avoiding political conflict, and/or intermarriage, and so on. The cross-border human flow is quite visible especially between the east coast of Sabah and the southern parts of the Philippines. For example, a lot of local people in Semporna have relatives and even families in Sitangkai, the southernmost part of the Tawi Tawi, through marriage and other social linkages. Nowadays, a lot of these fishermen in the border zone are easy targets for pirates.

Besides this relatively traditional pattern, a new factor has emerged in the human flow across borders: refugees, illegal immigrants, and smuggle. Since the early 1970s, tens of thousands of Muslim Filipino refugees have fled war-torn southern Philippines and settled in Sabah as refugees. These refugees escaped a kind of civil war or an ethno-religious conflict between MNLF (Moro National Liberation Front) and the Philippine government that was going on in Mindanao and Sulu during the 1970s. This conflict had actually literally brought catastrophic, devastating effects to the local economy in Sulu. Besides direct casualties, many local people lost their homes, lands, and evacuated to Sabah. As for Filipino refugees, there are various estimates of their total number. The Sabah State Government estimated that there were 70,000 of them living in Sabah in the 1970s while the United Nations High Commissioner for Refugees (UNHCR) estimated their number to be closer to 100,000. On the other hand, community leaders in Sabah alleged that their number might have exceeded 130,000.

It was relatively easy for them to evacuate to Sabah, because of both geographical proximity and the traditional social ties between the both sides of the border. Up to the present day, the refugees from Sulu are not unknown because of the ongoing sporadic fighting between those on Muslim separatist organizations and the Philippine military in Sulu. This deteriorating security and economic situation in the Philippine side of border is one of the main factors pushing people to resort to illegal informal economic activities, such as illegal migration, smuggling, and piracy.

In regard to cross-border trading, some of these activities are officially sanctioned and endorsed under the name of "barter trade". This barter trade between the southern Philippines and Sabah is quite active. Due to the geographical proximity with the Southern Philippines, Sandakan and Tawau are the two main ports of this barter trade. The monthly average value of goods exported from Sandakan to the southern Philippines is about two million Malaysian Ringgit (RM). These exported goods include cigarettes, sugar, biscuits, second-hand clothing, generators, radios, cassettes tapes, and other appliances. The value of goods imported from the southern Philippines to Sandakan is about RM30,000 to RM40,000. These imported goods include household goods such as Philippine-made skin lotions, perfumes, candies, and small goods, which are mainly for the consumption of the Filipino immigrants in Sabah. Most of the boats used for barter trade are of sizes ranging from fifteen to twenty tons which are known as *kumpits*. There are about thirty-six shipments per month in average. The licenses for barter trade are issued by the State Ministry of Finance and under the proper co-authorization by other agencies such as the Customs department, Police, and Immigration. The Sabah State Government encouraged this barter trade under the framework of the BIMP-EAGA (Brunei Darussalam-Indonesia-Malaysia-Philippines East ASEAN Growth Area) economic cooperation.

Except this barter trade or officially endorsed trade, other cross-border trading is, generally speaking, considered "smuggling", at least, from the government's point of view. Therefore, in theory, unauthorized cross-border trade would be an object of strict control and suppression by the respective government authorities. During my fieldwork between 1993 and 1994 in Sulu, it was not difficult for me to find these "smugglers" or illegal cross-border traders in the villages. Even during the 1990s, illegal cross-border trade was nothing if not the order of the day. Though goods and articles of trade depend mainly on time and route, various marine products, manufactured foods, and clothing are typical items.

As it is a kind of informal economy, exact statistical data on the cross-border trade do not exist. However, we can see that even today this cross-border trade plays a significant role in the local economy in and around the border zone of Sulu. Generally speaking, it can be recognized that cross-border trade is more active in the border area between Sabah and Sulu, than that between Sulu and Indonesia. This might be because of the difference in the strength of border controls and also that of the economic conditions between Indonesia and Malaysia.

The advantage for cross-border trading is by no means limited to marine products. For example, some kinds of beer, liquor, and cigarettes are relatively cheap in the Philippines compared with Malaysia. Taking advantage of this price differences, many traders of Sulu have engaged in exporting these "contraband" goods to Sabah, Malaysia. Of course, cross border trade of "contraband" goods is illegal, and is nothing but "smuggling" from a governmental point of view. So this "smuggling" is risky business. When I conducted field research in Sulu, I happened to know one such trader who conducted the cross-border trade in liquor between Sitangkai Island (the Philippine side) and Semporna, an east coast town of Sabah. On average, the frequency of the trade is three to four times a month during the year 1993. At that time, he procured twenty boxes of whisky for one trading trip, which cost about 4,300 Philippine pesos at that time. When he brought that whisky to Sabah, he could easily sell it for RM800 which was, at that time, equivalent to about double the original cost.

In other words, the existence of the nation state system and national borders has two ambiguous, or even contradictory, effects on local maritime people who do illegal smuggling. On the one hand, each national government and/or state-authority tries to control and suppress illegal maritime activities such as smuggling. However, the existence of this national border itself creates the relative gap/difference of economic conditions on both sides of the border. And smugglers utilize these very gaps/differences for economic profits.

We can recognize the same ambiguous function of national borders in the case of piracy, too. On the one hand, the security apparatus of each nation state, such as its marine police, navy, and border control system are, in theory at least, designed and created as effective means to suppress any illicit activities such as piracy. But if we look at the situation of piracy in Sulu, we have to acknowledge the more complicated and even the paradoxical nature of the nation state and its national border system. As we have already examined in the case of Usman, we cannot exclude the possibility that the corrupt elements of the local security apparatus (police /military) would themselves be involved in, or collude with pirates in a particular situation. Or, as it is shown in the case of Dato Hassan, a government sanctioned vigilante group such as ICHDF sometimes has counter-productive effects on suppressing piracy, because the very members of the vigilante group commits piracy themselves. Besides these facts, some contemporary pirates know quite well that the efficacy of national power ends at the national border. For example, if pirates from Sulu attack a target in Sabah (Malaysia), and then escape to Sulu, the Philippine side of the border, the Malaysian marine police cannot pursue them beyond the territorial jurisdiction of the national border. Thus, in other words, the pirates in contemporary Sulu take advantage of this "clack" of nation states system and their borders.

Conclusion: Change and Continuity in Piracy in Sulu

In the pre-colonial Sulu society, piracy was a large-scale raiding activity sometimes sponsored by the *dato* of the Sulu sultanates. The purpose was to get slaves whose manpower is decisive for gathering/collecting of marine products such as sea-cucumbers, shark fins, etc. Thus piracy or, more precisely, large-scale slave raiding, was strongly connected to the maritime trade of the Sulu sultanates (Warren 1982).

In contemporary Sulu, piracy is relatively small-scale activity. The purpose is not for slaves, but for booty and money (or hostages for ransom in far fewer cases). And the main characteristics of contemporary piracy in Sulu are follows: On the one hand, pirates are appropriating modern technologies like outboard engines, automatic rifles, etc. However, on the other hand, there exists a strong continuity of "traditional" features, namely, until today, piracy has a strong connection/interrelation with maritime trade (though of a different type; copra trade, smuggling etc.). Another important point which one can easily be noticed is that there is a persistence of traditional (folk-Islamic) beliefs and rituals among contemporary pirates in Sulu. Here we could recognize a paradoxical juxtaposition or combination of modernity and tradition in piracy.

Notes

1. J.F. Warren, *The Sulu Zone, 1768–1898: The Dynamics of External Trade, Slavery, and Ethnicity in the Transformation of a Southeast Asian Maritime State* (Singapore: Singapore University Press, 1982).
2. Ibid. Also see various other works by J.F. Warren, including *Iranun and Balangingi: Globalization, Maritime Raiding and the Birth of Ethnicity* (Singapore: Singapore University Press, 2002).
3. The chapter by Stefan Eklof (in this volume) which describes the piracy in the Sulu Sea during the decolonization period (1959–63) from the political and international points of view is a rare and excellent exception to this general "disregard" on contemporary piracy in Sulu. Still, his study is, methodologically speaking, not based on ethnographical or anthropological field work, but on archival works.
4. What I mean by "contemporary period" in this chapter is, roughly speaking, the period between the 1950s and the 1990s, in which the "living memories" of local informants are relatively easy to recollect and trace.
5. One could that this chapter tries to present a "thick description" of piracy in the C. Geertz's sense. See C. Geertz, "Thick Description: Toward an Interpretive Theory of Culture", in C. Geertz, *Interpretation of Cultures: Selected Essays* (New York: Basic Books, 1973), pp. 3–30.
6. This part of maritime Southeast Asia which was interconnected and loosely incorporated by maritime trade and political influence of the Sulu sultanates was named "Sulu Zone" by Warren (Warren, op. cit.).
7. Ibid.
8. Besides these major groups, there are also other relatively minor groups in the Sulu Archipelago such as Ilanun (Iranun, Iranon), who are known for their maritime raiding during pre-colonial days. The Jama Mapun in the Cagayan de Tawi Tawi Island and the Yakan in the Basilan Island are usually recognized as distinct ethnic groups in terms of ethnic identities, though,

linguistically speaking, both groups speak dialects loosely belonging to a subdivision of the Sama dialects.
9. For a concise outlook of the transformation of the concept of "piracy" in both Western and Southeast Asian history, see Adam J. Young "Roots of Contemporary Maritime Piracy in Southeast Asia" in Derek Johnson and Mark Valencia, eds., *Piracy in Southeast Asia: Status, Issues, and Responses* (Singapore: Institute of Southeast Asian Studies, 2005), pp. 1–33.
10. We have no space to elaborate on this issue here. For this contemporary Western version of the definition of piracy, see Derek Johnson, Erika Pladdet, and Mark Valencia, "Introduction" in ibid. pp. ix–xx.

References

Andaya, Barbara W. and Leonard Andaya. Y. *History of Malaysia*. London: The Macmillan Press, 1982.

Che Man, W.K. *Muslim Separatism: The Moros of Southern Philippines and the Malays of Southern Thailand*. Oxford: Oxford University Press, 1990.

Geertz, Clifford. "Thick Description: Toward an Interpretive Theory of Culture". In *Interpretation of Cultures: Selected Essays*. (New York: Basic Books, 1973) pp. 3–30.

IDS (Institute for Development Studies, Sabah). *Migrant Labour Flows in the East Asian Region*. Kota Kinabalu: Institute for Development Studies, 1998.

Johnson, Derek, Erika Pladdet and Mark Valencia. "Introduction". In *Piracy in Southeast Asia: Status, Issues, and Responses*, edited by Derek Johnson and Mark Valencia. Singapore: Institute of Southeast Asian Studies, 2005, pp. ix–xx.

Kiefer, Thomas M. *Tausug Armed Conflict: The Social Organization of Military Activity in a Philippine Moslem Society*. Chicago: University of Chicago Press, 1969.

———. "Folk Islam and the Supernatural". In *The Readings on Islam in Southeast Asia*, compiled by Sharon Siddique, Ahmad Ibrahim, and Yasmin Hussain. Singapore: Institute of Southeast Asian Studies, 1985, pp. 323–25.

Laarhoven, Ruurdje. *Triumph of Moro Diplomacy: The Maguindanao Sultanate in the 17th Century*. Quezon City: New Day Publishers, 1989.

Majul, Cesar Adib. *Muslims in the Philippines*. Quezon City: University of the Philippines Press, 1973.

Saleeby, Najeeb. *The History of Sulu*. Manila: Filipiniana Book Guild, 1963.

Sather, Clifford. *The Bajau Laut: Adaptation, History, and Fate in Maritime Fishing Society of South-Eastern Sabah*. Oxford: Oxford University Press, 1997.

Tokoro, Ikuya Ekkyou. *Border-Crossings: A View From the Maritime World of Sulu*. Tokyo: Iwanami Syoten Publisher (in Japanese), 1999.

———. "Transformation of Shamanic Rituals among the Sama of Tabawan Island, Sulu Archipelago, Southern Philippines". In *Globalization in Southeast Asia: Local, National, and Transnational Perspectives*, edited by Shinji Yamashita and Jeremy S. Eades. New York, Oxford: Berghahn Books, 2003, pp. 165–78.

Warren, James Francis. *The Sulu Zone, 1768–1898: The Dynamics of External Trade, Slavery, and Ethnicity in the Transformation of a Southeast Asian Maritime State*. Singapore: Singapore University Press, 1982.

———. *Iranun and Balangingi: Globalization, Maritime Raiding and the Birth of Ethnicity*. Singapore: Singapore University Press, 2002.

Young, Adam J. "Roots of Contemporary Maritime Piracy in Southeast Asia". In *Piracy in Southeast Asia: Status, Issues, and Responses*, edited by Derek Johnson and Mark Valencia Singapore: Institute of Southeast Asian Studies, 2005, pp. 1–33.

Index

A

Abu Sayyaf, 251
Alhabshy, Said Hasan, 135
Amboina
    incursions by Papuans, 150
    raids into, 148–52
Americans, anti-piracy patrols, 224
Amirell, Stefan Eklof, 11
Amoy, trans-shipment hub, 37
Ancien Regime, 120
anchorage groups, 86
Anglo-Dutch treaty (1871), 139
Anglo-Philippine naval cooperation, 230
anti-piracy campaigns, 213
    indigenous allies, 213–16
Antony, Robert J., 8, 103
Armed Forces of the Philippines, battles with Abu Sayyaf, 251
arms trafficking, 139
artisanale piracy, 144
Arung Bakung, 203
    part of Bone's sphere of influence, 211
Australian territorial waters, 20

B

Bacan, 154
Bai Ben, 86
Bai Lang, 102
Bajak Laut, 134–36
Bajau, 240
Balangingi, 135, 178
    end of slave raiding, 195
    enemy of Spanish, 182
    expedition against, 185
    use of Taosug credit system, 186
Banda, raids into, 148–52
Banggai, expedition against, 212
Bangsa Moro Liberation Organisation (BMLO), 261
banishment, form of punishment, 117
Banjarmasin, resistance forces, 138
barbarian pirates, 43
Baron, Hendrick, 60
Baron, Samuel, 51
Barrera, Juan Bautista, 183
    description of Wyndham's efforts, 184
    record of slaves captured, 193
    report by, 188
barter trade, 282
Barthes, Roland, 100
Basilan, 184
Bengal silk, 55
Berau, 133
Biak, 156
Bias Bay, 107, 110
Billington, Ray Allen, 41
BIMP-EAGA, 283
birds nests, 183
black market, Giang Binh, 39
Blok, Anton, 102, 115
Boano, destruction of VOC guard post, 152
Boggs, Eli, 107
bombing campaigns, pirate settlements, 214
Bone, 202
Borneo Paradise Resort, 256
Bourgon, Jerome, 116
Boxer Rebellion, 100, 121
Braudel, Fernand, 102
British, steam boats, Suez to Singapore, 133

British-Philippine relations, 229
Brooke, James, 185
Brouwer, Bastiaan, 59
Buch, Willem, 63
Bugis, 201
Burney Treaty (1826), 138
Buton, sultan of, 203

C

Cai Qian, 83
Calanca, Paola, 9
cannibalistic practices, 45
Canton, opium trade, 43
Cao Bang, 52
Captain Every, 16
Captain Kidd, 16
Caribbean, Captain Kidd, 16
cartaz system, 21
Cencilli, Juan, 189
Cendrawasih Bay, 167, 169
Centre for Maritime Research (MARE), 7
Chalk, Peter, 4
Chen Laosan, 45
Chen Shaoyuan, 95
Chen Zhangfa, 45
Chen Zigong, 95
China
    civil strife, beginning of Sun Yat Sen's republic, 109
    history of corporal punishment, 116
Chinese gold, export to Tonkin, 53
Chinese Maritime Customs Service, 113
Chinese prison system, 117
Chua Trinh, 62
    fifth military campaign against Quinam, 66
Christian cultists, 248
cloves, Dutch monopoly, 152
Chun Fuk Yin, 112
clan networks, South Fujian, 76
coastal villages, attack on, 278–79

coastal societies, stress from economic sources, 21
coastal surveillance, South Fujian, 77
coastal zones, boundary areas, 4
Cochin, 19
colonial maritime expansion, impact of, 216–17
colonial powers, expansionistic ambitions, 132
convict labourers, Cape of Good Hope, 153
Conxinga, 57
copper zeni, 67
copyright, infringement, 15
copra
    ban in exporting, 227
    demand for, 215
    traders, 226
Coromandel Coast, 55
Cornelius, time in Buton, 211
Coromandel trade, 53
corsair, 19
Cos, Simon, 150, 159
    expedition, 155
Council of the Indies, 54
Coyett, Fredrik (Governor), 53
Crespo, Don Romualdo, 134
custom surcharges, South Fujian, 89

D

Daeng Magassing, 205–06
Dai Viet, 71
damar, demand for, 215
Dato Mama, 143
de Brito, Miguel Roxo, 159
de los Santos, Juan, 194
definitions
    hongi, 218
    piracy, 3
    piracy in Asian waters, 15–28
    raiding, 3
    robbery, 3
    state, 18

Deshima factory, 56, 67
Dirty Hollow, place of execution in Hong Kong, 119
Dickens, Charles, 120, 124
Discouar, Gonsalvo, 69
Douglas Steamship Company, 110
Doyle, Edward, 100
Drake, Francis, 104
Dutch
  clove, monopoly, 148
  first steam ship, 133
  monopoly of trade in fine spices, 137
Dutch-Ternaten anti-piracy measures, 204
Dutch East India Company (VOC)
  commercial activities in East, 55
  desire for permanent foothold in China, 70
  heavy losses, 66
  Japan trade, 70

E

East Africa, 22
East India Company, attack on ships, 22
Eastern Sulawesi
  arrival of Dutch, 202
  Bugis frontier, 202
  Dutch influence, 203
  location, 217
egg families, 105
emigration
  clandestine, 89
  inter and intra-provincial, 81
Esperanza, 187
European Convention of Human Rights, 120
Exclusive Economic Zone (EEZ), 23, 243
executions
  public, 118, 119
  ultimate punishment, 117

F

Feliz, Francisco, 194

Filipino pirates, arrest by British authorities, 225
Fong Yao (Admiral), 111
Formosa, loss of, 52–54
Foukere, 163
frontiers, definition, 40
Fujian, 9
  South *see* South Fujian
Fujian Province, map, 78

G

Ganj-i Sawai, 16
Galela, 205, 218
Gao Qizhou, 79
Gebe, 151, 156
General History of Fujian, 84
Ghalib Andang, 253
Giang Binh, 8, 9, 31–50
  citizens, 42–46
  common culture of inhabitants, 44
  importance of piracy, 37
  location, 36
  location just inside China's border, 39
  part of "water world» of South China Sea, 37
  as pirate haven, 34
  Qing representation in map, 35
  razing by royalist troops, 36
  Vietnamese jurisdiction, 40
  water world in late 18th century, 38
Gilbert, William Schwenk, 3
gold, 55–58
  Coromandel, 56
  export to Tonkin, 53
  Japan, 56
  shortage of, 68
Guangdong Pirate Federation, 105
guerilla warfare, MNLF, 250
Gurabesi, 156

H

Hadanga, 85
Hadji Taata, 217

Hai Tan Straits, 111
Halcombe, Charles J.H., 122
Halmahera, 152
  origin of Tobelo, 204
Hao Yulin, 90
harami, bandits, 132
Harmads, 21
Hartsinck, Carel (Director General), 65
Hashim Salamat, 249
He Xing, 32
He Xiwen, 42
Heaven and Earth Society, 77, 80
Hirado factory, 56
Ho Fat To, 112
Hoang Anh Tuan, 9
Hobsbawm, Eric, Bandits, 99
Hong Dizhen, 104
Hong Kong, cases of piracy, 108
Hong Kong Musuem of History, 100
hongi, definition, 218
Horn of Africa, motivation of pirates in, 5
Huang clan, 94
Huang Daxing, 42
Huang Shijian (Admiral), 84
Huang Wu, 94

I

Ida'an, 192
Ilanun, 135
Imperial Chinese Maritime Customs Service, 110
Indonesia
  number of pirate attacks, 142
  view of free trade, 12
  violence and armed robbery at sea, 131–46
Indonesian fishing boats, 20
Indonesian navy, 226
Indonesian-Philippine agreement, eradication of piracy, 230
International Chamber of Commerce (ICC), 140
international cooperation, 229–31
International Court of Justice, 248
International Maritime Bureau (IMB), 5, 6, 140, 243
  definition of pircay, 20
International Maritime Organization (IMO), 273
international relations, complicated, 233
international trade, Jolo, 178–99
Italian mafia, 12
Iranun (Ilanun), 178, 285
  end of slave raiding, 195
  enemies of Spanish, 182

J

Jama Mapun, 285
Jambi, resistance forces, 138
Japan
  ban on gold exports, 68
  gold, 56
  silver, ban on exports, 69
Japanese gold
  ban on export, 56
  export to India, 58
Japanese Occupation, Hong Kong, 109
Jiang Sheng, 42
Jiangnan, 91
joanga (lanong), 179
Jojo Island, 271
Jolo
  international trade, 178–99
  slave marekting, 183–86
  slave market, preferential basis, 189
  slave raiding, 178–99
Juc Ling, 42

K

kain timur system, 166
Kanhoji, 18
Kayan, 192
Kendari, 209
Kendari Bay, 206–12
  Bugis claim, 210

Kenyah, 192
Kepala Burung peninsula, 169
Khaddafy Janjalani, 251
Kidd, William, 16
kimelaha, 149
Kleinen, John, 10
Knaap, Gerrit, 10
Konfrontasi, 229
kulukulu, pirate attacks on ships, 275
Kunak, pirate raid, 228

L

La Ma'dukelleng, 136
Laiwui, population, 209
Lapian, Adrian B., 10
Latimammang, 211
Latu Kaysuku, 149
Latumana, 212
levend, activities sanctioned by government, 132
Leung Tuow,, 113
Li Tana, 41
Li Xing, 32
Li Youyong, 85
Lijn, Pieter, expeditions, 162–64
Liang Er, 44
Ligitan, 248
Lingard, William, 133
Lipsman, Samuel, 100
Liss, Carolin, 12
Liu Xingtang, 78
liumin, 42
Liuwudian, 86
Lizhang, 32
Lord Jim, 134
Low A Wai, 112
Lubra, 107
Luo Yasan, 44

M

Mac clan, 52
Macapagal, Diosdado (President), 229
Madagascar, 40

Madrid Protocol, 139
Maetsuycker, Joan (Governor General), 62
Maguindanao, 134
Magsaysay, Ramon (President), 227
Malaysia
    Defence Ministry, 254
    increased patrols, 254
Malaysian Enforcement Coordination Centre, 243
Malaysian Marine Police
    increased presence, 255
    Sabah Division, 244
Malaysian Maritime Enforcement Agency, 257
Malaysian waters, pump boats, ban on, 255
Mappilas, 18
Marine Police, Semporna, 240
Marine Police Sabah Division, 245
maritime activities, control of, South Fujian, 92
maritime coastal zones, *see also* coastal zones
maritime piracy *see also* piracy
    modern, 237–68
maritime terrorism, 24
    link to maritime piracy, 5
maritime coastal zones, frontier societies, 3
Mau Lau Yune, 112
Medomo, 215
migration, inter island, 281
Melisherken, 54
military entreprenuers, 8, 104
military officers, South Fujian, 84
Miller, Harry, Pirates of the Far East, 99
Ming-Qing conflict, 52
Minnan, 79
    during height of piracy, 80
    local life in, 93
Mirs Bay, 107

Misool, 155, 158
  Dutch expedition to, 161
Moluccas, 147, 152–55
Mong Cai, 8
Mongol Plain Yellow Banner, 85
Morgan, Henry, 104
Moro Islamic Liberation Front (MILF), 249
Moro National Liberation Front (MNLF), 249, 282
  peace agreement signed, 250
Moro Wars, 131
Moros, 222
MT Selayang, 141
MT Shan Ho, 141
MV Prima Indah, 142
mundu, 274
Murray, Dian, 6 40, 42
musk, 53, 58–60
  Chinese, 59
  improvement in trade, 70
  Laotian, 59
  shortage of, 69
Muslim rebels, turned into pirates, 280
Muslim ships, 18

N

Nadal, Goncal Lopez, 37
Nan Ming dynasty, 60
nakula, 278
Nanjing Treaty *see* Treaty of Nanjing
Nanning, 62
naval cooperation, British and Filipino, 230
Netherlands
  demand for musk, 58
  gold, demand for, 67
North Borneo, pirate attacks on, 225
Norton-Kyshe, James William, 102
Nova Guinea, VOC vessel, 164, 165
Nuku, Tidorese prince-rebel, 147
Nuku (Prince), 204
Nur Misuari, 249

O

Obi, 154, 215
O'Connor, Richard, 100
Old Summer Palace, 113
Oman, 22
  ruler of, 22
Ong-Webb, Graham Gerard, 6
Onin, 166
Opium War, 105
  Second, 106
Orang Laut, 136, 137

P

Padanan Island, 254
parallel underground economy, 4
Pax Neerlandica, 148
  establishment of, 11
Peace of Munster, Netherlands and Spain, 153
Peking, tribute to, 51
Peng Aju, 36
Perotin-Dumon, Anne, 223
Perry, Elisabeth, study of Bai Lang, 103
Philippines
  American colonialism, 231
  view of free trade, 12
piracy
  as an economic activity, 21
  Asia, suppressing, 222–36
  "Asian» type, 144
  benefits to some agents of state, 17
  Chinese, 8
  contemporary, 237–68
  characteristics, 285
  criminology of piracy, 12
  definition, 3, 15–28, 140
  definition by International Maritime Bureau, 20, 243
  importance in certain areas, 37
  Indonesia, modern day, 140–43
  motivation for, Somalia, 5
  Papua, seventeenth century, 147–77
  problem of definition, 273–75

Index

research on, 6
relation with religion, 132
resurgence, 281–84
return of, 224–26
role in state formation, 13
shaping, 246
social science perspective, 4–6
Southeast Asia, 8
state sponsored, 17
sub-culture, 9
voyage, 277
pirate, difference from privateer, 15
Pirate Round, 17
pirates
  barbarian *see* barbarian pirates
  Chinese, 21
  collection of annual "tribute", 43
  dependency on ports and black markets, 33
  Muslim, 19
  other names for, 134
  Portuguese, 21
  retired, 276–79
  sentenced to decapitation, 112
  subjective world, 279–81
  Qawasim, 22
pirate settlements, bombing campaigns, 214
Pires, Tome, 144
Plinlochiu, 64, 65
Police General Action Group, 254
political piracy, 23
Pocock, Susan, 111
Pocock, Thomas Guy (Captain), 110
political state, 232
Polo, Marco, 19
ports
  activities at, 4
  clandestine, 37
Portugal, method of payment to men, 16
Portuguese cartaz system, 21
Portuguese Water Police, 112

prison system, Chinese, 117
privateer, 15
  Captain Kidd as, 16
protection money, 256
protection taxes, 80
public executions, 118, 119

Q

Qawasim, 18
Qawasim pirates, 22
Qin dynasty, corporal punishment during, 116
Qin Shizhen, 86
Qing dynasty
  end of, 109
  management of coast, 91
Qing magistrates, 10
Quanzhou, residents, 78
Quedah Merchant, 16
queues, cutting of, symbol of disloyalty, 44

R

raiders, migrating, 212
raiding, definition, 3
Raja Ampat
  provision of slaves, 165–68
  tribute to Tidore, 157
Raja Ampat islands, 147, 148, 155
  conditions, 155–59
  first expedition reports, 159-165
Raja Jailolo, 204–05
Raja Laut, 133, 134
rak
  raiding expeditions, 167
  reasons for staging, 167
ransom system, 190, 191
rattan, demand for, 215
Rarakit, 150
Ras al-Khaimah, 18
Raychaudhuri, Tapan, 67
record books, use by local authorities, 88

Red Sea, Captain Every, 16
Resimon, 59, 62
   devaluation of silver, blame on VOC, 76
   letter to Director General Hartsinck, 65
robbery, definition, 3
Roebuck, 17
Ron, James, description of frontier, 41
Rooselaar, Pieter, Governor of Moluccas, 160
Royal Malaysian Marine Police, 247
Royal Malaysian Navy, 240, 247

S

Sabah
   attack by vessel type, 244
   contemporary maritime piracy, 237–68
   timber trade, 238
   tourism, 238
Sabah Marine Police, 247
Saigon, trans-shipment hub, 37
St. John, Spencer, 184
St. Marie Island, off Madagascar, 40
Salawati, 158
Samaritan, 17
Scott, James, 103
sea farms, 95
sea gypsies, 136
sea nomads, 136
sea power, types, 132–37
security improvements, impact of, 254–57
Sekfamneri, 156
Semporna, 238–42
   buildings in, 240
   geographical features, 241
   increase in security, 257
   piracy in 1990 to early 2000s, 242
   pirates, types of, 245
   police boats, 239
   population, 240
   tourism, 241

Semporna District Police Administration, 254
Sennacherib (King), 23
separatist movements, 249
Series on Maritime Issues and Piracy in Asia, 6
Sevilla, Mariano, 187
Shanghai Academy of Social Sciences (SASS), 7
Sheikh of Qadil, 19
Shi clan, 94
Shi Lang, 94
ship captains, documents, 88
ShipLoc, 141
silk
   Bengal, 55
   Chinese, 55
   export to Japan, 54
   Tonkinese, 60
      falling profit margins, 66
      production, 64
   Vietnamese, 54
silver, 55
   devaluation, 66
Sinama, 270
Sino-Vietnamese frontier, black market on, 31–50
Sipadan, 248
   kidnapping, impact, 249–54
slave raids
   end of, 195
   interior of Seram, 149
   Jolo, 178–99
   maritime, 178
   systematic movement of, 180
slavery, modification of traditional culture, 192
slave raiding, 269
slaves
   female, high value of, 190
   numbers captured, 193
   Raja Ampat, 165–68
   women, 189

smallpox epidemic, 210
smuggling, 20
social banditry, 102–04
Somalia, 5
Sonnerat, Pierre, 180
Sontag, Susan, 114
South China Sea, piracy during 18th century, 33
South Fujian, 76–98
   clandestine emigration, 89
   coastal surveillance, 77
   custom surcharges, 89
   illegal activities, 82
   sea-coastal security, 83–93
   social context, 77–83
Southeast Asia, piracy, difference with Chinese piracy, 8
S.S. Greyhound, 112
S.S. Iron Prince, 107
S.S. Namoa, 10, 102
   piracy case, 110–18
   seizure of, 108
S.S. Tai On, hijack of, 109
state, definition of, 18
states, legality of, 19
Sulawesi
   eastern, 200-217
      colonial periphery, 201–04
      see also Eastern Sulawesi
Sullivan, Arthur, 3
Sultan of Brunei, steamship, 133
Sultan of Buton, 209
Sultan of Gunung Tabur, 137
Sultan Hamza Fahrudin, 153, 154
Sultan Saifudin, Ternate, 153
Sultan Sibori, conflict with Dutch, 153
Sultan of Ternate, 149
Sultanate of Sulu, heterogenous society, 180
Sulu
   aristocrats, involvement in slave raiding, 271
   ethnic composition, 272
   ethnographical case study, 269–88
   maritime society, 271–73
   patterns of pirate acts, 275–79
   slave trade, sources of intelligence, 181–83
   visit by English traders, 180
Sulu Archipelago
   geographical background, 270–71
   historical background, 270–71
Sulu Sultanate
   maritime expeditions, 131
   Spanish expedition against, 133
Sulu-Mindanao region, 11
Sulu Sea, 222
Sun Yat Sen, 109
surplus percentages, 89
syabandar, Bugis, 212

T

Taiping Rebellion, 106, 108
Taiwan
   annexation of, 88
   dynamism of development, 80
Tausug, Philippines, 272
Tawau Division, Sabah, 238
Tay Son Rebellion, 33
Tay Son rebels, 33, 36
Tawi-Tawi, 231
Tawi Tawi province, 270, 276
Tanah Jampea, 206
Tarling, Nicholas, 131
Tay Son soldiers, cooperation with Qing navy, 47
taxes, unofficial, 89
Ternate, sponsoring of raids, 213
territorial zone, UN Convention on Law of the Sea (UNCLOS), 23
terrorist, differnce from ordinary criminal, 252
Thang Long, 64, 66
The Pirates of Penzance, 3
Thenlongfoe, 61
Tiandihui, 105

Tidore, 148
  hongi from, 157
  Prince Nuku, 204
Tik Aram, 119
tin trade, 135
Tinnam, location, 63
Tinnam strategy, 60–64
Toasug credit system, 186
Tobelo, 201
  origins, 204
Tokoro, Ikuya, 12
Tolaki, 219
Tombolongan, 211
Tong Shengru, 31, 34
Tonkin, 51–75
  alternative gold supplier, 57
  decline, 65–70
  export of musk, 59
  musk, shortage of, 69
  as permanent factory, 64–65
Tonkin-China border, trade, stagnation, 52
tourism
  Sabah, 238
  Semporna, 241
tourists, kidnapping of, 253
trade, cross border, 283
trading state, 232
tradition story, 3
Treaty of the Bogue, 111
Treaty of Nanjing, 105, 106
trepang, 183
  trade, 203
Tuanna-I-Dondang, 207
Tumenggung Abdul Rahman, 137
tutelary network, 81
Tyburn of Hong Kong, 199

U

United Dutch East India Company (VOC), 9
United Nations Convention on Law of the Sea (UNCLOS), 23, 229
  definition of piracy, 140

United Nations High Commissioner for Refugees (UNHCR), 282
University of Amsterdam, 7
USS Cole, 24

V

van Benthem, Jan, 161
van Dam, Pieter, 59
van der Laan, Johan, 161
  successful expeditions, 162
van Gijn, Jacob, expeditions, 162–64
Vanning, 62
Velthoen, Esther, 11, 18
Verenigde Oos-Indische Compagnie (VOC), 147
  alliance with Qing Dynasty, 54
Veth, P.J., 132
Vietnam
  An Quang province, 34
  price of Chinese gold sold in, 58
Vietnamese merchants, attack by Chinese soldiers, 53, 58
Vietnamese silk, 54
Viking, attack on West European coastal settlements, 132
VOC-Tidore alliance, 168
Vosmaer, J., 207
Vosmaer, J.N., 207–12
  alliances, 208
  complaints, 209
  plan for colonial trading post, 210

W

Waigama, 158
Walled City of Kowloon, 112
Wang Gungwu, 42
Wang Jun, 85, 86
Wang Yade, 31, 32
Wang Ya'er, 43
Wang Zhi, 104
Warren, James, 11, 131, 269
Waygeo, 158
water frontier, 46

Woodhead, H.G., 122
"water people", 41, 105
water world, 46
Weng Panda, 31
White Lotus, 105
White Lotus Rebellion, 42
women, slaves in Sulu Zone, 189
world trade, protectionist policies, 8
Wyndham, William, 184

X
Xiao Ji, 96
Xingke tiben, 46
Xiong Wencan, 86

Y
Yakan, 285
Yang Yazhang, 45

Z
Zanzibar, 22
Zeelandia Castle, 57
Zeeridder, 68
Zhang Yi, 102
Zhang Wang, 85
Zhangshan, 32
Zhangzhou, residents, 78
Zhejiang, 91
   ports of, 81
Zheng Chenggong, 53, 94
Zheng Qi, 42, 43
Zheng Yi Sao, 8, 48
Zheng Zhilong, 86
Zhu Yigui, 92